EPISTLES OF MAIMONIDES

CRISIS AND LEADERSHIP

TEXTS TRANSLATED AND NOTES BY

ABRAHAM HALKIN

DISCUSSIONS BY

DAVID HARTMAN

THE JEWISH PUBLICATION SOCIETY

PHILADELPHIA · JERUSALEM

EPISTLES OF MAIMONIDES
CRISIS AND LEADERSHIP

Originally published under the title
Crisis and Leadership: The Epistles of Maimonides
Copyright © 1985 by The Jewish Publication Society of America
First paperback edition, 1993
All rights reserved
Manufactured in the United States of America
Paperback, ISBN 0-8276-0430-0

Library of Congress Cataloging in Publication Data

Maimonides, Moses, 1135–1204.
   (Correspondence. English. Selections)
   Epistles of Maimonides: crisis and leadership/(texts translated
and notes by Abraham Halkin; discussions by David Hartman).
     p. cm.
   Previously published: Crisis and leadership. Philadelphia:
Jewish Publication Society of America, 1985.
   Includes bibliographical references.
   ISBN 0–8276–0430–0
   1. Judaism—Works to 1900.   2. Martyrdom (Judaism)—Early
works to 1800.   3. Judaism—Apologetic works—Early works to
1800.   4. Jews—Yemen—Persecutions—Early works to 1800.
5. Islam—Controversial literature—Early works to 1800.
6. Resurrection (Jewish theology)—Early works to 1800.
I. Halkin, Abraham S., 1903–1990.   II. Hartman, David.
III. Title.
(BM545.A2513 1992)
296.1'72—dc20   92-35436
                                                  CIP

Designed by Adrianne Onderdonk Dudden

To Shulamit Halkin of blessed memory, devoted wife and companion
A.H.

To Sol Lederman, constant friend and dedicated leader
D.H.

CONTENTS

PREFACE

For a long time, Professor Halkin and I have felt the need to present a more accurate and broader understanding of Maimonides, and thus to correct the widespread misconception that Maimonides was only a brilliant theoretician of Judaism. That he certainly was, but he was also a man of action who offered practical assistance and guidance to his own Jewish community and to Jewish communities in other lands. This other aspect of Maimonides is presented through this new English edition of his three epistles to communities in crisis.

The translation of the epistles, and the accompanying historical introductions and notes, are the work of Professor Halkin. The philosophical and theological analyses of the epistles and the general introduction to the book were written by myself.

Given the long and difficult period of preparation of the book, my appreciation is unbounded for the support of my wife, Bobbie, and our children and for the critical contributions of the students and research fellows at the Shalom Hartman Institute. Two of the latter deserve special mention. Elliott Yagod, my philosophical associate of many years, worked untiringly to help me clarify the ideas in these essays. Malcolm Lowe, known in his own right as a scholar of Greek philosophy and the New Testament, subsequently recast the essays and helped to give them their final form. We all also owe much to Ruth Sherer, who patiently typed and retyped the successive drafts but refused to let us get away with even the slightest obscurities of expression. I should also like to thank all those who read the essays and made helpful comments, and especially my own teacher, Professor Shlomo Pines.

I dedicate this volume to a dear and beloved friend, Sol Lederman, patron of Jewish scholarship and president of the Shalom Hartman Institute. His personal dedication and devotion to my *aliyah* and my philosophical activity in Jerusalem are but a small example of his serious commitment to making Israel and Jewish learning central to the meaningful survival of our people. It is most gratifying to be able to dedicate this work on leadership in times of crisis to a dear friend who has stood by me and the Institute through challenging and difficult times.

Professor Halkin dedicates this work to his beloved wife, Shulamit, who passed away on Tevet 13 (January 8), 1982. It is our tragic loss that Shulamit Halkin, who followed the development of the book up to its last stages, was denied the chance of seeing it appear in print. May her memory be a blessing to Israel. My hope is that Professor Halkin will continue to be blessed with strength and creativity for many years to come. His painstaking scholarship and concern for clarity will contribute to making Maimonides' epistles meaningful to all concerned with fully appreciating the leading Jewish philosopher of all times.

David Hartman

EPISTLES OF MAIMONIDES

CRISIS AND LEADERSHIP

INTRODUCTION

Maimonides is universally known for his remarkable contribution to Jewish intellectual history. The quantity and nature of the works he produced bear the unmistakable mark of genius. While still in his youth, he wrote a book on logic, and in his twenties he composed a major commentary to the Mishnah. His comprehensive knowledge of the entire Jewish tradition and his incisive powers of interpretation and classification are clearly revealed in his *Sefer ha-Mitzvot* (Book of the Commandments) and in his magnum opus, the *Mishneh Torah*, a code of Jewish law that is a landmark in the development of Jewish jurisprudence. In his great philosophic work, *The Guide of the Perplexed*, Maimonides shows his mastery of the scientific disciplines of his time as well as a profound knowledge of Islamic and Greek philosophy.

Maimonides is best known as the great codifier of Jewish law or as the brilliant philosophic master of Jewish and medieval thought, but the role he played as a statesman and leader is largely unappreciated. The bulk of Maimonidean scholarship is devoted to uncovering the deepest meanings in Maimonides' legal and philosophical works. Because of his rigorous and succinct style (he wrote that he would have reduced all his writings to a single page if he could), scholars find much to ponder in his deliberate choice of words and phrases. Far less attention is devoted to those texts—composed with equal care—that reveal Maimonides' empathic involvement with the community, his profound understanding of the psychology of the sufferer, and his mode of reaching decisions that affected the fate of whole communities and later generations. The material in this book, therefore, focuses primarily upon Maimonides' response to crisis. He was subtle and suggestive not only when composing legal or philosophical texts, but also when writing with passion as a political leader committed to the survival of an oppressed community.

Some of Maimonides' writings seem to express elitist sentiments. At times Maimonides even seems to be a detached aristocratic intellectual unconcerned with the greater community. For example, in the introduction to *The Guide of the Perplexed,* Maimonides writes:

> I am the man who when the concern pressed him and his way was straitened and he could find no other device by which to teach a demonstrated truth other than by giving satisfaction to a single virtuous man while displeasing ten thousand ignoramuses—I am he who prefers to address that single man by himself, and I do not heed the blame of those many creatures. For I claim to liberate that virtuous one from that into which he has sunk, and I shall guide him in his perplexity until he becomes perfect and he finds rest.

The *Guide* expresses a teacher's devotion to one talented student who is superior to the mediocrity of the masses. In the dedicatory epistle of the *Guide,* addressed to his student Joseph, son of Judah, Maimonides writes that his purpose in writing the work

> . . . was that the truth should be established in your mind according to the proper methods and that certainty should not come to you by accident.

Because Joseph was away, Maimonides had to accomplish his purpose by writing this book.

> Your absence moved me to compose this treatise, which I have composed for you and for those like you, however few they are.

The gifted few could claim the total attention of Maimonides. He was the guide of those who were sufficiently learned to recognize the conflict between revealed religion and medieval science and philosophy.

Throughout the *Guide,* Maimonides conveys a sense of disdain for ignorance and consequently a disdain for the ignorant masses. In describing how the prophet trains for leadership, Maimonides portrays a type of aristocratic detachment from the majority of people, whom the prophet is taught to regard as being like sheep and cattle (*Guide* 2:36). The community-at-large is not the intended audience of the book. The passion that informs its pages (e.g., *Guide* 3:51) is that of the philosopher who longs for solitude and peace in order to pursue intellectual and spiritual perfection. The author writes not as a leader of a nation, but as a concerned teacher who has devoted ten years of his life to composing a work that will enable a single student to preserve his loyalty to Judaism without sacrificing his intellectual integrity.

The aristocratic spirit of the *Guide* has contributed to the mistaken belief that Maimonides was far removed from the ordinary concerns of the community and indifferent to the interests of the uneducated masses living in a world of shadows. Although certain aspects of Maimonides' works might prompt such a description, as an overall picture of him it is a gross distortion. In order to correct that unbalanced characterization, one need only read the moving conclusion of his *Epistle to Yemen*.

> I beg you to send a copy of this missive to every community in the cities and hamlets, in order to strengthen the people in their faith and put them on their feet. Read it at public gatherings and in private, and you will thus become a public benefactor. Take adequate precautions lest its contents be divulged by an evil person and mishap overtake us. (God spare us therefrom.) When I began writing this letter I had some misgivings about it, but they were overruled by my conviction that the public welfare takes precedence over one's personal safety. Moreover, I am sending it to a personage such as you: *The council of the Lord is for those who fear Him*. Our sages, the successors of the prophets, assured us that persons engaged in a religious mission will meet with no disaster. What more important religious mission is there than this? Peace be unto all Israel. Amen. (p. 131)

The *Epistle to Yemen* is the work of a philosopher-statesman prepared to risk his life because of the responsibility he felt toward the community. Maimonides wrote as a leader who refused to remain silent or stand aloof from the frightened and disillusioned community that had turned to him for guidance. He permitted himself to launch a severe attack on Christianity and Islam in a manner that mirrored the pent-up hostility felt by Jews toward their religious oppressors. He referred to Muhammad as "the madman," dwelt on the idea of Judaism's uniqueness and superiority to other faiths, and insisted that the letter be read in public in order to strengthen the entire community.

Deliberately and knowingly, he placed himself in danger in order to aid the "ten thousand ignoramuses" he had dismissed in the *Guide*. Here is no erudite intellectual expounding complex philosophical arguments for the sake of "a single virtuous man," but a committed leader who enters the marketplace of the community and is prepared to suffer personal hardships for the sake of the welfare of the whole. Also in the *Epistle on Martyrdom* and the *Essay on Resurrection*, we do not meet the teacher of the few, but rather the compassionate and concerned leader of the many. Both aspects of Maimonides—his intellectualism and his statesmanship—are in truth integral components of the rich personality of this philosopher-halakhist.

A careful and sensitive reading of Maimonides' works reveals that commitment to the community is actually a leitmotiv of all his works. Even in the *Guide*, Maimonides does not advocate an ivory-tower existence, but instead tries to convince his reader to return to the community. The ultimate stage of philosophic perfection described at the end of the *Guide* emphasizes the centrality of practice within the social context of Jewish society. Throughout the book, Maimonides argues that Judaic law, as it is practiced, is not indifferent or hostile to the life of philosophy, but is truly in harmony with the spirit of the philosophic quest.

The needs of the community were never far removed from Maimonides' thoughts. He was a leader of his people in everything he did or wrote. His leadership took different forms depending on the needs of situation. In response to the need to reeducate the community, he wrote interpretations and commentary. In response to the social and intellectual problems of Jewish dispersion, he composed a masterful codification of rabbinic law. And given the seeming conflict between Judaism and the philosophy of his day, he wrote an analytic treatise that argued for the compatibility of Judaism with most of the concepts and methods of the Aristotelian world view.

Indeed, the very fact that Maimonides composed a work such as the *Guide* can be seen as qualifying him for political leadership. Maimonides may be said to have realized the ideal expressed by Plato (*Republic* 521): the best leader is the philosopher who, because he has discovered the incomparable pleasure of the quest for truth, has no craving for power. A leader who finds fulfillment in teaching a single student, who finds satisfaction as a solitary individual engaged in contemplative worship of God, can guide the community disinterestedly. A leader who has faith in the power of rational argumentation can distinguish between rational disagreement and subversion. In this sense, for both Plato and Maimonides it would be correct to say that only he who can be alone can be trusted with the power to lead others. While no person is immune from the corrupting influences of power or mass approval, there are conditions that militate against these dangers. Maimonides was well aware of the corruptibility of man. Nevertheless, he believed that intense learning and the cultivation of a philosophic spirit in a political leader could balance the corrupting influences inherent in political structures. A profound quest for spiritual excellence, a commitment to the dignity of the single student, an uncompromising regard for excellence and intellectual honesty—these traits could possibly exert a countervailing force to offset the allurements of political power.

The philosophic spirit of the *Guide* is also reflected in Maimonides' refusal to allow the nation to become an entity that takes precedence over the individuals who compose it. He emphasized repeatedly that national renewal in the messianic age will be only of instrumental value; it will create conditions conducive to the realization of the ideal of love and knowledge of God by individuals in the community. He warned against viewing messianism as a collective fantasy of national revenge and aggrandizement. National renewal and the acquisition of power had to be subservient to the ultimate purpose of Judaism: intellectual love of God expressed in the imitation of God's moral actions.

The community must find its fulfillment in the perfection of the individuals composing it. No national entity and no national normative system are self-justifying. They must always pass before the bar of universal rationality. For Maimonides, knowledge of philosophy provides a person with a conceptual framework that transcends particular national legal and cognitive frameworks. In this respect, the wisdom that grows from the study of nature (in the broad sense) can act as a corrective against the potential distortions resulting from normative structures that claim to be the exclusive source of truth. No law or nation can legitimately claim to be above rational criticism. This, then, is the political message of the *Guide* as well as of the introductory chapters of the *Mishneh Torah*.

The three epistles contained in this book each testify to how Maimonides' manner of harmonizing Judaism with philosophy, as expounded above all in the *Guide*, influenced his role as a statesman. The *Essay on Resurrection* is particularly interesting in this respect, because it shows how Maimonides—near the very end of his life—was obliged to reassess that manner of harmonization. The essay has to be seen in the context of one of Maimonides' primary aims as an educator:

to neutralize the community's religious fantasies and grandiose expectations. While fully aware of the gap that existed between the levels of worship of the masses and of the educated few, he nonetheless tried, throughout his life, to raise the level of the community closer to the ideal of love of God. His main philosophical enemies were the theologians known as the *mutakallimun,* because of their willingness to espouse doctrines that were contrary to the nature of reality (*Guide* 1:71). Maimonides waged a relentless battle against those who conceived of reality according to the excesses of the imagination and in disregard of the science of nature. He sought to inhibit human fantasies with respect both to nature and to God and to heal the disease of religious orientations that claimed to transcend the natural order.

Maimonides wanted to show that one could remain anchored in empirical reality and rationality and at the same time be loyal to the God of the Torah. God need not satisfy all human fantasies in order to be the object of religious love and passion. Despite elements in the Jewish tradition that supported the growth of fantastic expectations, and despite the rarity of religious persons who conceive of God in rational naturalistic terms, Maimonides struggled to purge the mythic propensity in the Jewish community. His concern with demythologizing Jewish consciousness was evident in his successive writings whenever he discussed eschatological themes, such as messianism, the resurrection of the dead, or the immortality of the soul.

When he came to write the *Essay on Resurrection,* however, Maimonides was faced with the painful realization that all this effort as a religious educator might have been a failure. The events that led Maimonides to write the essay showed that the community rejected his attempt at demythologization. The community realized that miracles played a secondary role in Maimonides' religious world view. It understood that although he listed belief in resurrection among the thirteen dogmas of the Jewish faith, he denigrated the miraculous in everyday religious life. For Maimonides, resurrection was not the culmination of Jewish aspirations; he rejected the fanciful belief in a resurrected body that would be eternal and capable of infinite gratification. But the community, after suffering great deprivation in history, was not prepared to follow Maimonides by giving up belief in a future state of limitless material wealth, sensual enjoyment, and political power. It was, in effect, telling him plainly: "You want us to aspire to love God and to appreciate the joys of knowledge of God and of being in His presence; we, however, are unable to listen to you if you deny us bodily gratification. We must have a God who will resurrect our bodies and thus justify our hope for material joy and pleasure."

The crucial and profoundly personal question that lies behind the

Essay on Resurrection is: What happens to a leader when he discovers the failure of his lifelong struggle to raise the aspirations of his community to a higher plane? Does he make his love for the community conditional upon the possibility of transforming it to accept the ideal of intellectual love of God? Does his love for his student, which plays such an important role in his political theory, lead him to reject the community that he no longer believes he can educate?

The discussion that follows the *Essay on Resurrection* in this volume explores whether Maimonides was discouraged by his failure to the point of cynicism and whether he abandoned the community, never again to return to the cave as pictured by Plato in the *Republic*. Does the essay reveal Maimonides finally accepting that the philosopher-halakhist must remain a lonely person with religious ideals and aspirations that must be realized within the narrow circle of his elite students, but cannot be implanted in the life of the community or polis? Or does he continue to struggle to be a halakhist-statesman even after defeat? If so, what new form does his leadership take? What vessel does he provide for the mythic sensibility he was unable to eliminate?

In the *Epistle to Yemen*, Maimonides confronted the dilemma that the community faced as a result of the triumph of Islam and the consequent policy of forced conversion. The community's faith had been shaken by the ascendance of rival monotheistic faiths whose spokesmen could allege in their favor enormous material wealth and political power. The doubts engendered by this historical situation could have two dangerous consequences. First, it could lead to apostasy, either out of fear alone or out of the belief that historical power and success are signs of religious truth. Second, it could lead to the profound despair that renders a person vulnerable to wild apocalyptic movements and ideologies.

Maimonides thus had to deal with a twofold danger. He had to secure the community's belief in the integrity of the Sinai revelation, even though its lived reality seemed so incongruous with all that the Torah had promised. At the same time, he had to neutralize the appeal of charismatic messianic pretenders, who preyed upon the community's susceptibility to follow any forceful personality who promised them an end to their suffering and humiliation.

Maimonides was addressing an audience paralyzed by disillusionment and doubt. The approach that he adopted was to enter into the world of the sufferers and restore their dignity despite their inability to act or express themselves freely. Maimonides, the philosopher who naturalized so much of the mythic in Judaism, entered into the dungeon of the suffering community in order to teach it how to persevere in its loyalty and trust in Judaism without vainly acting out its messianic aspirations. His approach in the *Epistle to Yemen* can be seen as an imitation of the model of God as educator that is described in the *Guide:* Maimonides does not teach from a position far removed from the situation of his audience, but listens to it carefully and attentively and speaks in a language that it can understand.

A striking sense of realism and compassion is also found in the *Epistle on Martyrdom,* one of his earliest writings. The Moroccan Jewish community was undergoing a crisis precipitated by the Almohad persecution, which had led a number of Jews to adopt a Marrano-type existence. As a halakhic leader, Maimonides was faced with a difficult choice in offering guidance to a community that lacked the courage to defy the Islamic persecutor. Should he demand heroism as a necessary condition for remaining a genuine member of the Jewish people? Or should he permit compromise? Could a stateless and powerless people tolerate weakness of will without destroying one of its essential means of survival? Or could the community make concessions to its persecutors in a way that would not destroy the future of Judaism? And if that was the case, then what forms of expression might its commitment to Judaism take in such compromise situations?

Maimonides' willingness to tolerate compromise and to salvage whatever dignity was possible in such circumstances was in many respects an application of the rabbinic principle: "The Torah spoke only with respect to the *yetzer ha-ra*" ("evil inclination," i.e., human passions) (BT Kiddushin 21b). This principle, which is discussed in the talmudic treatment of the law of the captive woman (Deut. 21:10–14), evinces a fundamental rabbinic understanding of Judaic law: the Torah is not a law for ideal people living in idyllic conditions, but rather a normative system that guides people in imperfect situations and through personal crises of the will and spirit. Rather than legislate a law that a normal person in the heat of battle would be unable to abide by, the Torah restricted the soldier's conduct with respect to the captive woman and thus lent a degree of dignity and morality to an otherwise brutal situation. Compromise was preferable to total demoralization. This legislative model may have guided Maimonides in trying to salvage some form of dignified Jewish life for a community that was not prepared to make the heroic choice of martyrdom.

Although accepting compromise and struggling to restore the compromiser's self-respect, Maimonides does not allow him to feel comfortable and complacent. Maimonides insists, in the *Epistle on Martyrdom,* that those who gave way under persecution have committed a serious sin, even though they should not be branded as idolaters. He tells them that it is their duty to flee at the first opportunity to a place where they will be able to resume their life as full Jews and put aside compromise. But if they do not flee, they should nonetheless continue to perform as many of the commandments of Judaism as they can. His guidance thus creates the capacity for permanent struggle and new forms of heroism in contexts of compromise and weakness. He never permits his audience to escape the need for moral vigilance and discrimination. While tolerating compromise, he simultaneously strives to keep alive a sense of dissatisfaction with the given conditions. He bases his attempt to rescue the community not only on legalistic reasons, but also on a prudent evaluation of what its moral strength will permit.

Judicious statesmanship pervades Maimonides' advice to the community from his earliest to his last epistles. He shows an enormous capacity to identify with the sufferings of others and to understand their fears and needs. Yet he is never wholly overwhelmed by the sufferer's perspective and maintains a critical distance from his audience, enabling him to provide anchor points from which to transcend their immediate framework of experience. In all three epistles, Maimonides weaves together this twofold attitude of the leader toward his community. In all three situations, he enters into the world of his audience and, in the midst of crisis, moves them slightly beyond the level at which they were before.

In all his responses to crisis, Maimonides upheld his commitment to a realistic approach and sought to impart it to his readers. Even in the *Essay on Resurrection*, where he accepted the community's resistance to his attempt to restrict the use of the concept of the miraculous, he formulated a way of using the concept of miracle without undermining the concept of the natural order. This commitment to realism is related to the concerns of the *Guide*, but also has a firm basis in the rabbinic tradition. To the questions: "Why does God not destroy the objects of idolatry? Why does stolen wheat grow? Why do violated women conceive?" (BT Avodah Zarah 54b), the Talmud replies: "The world conforms to its usual course" (*olam ke-minhago noheg*). The crucial point of this text is the willingness of talmudic sages to admit that natural causality does not always mirror the biblical promise. The conformity of the natural order to the moral law is simply an aspiration, or, as the Talmud says, it is what rightfully should be the case (*din hu*); it is not always confirmed by empirical reality.

The challenge facing a religious person as a result of this type of realism is whether he can genuinely hope for a world governed by moral principles without misusing the notion of the miraculous and thus choosing religious fantasies and distortions above the real world. Maimonides constantly responded to that challenge. His writings in general and these epistles in particular testify to his conviction that Judaism could grow and flourish without exaggerated apocalyptic myths or nationalistic fantasies. One could be loyal to God without disparaging the natural order. One could love God with a profound passion without granting the Judaic tradition the exclusive authority to define the nature of truth.

Maimonides recognized the distortions of reality that could enter a tradition that claims: "God only has in His world the four cubits of the Law" (BT Berakhot 8a). The total claim of Halakhah upon the Jewish people could create an insulated culture and a self-righteous disregard for empirical reality. The danger is that for such a mind, the possible is defined by imagination and not by empirical experience.

Maimonides was a leader who could move a people that had tasted the brutality of oppression, yet he did not need to resort to delusion and fantasy. His sobriety and compassion in the midst of crisis testify to the way an intellectual giant merged love for the community with the quest for intellectual integrity.

THE EPISTLE
ON MARTYRDOM

Maimonides was born in April 1135 C.E. in Córdoba, a city
which, like most of the Iberian peninsula at that time, was under
Muslim rule. A few years later, Spain was invaded by a funda-
mentalist Muslim sect that had already seized power in Northwest
Africa. This sect, the Almohads (*Al-Muwaḥḥidun:* those who
assert the unity of God), adopted a policy of forced conversion
to Islam. Many Jews were coerced into making a public affirmation that Muhammad was the prophet of God; others refused
and suffered martyrdom. In order to survive, Maimonides' family
wandered from place to place, reaching Fez in 1160 and going
from there in 1165 to the Land of Israel and to Egypt, where
they could again practice their faith openly.

One of the forced converts inquired of a rabbi—a distinguished talmudist—whether he would gain merit by observing
secretly as many commandments of Judaism as he could. The
rabbi gave a halakhic ruling that any Jew who had made a profession of Islam would thereafter commit an additional sin with each
commandment of Judaism that he performed. Horrified by this
ruling, Maimonides composed his *Epistle on Martyrdom* to refute
it and to offer sounder advice to the forced converts. The epistle
was probably written in 1165, shortly before Maimonides and
his family left Fez.

I

A contemporary of mine[1] inquired regarding this persecution[2] in which he is forced to confess that that man[3] is God's messenger and that he is a true prophet. He addressed his query to one whom he calls a sage[4] and who was not touched by the tribulations of most of the Jewish communities in this violence, may it pass soon, and he wished to learn whether he should make the confession in order not to die, although his children will be lost among the gentiles, or should he die and not acknowledge what he demands, seeing that in this way he does what he is required by the Torah of Moses, and that the confession leads to the relinquishment of all the commandments.[5]

The man of whom the inquiry was made offered a weak and senseless reply, of foul content and form. He made statements in it distinctly harmful, as even light-minded women can realize.[6] Although his reply is weak, tedious, and confused, I thought I should quote him at length, but I spared the gift that God, blessed be He, bestowed on mankind. I mean speech, of which our sacred Torah states: *Who gives man speech? . . . Is it not I, the Lord?* [Exod. 4:11].[7] A man should be more sparing of his speech than of his money, and should not speak much yet do little. Indeed the Sage[8] has condemned verbosity with little content in his declaration: *Just as dreams come with much brooding, so does foolish utterance come with much speech* [Eccles. 5:2]. You know of course what Job's friends said as he talked on and on:[9] *Is a multitude of words unanswerable? Must a loquacious person be right?* [Job 11:2]; *Job does not speak with knowledge; his words lack understanding* [Job 34:35].[10] There are many such reflections.

Since I am well informed regarding this issue, and am not ignorant of it as this man is, I think it is proper to cite something of the gist of what he said, and omit the rest, which does not merit a response, although on close examination nothing of what he said deserves an answer. Such is his assertion that whoever acknowledges his[11] apostleship has *ipso facto* disavowed the Lord, God of Israel. In support he brings the statement of our sages, "Whoever professes idolatry is as if he denied the entire Torah."[12] Judging from this analogy, he apparently finds no distinction between one who turns to idolatry not under duress but voluntarily, like Jeroboam and his associates,[13] and one who will under compulsion say of someone that he is a prophet, because he is afraid of the executioner's sword.

When I read this first statement of his, I decided not to challenge him before I read all of it, heeding the instruction of the Sage: *To answer a man before hearing him out is foolish and disgraceful* [Prov. 18:13]. So, when I looked further into his remarks, I noted that he said the following: "Whoever utters that confession is a gentile, though he fulfills the entire Law publicly and privately."[14] This "clear-headed man"[15] evidently sees absolutely no difference between one who does not observe the Sabbath out of the fear of the sword and one who does not observe it because he does not wish to.[16] I read on: "If one of the forced converts enters one of their houses of worship,[17] even if he does not say a word, and he then goes home and offers his prayers, this prayer is charged against him as an added sin and transgression." His proof text is the comment of our sages on the verse, *For My people have done a twofold wrong* [Jer. 2:13]:[18] They bowed to the idol and they bowed to the Temple.[19] This interpretation again does not discriminate between one who bowed to the idol and the Temple because he is a heretic and wants to defile God's ᴉame and desecrate His holiness and one who comes to a house of worship in order to behave like someone zealous[20] for the glory of God,[21] but does not utter or say a word that is in any way contrary to our religion, yet he must of necessity go to that house.[22] I likewise found him saying that anyone who avows that that man is a prophet,[23] though he does it under compulsion, is a wicked person, disqualified by Scripture from serving as a witness, since the Torah rules: *You shall not join hands with the guilty* [Exod. 23:1], that is, do not make a wicked man a witness.[24]

Even as I read his abuses, his long-winded foolish babbling and nonsense, I still believed it was not correct to challenge him before I read all the rest; perhaps it might be an example of what Solomon described: *The end of a matter is better than the beginning of it* [Eccles. 7:8].[25] But I found him saying toward the end of his missive that heretics and Christians likewise assume that they will choose death rather than grant his apostleship.[26] When I learned this I was struck with amazement and wondered: Is there no God in Israel? [2 Kings 1:3, 6].[27] If an idol-worshiper burns his son and daughter to his object of worship,[28] do we even more certainly have to set fire to ourselves for service to God? Alas for the question, alas for the answer! Considering that he began by finding support in something irrelevant to his argument, and concluded by approving the thinking of heretics and Christians, I decided that God's judgment is right: his talk begins as silliness and ends as disastrous madness.

You ought to know that no one has the right to speak in public before he has rehearsed what he wants to say two, three, and four times, and learned it; then he may speak. This is what the rabbis taught, and took their proof text from the verse: *Then He saw it and gauged it; He measured it and probed it*. And afterward: *He said to man* [Job 28:27].[29] So much for what a person is required to do before he speaks. But if a man legislates on his own, and puts it down in writing, he should revise it a thousand times, if possible. This man, however, did nothing of the kind. He reduced all this important advice to writing, and did not think it necessary to prepare a first draft and then revise it. Evidently he considered his remarks free from doubt, in no need of correction. He handed them to someone who was to convey them in every city and town, and in this way brought darkness into the hearts of men. *He sent darkness; it was very dark* [Ps. 105:28].[30]

II

I shall now undertake to define the magnitude of the error that misled this poor wretch, and how he hurt himself unknowingly.[31] He thought he was doing one kind deed, but instead became guilty of many wrongs, marshalling much irrelevant evidence, spouting words, and becoming the slave of his pen. It is well known from the account of our rabbis that before the Israelites left Egypt, they corrupted their ways and violated the covenant of circumcision,[32] so that none of them save the tribe of Levi[33] was circumcised. Only when the Passover commandment was promulgated, in connection with which God instructed Moses: *No uncircumcised shall eat of it* [Exod. 12:43],[34] he ordered them to perform the rite. Our rabbis described the performance: Moses did the cutting, Joshua the ripping, Aaron the sucking.[35] The foreskins were collected in heaps.[36] The blood of circumcision got mixed with the blood of the paschal lamb, and this made them deserving of the redemption.[37] This is the implication of God's narration through Ezekiel: *When I passed by you and saw you wallowing in your blood, I said to you: "Live by your blood," Yea, I said to you, "live by your blood"* [Ezek. 16:6].[38] Our rabbis added that they became degenerate with incest, deriving it from the the verse: *O mortal, once there were two women, daughters of one mother* [Ezek. 23:2].[39] Nevertheless, although they were corrupt as all this, God rebuked Moses for saying: *What if they do not believe me?* [Exod. 4.1].[40] And he retorted: They are believers, children of believers;[41] believers, as Scripture reports: *and the people . . . believed* [Exod. 14:31]; sons of believers: *because he believed, He reckoned it to his merit* [Gen. 15:6].[42] But you will end up not believing; it is told in Scripture: *Because you did not believe Me enough to affirm My sanctity* [Num. 20:12].[43] In fact, he was punished at once, as the rabbis understood:[44] "He who suspects the innocent suffers physically. What is the proof? Moses."[45]

Again, in Elijah's time, they were all sinfully deliberate idolaters, all but the *seven thousand—every knee that has not knelt to Baal and every mouth that has not kissed him* [1 Kings 19:18].[46] Notwithstanding, when he was about to hurl accusations against Israel at Mt. Horeb, the following dialogue was carried on between God and him. God: *Why are you here, Elijah?* Elijah: *I am moved by zeal for the Lord, the God of Hosts, for the Israelites have forsaken Your covenant.* God: Is it your covenant by chance? Elijah: *Torn down Your altars.* God: Your altars perhaps? Elijah: *And put Your prophets to the sword.* God: But you are alive!? Elijah: *I alone am left, and they are out to take my life* [1 Kings 19:10].[47] God: Instead of hurling accusations against Israel, would it not have been more reasonable to direct them against the gentile nations? They have maintained a house of prostitution, a house of idol worship, and you plead against Israel! For the text reads: *The towns of Aroer shall be deserted* [Isa. 17:2]. *Go back by the way you came, and on to the wilderness of Damascus* [1 Kings 19:15].[48] This is all explained by the sages in Midrash Ḥazita.[49]

Similarly in Isaiah's time, they indulged heavily in sin, as the text accuses: *Ah, sinful nation! People laden with iniquity!* [Isa. 1:4];[50] they worshipped idols (*behind the door and doorpost you have directed your thoughts* [Isa. 57:8]);[51] they were also murderers (*Alas, she has become a harlot, the faithful city that was filled with justice, where righteousness dwelt—but now murderers* [Isa. 1:21]);[52] they even desecrated God's name (*Eat and drink, for tomorrow we die* [Isa. 22:13]);[53] and they disdained God's law (*Leave the way! Get off the path! Let us hear no more about the Holy One of Israel* [Isa. 30:11]).[54] Despite this, in punishment of his complaint: *And I live among a people of unclean lips,* immediately *one of the seraphs flew over to me with a live coal. . . . He touched it to my lips and declared: "Now that this has touched your lips, your guilt shall depart and your sin be purged away"* [Isa. 6:5–7].[55] According to the sages, his sin was not forgiven until Manasseh killed him.[56]

When the angel appeared[57] to plead against Joshua son of Jozadak because his sons married girls who were unworthy to be the wives of priests,[58] God silenced him, since the text continues: *The Lord rebuke you, O Accuser; may the Lord who has chosen Jerusalem rebuke you! For this is a brand plucked from the fire* [Zech. 3:2].

If this is the sort of punishment meted out to the pillars of the universe—Moses, Elijah, Isaiah, and the ministering angels[59]—because they briefly criticized the Jewish congregation, can one have an idea of the fate of the least among the worthless who let his tongue loose against Jewish communities of sages and their disciples, priests, and Levites, and called them sinners, evildoers, gentiles, disqualified to testify, heretics who deny the Lord God of Israel?[60] These are verbal quotations from his response; can you picture his punishment? They[61] did not rebel against God to seek satisfaction and delight, they did not abandon our faith to achieve status and worldly pleasures. *For they have fled before swords: before the whetted sword, before the bow that was drawn, before the stress of war* [Isa. 21:15].[62] This man did not realize that they are not rebels by choice. God will not abandon nor forsake them, *for He did not scorn, He did not spurn the plea of the lowly* [Ps. 22:25]. It is as the sages, peace be upon them, interpreted the verse, *And he smelled his clothes* [Gen. 27:27];[63] and pronounced it "his traitors" not "his clothes."[64] But this person wrote only what he invented and concocted.

It is common knowledge that in the course of a persecution during which Jewish sages were executed, Rabbi Meir was arrested.[65] Some who knew him said: "You are Meir, aren't you?" and he replied: "I am not."[66] Pointing to ham they ordered: "Eat this if you are not Jewish." He responded: "I shall readily eat it," and he pretended he was eating, but did not in fact. In the view of this modest person who knows the true meaning of Torah, Rabbi Meir is undoubtedly a gentile, for so his responsum rules: He who acts openly as a gentile, although secretly he behaves like a Jew, is a gentile, since according to him worship of God is open,[67] and he[68] hides it, as Rabbi Meir did.

It is likewise well known that Rabbi Eliezer was seized for heresy, which is worse than idolatry.[69] The heretics—may God destroy them—mock religion, and call anyone who adheres to it a fool, anyone who studies it deranged. They reject prophecy utterly. Rabbi Eliezer was a celebrated scholar in the sciences.[70] They inquired: "How can you be at your level in learning and still believe in religion?" He answered them in a way that made them believe that he adopted their doctrine, whereas in his reply he was really thinking of the true religion and no other. This incident is recounted in the midrash on Ecclesiastes[71] as follows: Rabbi Eliezer was seized in order to be converted to heresy. The chief brought him to the capital and said to him: "Say, old man, is a person like you engaged in this stuff?" He replied: "I have faith in the judge." The chief thought he meant him, whereas he was really thinking of God, and the chief continued:[72] "Rabbi, in view of your having faith in me, I was indeed wondering, can he possibly have been misled by such stuff? By God, you are free!" It is clear that Rabbi Eliezer feigned before the chief that he was a heretic, although he was sincerely devoted to God. Now heresy is far more grievous than idolatry; it has been clearly expounded in the entire Talmud.[73] Yet according to this virtuous individual, Rabbi Eliezer is definitely disqualified. But in this persecution to which we are subjected we do not pretend that we are idolaters, we only appear to believe what they assert.[74] They fully understand that we do not mean it at all, and are simply deceiving the ruler. *Yet they deceived Him with their speech, lied to Him with their words* [Ps. 78:36].[75]

We know what happened to Israel in the reign of the wicked Nebuchadnezzar, when all the inhabitants of Babylon, except Hananiah, Mishael, and Azariah bowed before the molten image. The Lord, blessed be He, foretold it: *No more shall Jacob be shamed, no longer his face grow pale* [Isa. 29:22].[76] It may be that even the artisans and laborers[77] were among those who prostrated themselves in Babylon, if they were there at the time. Despite this, I have not come across anyone who named them wicked, gentiles, disqualified to give testimony. God did not charge them with the sin of idolatry, because they acted under duress. The sages put it this way, reflecting on the time of Haman: They only pretended, I also shall only pretend.[78] That man,[79] however, is undoubtedly God-fearing. *Shame on him who argues with his Maker, though naught but a potsherd of earth! Shall the clay say to the potter, "What are you doing?"* [Isa. 45:9].[80]

We likewise know of the evil, cruel decrees during the wicked rule of the Greeks,[81] including the order that none was to shut the door of his house, so he would not be alone, fulfilling a divine command. Nevertheless our sages did not label them gentiles, or sinful, but absolutely righteous. They prayed for them and added the thankful prayer—recited on Hanukkah—"for the Miracles,"[82] which one can read down to "and the wicked in the hands of the righteous."

If in my opening remarks I had not decisively stated that I would not repeat all of his prattle, I would let you read it *in extenso* how one can be fool enough to speak in this manner or let himself go and write or respond to irrelevant matter in answer to a simple question that was asked of him. He cited proof from "contradicted witnesses,"[83] one who reviles his father and mother,[84] the law of fringes,[85] one who plows with an ox and an ass together,[86] letting one's cattle mate with a different kind,[87] as if the man asked him to compose *azharot*,[88] in which all the precepts would be enumerated. He reported that the Muslims have an idol in Mecca and in other places; was he asked whether he should go on a pilgrimage to Mecca? He informed him that Muhammad[89] killed 24,000 Jews, as if he wished to know if Muhammad would share in the world-to-come, and many such unrelated items. He should have more properly paid much heed to Solomon's admonition: *Keep your mouth from being rash, and let not your throat be quick to bring forth speech before God* [Eccles. 5:1]. Had he heeded this verse, he would have realized that whoever answered an inquiry or engaged in an analysis of the allowed and the forbidden was bringing forth speech before God, and he would not fail as he did.[90]

God knows and bears witness—"He is an adequate witness"[91]— that even if he rebuked and spoke more chattily than he did, it would not hurt me. I am certainly not seeking victory. On the contrary, I feel, *Let us lie down in our shame, let our disgrace cover us; for we have sinned against the Lord our God, we and our fathers* [Jer. 3:25].[92] I should have respected and esteemed him more, believed that his objective was to do God's bidding. Thank God, I know my personal worth very well. *We acknowledge our wickedness, O Lord—the iniquity of our fathers* [Jer. 14:20].[93] It would not have been right of me to find fault with him had he not written things that I have no right to overlook or disregard, like ruling that any victim of the persecution who prays receives no reward but is, on the contrary, guilty of committing a sin. I know that whatever is published in a book—correct or incorrect— will most certainly become public knowledge. This is why so many wrong ideas are popular among people. Only what is recorded in writing makes the difference between you and the wrong views,[94] and they will gain him a following. Therefore I was afraid that the response that turns people away from God would fall into the hands of an ignorant individual, and he would conclude that he will receive no reward for praying, so he will not pray. This, he will assume, is true of the other commandments; if he performs them, he will get no reward for performing any of them.

III

I shall now expose what this ranter of nonsense went astray in. It is explicitly reported in the Bible that Ahab son of Omri who denied God and worshiped idols, as God attests: *Indeed there never was anyone like Ahab* [1 Kings 21:25],[95] had the decree against him rescinded after he fasted two and a half hours.[96] The Bible informs us: *Then the word of the Lord came to Elijah the Tishbite: "Have you seen how Ahab has humbled himself before Me? Because He has humbled himself before Me, I will not bring the disaster in his lifetime; I will bring the disaster upon his house in his son's time* [I Kings 21:28–29].[97]

Eglon, king of Moab, who oppressed Israel, was handsomely rewarded by God because he honored Him and rose from his seat when
Ehud said to him: *I have a message for you from God* [Judg. 3:20].[98]
He had the throne of Solomon, which is a divine throne (*and Solomon
sat on the divine throne* [1 Chron. 29:23]),[99] and the throne of the
Messiah come from his descendants. For, as the rabbis teach us, Ruth
the Moabite was his daughter.[100] God did not withhold his reward.

The wicked Nebuchadnezzar, who killed vast multitudes of Israel
and burned the Temple that is the footstool of God,[101] was rewarded
with a forty-year reign like King Solomon, because he ran a short
distance to meet God for the sake of Hezekiah, as the rabbis state:
"He ran after him a distance of four paces. God did not withhold his
reward."[102]

Wicked Esau—God certified His rejection of him, as is written: *And
I have rejected Esau* [Mal. 1:3]—had his outrages spelled out by the
rabbis. That day he committed five crimes: murdered, worshiped idols,
ravished an engaged girl, denied resurrection, and despised the rights
of primogeniture. He then enwrapped himself in his cloak, came to
his father Isaac, and asked him: "Father, is salt subject to the tithe?"
His father reflected: "How strict my son is in religious observance."[103]
Yet, as reward for the one commandment—honoring his father—which
he fulfilled, God has granted him uninterrupted dominion until the
Messiah the king arrives.[104] This is confirmed by the rabbis: David's
descendant will not come before Esau receives his reward for honoring
his father and mother, as the text reads: *He sent me after glory unto
the nations* [Zech. 2:12].[105] Several times our sages repeat this principle: "The Holy One blessed be He, does not withhold the reward of
any creature.[106] He always rewards everyone for the good deed that
he performs, and punishes everyone for the evil he does, as long as
he continues to do it."[107]

If these well-known heretics were generously rewarded for the little
good that they did, is it conceivable that God will not reward the Jews,
who despite the exigencies of the forced conversion perform commandments secretly? Can it be that He does not discriminate between
one who performs a commandment and one who does not, between one
who serves God and one who does not? So it appears from the writing
of this man, nay, that when he prays he commits a sin, and he cites

the verse: *For My people have done a twofold wrong* [Jer. 2:13].[108] Now his error has been exposed to you and that he has not ceased to disparage his contemporaries, going so far as to speak against the sages, as we pointed out; nay, he even dared to ascribe to the Creator that He punishes for the performance of a commandment, as he expressed himself: The prayer of any of us is a sin. Indeed, it is of this that Solomon said: *And don't plead before the messenger that it was an error* [Eccles. 5:5].[109]

IV

Realizing this amazing matter that hurts the eyes, I undertook to gather pharmaceutics and roots from the books of the ancients, of which I intend to prepare medicine and salve helpful for this sickness, and heal it with the help of God.[110]

I think it right to divide what I have to say on this subject into five themes: 1. the class of the laws related to the time of forced conversion; 2. definitions of the desecration of God's name and the punishment; 3. the ranks of those who die a martyr's death, and those who are forcibly converted in a persecution; 4. how this persecution differs from others, and what is to be done in relation to it; and 5. a discussion of how advisable it is for one to be careful in this persecution, may God soon put an end to it. Amen.

Theme one, the distribution of the precepts during a time of duress, is divided into three classes: A. One class of precepts, those concerning idolatry, incest, and bloodshed, requires that whenever a person is forced to violate any of them, he is at all times, everywhere, and under all circumstances obliged to die rather than transgress. *At all times* means in a time of persecution or otherwise; *everywhere* means privately or publicly; *under all circumstances* means whether the tyrant intends to have him act against his faith or not; in these situations he is obliged to die rather than transgress.[111] B. All the other commandments, any of which an oppressor may compel him to transgress, he is to judge. If the tyrant does it for his personal satisfaction, be it a time of persecution or not, privately or publicly, he may violate the Torah and escape death.[112] Support of this procedure is found in the chapter on the wayward son:[113] "But the case of Esther was public!

Yes, but she was always passive."[114] Rava maintained: "If it is for his personal satisfaction it makes a difference; otherwise how do we allow ourselves to give them the censers and the coal-containers?"[115] Clearly, it is because it makes a difference when it is for their personal satisfaction. In the case of Esther the similar difference exists: It is for their personal satisfaction. Rava is following his own reasoning, for he rules that if a non-Jew orders a Jew to cut the alfalfa on a Sabbath day and throw it before his beasts or he will kill him, he is to cut it and not have himself killed. But if he orders him to cast it into the river, he is to prefer death to obeying him, since he wants him to commit a sin.[116] It is our principle to follow Rava's decision. It is clear that as long as the oppressor is doing it for his personal satisfaction he is to transgress and to shun death, even if it is in public and in the course of a persecution.[117] C. If it is the aim of the oppressor to have him transgress, it is for him to deliberate. If it is a time of persecution he is to surrender his life and not transgress, whether in private or in public, but if it is not, he should choose to transgress and not die if it is in private, and to die if it is in public.[118] This is how the sages formulate it: When R. Dimi arrived he ruled in the name of R. Johanan that even if it is not a time of persecution, he may transgress rather than die only in private; in public he may not violate even a minor rabbinic precept, even changing the manner of tying the shoes. In public is defined as a body of ten, all Israelites.[119]

The second theme covers the definitions of the profanation of God's name and the punishment. Profanation[120] divides in two classes, general and particular. The general has two subdivisions: Commission of a sin for spite, not for pleasure or any satisfaction to be derived from the act, but because one thinks little of it and scorns it. This individual has profaned God's name, for He warns: *You shall not swear falsely by My name, profaning the name of your God* [Lev. 19:12]; it is an act that yields no pleasure or satisfaction.[121] If he does it in public he is profaning God's name. It has been made clear that in public means before ten Israelites. The second subdivision is of people who are neglectful and do not improve their behavior, so that others grumble about them very critically.[122] They may not have committed a sin, but they have profaned God's name. In the matter of transgressions a person is required to be as heedful of human beings as he is of God.[123]

He, blessed be He, ruled: *You shall be guiltless before the Lord and before Israel* [Num. 32:22].[124] It is related in the tractate Yoma[125] that Rabbi Naḥman ben Yitzhak pointed to the proverb people use: "May God forgive so-and-so."[126] Another expression is: "When friends are embarrassed by his reputation."[127]

The particular is of two kinds. The first is when a learned person does something that others may do without demur, but that a person like him ought not to do, because he enjoys a widespread reputation of piety, so that more is expected of him. He has profaned God's name. Rav offered this definition of profanation: "When I, for example, buy meat and do not pay at once."[128] In other words, a person of his stature should not purchase anything unless he can pay at once at the time of purchase, although it is a quite acceptable practice (to buy on credit). A similar point of view is reflected in R. Joḥanan's statement: "When I, for example, walk four ells without wearing my phylacteries,"[129] implying that it is not proper for a man like him to do this. Many times we find the explanation that it is different when the party concerned is an important individual.[130]

The second kind is when a learned man behaves disgustingly in matters of trade or negotiation, receives people sullenly and insolently, is not of a friendly disposition, and has relations with others that are not founded on respect and mutual regard. A person of this character has profaned God's name. This is what the rabbis, peace be upon them, say: "When a person is learned but does not deal creditably, and does not speak softly to people, how is he judged? 'Woe to so-and-so who is educated, woe to his father who had him study, woe to his master who taught him. How perverse his actions are! How ugly his ways!' "[131] Scripture speaks of him in this passage: in that it was said of them, these are the people of the Lord and they left His land.[132]

If I were not concerned about verbosity and rambling, I would outline in detail how an individual ought to deal with others, what all his actions and words should be like, and how he should receive people, so that anyone who spoke to him or had dealings with him would have only words of praise. I would explain what the rabbis mean by their expression "dealing creditably" or "speaking softly to people." But this would require a full-length book. So I resume.

Sanctification of God's name is the contrary of profanation. When a person fulfills one of the commandments, and no other motive impels him save his love of God and His service, he has publicly sanctified God's name.[133] So also if he enjoys a good reputation he has sanctified God's name. The rabbis phrase it this way: "When a person has studied Bible and Mishnah, ministered to scholars, dealt gently with people, what is the general judgment of him? Happy is his father who taught him Torah, and woe to those who have not studied. See how lovely are the ways of so-and-so who is learned in Torah, how proper his deeds."[134] It is he who is meant by the verse: *And He said to me, "You are My servant, Israel in whom I glory* [Isa. 49:3].[135] Similarly, if a great man shuns actions that others think ugly, even if he does not think so, he sanctifies God's name. Scripture counsels: *Put crooked speech away from you* [Prov. 4:24].[136]

Profanation of God's name is a grievous sin for which the inadvertent sinner and the deliberate sinner are equally punished. The rabbis rule that in the sin of the profanation of God's name it makes no difference whether it is accidental or purposeful.[137] A man is granted a delay in punishment of all sins, but not for the profanation of God's name. This is how the rabbis formulate it: "For the profanation of God's name no credit is extended. What does it mean? He is not treated as he is by the storekeeper who extends credit."[138] The rabbis also teach that whoever profanes God's name in secret is punished in the open.[139] It is a more serious sin than any other. Neither the Day of Atonement,[140] nor suffering, nor repentance procures forgiveness. This is the dictum of the rabbis: "He who is guilty of the profanation of God's name cannot find forgiveness by either repentance or the Day of Atonement, nor can suffering wash it away; they all suspend punishment until death provides the forgiveness, and its biblical support is: *Then the Lord of Hosts revealed Himself to my ears: 'This iniquity shall never be forgiven you until you die"* [Isa. 22:14].' "[141] The entire exposition is in reference to the person who voluntarily profanes God's name, as I shall elucidate.

As profanation of God's name is a grievous sin, so is sanctification of His name a most meritorious deed, for which one is generously rewarded. Every Jewish individual is required to sanctify God's name. It is stated in Sifra:[142] "I the Lord am your God, who brought you out of the land of Egypt, to give you the land of Canaan, to be your

God,"[143] that is, on condition that you sanctify My name publicly. In the chapter on the rebellious and defiant son we are told that Rabbi Ami was asked if a Noahide[144] is commanded to sanctify God's name. It may be concluded from this question that regarding an Israelite no similar doubt is raised; he is indeed bidden to sanctify His name, and this is what the verse implies: *That I may be sanctified in the midst of the Israelite people* [Lev. 22:32].[145]

Theme three is about the gradation of those who are martyrs for God's name and those whom persecution forces to convert. You have to realize that wherever the sages rule that one is to surrender his life and not transgress, one who was executed has sanctified God's name. If ten Israelites witnessed his death he has sanctified His name publicly. It includes Hananiah, Mishael, Azariah,[146] Daniel,[147] the ten martyrs by government order,[148] the seven children of Hannah,[149] and all the other victims of Israel, may God avenge their blood in the near future. It is to them that the verse refers: *Bring in My devotees, who made a covenant with Me over sacrifice* [Ps. 50:5].[150] To the rabbis this verse seemed appropriate: *I adjure you O maidens of Jerusalem, by gazelles or by hinds of the field* [Song of Songs 2:7],[151] which means—*I adjure you, O maidens of Jerusalem*, the persecuted generations; *by gazelles*, those who did for Me what I desired, so I did what they desired; *by hinds of the field*, those who shed their blood for Me[152] like the blood of the gazelles and the hinds.[153] To them this verse also refers: *It is for Your sake that we are slain all day long* [Ps. 44:23].[154]

A person to whom God grants the privilege of ascending to this high rank, in other words, to suffer a martyr's death, even if he is as sinful as Jeroboam ben Nebat and his associates,[155] is surely one of the members of the world-to-come, although he may not be learned.[156] The rabbis infer[157] this from the tradition that no creature is qualified to attain the status of the martyrs by government order: "Is it Rabbi Akiva and his colleagues? But of course not! They are beneficiaries of learning and good deeds.[158] No, it is the martyrs of Lydda."[159]

Now, if he did not surrender himself to death but transgressed under duress and did not die, he did not act properly, and under compulsion he profaned God's name. However, he is not to be punished by any of the seven means of retribution.[160] Not a single instance is found in the Torah in which a forced individual is sentenced to any of the punishments, whether the transgression was light or grave. Only he who acts voluntarily is subject, as Scripture directs: *But the person . . . who acts defiantly . . . that soul shall be cut off* [Num. 15:30], but not of one who was forced.[161] The Talmud often says: The Torah rules that the forced individual is not culpable, *for this case is like that of a man attacking another and murdering him* [Deut. 22:26],[162] and frequently the ruling is repeated; a forced individual is excused by the Torah.[163] He is not dubbed a transgressor, nor a wicked man, nor is he disqualified from giving testimony, unless he committed a sin that disqualifies him from serving as a witness.[164] He simply did not fulfill the commandment of sanctifying God's name, but he can under no circumstance be named a deliberate profaner of God's name.[165]

Therefore, anyone who claims or thinks that a person who transgressed is to be condemned to death, because the sages established the principle that one must surrender himself to death and not transgress, is absolutely wrong. It simply is not so, as I shall explain. True, it is upon him to surrender to death, but if he does not he is not guilty.[166] Even if he worships idols under duress his soul will not be cut off, and he is certainly not executed by court order. This principle is clearly stated in the Sifra:[167] The divine Torah rules regarding one who gives of his seed to Molech: *I Myself will set My face against that man* [Lev. 20:5], not if he was forced, nor if it was unwittingly, nor if he was taught wrong. Plainly then, if he was forced or was taught wrong his soul will not be cut off, although it will be if he does it presumptuously and voluntarily. It is even plainer that if he forcibly committed sins that, if presumptuously and voluntarily committed, are punished by forty lashes, he is not at all subject to this punishment. The law against profanation is stated prohibitively in the declaration of God, blessed be He: *You shall not profane My holy name* [Lev. 22:32].[168]

Now it is known that a false oath is profanation, as we read in the Torah: *You shall not swear falsely by My name, profaning the name of your God: I am the Lord* [Lev. 19:12].[169] Yet the text of the Mishnah reads: "Men may vow to murderers, robbers, and tax-gatherers that what they have is heave-offering. . . ."[170] The school of Shammai qualifies that they may confirm this with a vow; the school of Hillel broadens it to include even an oath. This is explicitly written. These matters are clear and in no need of supportive argument of any kind, for how can anyone suggest that the law with respect to a person who acted under duress and one who acted voluntarily is the same? And our sages ruled: "Let him transgress and surrender his life." So you see, this man[171] is of higher status than the sages, and more punctilious about the Law. By word of mouth and the use of his tongue, he surrenders himself to death and claims to have sanctified God's name. But by his actions he is a sinner and rebellious, and he makes himself guilty against his life, because God, exalted be He, established *by the pursuit of which man shall live* [Lev. 18:5], and not die.[172]

Theme four deals with the difference between this persecution and others, and what a person should do. Remember that in all the difficulties that occurred in the time of the sages, they were compelled to violate commandments and to perform sinful acts. The Talmud lists the prohibitions, that they may not study Torah, that they may not circumcise their sons,[173] and that they have intercourse with their wives when they are ritually unclean.[174] But in this persecution they are not required to do anything but say something, so that if a man wishes to fulfill the 613 commandments[175] secretly[176] he can do so. He incurs no blame for it, unless he set himself without compulsion to desecrate the Sabbath, although no one forced him.[177] This compulsion imposes no action, only speech. They[178] know very well that we do not mean what we say, and that what we say is only to escape the ruler's punishment and to satisfy him with this simple confession. Anyone who suffered martyrdom in order not to acknowledge the apostleship of "that man,"[179] the only thing that can be said of him is that he has done what is good and proper, and that God holds great reward in store for him. His position is very high, for he has given his life for the sanctity of God, be He exalted and blessed. But if anyone comes to ask me whether to surrender his life or acknowledge, I tell him to confess and not choose death. However, he should not continue to live in the domain of that ruler.[180] He should stay home and not go out, and if he is dependent on his work let him be the Jew in private. There has never yet been a persecution as remarkable as this one, where the only coercion is to say something. When our rabbis ruled that a person is to surrender himself to death and not transgress, it does not seem likely that they had in mind speech that did not involve action. He is to suffer martyrdom only when it is demanded of him to perform a deed, or something that he is forbidden to do.[181]

A victim of this persecution should follow this counsel: Let him set it as his objective to observe as much of the Law as he can. If it happens that he has sinned much, or that he has desecrated the Sabbath, he should still not carry what it is not allowed to carry.[182] He must not think that what he has already violated is far more grievous than what he observes;[183] let him be as careful about observance as possible. Remember, a person must learn this fundamental principle. Jeroboam ben Nebat[184] is chastised for making the calves, and for disregarding the regulations regarding the Sabbath that come immediately after a holiday, or the like.[185] None can claim that he was guilty of a more serious sin.[186] This principle is applicable only in man-made laws in this world. God inflicts punishment for grievous sins and for minor ones, and He rewards people for everything they do. Hence it is important to bear in mind that one is punished for every sin committed and is rewarded for every precept fulfilled. Any other view of this is wrong.

What I counsel myself, and what I should like to suggest to all my friends and everyone that consults me, is to leave these places and go to where he can practice religion and fulfill the Law without compulsion or fear. Let him leave his family and his home and all he has, because the divine Law that He bequeathed to us is more valuable than the ephemeral, worthless incidentals that the intellectuals scorn; they are transient, whereas the fear of God is eternal.[187] Moreover, when two Jewish cities are at one's elbow, one superior to the other in its actions and behavior, more observant and more concerned with the precepts, the God-fearing individual is obliged to depart from the town where the actions are not at their best, and move to the better township.[188] We are guided by the admonition of the rabbis not to dwell in a city in which there are fewer than ten righteous residents.[189] They derive this from a dialogue between God and Abraham, which concludes the account of Sodom. *What if ten righteous people should be found there? And He answered: "I will not destroy, for the sake of the ten"* [Gen. 18:32]. This is the proper thing to do when both cities are Jewish. But if the place is gentile, the Jew who resides there must by all means leave it and go to a more suitable location. He must make every effort to do so although he may expose himself to danger, so that he can get away from this bad spot where he cannot practice his religion properly, and strive to reach a comfortable place. Indeed, the prophets have spelled out that a person who resides among nonbelievers is one of them,[190] and so King David complained: *For they have driven me out today, so that I cannot have a share in the Lord's possession, but am told, "Go and worship other gods"* [1 Sam. 26:19]; he equated his dwelling among the gentiles with the worship of other gods. The pious and the God-fearing are required to despise evil and its doers, for so David declared: *O Lord, You know I hate those who hate You, and loathe Your adversaries* [Ps. 139:21].[191] He also announced: *I am a companion to all who fear You, to those who keep Your precepts* [Ps. 119:63].[192] Likewise, our father Abraham, we find, despised his family and his home and ran for his life to escape from the doctrines of the heretics.[193]

This is the effort he must make to separate himself from the heretics when they do not coerce him to do as they do; he should leave them. But if he is compelled to violate even one precept it is forbidden to stay there. He must leave everything he has, travel day and night until he finds a spot where he can practice his religion. The world is sufficiently large and extensive. The appeal of the person who pleads his duties to his family and his household is really no excuse. *A brother cannot redeem a man, or pay his ransom to God* [Ps. 49:8].[194] I do not think it is right to make this plea in order to avoid the obligation and not flee to a reasonable place. He must under no circumstance continue to reside in the land of persecution. If he does, he is a transgressor, profanes God's name, and is almost a presumptuous sinner.

Those who delude themselves to think that they will remain where they are until the king Messiah appears in the Maghreb, and they will then leave for Jerusalem[195]—I simply do not know how they will rid themselves of the present difficulties. They are transgressors, and they lead others to sin. The prophet Jeremiah's criticism: *They offer healing offhand for the wounds of My people, saying, "all is well, all is well," when nothing is well* [Jer. 6:14 and 8:11],[196] fits them and others like them very well. There is no set time for the arrival of the Messiah that they can count on and decide that it is close or distant. The incumbency of the commandments does not depend on the appearance of the Messiah. We are required to apply ourselves to study and to the fulfillment of the precepts, and we must strive for perfection in both. If we do what we have to, we or our children or grandchildren may be privileged by God to witness the coming of the Messiah, and life will be more pleasant. If he does not come we have not lost anything; on the contrary we have gained by doing what we had to do. But it is wicked and hopeless and a renunciation of the faith for anyone to stay on in these places and see the study of Torah cease, the Jewish population perishing after some time, he himself unable to live as a Jew, but continue to say: "I will stay here until the Messiah appears and then I shall be relieved of the situation I am in."

Theme five is concerned with how a person should regard himself in this persecution. Anyone who cannot leave because of his attachments, or because of the dangers of a sea voyage, and stays where he is,[197] must look upon himself as one who profanes God's name, not exactly willingly, but almost so.[198] At the same time he must bear in mind that if he fulfills a precept, God will reward him doubly, because he acted so for God only, and not to show off or be accepted as an observant individual.[199] The reward is much greater for a person who fulfills the Law and knows that if he is caught, he and all he has will perish. It is he who is meant in God's qualification: *If only you seek Him with all your heart and soul* [Deut. 4:29]. Nevertheless, no one should stop to plan to leave the provinces that God is wroth with, and to exert every effort to achieve it.[200]

It is not right to alienate, scorn, and hate people who desecrate the Sabbath. It is our duty to befriend them, and encourage them to fulfill the commandments. The rabbis regulate explicitly that when an evil-doer who sinned by choice comes to the synagogue, he is to be welcomed and not insulted.[201] In this ruling they relied on Solomon's counsel: *A thief should not be despised for stealing to appease his hunger* [Prov. 6:30]. It means do not despise the evildoer in Israel when he comes secretly to "steal" some observance.

Ever since we were exiled from our land persecution is our unending lot,[202] because *from our youth it has grown with us like a father and from our mother's womb it has directed us* [Job 31:18].[203] But we frequently find in the Talmud, "a persecution is likely to pass."[204] May

God put an end to this one, and may the prediction be realized. *In those days and at that time—declares the Lord—the iniquity of Israel shall be sought, and there shall be none; the sins of Judah, and none shall be found; for I will pardon those I allow to survive* [Jer. 50:20]. May it be His will. Amen.

NOTES

1. Maimonides employs the first person plural in most references to himself (literally, ours). This was the usage developed among speakers of Arabic in medieval times, especially in northwestern Africa. In the translation, English practice is followed.
2. The reference is to the Almohads (al-Muwaḥḥidun) and their destructive conquest of North Africa and Spain (see Abraham ibn Ezra's poem: "Alas, calamity from heaven has struck Spain, an elegy for the victims of the persecution"). The Almohads (1130–1223) early in their history instituted forced conversion.
3. *That man* in this context is Muhammad, founder of Islam, whose name Maimonides avoids mentioning.
4. By qualifying the "sage" with "whom he calls," Maimonides indicates that he himself does not think so.
5. The question raised by the forced convert is either/or, as if there is no alternative, as Maimonides will point out.
6. It is to be noted that Maimonides begins with his opinion of the sage, and follows it with evidence that supports his judgment. His evaluation of women's capacity was common in the ancient and medieval world.
7. The verse from the Bible is used by Maimonides to support his thinking. This reflects the view, held by generations of rabbis and scholars, that Scripture is a storehouse of all knowledge and doctrine.
8. The reference is to King Solomon, recognized by tradition as the author of Song of Songs, Proverbs, and Ecclesiastes.
9. Maimonides may be referring to Job's response to his friends after every speech they made, or he may be thinking of the length of Job's answers compared with the briefer statements of the friends.
10. The first passage is Zophar's opening rebuke and the second is by Elihu.
11. I.e., Muhammad.
12. BT Nedarim 28a; BT Kiddushin 40a; and elsewhere.
13. See the relevant account in 1 Kings 12:20ff.
14. The rabbi's reasoning is that the person who pronounces the Muslim confession of faith thereby reads himself out of the Jewish religious community, so that his fulfillment of the Law, or any part of it, is no more efficacious than its fulfillment by any Muslim or gentile.
15. An ironical characterization, implying the opposite.
16. Maimonides' judgment of the case is very different from that of the

rabbi. Maimonides regards the utterance of the confession as insignificant because it was not spoken in sincerity. The question to be determined is why an individual in this critical situation refrains from observing Jewish laws. Is it because he does not want to, or because he is afraid? Maimonides is persuaded that the judgment of the issue is related to this difference.

17. I.e., he attends Muslim services in a mosque.

18. In JT Sukkah 5, section 5, the verse is applied to those who bow before the sun and also bow down before the Temple.

19. I.e., they play the role of the truly pious Muslim.

20. A pious Jewish individual.

21. Literally: the magnificence of God, the name of the declaration that the Muslim makes: Allah Akbar—God is most magnificent.

22. Namely, the mosque.

23. I.e., Muhammad. The avowal is part of the confession that the convert to Islam recites.

24. This is the meaning that the rabbis derive from the verse. Cf. BT Bava Kamma 72b and BT Sanhedrin 27a.

25. Maimonides renders the verse "the end may be better."

26. The suggestion in the rabbi's introduction of "heretics and Christians" is that the confession is such grievous betrayal of their convictions, that a Jew should certainly act the same way, and if he fails to, he excludes himself from the Jewish religion.

27. The protest is made by Elijah against King Ahaziah's inquiry of ⸍ foreign deity. The phrase is expressive of Maimonides' inner pain.

28. The Torah, Lev. 20:1–6, very vigorously condemns this act anᴅ behavior of those who disregard this hideous deed.

29. The caution Maimonides expresses is consistent with his own practice, and he explicitly declares in his Introduction to the *Guide of the Perplexed:* "The diction of this treatise has not been chosen haphazardly, but with great exactness and exceeding precision . . . and nothing has been mentioned out of place." He reads the advice in Job as it was explained by R. Aha in Genesis Rabbah 24:5: God would repeat every statement He made to Moses. See also BT Eruvin 54b.

30. The verse speaks of the plague of darkness inflicted on Egypt. Former generations did not hesitate to use any apt biblical passage, even though its original use was in a different context.

31. Maimonides is referring to the sin that he committed by hurling insults at Jews and naming them gentiles.

32. Exodus Rabbah 1:10 charges the Jews in Egypt with deliberately discontinuing the rite of circumcision because they wished to imitate the Egyptians.

33. Exodus Rabbah 19:6.

34. The verse occurs in the section that teaches the proper treatment of the Paschal lamb.

35. Numbers Rabbah 11:6, in which Song of Songs 3:7 is said to be a summary of the story of the Exodus.

36. Josh. 5:3 reports that Joshua circumcised the people at the "Hill of

Foreskins." The corresponding Midrash accounts for its name by this explanation.

37. This is stated in Exodus Rabbah 19:6.

38. The Midrash supports its statement by this verse, as "your blood" is in the plural, to indicate its two sources.

39. Ezekiel relates in detail the sexual excesses in the northern and southern states of the land of Israel. Although his graphic description was meant to be taken metaphorically, the rabbis utilized it for their homiletic needs.

40. This is another illustration of the method of taking an apt phrase out of its context.

41. The dialogue comes from BT Shabbat 97a and Exodus Rabbah 3:12.

42. The verse is concerning Abraham who trusted God's promise that he was going to have offspring.

43. These words are directed to Moses and Aaron after they had struck the rock to draw water from it.

44. BT Shabbat 97a.

45. The author briefly gives the conclusion of the dialogue in the Talmud.

46. Maimonides' contention that the general worship of the Baal was voluntary is based on the lack of any reference to an outside force, unlike the situation in his day.

47. The verse is Elijah's reply to God's question: *Why are you here, Elijah?* And Elijah explains: *I am moved by zeal for the Lord, the God of Hosts, for the Israelites have forsaken Your covenant, torn down Your altars, and put Your prophets to the sword. I alone am left, and they are out to take my life.* The reported dialogue here is built on the phrases of the biblical verse.

48. The biblical verse is a continuation of the conversation between God and Elijah.

49. An alternate name for Song of Songs Rabbah, whose first word is *hazita* [Prov. 22:29]. The dialogue in our text is one of several in the Midrash that are meant to prove that God resents the slander of prophets against Israel.

50. This begins the first criticism of the people in the text.

51. The rendering of the verse by Maimonides is suggested by the Aramaic Targum to the verse.

52. The verse is from the elegy for the city of Jerusalem.

53. The wantonness voiced in the verse is a desecration of God's name since it indicates no realization of the seriousness of their position.

54. "The way" they reject is clearly God's way.

55. The verse is from the vision of the heavenly scene.

56. Both BT Yevamot 49b and JT Sanhedrin 28c (ed. Krotoshin) report it. In the former, Rava relates that a trial took place in which Menasseh accused Isaiah of acting against the laws of Moses.

57. Zech. 3:1 tells of a vision in which the prophet sees the high priest Joshua and Satan standing at his right to accuse him.

58. In Ezra 10:18 we read that some descendants of the sons of Joshua took non-Jewish wives. The Aramaic Targum to Zech. 3:3 informs us of this.

59. He probably has Satan in mind. In the incident with Joshua, Satan is

more an adversary than a ministering angel, but he is, of course, subject to God.

60. Maimonides enumerates these groups either because some from among them were forced to convert, or because by issuing his decision he is in fact disparaging scholars who think otherwise.

61. I.e., the forced converts.

62. The biblical quotation speaks of refugees who fled before the raiders, and there is a strong similarity to the situation in the text.

63. The quotation is from the story of the contest over the blessing of Isaac.

64. BT Sanhedrin 37a. R. Ze'eira suggests that since the consonants of *his clothes* (Gen. 27:27) are the same as of *his traitors*, the idea is implicit that even when Israelites act wrongfully against God, they are still under His protection. The verse continues: *and he blessed him*.

65. Stories of the Roman persecution of scholars, and the incidents connected with it, are found in BT Avodah Zarah 16b-18b, including the involvement of R. Meir. It is related that in his effort to free his wife from a house of prostitution to which she had been sentenced, he tried to bribe the guard. When the guard sounded his fear that he might be punished by his superiors, R. Meir told him that in that case he should call out: "O God of Meir, help me." Evidently this created the impression that R. Meir had his God, as they had theirs.

66. This exchange is not recorded in the Talmud.

67. The Hebrew text reads "secretly," but the rendering must be as translated here, for this is what Maimonides is seeking to establish.

68. I.e., the convert who addressed his question to the rabbi.

69. Although idolatry is thoroughly condemned in the Jewish tradition, it has at least the redeeming feature of belief in superior powers, whereas heresy is agnosticism, and often atheism, and a rejection of prophecy.

70. See S. Lieberman, *Greek in Jewish Palestine* (New York: Philipp Feldheim, 1965), pp. 15-19, where the examination of sources leads to the conclusion that R. Eliezer "acquired his secular learning in his youth," and was "even qualified to pass judgment on the style and exactness of Aquila's translation of the Torah into Greek."

71. To verse 1:8; it is the third midrashic development of the implications of the verse.

72. He is now addressing his associates, but the verdict is pronounced to R. Eliezer.

73. In the time of the tannaim, it generally referred to Christianity. In his comment on Mishnah Hullin 1:2 (ed. Kafih) Maimonides identifies them with the Christians, but in his comment on Avot 1:3 he reports about the two disciples of Antigonos, Zadok and Boethus, and concludes: From that time, these cursed groups rose, the heretics, that are called Karaites in our district, I mean Egypt.

74. Later in this essay Maimonides teaches that in Islam monotheism is absolute, and he expresses a similar view in his responsum to the proselyte Obadiah. Cf. J. Blau, *Maimonides' Responsa* (1957-61), no. 448 (p. 725),

and A. Freimann, *Maimonides' Responsa* (1957–61), no. 369 (p. 335). Islam differs from Judaism with respect to the belief in the revelation to Muhammad, the man, and the Koran.

75. He implies that they lie when they also avow that Muhammad is the apostle of God.

76. The trial related in Daniel is fully developed by Maimonides in his *Sefer ha-Mitzvot*. (Hebrew translation and commentary by J. Kafiḥ [Jerusalem: Mossad Harav Kook, 1971] pp. 63–99). The enumeration of the 613 commandments, at precept 9, states: The Sanctification of God's Name, incumbent on all Israel, requires that we surrender ourselves to death by the hand of the tyrant for the sake of our love of Torah and our belief in His unity. This is what Hananiah, Mishael, and Azariah did in the reign of Nebuchadnezzar, when he demanded that they bow to the image. All the people, including the Jews, obeyed him, and they brought great shame on Israel since the commandment that was designed for this kind of crisis was disregarded. The proper action was to publicize and demonstrate God's unity at that juncture. God has promised them through Isaiah that the shame of Israel would not be total, and that young men would arise in that difficult situation whom death would not daunt, and they would surrender their blood, and thus publicize the faith and sanctify God's Name in public as we were ordered by Moses.

77. Maimonides took these two groups, exiled by the Babylonians, 2 Kings 24:14, to be the great scholars, as the rabbis explained, BT Gittin 87a.

78. This explanation of the rabbis in connection with Nebuchadnezzar's decree is found in BT Megillah 12a.

79. He writes of the man who wrote that responsum.

80. Maimonides applies to the author of the responsum a verse in which the prophet reprimands those who criticize God for choosing the gentile Cyrus to proclaim the right of Israelites to return to their homeland.

81. The sources are listed in Moses Maimonides, *Epistle to Yemen*, ed. A. Halkin, trans. B. Cohen (New York: Proceedings of the American Academy for Jewish Research, 1952), p. 22.

82. Throughout the holiday of Hanukkah a prayer of gratitude, recited during the services and in the grace after meals, begins: [We thank You] for the miracles,...

83. Deut. 19:15–21 states that if testimony given by witnesses is proved false by others, *you shall do to him as he schemed to do to his fellow* [Deut. 19:19]. In BT Makkot 2a–7a, the law as detailed in the Mishnah is further elaborated.

84. The root of the law is Exod. 21:17. It is one of the negative commandments (number 319 in Maimonides' list, ed. Kafiḥ, p. 329).

85. Num. 15:37–41 and Deut. 22:12. The rabbinic exposition is in chapter 4 of BT Menaḥot 38a–44a, b.

86. Deut. 22:10. Rashi's comment on the verse enumerates additional rabbinic prohibitions.

87. Lev. 19:19, which opens with the admonition: *You shall observe My*

laws. Rashi points out that these laws are God's command and are not rationally understandable.

88. *Azharot* are a literary genre of poetical enumerations of the 613 commandments developed by Jews in the Middle Ages. Several collections are known.

89. In the Hebrew text a derogatory epithet appears, and it is difficult to determine whether the author, translator, or copyist is responsible for it.

90. I.e., he would be conscious of the responsibility resting on him, and would be careful to write only what is relevant and to the point.

91. This is a frequent exclamation of Arabic literature.

92. The verse is taken out of context, but is appropriate here as an expression of Maimonides' embarrassment at the letter of the rabbi, whom he is excoriating.

93. Evidently the author seeks to take the edge off what sounds like boastfulness.

94. In his *Epistle to Yemen* (ed. Halkin, p. ix), he informs us of his realization that "the liar is as little restrained with his pen as with his tongue." Here he emphasizes the prestige that books enjoy, at times undeservedly.

95. The verse continues: *who committed himself to doing what was displeasing to the Lord, at the instigation of his wife Jezebel.* It is the concluding summary of the story of the vineyard of Naboth, which Ahab coveted, and Jezebel prevailed on him to set up a trump court, which condemned Naboth to death. Elijah pronounced the celebrated rebuke: *Would you murder and take possession?* [1 Kings 21:19].

96. Basing themselves on *Have you seen how Ahab has humbled himself before Me* [1 Kings 21:29], and on the practice of royalty to rise late, the rabbis, BT Ta'anit 25b, conclude that Ahab fasted from 9 A.M., but do not report how many hours he fasted.

97. JT Sanhedrin 10, Halakhah 2, tells that it lasted three hours. The number here may represent what Maimonides had in his copy of the Jerusalem Talmud.

98. It is the story of Ehud ben Gera who brought the tribute paid by Israel to Eglon, and then revealed he had a message for him from God. He rose and Ehud stabbed him fatally. See Judg. 3:15–22.

99. Maimonides cites this phrase to prove the truth of his statement.

100. BT Sanhedrin 105b says so, but in BT Nazir 23b the Tosafot speak of the genealogy ("his daughter or his son's daughter") as not exact, because of the several generations that elapsed between the time of Eglon, King of Moab, and the time of King David or Solomon.

101. See 2 Kings 25:9 and Isa. 66:1. Leviticus Rabbah 20:1 points out that like Solomon, the builder of the Temple who reigned forty years, the king of Babylonia who destroyed the Temple also reigned forty years.

102. BT Sanhedrin 96a. It cannot be told whether Maimonides drew his own conclusion or found in some source the relation between deed and reward.

103. The source of the catalog of sins is BT Bava Batra 16b, and in Tanḥuma to Gen. 27:1 (no. 8) is the halakhic question he asked of his father.

104. Cf. G. D. Cohen, "Esau as Symbol in Early Medieval Thought" in

Jewish Medieval and Renaissance Studies, ed. A. Altmann (Cambridge: Harvard University Press, 1967), pp. 19–48.

105. In his comment on the verse Rashi cites an aggadic midrash that treats its content as the reward to Esau for honoring his father.

106. Cf. BT Pesaḥim 118a, Nazir 23b, Bava Kamma 38b, and Horayot 10b.

107. Maimonides voices his view here that every human act is judged, and that actions do not cancel one another; see his comment on the last Mishnah in Mishnah Avot, 4.

108. The rabbi thought the converts would be punished for a prescribed act as they would be for their conversion.

109. Maimonides regards the verse as very apt for the rabbi.

110. Maimonides here indulges in medical jargon, but the sense is clear.

111. The Hebrew formula is *yehareg ve-'al ya'avor*—let him get killed but let him not transgress, see BT Yoma 82a.

112. I.e., he is to submit to the force demanding the act.

113. BT Sanhedrin 74a–b, where the discussion is to be found.

114. In BT Sanhedrin 74a–b, where the definition of "public" is accepted as ten Jewish adults, the question is raised, why is Esther, who in public became the queen of Ahasuerus, not criticized; the answer given is that she did not actively participate, that she was passive.

115. During the Zoroastrian Sassanian rule in Persia (226–651 C.E.), the Persians provided fire and heat in their place of worship, and Jews had to participate along with the others. It was seemingly service to the idol worshiper, but the ruling authorities did not compel the Jews to cooperate out of malice, but for their own benefit.

116. This completes the passage from the Talmud.

117. This individual, when he realizes that the oppressor is not intent on converting him, is to yield to his demands under all circumstances and thus save his life.

118. Since he is not serving as an example to others, he may yield to the oppressor.

119. BT Sanhedrin 74a. In its text the rabbi who cites R. Joḥanan is Rabin.

120. The concept of profanation derives from a prohibition in the Torah: *You shall not profane My holy name* [Lev. 22:32 and elsewhere]. Like its opposite, *kiddush ha-Shem*, also deriving from the Torah, the concept was fashioned in rabbinic times.

121. As Maimonides explains, the juxtaposition of a false oath and desecration indicates that something done for no gain or pleasure to the doer is an act of profanation.

122. This category of people are within the law yet they do not act creditably. It is what Naḥmanides defines (in his comment on Lev. 19:2) as "a scoundrel within the requirements of the Torah."

123. It is the discussion of an act that is not sinful but may be regarded by others as sinful, or at least raise the suspicion that it is sinful.

124. Israel is mentioned together with God as requiring the guiltlessness of actions.

125. BT Yoma 86a. Several examples are given of this variety of desecration.

126. The saying prays that God will forgive such actions.

127. This definition of profanation was given by R. Yannai in BT Yoma 86a.

128. This and the rest of the material gathered here are collected in BT Yoma 86a.

129. This is one of the several statements in the Talmud by men who out of respect to the Almighty covered their heads. It was gradually popularized until it became the accepted practice of Orthodox Jews not to walk or sit with bare heads.

130. BT Berakhot 19a and elsewhere.

131. The same judgment is passed by Maimonides in *Mishneh Torah, Hilkhot Yesodei ha-Torah* 5:11.

132. The statement of the rabbis is in the same context, in BT Yoma 86a: see note 128.

133. The idea sounded here is also found in Maimonides' comment on Mishnah Makkot 3:17, in which he lays down the principles listed here.

134. This is from BT Yoma 86a.

135. In this particular prophecy the prophet speaks of God's choice of him (or the people) and of the praise bestowed.

136. The verse appears among counsels of caution.

137. BT Kiddushin 40a, in a discussion of the commission of sins and its negative consequences.

138. The assertion of the rabbis is likewise found in BT Kiddushin 40a. It is taken from Mishnah Avot 4:4, and reads not "extending credit," but "is punished."

139. This assertion is also in Mishnah Avot 4:4.

140. Maimonides begins with the inability to find forgiveness for this kind of profanation on the Day of Atonement because in Mishnah Yoma 8:8 we are told that sins of man against God are forgiven on the Day of Atonement. Its ineffectiveness in sins of profanation demonstrates the grievousness of such sins.

141. BT Yoma 86a. The verse from Isaiah is the last verse of the prophet's condemnation of Judah, during the preparations for defense against the Assyrian siege of Jerusalem. In the course of it the prophet protests: *But you gave no thought to Him who planned it, you took no note of Him who designed it long before* [Isa. 22:11]. This is profanation of God's name.

142. In its comment on Lev. 25:28. Its simple sense is that God's purpose in the Exodus was to give the Israelites the land of Canaan and to assert that He was their God. Maimonides explains it *on condition that* I be your God, and he finds support in the Sifra for his introduction of the condition; it contains the specific stipulation that He makes: on condition that you sacrifice yourselves in order to sanctify My name.

143. This is in chapter 8 of Mishnah Sanhedrin.

144. Jewish tradition teaches that the descendants of Noah, in other words, all of humankind with the exception of the Israelites, are obliged to observe seven commandments. The Noahide laws prohibit the rabbinic expansion of the law, blasphemy of God, idolatry, incest, bloodshed, robbery, and cutting off a part from a living animal. The problem of whether Noahides are also required to sanctify God's name and are forbidden to profane it is discussed in BT Sanhedrin 74a. It is first suggested that if they are, the total will be eight, but that objection is obviated by explaining that essentially all seven are for the purpose of sanctification.

145. BT Sanhedrin 74b invokes this verse as evidence that ten Israelites are needed to make an act public. Maimonides emphasizes that this indicated the duty of Israelites to sanctify God's name.

146. Exiles from the land of Israel, they are the heroes of Daniel 3, which recounts the order of Nebuchadnezzar to his people to prostrate themselves before an image, the refusal of the three to obey, and their miraculous escape from the fire in the furnace.

147. Daniel, after whom the book is named, succeeded in interpreting the mystifying dreams of Nebuchadnezzar and the mysterious writing on the wall that Belshazzar beheld; he survived a night in the den with the lions and saw visions that predicted the future fate of the people of Israel.

148. Although the story of the ten rabbis executed by the Roman administration is widely accepted, the earliest source is a late midrash, *Eleh Ezkerah* in A. Jellinek's edition of small midrashim, *Bet ha-Midrash* (Leipzig, 1853; reprint ed., Jerusalem: Wahrmann, 1967), 2:62–74. For an analysis of the material, see L. Finkelstein, "The Ten Martyrs," in *Essays and Studies in Memory of Linda R. Miller*, ed. I. Davidson (New York: Jewish Theological Seminary, 1938), pp. 29–55.

149. The seven children of Hannah (for the variations in the mother's name and story, see G. D. Cohen, "The Story of Hannah and Her Seven Sons in Hebrew Literature," in *Mordecai M. Kaplan Jubilee Volume*, ed. M. Davis [New York: Jewish Theological Seminary, 1953], pp. 109–22, Hebrew), all refused to worship idols during the persecution of Antiochus IV (168 B.C.E.). They wouldn't even pick up a ring that the king dropped and they were all executed. See 2 Macc. 7.

150. The application of this verse to these martyrs is made in BT Sanhedrin 110b.

151. This verse is repeated three times (with variations) in Song of Songs.

152. Song of Songs Rabbah to 2:5. The explanation offered here is one of several in the Midrash. "What they desired" is explained as what I decided for them.

153. The phrase is from Deut. 15:22–23.

154. The exposition is developed in BT Pesahim 50a.

155. See 1 Kings 12:20 ff. He is notorious as the man "who sinned and he led the many to sin," Mishnah Avot 5:18.

156. Although the unlearned person is not esteemed, as many declarations in the Talmud express it, especially BT Pesahim 49a–b.

157. BT Pesahim 50a and BT Bava Batra 10b.

158. In BT Bava Batra 10b a phrase is added: "without these as well," i.e., even if they were not martyrs they would be in Heaven.

159. See S. Lieberman "The Martyrs of Caesarea" in *Annuaire de l'Institut de Philologie et d'Histoire Orientales et Slaves* 7 (1939), and in a revised Hebrew translation, *Salo Wittmayer Baron Jubilee Volume on the Occasion of His Eightieth Birthday*, ed. S. Lieberman and A. Hyman (Jerusalem: American Academy for Jewish Research, 1974), pp. 213–46.

160. According to the rabbis, four of the seven punishments are public executions (by sword, stoning, strangulation, and burning), and the others are premature death, divinely caused death, and lashes.

161. The deduction is made by Maimonides.

162. BT Nedarim 27a. From the verse cited in the text, *Sifrei* ad versum states "that all people described in the sources as forced are guiltless, and their lives are to be spared."

163. Deut. 22:26, cited several times in both the Babylonian and Jerusalem Talmuds, is explained to teach us that the attacker, like the girl, is not, so far as possible, killed, and that the girl, like the attacker, is subject to the principle of "let him surrender his life and not transgress." See BT Pesaḥim 25b.

164. BT Bava Kamma 28b, Avodah Zarah 54a.

165. In *MT Hilkhot Edut* 10, Maimonides discusses at length the people disqualified to testify because they violate Mosaic or rabbinic laws.

166. Maimonides does not exonerate the person from the guilt of profanation because in acknowledging Islam that person has acted against God's sanctity. However, Maimonides discriminates between him, a forced convert, and the deliberate sinner.

167. Sifra, Lev. 10, in the section dealing with people who dedicate their offspring to Molech.

168. Rashi explains the verse as follows: by transgressing presumptuously.

169. The second half of the verse is the result of the first.

170. Mishnah Nedarim 3:4. In his comment on this mishnah, Maimonides states explicitly that they are oppressors. In the case of the tax-gatherer he specifies that if he is a legal emissary of the government no attempt to shirk is allowed.

171. The rabbi who wrote the response to the convert.

172. This conclusion was added by the rabbis, cf. BT Sanhedrin 74a. Lev. 18:5 begins: *You shall keep My laws and My rules.*

173. This text is a conflate of the versions in BT Rosh ha-Shanah 19a and Ta'anit 18a and Me'ilah 17a.

174. Maimonides also speaks of these prohibitions in the *Epistle to Yemen*.

175. Based on a statement in BT Makkot 23b, the belief that there are 613 commandments (248 positive and 365 prohibitory) was universally accepted in the Jewish world.

176. Despite his insistence that these converts can continue to live as Jews, he is cautious enough to advise secrecy because the government authorities will not tolerate public behavior as Jews.

177. Maimonides here grants the individual the right to save his life, but in *MT Hilkot Yesodei ha-Torah* 5:7 he rules that one who chooses martyrdom is actually committing a sin.

178. The Moslems and their rulers.

179. Muhammad.

180. Cf. the *Epistle to Yemen*, where Maimonides urges a similar course. It may be suggested that his own departure from Spain, and later from Fez, resulted from a fear that he was in danger of being recognized as a Jew.

181. This includes the positive as well as the prohibitory laws.

182. In Mishnah Shabbat and BT Shabbat many laws and discussions are found that have to do with the general principle that it is forbidden to move things from the home to a public area and conversely.

183. It is the principle that when a person is guilty of a grievous sin or crime and incurs severe punishment, he must not be chastised for a minor offense and its lighter retribution, cf. BT Gittin 53bf.

184. Cf. 1 Kings 12:28–33.

185. It is the practice instituted by the rabbis of preparing a dish on the day before the holiday, which will be consumed on the Sabbath immediately following, and by means of it the dishes prepared for the Sabbath on the holiday (Friday) are regarded as a continuation of the cooking begun on the day before the holiday (Thursday). This is called the "fusion of cooked dishes." They have similarly provided for a "fusion of areas," which can be set up so as to extend the stretch within which carrying on the Sabbath becomes permissible.

186. So that the rule mentioned in note 183 would be in force, Maimonides limits its effectiveness only to man-made laws; God is not bound by them.

187. Maimonides knows very well that in the evaluation of the goods of this world a difference exists between the common folk and the intellectuals. His analysis is contained in the last chapter of his *Guide of the Perplexed*.

188. See Maimonides' Introduction, called "Eight Chapters," to the commentary on Mishnah Avot, chapter 4, which deals with the choices that confront a person.

189. Maimonides probably relied on the admonition of *Pirkei de-Rabbi Eliezer*, chapter 26.

190. The rabbinic judgment that whoever dwells outside the land of Israel is like one who has no God (BT Ketubbot 110b), is the source of Maimonides' statement.

191. In *Avot de-Rabbi Natan* (ed. S. Schecter [Vienna: 1887], p. 64, version A) the force of the expression is mitigated and limited to converts and Christians.

192. See Tanhuma, Tzav, 8, discussing some of the ancients whom God chose but who did not draw close to Him (in reference to Ps. 65:5: *Happy is the man You choose and bring near*), and they made the effort to draw close. One of them was David, and the verse indicates that he strove to come close to God.

193. See *Pirkei de-Rabbi Eliezer*, 26.

194. Sifrei Deut. to verse 32:39 derives from this sentence that parents cannot save children nor can brothers save one another from the consequence of their deeds.

195. In the *Epistle to Yemen*, Maimonides derives from a biblical verse that the Messiah will appear in the land of Israel.

196. Jeremiah attacks the profiteers and false prophets who mislead the people with promises of peace and prosperity.

197. Maimonides is well aware of the obstacles in the way of rational conclusions and truly important decisions.

198. In *MT Hilkhot Yesodei ha-Torah* 5:9, he seems to take a harsher position, identifying the individual who is reluctant to leave as *a dog [that] returns to his vomit* (Prov. 26:1), and names him a "deliberate idolator."

199. The assurance given the observant convert and Jew finds its parallel in the position of R. Judah Halevi (c. 1075–1141) who, although he deplores the choice of Jews to live away from the land of Israel, contends that the fulfillment of God's laws in exile earns double reward, *Kuzari* 1:114.

200. Maimonides does not concede the right to transgress and make peace with the idea of continuing to live in "the provinces that God is wroth with."

201. See *Tosefta* (ed. Zuckermandel), BT Bava Kamma 7:3.

202. In the *Epistle to Yemen*, Maimonides dates the opposition to Judaism and its followers from the time of the Revelation at Mt. Sinai.

203. Maimonides takes the verse, Job 31:19, from the personal confession of Job to refer to the people of Israel and their history.

204. BT Ketubbot 3b; see *Epistle to Yemen*.

DISCUSSION OF
THE EPISTLE ON MARTYRDOM

Throughout his works Maimonides was able to combine mastery of the intricate details of talmudic legal thought with a philosophic theocentric passion. In reading Maimonides, one is not forced into an either/or position: either God or the law, either the individual or the community, either history or immortality. His great genius was his ability to unite and keep alive the profound tensions and subtle dialectic underlying Jewish spirituality.

The *Epistle on Martyrdom* exemplifies that genius in its approach to the principle of *kiddush ha-Shem*, sanctification of God's name, of which the highest form is martyrdom. Maimonides' treatment of *kiddush ha-Shem* in his legal writings would seem to indicate that this principle was central to his understanding of halakhic practice.[1] Israel must defy the world and bear witness to its covenantal destiny. Israel must have the courage to oppose all attempts to overthrow the supremacy of God in the world.[2] The concept of election—which is the foundation of *kiddush ha-Shem*—casts Jews in the role of witnesses to the divine reality.[3] Yet, while emphasizing and expanding the heroic in Judaism, Maimonides was able to make allowances for the fragility and vulnerability of human beings. In the *Epistle on Martyrdom* we meet a compassionate and patient leader who enables those who fall short of heroism to find their way in a tradition that focuses on the heroic. This epistle testifies to Maimonides' ability to unite an intense compassion for human beings with his basic commitment to a heroic life in sanctification of God.

Consequently, we must dissent from Haym Soloveitchik's interpretation of this epistle in which he says that Maimonides, the master halakhist and codifier of Jewish law, disregarded the authority of Halakhah in a moment of crisis and argued for a position that he knew to be legally (halakhically) invalid.

As a legal defense the *Iggeret ha-Shemad* [The Epistle on Martyrdom] is inexplicable, but not as a work of rhetoric, in the classic (and medieval) sense of the term—as a pamphlet aimed not at truth but at suasion, at moving people by all means at hand toward a given course of action. The *Iggeret ha-Shemad* is not a halakhic work, not a responsum, but to use a modern term, a propagandist tract, written with a single purpose in mind—to counteract the effects of a letter of indictment that had gained great currency and threatened to wreak havoc on the Moroccan community.[4]

To draw a distinction between "Maimonides the halakhist" and "Maimonides the rhetorician" is to add to the list of schematic dichotomies often used to explain different aspects of Maimonides' writings (e.g., the philosopher of the *Guide of the Perplexed* versus the legalist of the *Mishneh Torah*). Instead, we will treat the *Epistle on Martyrdom* as a classic example of the rich interconnection between halakhic (legal) and aggadic (narrative-homiletic) rabbinic material in halakhic decision-making.

What is at stake in approaching the *Epistle on Martyrdom* is how to understand the relationship of the formal body of halakhic rules to the broader framework of concerns, values, and interests of the living tradition. The fact that Maimonides wove numerous aggadot and other allegedly "extralegal" material into the fabric of his legal presentation need not oblige the conclusion that the epistle is a work of rhetoric or that, as Haym Soloveitchik puts it, Maimonides was "aware that his whole position was of a flimsy and makeshift nature, with little more than an aggadic loincloth to cover its nakedness."[5] Rather, it testifies that the halakhic jurist is not confined exclusively to the explicit legal rules of the halakhic code, but may legitimately ascribe *legal* weight to the other principles, values, and goals that are integral to the halakhic tradition.

To justify this approach to understanding the epistle, it is necessary first to reconstruct the nature of the problem facing Maimonides and the kinds of considerations that led him to present his argument in the manner he did.

THE DILEMMA

The Almohad persecutors demanded that Jews publicly proclaim that there is no God but Allah and that Muhammad is the prophet of Allah.

Although no attempt was made to prevent Jews from continuing to maintain their religious way of life in secrecy, they were forced to make this public declaration or face death.

One must understand the vast differences between the place of religion in modern Western society and in medieval North Africa in order to comprehend the terrible dilemma facing Jews under the Almohads. In the modern world, it makes sense to speak of religious pluralism and to acknowledge the legitimacy of faiths other than one's own.[6] In a medieval context, however, acknowledging the validity of a rival religion involved much more than admitting the "legitimacy" of different faith traditions. "Judaism for the Jews, Christianity for the Christians, and Islam for the Muslims" was foreign to the religious climate of twelfth-century North Africa.

The medieval world was one where religion and politics were inseparably interwoven; a person's theology was not a private affair, but integral to defining his social and political status. In addition, Judaism, Christianity, and Islam all claimed to be exclusive heirs to the same tradition. Admitting the truth of one of these faiths entailed admission of the invalidity of the others. "Who are the authentic inheritors of the biblical covenant?" was a question allowing for but one unequivocal answer. Christianity claimed to be the "new Israel." Islam accused the Jews of falsifying scripture, e.g., by removing mention of Muhammad from the biblical text.[7]

The Islamic claims alleging Jewish falsifications of scripture threatened the very mainstay of Jewish identity. Jews were being asked to admit that they, their parents, their grandparents, and all previous generations had the false belief that their beloved Torah was complete and eternal. Their very own scripture was said to confirm the authenticity of Islam. If Islam was the ultimate fulfillment of the biblical covenant, then their persistent and heroic loyalty to Judaism in the midst of crisis was meaningless. Conversely, loyalty to Judaism implied that the Jewish tradition had not been superseded by any other historical religion; it was thus perceived as a scandalous repudiation of the rival religious claims of Islam.

In the light of such religious rivalry and antagonism, the choice of whether to submit publicly to the Almohads was a difficult and painful dilemma. It could be argued that, given the specific historical context, anything short of heroism would strengthen the hand of Israel's adversaries and undermine the steadfast determination necessary for the Jewish community's survival. As will be explained further on in this discussion, Halakhah demands the heroism formulated in the laws of *kiddush ha-Shem* (sanctification of God's name). Allegiance to Judaism must transcend the value of life itself. If compelled to commit idolatry, murder, or certain illicit sexual acts or if, during times of persecution, Jews are forced to commit acts aimed at undermining their loyalty to the Torah, they are required to resist the will of their oppressors even at the cost of death.[8]

God becomes sanctified by the supreme expression of love of God—martyrdom. The heroic courage to suffer death rather than transgress testifies to a Jew's profound love for God and for a way of life whose value stands above the value of life. At such moments his love for God becomes the supreme value in life and all else becomes secondary by comparison.

Maimonides was fully aware of the fact that there are moments in history when a response less than the heroic endangers the Jewish community's continuity. Failure to act heroically can be said to constitute *hillul ha-Shem* (desecration of God's name), insofar as it reinforces the adversary's belief that he can manipulate Israel through brute force and weaken its ability to sustain its covenantal relationship with God.[9] Giving way under the threat of death may create a historical precedent for undermining Israel's commitment to its way of life by intimidation and the use of threats. The community sanctifies God's name by bearing witness to the futility of using brute force to break Israel's will to remain loyal to its tradition. It desecrates God's name if, by not demonstrating heroic resistance, it loses the crucial battle in the war against naked power. Given certain historical circumstances, any act of resistance or acquiescence may become a decisive test of the community's ability to survive and may serve as a watershed in the prophetic war against the "pharaohs" of history.

This, then, was Maimonides' dilemma: should he remind the community of its historical obligation to accept death and bear witness to its eternally binding covenant with God, or should he tell the people to remain alive? If the latter, then at least the Moroccan Jews, although losing this battle, might emerge victorious in subsequent ones. If they made the public declaration demanded by the Almohads, but continued in private to live as Jews, then future generations might be able to continue Jewish history when the power of Israel's enemies would abate.

There was an authoritative rabbi of the time who had issued a categorical and unequivocal decision on the issue: the Jewish community must publicly resist the Almohads and bear the burden of God's covenant with Israel, even if the cost be death. The tragic predicament of the Moroccan Jews was not particular to this community or to this generation of Jews; it was the common fate of all Jewish communities and generations both past and future. A loyal religious Jew feels the weight of being God's witness in history. He believes that his actions

affect the destiny of his people throughout history. The rabbi's ruling
may thus be explained in terms of the view that allowing the Moroccan
Jews to succumb to their persecutors would so weaken the structure
and courage of the Jewish community that its extinction would inevitably follow.

Maimonides decided to challenge the rabbi's halakhic judgment and
to fortify the Moroccan Jews by arguing that martyrdom was not absolutely required under the particular conditions of this persecution.
To a considerable extent, his decision was based on a political judgment. The question was not simply one of determining whether the
logic of certain halakhic concepts implied that martyrdom was required
during the Almohad persecutions. Maimonides and the rabbi were
forced to make a practical political judgment of whether choosing not
to act heroically in the existing situation might create social conditions
leading to the disappearance of the community.

The important point to bear in mind is that judging whether to regard
the Almohad persecution as a crucial test of the viability of Jewish
history involves considerations that transcend legality in the strict sense.
No set of legal rules is sufficient to determine how to resolve this
dilemma. All the same, the halakhic judge must accept his responsibility to pronounce a judgment in such circumstances. The decisions
of both Maimonides and the rabbi were products of Judaic values,
attitudes, precedents, and principles, and not only of halakhic rules.

A major halakhic issue around which the arguments of the *Epistle
on Martyrdom* turn is the status of the nonhero. For Maimonides, one
of the key considerations was how the community would perceive itself.
How should they regard the decision not to act heroically? Does Halakhah in the broadest sense of the term indicate what considerations
are relevant for evaluating the status of nonheroic behavior? What most
perturbed Maimonides about the rabbi's ruling was not his legal decision requiring martyrdom, but the fact that he (the rabbi) stripped
any positive significance from the religious behavior of those who failed
to become heroes. As Maimonides claims, he became enraged by the
rabbi's declaration that if a Jew failed to accept martyrdom, all his
secret prayers and religious practices thenceforth became loathsome
in God's eyes.

God knows and bears witness—"He is an adequate witness"—
that even if he rebuked and spoke more chattily than he did, it
would not hurt me. I am certainly not seeking victory. On the
contrary, I feel, *Let us lie down in our shame, let our disgrace
cover us; for we have sinned against the Lord our God, we and
our fathers* [Jer. 3:25]. I should have respected and esteemed

him more, believed that his objective was to do God's bidding.
Thank God, I know my personal worth very well. *We acknowledge
our wickedness, O Lord—the iniquity of our fathers* [Jer. 14:20].
It would not have been right of me to find fault with him had he
not written things that I have no right to overlook or disregard,
like ruling that any victim of the persecution who prays receives
no reward but is, on the contrary, guilty of committing a sin. I
know that whatever is published in a book—correct or incorrect—will most certainly become public knowledge. This is why
so many wrong ideas are popular among people. Only what is
recorded in writing makes the difference between you and the
wrong views, and they will gain him a following. Therefore I was
afraid that the response that turns people away from God would
fall into the hands of an ignorant individual, and he would conclude that he will receive no reward for praying, so he will not
pray. This, he will assume, is true of the other commandments;
if he performs them, he will get no reward for performing any of
them. (p. 22)

Maimonides seems less disturbed by the legal technicalities ad-
duced by the rabbi than by the devastating impact of the rabbi's ruling
on the community. That impact was for him a halakhically relevant
fact of major importance. The status of nonheroic, compromising behavior is, as Maimonides shows, a legitimate halakhic issue. Judaism
not only stipulates legal rules for conduct, but provides principles for
assessing the religious significance of the behavior of a person who
fails to live a heroic religious life. Such principles may be explicit in
the tradition or may be implicit in the descriptive body of Aggadah
that constitutes an integral part of Judaism.

THE REFUTATION OF THE RABBI

Maimonides begins his argument aimed at rehabilitating the status of
nonheroic persons by undermining the authority of the rabbi. The first
three sections of the epistle are entirely devoted to this purpose. Although he appeals to many sources to support his position, he departs
from his usually restrained manner of writing by casting aspersions on
the rabbi's character and wisdom. His vituperative attack on the rabbi
should be understood in the light of his overriding interest in restoring
the community's sense of dignity and worth. He resorts to abusive *ad
hominem* arguments as a means of freeing the community from the
desperate anxiety and sense of guilt that an alleged rabbinic authority
had aroused in it.

The community's feelings of guilt and discouragement were rooted in its perception of the burden of its sinful actions and of the authoritative weight of that rabbi as a mediator of Halakhah. Maimonides' task was to free the Moroccan Jews from their paralyzing guilt for failing to be heroes. He had to counteract the damning verdict of the rabbi and show that Halakhah confirms the worth of partial, nonheroic behavior.[10]

The first section of the epistle is concerned with exposing what Maimonides regards as a basic error vitiating all of the rabbi's pronouncements: his failure to distinguish between coerced and voluntary idolatry.

> . . . Such is his [the rabbi's] assertion that whoever acknowledges his apostleship has *ipso facto* disavowed the Lord, God of Israel. In support he brings the statement of our sages, "Whoever professes idolatry is as if he denied the entire Torah." Judging from this analogy, he apparently finds no distinction between one who turns to idolatry not under duress but voluntarily, like Jeroboam and his associates, and one who will under compulsion say of someone that he is a prophet, because he is afraid of the executioner's sword. (pp. 15–16)

While acknowledging that the two cardinal norms of Judaism are the love of God and the repudiation of idolatry, and granting the validity of the rabbinic judgment that one who submits to idolatry thereby denies the entire Torah, Maimonides emphasizes in the epistle, as in the *Book of the Commandments* and the *Mishneh Torah*, that one must not ignore the fundamental distinction between acting out of conviction and acting under duress. The relevance of the fact of coercion for assessing guilt is basic to our understanding of human agency and responsibility. Consequently, even if what the Almohads had demanded constituted idolatry (although Maimonides suggests good reasons to believe that it did not), those who acquiesced in their demand may not be called idolaters. Though they may have failed to fulfill the heroic norm of martyrdom, their sin is not that of worshiping idols.[11] Maimonides goes so far as to argue that even with regard to the norm of *kiddush ha-Shem*, which presupposes coercion ("Choose death rather than transgress"), if one fails to act heroically and thus is guilty of *ḥillul ha-Shem* one is exempt from punishment. Coercion is an overriding consideration in any evaluation of human action and responsibility.

> Where one is enjoined to suffer death rather than transgress, and commits a transgression and so escapes death, he has profaned the name of God. If the transgression was committed in the pres-

ence of ten Israelites, he has profaned the name of God in public,
failed to observe an affirmative precept—to sanctify the name of
God—and violated a negative precept—not to profane His Name.
Still, as the transgression was committed under duress, he is not
punished with stripes and, needless to add, he is not sentenced
by a court to be put to death, even if, under duress, he committed
murder. (*MT Hilkhot Yesodei ha-Torah* 5:4)

In the second section of the epistle, Maimonides weaves together a
rich variety of aggadic material that indicates the proper way for a
Jewish leader to react to the community's sinful behavior. To begin
with, he cites aggadot that can be used to cast discredit upon the rabbi
personally.

First, he mentions a rabbinic Aggadah that claims that Moses, the
greatest of all prophets, was punished for expressing doubt about the
community's faithfulness. The community in Egypt had, according to
a midrash, forsaken the covenant of circumcision and had undermined
the very cornerstone of Jewish communal life, the family, by engaging
in illicit sexual relations. Nevertheless, for branding them as a faithless
community [Exod. 4:1], Moses was reprimanded by God and punished.

Next, Maimonides cites a midrash showing that Elijah, the zealous
prophet of God who challenged and defeated the prophets of Baal, was
castigated by God for hurling accusations against Israel. Even though
practically all the Jews in Elijah's time were deliberate idolaters, Elijah was severely admonished by God for singling out Israel for condemnation when the behavior of other nations was worse. Similarly,
Isaiah was punished for saying "I live among a people of unclean lips"
(Isa. 6:5), even though the community had in fact become idolaters,
murderers, desecrators of God's name, and disdainful of His law.

The common motif of these three aggadot is the critique of the leader
who loses faith in the community on account of its current failures. In
each of the cases cited, God castigates the prophet for branding the
people as a sinful people. God, as it were, demands that the leader
must never adopt a rejecting attitude toward the community, irrespective of its behavior. As the aggadot in question reveal, Moses, Elijah,
and Isaiah did not misrepresent what the community was like; their
sin consisted in their lack of confidence in and respect for the community during moments of moral weakness. They erred, we may say,
in stigmatizing the people as if its failures went beyond all possible
teshuvah (return to God, repentance) and warranted divine rejection.

To drive home his point, Maimonides cites a fourth Aggadah, according to which even one of the ministering angels was rebuked by
God for his eagerness to bring accusations against Jews. In the light

of such examples, it is easy for Maimonides to discredit the rabbi who
had castigated the Moroccan Jews:

> If this is the sort of punishment meted out to the pillars of the
> universe—Moses, Elijah, Isaiah, and the ministering angels—
> because they briefly criticized the Jewish congregation, can one
> have an idea of the fate of the least among the worthless who let
> his tongue loose against Jewish communities of sages and their
> disciples, priests, and Levites, and called them sinners, evil-
> doers, gentiles, disqualified to testify, heretics who deny the Lord
> God of Israel? These are verbal quotations from his response;
> can you picture his punishment? (p. 19)

So far, the aggadot recalled by Maimonides suffice only to call in
question the manner in which the rabbi gave his ruling. Had he stopped
at this point, his readers could have noticed that he had not challenged
the rabbi's evaluation of how the community should behave in response
to the Almohad demands. But now Maimonides recalls further stories
from the Jewish tradition to show that the rabbi's call for unconditional
resistance, culminating in martyrdom, was not the only option permitted by Halakhah. The incident he reports is related as follows in
tractate Avodah Zarah:

> When R. Eliezer was arrested because of *minut* [heresy] they
> brought him up to the tribune to be judged. Said the governor to
> him, "How can a sage like you occupy himself with those idle
> things?" He replied, "I acknowledge the Judge as right." The
> governor thought that he referred to him—though he really re-
> ferred to his Father in heaven—and said, "Because thou hast
> acknowledged me as right, I pardon; thou art acquitted." [16b]

> They [the Romans] engraved R. Meir's likeness on the gates of
> Rome and proclaimed that anyone seeing a person resembling it
> should bring him there. One day [some Romans] saw him and
> ran after him, so he ran away from them and entered a harlot's
> house. Others say he happened just then to see food cooked by
> heathens and he dipped in one finger and then sucked the other.
> Others again say that Elijah the prophet appeared to them as a
> harlot who embraced him. "God forbid," said they, "were this
> R. Meir, he would not have acted thus!" and they left him. He
> then arose and ran away and came to Babylon. [18b]

R. Eliezer outwitted his accusers by playing with double en-
tendres.[12] He made a statement that would sound to them like an
acknowledgment of guilt, but that he could privately understand in a

completely different sense. This enabled him to evade punishment without sacrifice of principle. R. Meir, too, resorted to trickery in order to escape his pursuers. Whether his trick consisted in entering a harlot's house or in pretending to eat unkosher food, the point is that he chose a nonheroic alternative to martyrdom. The stratagem gave him a chance to flee to Babylon, where he could live freely according to his beliefs.

Maimonides was deliberately selective in choosing to quote only these two passages from Avodah Zarah. For in that tractate one finds, interposed between the stories of R. Eliezer and R. Meir, the story of how R. Hanina b. Teradion openly challenged the Roman authorities and heroically suffered martyrdom. The story that Maimonides chose not to recall is significant for understanding his response to the predicament of the Moroccan community.

> When R. Jose b. Kisma was ill, R. Hanina b. Teradion went to visit him. He said to him: "Brother Hanina, knowest thou not that it is heaven that has ordained this Roman nation to reign? For though she laid waste His house, burnt His temple, slew His pious ones and caused His best ones to perish, still is she firmly established! Yet, I have heard about thee that thou sittest and occupiest thyself with the Torah, dost publicly gather assemblies, and keepest a Scroll of the Law in thy bosom!"
> He replied, "Heaven will show mercy." "I," he remonstrated, "am telling thee plain facts, and thou sayest 'Heaven will show mercy!' It will surprise me if they do not burn both thee and the Scroll of the Law with fire." . . . It was said that within but a few days R. Jose b. Kisma died and all the great men of Rome went to his burial and made great lamentation for him. On their return, they found R. Hanina b. Teradion sitting and occupying himself with the Torah, publicly gathering assemblies, and keeping the Scroll of the Law in his bosom. Straightaway they took hold of him, wrapt him in the Scroll of the Law, placed bundles of branches round him and set them on fire. They then brought tufts of wool, which they had soaked in water, and placed them over his heart, so that he should not expire quickly. His daughter exclaimed, "Father, that I should see you in this state!" He replied, "If it were I alone being burnt it would have been a thing hard to bear; but now that I am burning together with the Scroll of the Law. He who will have regard for the plight of the Torah will also have regard for my plight." His disciples called out, "Rabbi, what seest thou?" He answered them, "The parchments are being burnt but the letters are soaring on high." [18a]

The proximity of these three stories in tractate Avodah Zarah sug-

gests that the tradition was able to join together into one community
of faith individuals like Hanina ben Teradion, who chose death in
defiance of Roman oppression, and individuals like R. Eliezer and
R. Meir who compromised for the sake of survival.[13] For Maimonides,
R. Eliezer and R. Meir are symbols of the possibility of spiritual
renewal for people who chose life above martyrdom. By evading punishment they were able to continue to live as Jews, when necessary
by fleeing to a place where Jews were free from persecution. The
relevance of these examples is that Maimonides wanted the Jews of
Morocco to retain their commitment to Judaism and to flee the country
at the first opportunity. His effort is directed toward setting into motion
a spiritual process of renewal for those who felt the guilt of having
publicly acknowledged Islam.

In the third section of his epistle, Maimonides goes on to refute the
rabbi's claim that those Jews who had succumbed to the Almohad
demands could gain no merit with God—but rather only double condemnation—if they subsequently continued to perform *mitzvot* (commandments). Maimonides presents rabbinic statements whose common
motif is the principle that divine judgment is meted out on the basis
of each and every act a person does. In Jewish jurisprudence, admit-
tedly, if a person is culpable for two or more crimes, the greater
supersedes and overrides the lesser (e.g., someone guilty of theft and
murder is punished for murder alone). But this is merely the practice
of human courts, whereas God judges and evaluates anything and
everything a person does.

Maimonides quotes midrashim to show that the divine judgment on
Ahab son of Omri, a denier of God and an idolater, was rescinded
because of the two-and-a-half hours in which he fasted and humbled
himself before God. Nebuchadnezzar, who killed many Jews and destroyed the Temple, was nonetheless rewarded for the few steps he ran
in deference to God. Even Esau, who in rabbinic lore epitomized moral
corruption and sacrilege, was said to have been rewarded for having
shown honor to his parents.

Maimonides repeatedly emphasizes that a person who is guilty of
transgressions—even transgressions against cardinal norms of Judaism—does not warrant a judgment that destroys his future options.
The notion of divine judgment is open-ended: because of its attention
to details and to the ever-present possibility of *teshuvah*, it never
involves a final, irreversible verdict. He rejects the claim that if a Jew
cannot realize the whole, then the part has no significance. In contrast
to the rabbi who declared that praying or observing any other *mitzvah*
was detestable in the eyes of God after public acquiescence in the
Almohad demands, Maimonides argues that God values every *mitzvah*

a Jew performs even if he has been guilty of nonheroic behavior. Heroic defiance of religious persecution is a normative ideal in Judaism, but it is not a precondition for being a commanded one (*metzuvveh*). On the contrary, a Jew always remains responsible to the Halakhah and obligated to perform *mitzvot*, regardless of his past sins.

THE HALAKHIC ISSUE

Despite the abuse that Maimonides heaps upon the rabbi, their distinct approaches can be seen as being based upon a common concern—the continued existence of the Jewish people—and both gave rulings derived from their understanding of Halakhah. Before explaining the nature of the halakhic issue involved, however, it is necessary to discuss an interpretation of the epistle according to which there was no such issue. Haym Soloveitchik has claimed that Maimonides resorted to arguments based on aggadot because he knew that from a strict halakhic viewpoint the rabbi's ruling was incontestable. Soloveitchik considers that rabbinic aggadot are by their nature incapable of playing a major role in the process of halakhic decision-making; they "may be used occasionally with some effectiveness in a peroration as the *coup de grace* of a sharp legal duel," but because of their "amorphousness and subjectivity," they "lack the hard substantiveness to bear the brunt of juridic combat."[14] He supposes that Maimonides shared this evaluation of aggadot and therefore took recourse to them only as a makeshift expedient. However, in another reading of the *Epistle on Martyrdom*, Maimonides can be seen to have entered into genuine "juridic combat" armed with numerous aggadot. These enabled him 1) to differentiate between judging a person's actions and judging his status, and 2) to ascribe value to action taken in compromise situations.

According to Soloveitchik, Maimonides presented aggadic material dealing with the theme of God's rewarding sinners for each and every good deed they performed in order to suggest that the rabbi's harsh judgment comes close to being a negation of providence.

> The message of these homiletical passages is that when man appears before the Heavenly court (and he does so every day), he is judged not on the basis of his predominant actions but for all of them—every petty crime or merit is taken into consideration. This is nothing but the idea of divine retribution, and the midrashim quoted by Maimonides only portray vividly its exactness.[15]

Maimonides, claims Soloveitchik, is indirectly accusing the rabbi of heresy. Rather than deal directly with the issues raised by the rabbi, Maimonides resorts to *ad hominem* arguments aimed at undermining the rabbi's authority in the eyes of his intellectually unsophisticated readers. By such sleight of hand, Maimonides hoped to divert his reader's attention from the rabbi's devastating though incontrovertible halakhic decision.

> But Maimonides could discover no *ad hoc* distinctions with which to deflect his opponent's charges. The polemical gifts of the accuser came unexpectedly to his aid. His antagonist had summed up his views in a sentence wisely calculated to go straight to the hearts of the masses: "Even if he performs a commandment he will receive no reward for it." Maimonides picked up the phrase and turned his opponent's flank. He cited the statement quite justly as the core of the accusation, but in doing so he estranged it from its context and altered its very nature. No longer did the claim now center upon the legal worth of the Marrano's ritual but upon the nature of divine bookkeeping. Having transformed the charge, Maimonides could dispose of it with ease, yet he took care never to press his advantage too hard. He refused even once to mention the central issue of reward and punishment, but rested content with simply citing the aggadic passages and letting them tell their own tale. On the surface the simplest line of defense would have been to charge that the accusations ran counter not just to several midrashim, but to the incontrovertible principle of divine retribution, and then to swing into a crushing offensive by pointing out that the very person who had condemned whole communities to heresy was himself a heretic, for by his charges he had denied one of the fundamental tenets of the faith. Maimonides eschewed doing so, for to bring out too clearly the fatal absurdity of his antagonist's claim would serve only to make his own victory suspect. He declined to delineate too sharply just what it was that he was refuting, for fear that his readers might become aware that this was not at all what had been charged. He left his opponent's charge untouched in form but vitiated in substance, so that when the time came, despite its outer impressiveness, it would topple dramatically under the blow of a few tales.
>
> Aware that his whole position was a flimsy and makeshift nature, with little more than an aggadic loincloth to cover its nakedness, Maimonides took care to quietly lay the foundation for a more substantial, if less showy, defense. When mentioning that the Jews had only professed belief in the mission of Mohammed, he remarks, almost as an afterthought, that at any rate it was done under coercion. . . .[16]

This is a dramatic and ingenious interpretation of Maimonides' ar-

gument against the rabbi, but it fails to do justice to the substance
and spirit of the *Epistle on Martyrdom*. Maimonides does not try to
conceal the truth from his readers, nor does he try to discredit his
opponent by cleverly distorting his words so as to "catch" him at
heresy. The differences between Maimonides' and the rabbi's position
are of a substantive nature and are not reducible to mere rhetoric.
They touch upon the religious worth of the halakhic acts of the forced
convert: Maimonides affirmed the religious significance of his performance of *mitzvot*, whereas the rabbi declared that Judaism excludes
the forced convert from the community and that all his *mitzvah* performances are null and void.

Maimonides attacked the rabbi not for denying the doctrine of reward and punishment, but first and foremost for ignoring the distinction
between practicing idolatry out of conviction and practicing idolatry
as a result of coercion. The distinction is not introduced "almost as
an afterthought" by Maimonides, but is discussed at length in the
opening section of this epistle. Here he vehemently rejects the rabbi's
use of the talmudic interpretation of the verse in Jeremiah: *For my
people have done a twofold wrong* [Jer. 2:13], where the prophet condemns the community for combining the worship of God with pagan
idolatry. The rabbi totally disregarded the context of Jeremiah's condemnation. Maimonides' anger was aroused by a seemingly deliberate
attempt to ignore the motives behind a person's performing idolatrous
acts.

> . . . This interpretation again does not discriminate between one
> who bowed to the idol and the Temple because he is a heretic
> and wants to defile God's name and desecrate His holiness and
> one who comes to a house of worship in order to behave like
> someone zealous for the glory of God, but does not utter or say
> a word that is in any way contrary to our religion, yet he must
> of necessity go to that house. (p. 16)

In this context, it was appropriate for Maimonides to draw upon
aggadic material that shows Judaism's sensitivity to a person's total
religious personality and not only to those aspects of his behavior that
fall within the circumscribed jurisdiction of the law. The fact that God
does not judge a person in an all-or-nothing manner is not an "aggadic
loincloth" conjured up by Maimonides, but part of the aggadic fabric
in which Halakhah is generally woven. For Maimonides, Judaism is
not merely a compilation of legal rules and regulations; it is rather a
comprehensive religious way of life in which Halakhah is an instrument
that organizes and provides a framework for expressing the relationship
between Israel and God.

Soloveitchik also offers a rationalization of the rabbi's decision that the private prayers of the forced convert are halakhically null and void.

Every Jew is commanded to eat unleavened bread (*matzot*) on the eve of Passover. Suppose an atheist should be invited to a house in which the holiday is celebrated. Upon arrival he says to himself: "Of course, I do not believe in the Mosaic revelation, much less in the divine nature of the Bible. The entire holiday is a holdover of a tribal superstition. But I am a guest, so I'll participate in the ritual tonight and eat whatever I'm supposed to." The question that poses itself is whether he will have, by his social supping, fulfilled the commandment of eating *matzot*.

If charity is given not out of a sense of religious obligation but from a desire to help a fellow man, little doubt can be entertained as to its merits. However, when we come to purely religious matters, the meaningfulness of one's deeds becomes much more suspect. One wonders whether one can fulfill his religious duty via some technical act though he denies his religion, or whether the act takes on substance only within the context of conviction. In short, can one be "observant" without believing?

The instinctive answer, I think, would be in the negative. Fulfillment of a commandment becomes meaningful within, and only within, the matrix of admission of its divine and obligatory character. A commandment whose essential nature has been denied is meaningless when performed, for ritual without belief is a game and not a religious act.

At any rate, this is the opinion, I venture to suggest, of Maimonides' opponent and the point he was actually making. His position was not just a vague forecast of the millennial fate of the Marranos, but a consequence of his previous stand. The Jews in Morocco had admitted the prophetic character of Mohammed's mission. They had by this disavowed the eternal validity of their religion and their Law, and for this they were to be deemed apostates. This led to one inescapable conclusion: that their religious observances were of no value. Having denied their religion, their attempts to fulfill its dictates were not only worthless but ridiculous, indeed they verged close to mockery. There is no room in the faith, he claimed, for Orthodox Jewish heretics.

In this charge he was assessing not simply the moral standing of the Marrano generally, but also the meaningfulness of his religious conduct, the precise legal standing of his actions. He was focusing on the deed as much as on the man. The conclusions he arrived at were highly negative, and he spared nothing to make this brutally clear to his readers. With his gift for effective statement he summed up his position in a phrase calculated to drive deepest into the hearts of the simple people: "Even if he performs a commandment he will receive no reward for it."[17]

Without going into all the complex halakhic questions involved, I shall briefly indicate some of the questionable points in this argument. One such point is whether a Jew can legitimately be said to have observed a *mitzvah* if he does not believe in God. The answer to this question is not a foregone conclusion, especially if one seriously considers the midrashic statement: "Would that they [Israel] had forsaken Me [God] but kept my Torah."[18] Does a description of an act as religious presuppose that the act grows out of certain types of motives, or is it sufficient if the act conforms to the accepted religious practice of the community? Given the centrality of practice and community within Judaism, there is some plausibility in the argument that the community's perception of and response to a person's behavior play important roles in defining the act as a *mitzvah* performance.[19]

Even if it be granted that a convinced atheist cannot perform the commandment of eating *matzah* on Passover, and that belief in God and revelation are prerequisites for endowing an act with religious significance, this does not justify Soloveitchik's analogy between the atheist and the person who practices idolatry under duress.

Soloveitchik's analogy would be valid only on the assumption that a verbal profession of belief is *ipso facto* definitive of the personal conviction of the individual who makes it and that it can suffice to categorize his character. According to Soloveitchik, if the person who succumbs to the Almohads is formally guilty of *avodah zarah*, then for all intents and purposes he is like an atheist; his private religious performances have no more validity than the religious performances of an avowed atheist.

But this is to confuse the nature of a person's individual acts when judged in terms of formal legal categories and the status of that person as a total religious personality. Legal considerations are not sufficient for evaluating a person's religious convictions. A halakhic court may decide that a person who acted under coercion is nonetheless guilty of idolatry. But it has not thereby pronounced that that person is equivalent to an atheist who rejects the divine and obligatory character of the commandments. That is an issue lying outside the scope and purpose of a judicial decision. Courts necessarily operate within a circumscribed area of life. A legal judgment that finds a person guilty or innocent of a particular transgression is not in itself a judgment of the religious character of the person in question. There is a clear distinction between finding a person guilty of an idolatrous act and declaring him to be a heretic or idolater.

The suggested analogy between the atheist and the person who suc-cumbs to the Almohads belongs to a type of legal reductionism that draws no distinction between judgments of character and judgments of acts, defines reality using legal categories, and assesses persons by formal legal criteria without considering the dynamics of their total personalities. To argue that a person forced to utter a heretical formula is on par with a person who does not believe in God is to disregard the complexity of religious behavior and to reduce a person to a formal legal category.

Even if such a formalist approach to Halakhah is theoretically pos-sible, it cannot be ascribed to Maimonides. He forcefully rejected the rabbi's decision because it equated the idolater who acts out of con-viction with the person who is coerced to enter an idolatrous house of worship. He was appalled by the rabbi's use of the talmudic interpre-tation of the twofold sin referred to by Jeremiah—"They bowed to the idol and they bowed to the Temple"—in order to nullify the religious significance of the forced convert's prayers. According to Maimonides, this was a gross distortion of the intended meaning of the talmudic text.

Indeed, it is not certain that even the rabbi himself was a legal reductionist. He was presumably aware, not less than Maimonides, that there were differences between the duplicity denounced by Jere-miah and the Marrano-type compromise adopted by those Moroccan Jews who had succumbed to Almohad pressure. If he disregarded the differences, it was because he judged that the behavior of the Moroccan Jews would have the same long-term consequences as willful idolatry: the disintegration of the Moroccan Jewish community and a weakening of the resolve of Jews elsewhere who might follow their example. He therefore told them that whoever made the Islamic profession of faith was no better than an idolater. The failure to act heroically by suffering martyrdom was, according to this view, sufficient grounds for claiming that the relationship to God and to the covenantal community of Israel had been severed. The rabbi drew upon halakhic sources to show that a *rasha*, a wicked person, was excluded from communal life (e.g., his testimony was not accepted in courts), and his prayers had the de-testable quality of a paganized Jew who "hedges his bets" by combining idolatrous worship with evening Sabbath prayers at the synagogue. This responsum was meant to create in the community a sense of revulsion for any member who publicly acknowledged Islam, regardless of his reason.

Maimonides, in contrast, did not regard the Almohad persecution as the crucial and final battle of Jewish history. He therefore rejected an either/or attitude to the problem at hand and tried to convince the

Moroccan Jews that their inability to act heroically did not mean they were *reshaim*, wicked. He believed also that the rabbi's theology was mistaken and that his halakhic decision denying the validity of the community's partial performance of the commandments was a dreadful error. Accordingly, Maimonides marshaled numerous sources to show that the Judaic tradition drew a sharp line between sinful behavior and divine rejection. If the communities at the times of Moses, Elijah, and Isaiah were deemed to be beloved unto God despite their willfully committed grave sins, then the Moroccan community that acted under duress was *a fortiori* beloved and esteemed by God. Maimonides told the Moroccan Jews not to despair or lose their sense of dignity, since their status as God's covenantal people remained eternally valid.

> . . . This man did not realize that they are not rebels by choice. God will not abandon nor forsake them, *for He did not scorn, He did not spurn the plea of the lowly*. (p. 19)

Although Maimonides so emphatically contradicted the rabbi, their different rulings can be seen as addressed to the same basic issue: would defiance or accommodation to persecution be in the best interest of the Jewish people? Whenever a Jewish leader is faced with this issue, no decision he makes is free from risks. Yet he must make decisions—decisions that may alter the fate of an entire Jewish community. Should he gamble on the temporary nature of the present persecution and tell the community to choose survival whatever the cost? Or should he tell it to defy its oppressors and demonstrate to the world its unshakable loyalty to its way of life by accepting death with courage and determination? When do you advise a community to walk the path of the *akedah* (binding of Isaac) and when do you advise it to struggle to survive within an ugly and brutal world and salvage whatever dignity it can?[20]

There are no rules or formal guidelines that dictate what decision ought to be made under such circumstances. There is no escape from the need for personal judgment in evaluating a particular historical situation. The rabbi's decision did not necessarily reflect narrow-mindedness and lack of compassion, although Maimonides, for his own purposes, portrayed it as such. He may have felt that if the Jewish people were to survive in a hostile world, the Moroccan community would have to set an example for other Jewish communities as well as for the enemies of Israel, by showing that Jews can transcend the natural instinct for life because of their love for God and the Torah. Maimonides, however, chose a different course of action; he provided the community with other outlets for expressing heroic love for God even in the midst of compromise.

Both Maimonides and the rabbi may be seen as leaders who recognized their responsibility to the community. Both sought support from their tradition in their responses to the crisis. The vast difference between their respective applications of the tradition reflects a difference in their personal judgment with respect to the nature of the situation at hand. The halakhist cannot simply apply the law in a mechanical fashion, but must boldly accept responsibility for his creative role in making decisions for a community that chooses to live by the Torah in an unredeemed world. Halakhic problems involving borderline situations, such as the one dealt with in the *Epistle on Martyrdom*, demand that the halakhist listen attentively to both the Halakhah and the Aggadah of his tradition in order to gain a sense of direction that reflects the spirit of Judaism. Although he listens attentively to every aspect of his tradition, his decision is not a mechanical application of rules, but rather a creative act that grows out of the interaction between the weight of the tradition and the complexity of the present.

The crucial question facing Maimonides was whether the public acknowledgment of Islam, as the Almohads demanded, would transform the people involved and effect profound changes in their basic attitude to Judaism. Would they treat the acknowledgment as a temporary expedient, to be cast aside once the threat of persecution was removed? Or would it set into motion an irresistible process leading to eventual assimilation?

Maimonides had to consider the social and psychological effects on the character of the sinner as well as the religious consequences of the prevailing form of apostasy. He had to consider what process of behavioral conditioning was being set into motion by compliance with the Almohad demands. Assessing the impact of the community's submission to the Almohads upon the character of its members was in many respects a more important legal consideration than whether Islam was technically a form of idolatry or whether public verbal pronouncements without conviction constitute religious worship.[21]

In deciding to oppose the rabbi's either/or attitude to the Moroccan community, Maimonides had to assess the compromise required not only in terms of the legal status of the particular acts involved, but also, and most importantly, in terms of its conditioning effects. A person can become conditioned to living a certain way and thus resist changing his behavior even when the original conditions justifying such behavior no longer obtain. The problem facing Maimonides, therefore, involved not only formal legal rules and definitions, but also social, political, and psychological considerations. Maimonides realized that in permitting the community to succumb publicly to the Almohads, he ran the risk of undermining the community's perception of the importance of Judaism and impeding its eventual return to a totally halakhic way of life. Would their formal acknowledgment of Islam lead people to adopt habits that would irreparably undermine their commitment to a traditional halakhic way of life? Would acquiescence encourage the oppressors to intensify their efforts at weakening Judaism? And would the Marrano-type way of life of this community serve as a dangerous precedent legitimating weakness and compromise in the face of adversity?

Maimonides judged that the risk was sufficiently small to be worth taking. Unlike what had happened during earlier persecutions, the Jews were not being compelled to perform acts violating the commandments of Judaism, but only to utter a form of words acknowledging Islam.

. . . Remember that in all the difficulties that occurred in the time of the sages, they were compelled to violate commandments and to perform sinful acts. The Talmud lists the prohibitions, that they may not study Torah, that they may not circumcise their sons, and that they have intercourse with their wives when they are ritually unclean. But in this persecution they are not required to do anything but say something, so that if a man wishes to fulfill the 613 commandments secretly he can do so. He incurs no blame for it, unless he set himself without compulsion to desecrate the Sabbath, although no one forced him. This compulsion imposes no action, only speech. They know very well that we do not mean what we say, and that what we say is only to escape the ruler's punishment and to satisfy him with this simple confession. (p. 30)

In distinguishing here between speech and action, Maimonides is not claiming that statements uttered without conviction can never count as idolatrous acts. His point is that there are historical circumstances where speech—especially when uttered without conviction—has far less effect on a person's character than action. Had the Almohads required Jews to participate in Islamic rituals and practices, and had they forbidden Jewish observances even in private, then the consequences of such behavioral conditioning would constitute a much greater threat to the community than the simple recitation of a faith formula. In the light of these circumstances, Maimonides believed that the speech/action distinction was relevant to a halakhic evaluation of the situation of the Moroccan community. He was prepared to legitimate compromise and weakness of will in a situation where a person's private halakhic practices were not under attack.

He strengthens his argument by adding that the Almohads evidently did not insist on conviction. They were satisfied with the public utterance of the specified faith formula, even when it was apparent to all that the Jews disavowed in their hearts what they publicly proclaimed.

Since the Almohads did not forcibly inhibit the private observance of Judaism, nor did they require Jews to participate in Islamic religious practices, there was good reason to believe that succumbing to their demands would not result in an irreparable transformation of the Jewish community. In other words, the Almohad form of apostasy did not destroy the potential to perform *teshuvah* when opportunity occurred. In the light of these considerations, as well as the fact that Maimonides held that Islam does not contradict the belief in the unity of God, he was prepared to run the risk of advising the community to submit to the Almohad demands rather than choose death. The speech/action distinction, the fact that the oppressors did not insist on Israel's becoming true believers in Islam, the community's ability to retain some semblance of *mitzvah* observance in private—these factors influenced the decision of a religious statesman who recognized his responsibility not only to uphold a formal legal system, but also to promote the community's future spiritual renewal. Considerations regarding how actions affect the possibilities for *teshuvah* are halakhically relevant for a judge who is required not only to apply the law, but above all to guide people in the worship of God.

Lest anyone conclude that this decision was an easy, straightforward one, Maimonides makes it quite clear to his readers that their situation is complex and in many respects unique and that it should be viewed as a borderline situation. Maimonides did not question the fact that the conditions imposed on the Moroccan Jews by the Almohads constituted a situation where martyrdom would be considered a legitimate and noble act. In the *Mishneh Torah* he regards a person who chooses death when halakhically required to evade it as being guilty of a serious violation of Halakhah.

> When one is enjoined to transgress rather than be slain, and suffers death rather than transgress he is to blame for his death. Where one is enjoined to die rather than transgress, and suffers death so as not to transgress, he sanctifies the name of God. (*MT Hilkhot Yesodei ha-Torah* 5:4)

Thus, Maimonides was clearly opposed to a person choosing to be a martyr in situations when, according to Halakhah, such behavior was forbidden. In the *Epistle on Martyrdom*, however, he states that all Jews who had suffered under the Almohads had performed a bona fide act of *kiddush ha-Shem*. It was a borderline situation in which martyrdom was permitted and to be greatly honored, yet he preferred to recommend its avoidance.[22]

> . . . Anyone who suffered martyrdom in order not to acknowledge the apostleship of "that man," the only thing that can be said of him is that he has done what is good and proper, and that God holds great reward in store for him. His position is very high, for he has given his life for the sanctity of God, be He exalted and blessed. But if anyone comes to ask me whether to surrender his life or acknowledge, I tell him to confess and not choose death. (p. 30)

SANCTIFICATION OF GOD'S NAME

In the fourth and last section of the epistle, from which the quotation just given is taken, Maimonides ceases his attacks upon the rabbi and turns to the positive task of formulating his own advice to the community. This section, which is as long as the first three together, successively discusses five distinct but related themes:

> I think it right to divide what I have to say on this subject into five themes: 1. the class of the laws related to the time of forced conversion; 2. definitions of the desecration of God's name and the punishment; 3. the ranks of those who die a martyr's death, and those who are forcibly converted in a persecution; 4. how this persecution differs from others, and what is to be done in relation to it; and 5. a discussion of how advisable it is for one to be careful in this persecution, may God soon put an end to it. (p. 24)

As may be seen, the whole discussion hinges upon the concepts of *kiddush ha-Shem* (sanctification of God's name, of which the highest form is martyrdom) and *ḥillul ha-Shem* (desecration of God's name). Haym Soloveitchik has suggested that the attitude of the epistle to these concepts differs from that of Maimonides' major works. In fact, however, Maimonides always expounds the same basic doctrine of *kiddush ha-Shem* and *ḥillul ha-Shem*, though the manner in which he expounds it may differ according to circumstances. It will be convenient, therefore, first to state his general views on this matter in a systematic form and then to deal with the particular features that distinguish his exposition in the epistle.

In philosophical discussions of ethics, it is possible to distinguish between duties that a person owes to any and every individual and duties that he owes only to those who stand in some specific relationship to him. For instance, it may be argued that a person should be truthful in his dealings with everybody, but the duty to sacrifice one's life arises only in the context of certain relationships. A father may have a duty to sacrifice his life in order to save that of his child, as an obligation that derives from the parental relationship. But if a man sacrifices his life for the sake of a complete stranger to whom he has no obligations, he is going rather "beyond the call of duty" by performing an action that the stranger could not have expected as of right. J. O. Urmson correctly points out the distinction between "rock-bottom duties which are duties for all and from every point of view" and what he calls "heroic" or "saintly" actions.[23] What he fails to mention, however, is that a relationship between individuals or within a group may constitute a framework within which such heroic behavior becomes itself normative. In particular, the relationship of love for another human being or for God can so dominate a person's consciousness that sacrificial action for one's beloved can take precedence over the natural instinct of self-preservation.

Kiddush ha-Shem is a case in point. The norms of *kiddush ha-Shem* are not natural outgrowths of an ethic revolving around the autonomous self-legislating individual. They are not ethical imperatives that the solitary individual discovers in the course of reflection, but appear to presuppose the existence of a covenantal relationship with God. The Talmud restricts the laws of *kiddush ha-Shem* to Israel and does not include them among the Noahidic laws incumbent upon all human beings. It is because of the covenantal framework between God and Israel that martyrdom becomes a duty for all Jews.[24] In specific circumstances, the Jew must be prepared to make the ultimate sacrifice and thereby express his fundamental conviction that life has no meaning outside of his covenantal relationship with God.

Martyrdom is often taken to be virtually synonymous with *kiddush ha-Shem*. Maimonides, however, is always at pains to show that the latter is a broader concept applying to all domains of human activity. *Kiddush ha-Shem* as understood by Maimonides also demonstrates the triumph of a person's passionate love for God over all his other concerns and interests. This is his view not only in the *Epistle on Martyrdom*, but also in the *Mishneh Torah* and *Sefer ha-Mitzvot*.[25]

The concept of *kiddush ha-Shem* is for Maimonides intimately connected with the concepts of *ahavah*, love, and *yirah*, fear or awe, and

simḥah shel mitzvah, the joy of performing a commandment. The pair
of concepts *ahavah/yirah* is particularly important for understanding
Maimonides' psychology of religious behavior and his approach to *kiddush ha-Shem*. He uses *yirah* to designate two distinct stages of religious worship. *Yirah* can connote a fear of God that is the opposite of
ahavah, love of God, or it can connote *yirat ha-romemut*, an awe and
humility before God, which complements the experience of love.[26]

Yirah in the sense of fear of punishment suggests a self-interested
orientation both to religion and to life in general. The *yirah* personality
is, in many respects, like a child trapped within a net of subjective
hungers and fears. He perceives the world through a grid of personal
wants and needs. He cannot step beyond himself nor can he be motivated to act save by appeals to his immediate needs and interests,
e.g., the promise of rewards and punishments. "There are no atheists
in the foxhole" conveys the fundamental religious perspective of *yirah*.
The person who never transcends this level of religion expands the
image of the foxhole into a worldview that defines his basic attitude
toward his self, his community, and God.

The other and higher level of *yirah—yirat ha-romemut*—indicates
the "fear and trembling" felt when one becomes conscious of the infinite wisdom and power of the divine reality. In contrast to the fear
of punishment, fear in the reverential sense presupposes the ability to
transcend considerations of self-interest and to be completely absorbed
by what Rudolph Otto calls the mystery of the "wholly other." *Yirah*
of this kind emerges only after the egocentric sense of *yirah* has been
superseded by love. Such *yirah* is thus an outgrowth of love. *Ahavah*
presupposes sufficient freedom from egotistical attitudes and concerns
to appreciate and know an other with full objectivity; *yirat ha-romemut*
emerges when one recognizes the necessary limits of knowledge as a
result of the inexhaustible mystery of God.

Maimonides stresses the intimate connection between love and
knowledge of God and explains *yirah* as being a consequence both of
the essential limits of human knowledge and of being conscious of the
vast difference between human finitude and divine infinitude. While
all of Halakhah may be viewed as being conducive to this experience
of *yirah*, the norms of *kiddush ha-Shem* are conspicuous examples of
how love of God becomes integrated into halakhic practice. As Maimonides understands them, these norms mirror the particular orientation of one who loves God. The psychological dispositions and attitudes that provide the necessary background for fully appropriating
the letter and spirit of *kiddush ha-Shem* in all its forms are equally
necessary in order to internalize the two cardinal norms of Judaism:
the love and the fear of God. The laws of *kiddush ha-Shem* thus throw

light on the ultimate goals of Judaism and on how halakhic man acts and thinks when he loves God with all his heart.

Maimonides distinguishes between three categories of laws of *kiddush ha-Shem*. The first and highest category consists of the laws involving the requirement of martyrdom. Under special circumstances, which will be specified later, the community as a whole is expected to show that its passionate love of God supersedes the value of life itself.

The second category of *kiddush ha-Shem* expresses love of God in terms of what motivates a person to perform *mitzvot*. A person sanctifies God's name when he no longer feels that reward and punishment are necessary for motivating his observance of commandments. Valuing a *mitzvah* apart from its utility in gratifying extraneous needs and wants mirrors the self-transcending attitude of one who loves God. Whereas in martyrdom a Jew transcends the instinct of self-preservation, in disinterested worship of God he transcends egocentric needs and hungers. This form of *kiddush ha-Shem* is equivalent to Maimonides' description of *avodah me-ahavah*, service of God out of love.

> Whoever serves God out of love, occupies himself with the study of the law and the fulfillment of commandments and walks in the paths of wisdom, impelled by no external motive whatsoever, moved neither by fear of calamity nor by the desire to obtain material benefits; such a man does what is truly right because it is truly right, and ultimately, happiness comes to him as a result of his conduct. (*MT Hilkhot Teshuvah* 10:3)

He who "does what is truly right because it is truly right" and believes that "the reward of a *mitzvah* is the *mitzvah* itself" becomes wholly absorbed in the performance of the *mitzvah* apart from the extraneous benefits that may subsequently follow. The notion of *simḥah shel mitzvah*, the joy of performing a commandment, is also intimately connected to love of God. There is a particular feeling of joy that arises when one's mind is totally fixed on an act and nothing other than the value of the act itself claims one's attention. A person partakes of such joy when he performs a *mitzvah* without anticipating any extraneous benefits from it.[27] Such is the attitude toward *mitzvot* of a person who worships God out of love.

The third category of *kiddush ha-Shem* involves the actions of a person for whom reciprocity is not a necessary condition for moral conduct. In philosophical discussions, the domain of moral action is often limited to people who share a common commitment to moral or legal rules and are thus prepared to act morally because of their belief that others will reciprocate. The expectation that people to whom I act morally feel bound by the same rules and principles as those I accept often acts as a necessary condition for moral behavior. According to Maimonides, anyone who transcends this attitude in his dealings with othes sanctifies God's name. He defines the *ḥasid* as the Jew whose conduct is not limited to duties incumbent on everyone by virtue of the explicit norms of Halakhah, but who acts regularly *li-fnim mi-shurat ha-din*, beyond the requirements of the law.[28] The person for whom such behavior becomes the rule rather than the exception sanctifies the name of God; his unbounded love of God is reflected in his becoming a *ḥasid* whose love of God impels him to do "more than his duty in all things." The word *ḥasid* is derived from the word *ḥesed*, here understood as meaning an excess or overflowing abundance of kindness. In contrast to the "balance-sheet" characterization of moral conduct, which depicts the moral agent as a person weighing losses against gains in order to determine the relative advantages of moral conduct, the image suggested by the notion of a *ḥasid* is that of an overflowing spring, which pours forth a copious stream of water.

Maimonides' definition of the *ḥasid* is based upon the fact that the normative framework of Halakhah may be divided into *din* (law) and *li-fnim mi-shurat ha-din* (beyond the requirements of the law). *Din* is law—rules and regulations—that all members of the community are formally required to obey. *Li-fnim mi-shurat ha-din* comprises actions that are praiseworthy although not formally required. The distinction between *din* and *li-fnim mi-shurat ha-din* cannot be adequately explained in terms of the distinction between law and morality.[29] The Torah cuts across the latter dichotomy and legislates behavior that many today would exclude from legal jurisdiction, e.g., private morality, symbolic ritual behavior, and various forms of ethical conduct.

Din is rather to be distinguished from *li-fnim mi-shurat ha-din* by the extent to which rules predominate in determining one's obligations and to which reciprocity acts as a necessary condition of moral conduct. *Din* may be characterized as a rule-dominated ethic of reciprocity. *Li-fnim mi-shurat ha-din* grows out of a particular attitude to life; it flows from the individual and may not be imposed on someone. The *ḥasid*'s actions go beyond the requirements of the law; yet he does not expect that in similar circumstances he can require the same from others.

While *li-fnim mi-shurat ha-din* by its very nature cannot be legislated, in its absence Halakhah loses its soul and religious character. The Talmud states that the Temple was destroyed because people lived entirely according to *din* and not according to *li-fnim mi-shurat ha-din*.[30] Or as Naḥmanides claimed, one can become a degenerate within the framework of the law.[31] The spirit of Judaism is lost when communities mirror the "rule of law" alone, when people only demand of themselves what they believe they can expect from others. *Din* alone is a form of religious behaviorism that lacks convenantal religious passion; *li-fnim mi-shurat ha-din* mirrors the internalization of the spirit and purpose of the *mitzvot:* love of God.

All three categories of *kiddush ha-Shem* are connected to the relational passion of love of God. The ability to transcend the natural instinct for self-preservation, the overcoming of self-interested needs and hungers, which block an objective appreciation of what is independent of oneself, and the transcendence of reciprocity as a necessary condition for moral religious behavior, constitute for Maimonides three modes of expressing *kiddush ha-Shem*. The Talmud understood that such behavior not only reflects love of God, but makes God beloved to others. When people sanctify God's name through their conduct, they not only bear witness to their personal passion for God, but influence others by virtue of the exemplary character of their life. They make love of God into a contagious aspiration; they captivate others by showing how belief in God can transform a human being. Love of God is both an antecedent and a consequent of *kiddush ha-Shem*.

SANCTIFICATION AND DESECRATION IN THE EPISTLE

Of the five themes of the last section of the *Epistle on Martyrdom*, the first specifies the circumstances in which a Jew is commanded to suffer martyrdom, the second gives Maimonides' broad definition of *kiddush ha-Shem* and *ḥillul ha-Shem*, and the third subsumes martyrdom under the general definition of *kiddush ha-Shem*. In the fourth and fifth themes, Maimonides gives advice to the community.

Because Maimonides does not state at the outset that martyrdom is a form of *kiddush ha-Shem*, although Jews have commonly regarded the two notions as virtually synonymous, Haym Soloveitchik has suggested that the second theme is a kind of smoke screen invented by Maimonides in the special circumstances of the Almohad persecution. Maimonides wanted to save the Moroccan Jews from "waves of despair" over the realization that they had committed desecration of God's name, the gravest of all sins. To this end, he expanded the definition of *kiddush ha-Shem* to include all kinds of behavior other than martyrdom, and mentioned the latter as a special case as a kind of afterthought. By this dubious device, Maimonides made the guilt-ridden Marrano feel relaxed and serene in the knowledge that God would reward him for his actions. Here as elsewhere in the epistle, according to Soloveitchik, Maimonides "distorted the facts to whose ascertainment he had dedicated his life, in the hope of saving a host of sinners from despair and conversion."[32] The whole epistle has no basis in Halakhah; its intellectual roots lie rather in the Aristotelian tradition and specifically in Aristotle's *Rhetoric*, with which Maimonides was familiar.

> Rhetoric was a recognized literary and intellectual genre and Maimonides could well feel that his mode of argumentation no less than his ultimate goal was in one sense valid and that in writing as he did he stood not only religiously but intellectually as well in a reputable tradition—a tradition which, given every instinct and inclination of his, he would ideally have preferred not to involve himself in but a respectable one nonetheless.[33]

In rejecting Soloveitchik's often ingenious interpretation of this epistle, it can be maintained that far from being a distortion of Maimonides' beliefs *qua* halakhist, it reveals the depth of his approach to the scope and purpose of halakhic spirituality. The expanded notion of *kiddush ha-Shem* is not peculiar to the epistle, but is also found (as already noted) in the *Mishneh Torah* and *Sefer ha-Mitzvot*. If there is a difference between those other writings and the epistle, it is that in the *Mishneh Torah* and *Sefer ha-Mitzot* he talks of *kiddush ha-Shem* in the broad sense in connection with the way of life of the *ḥasid*, the especially pious and learned Jew, whereas in this epistle he presents it as a concept relevant to all Jews. The argument of the *Epistle on Martyrdom* thus has nothing to do with Aristotelian rhetoric. It derives instead from Maimonides' comprehensive view of *kiddush ha-Shem* as a category fundamental for the proper understanding of Halakhah and for the development of a total religious personality.

Maimonides does not hide his motives behind a subterfuge of misleading rhetoric. His expanded explication of the notions of *kiddush ha-Shem* and *ḥillul ha-Shem* reflect his genuine understanding of these comprehensive religious notions. The central issue was not whether the label of *ḥillul ha-Shem* was applicable to the forced convert, but rather, whether the failure to act heroically (by becoming a martyr) condemned a person to a form of irredeemable guilt that emptied anything he might do subsequently of all religious significance. By focusing exclusively on martyrdom as the test of whether one is a sanctifier or desecrator of God's name, one creates an all-or-nothing situation where failure to become a martyr engenders total despair and feelings of worthlessness.

Maimonides sought to correct this dangerous and distorted orientation to heroism. He understood the concepts of *kiddush ha-Shem* and *ḥillul ha-Shem* to imply that heroism is not only confined to those singular moments when one may choose to make the supreme sacrifice for the sake of Judaism, but is also manifest in the less dramatic "prose" of everyday life. Heroism is not only a response to conditions imposed from without, but may also be manifest in sanctifying God's name in the manner in which a person conducts his life, in his interaction with others, in his business dealings, in his speech, and in his personal morality.

The ultimate sacrifice of one's life under extreme circumstances does not exhaust the significance of *kiddush ha-Shem*. In the concluding section of the epistle, Maimonides explains the comprehensive nature of heroïc behavior in Jewish law and thereby tries to awaken his readers to the potential heroic dimensions of love of God present in compromise situations and in partial fulfillment of the *mitzvot*. The concepts of sanctification and desecration of God's name are explicated in terms of a person's mode of worship of God and his mode of personal and interpersonal behavior. Love of God, humility, and scrupulous ethical conduct constitute sanctification of God's name and make God beloved to others. Desecration consists in the opposite manner of worship and conduct. By explicating these notions in terms of scrupulous conduct and spiteful, sinful behavior respectively, Maimonides makes his reader aware of the essential connection between *kiddush ha-Shem* and disinterested worship of God. Total devotion to God, even if this be expressed in seemingly prosaic daily performances of the commandments, constitutes the essence of *kiddush ha-Shem*. Sanctification of God's name is not confined to heroic moments of defiance. A person can demonstrate heroic love for God and Torah by performing any *mitzvah* for its own sake. The crucial test of sanctification of God's name is whether one feels totally claimed by God.

In his commentary to the concluding mishnah in tractate Makkot, Maimonides states that God gave 613 commandments in order to enable each and every individual Jew to discover at least one commandment that he could perform out of love.[34] Rather than viewing the large number of commandments as an oppressive burden imposed by an authoritarian God, Maimonides sees it as a divine act of love that provides opportunities for different types of individuals to worship God out of love.

The position he adopts with respect to *kiddush ha-Shem* and *ḥillul ha-Shem* may be viewed as a particular instance of his general approach to Judaism, which is opposed to formal legalism and focuses on the total character of the observant person. Maimonides' conception of the highest level of observance of the law is exemplified by the *ḥasid* who internalizes the spirit of the law to such an extent that he habitually acts beyond the strict requirements of the law. In *MT Hilkhot Teshuvah* (7:3), he does not restrict his discussion of repentance to particular acts, but includes as well dispositions and character traits that he claims are far more resistant to change. One need only read his analysis of Halakhah in the fourth and fifth chapters of the *Eight Chapters* to realize that he eschewed halakhic behaviorism and perceived the law as a normative system that aimed at influencing the total character of an observant Jew.[35]

It is, therefore, not surprising that he explicates the concepts of *kiddush ha-Shem* and *ḥillul ha-Shem* in terms of a comprehensive religious orientation to life. These concepts point to a religious posture toward life and not simply to certain acts that one is legally required to perform. It is for this reason that Maimonides, in the midst of his discussion of *kiddush ha-Shem* and *ḥillul ha-Shem* in the epistle, informs his readers that it would require a full-length book to "outline in detail how an individual ought to deal with others, what all his actions and words should be like, and how he should receive people, etc." This statement reveals Maimonides' appreciation of the relationship of *kiddush ha-Shem* to the development of an ethical personality.[36] Although he does not elaborate on the details of ethical interpersonal relations in the epistle, he clearly communicates to his readers the spirit in which he wants them to behave. *Kiddush ha-Shem* and *ḥillul ha-Shem* are all-pervasive principles and should not be reduced to formal legal categories.

The crucial question in the epistle is not whether the forced convert believes that his weakness of will constitutes desecration of God's name, but whether his failure to become a martyr marks him as a *rasha*, a wicked person cast beyond the pale of the spiritual community of Israel. Maimonides argues repeatedly that the covenantal relationship to God and the significance of a person's performance of *mitzvot* are not nullified because he lacks the courage to sacrifice his life for the sake of his faith. The central thrust of the epistle is that guilt for not accepting to die a martyr's death should not lead a person to reject the significance of everything else he does.

Maimonides was not seeking to hide the guilt of the forced converts, but rather to ensure that their feeling of guilt would have constructive and not destructive consequences. In order to appreciate the purpose of his advice to the community, it is relevant to consider some basic features of the psychology of moral behavior. The dynamics of moral behavior involve a person's relationship to a social framework and not simply the internalization of moral rules and principles. The language of morals is oversimplified and incomplete if one focuses exclusively on the logic of moral rules. While rules undoubtedly constitute a significant aspect of moral conduct, there are important psychological and sociological factors that influence the motivational matrix of moral action.

In Judaism, moral and religious behavior are embedded within certain relational religious frameworks, which serve as essential backgrounds for such behavior. A person's relationship to the historical community of Israel and to God penetrates deeply into his attitude to moral religious action. While it is true in general that a person's self-regard affects his motivation to act morally, in Judaism such self-regard is intimately bound up with how he perceives his relationship to the community and to God. When a Jew loses a sense of personal dignity and becomes detached from the community and from God, his moral will is thereby weakened.

In other words, morality in the Jewish tradition cannot be reduced to the dynamics of the self-legislating autonomous will; the moral agent participates in frameworks of meaning that transcend the isolated self. Communal membership is an essential source of moral energy. The impetus to act is intensified or reduced depending on the strength of one's bond to the community and to God. When the individual feels cut off from his social environment, when he experiences social isolation and alienation, he becomes morally vulnerable and weak.

The definition of man as a social animal has particular implications for moral behavior in general. The sociological notion of "significant others" is relevant for moral theory, insofar as people tend to act differently when they feel estranged from their environment. While leaving his familiar social environment may free a person from suffocating patterns of conduct to which he has become accustomed, it can also result in moral disintegration and feelings of anomie. A person may feel morally enervated when deprived of a supportive social environment; his motivation to withstand moral corruption may be seriously weakened if he feels socially rootless and fragmented.

The moral will is nurtured within contexts that provide the individual with frameworks of relationship in which his personal history develops. Moral authenticity is often a gift that the community and memory bestow upon the individual; it is rarely achieved when an individual falls victim to existential loneliness, when his world view limits him to a vertical dimension of experience with no access to the past or a community.

The relational component of moral religious behavior can also lead to a specific form of guilt beyond the guilt one normally feels as a result of moral failure. A person may naturally feel guilt for failing to meet certain standards or for violating accepted norms. Guilt for having "missed the mark" is a normal part of moral behavior and is compatible with continuing to view oneself as a moral person. "For there is not one good man on earth who does what is best and doesn't err" [Eccles. 7:20]. Normative moral and religious systems allow for such failures. The very fact that Judaism contains detailed laws of *teshuvah* shows that moral-religious failure is not an irredeemable condition.

There is, however, another experience of guilt that goes beyond specific transgressions and failures and attacks the very foundations of a person's moral life. This type of guilt paralyzes the moral agent because it involves the destruction of the essential relationships framing his moral-religious experience. This guilt is magnified by feelings of rejection; it crushes the guilty person's self-respect by declaring him unworthy of being a party to the relationship in question. When someone feels guilt in this sense, he feels personally condemned and unfit to be a moral-religious agent.

The normal experience of guilt may enhance a person's self-regard because it presupposes his being accountable and adequate to shoulder the burden of moral responsibility. Guilt in this sense can be a productive experience that focuses a person's attention on his ability to assume control of his life and to redirect his energies toward new goals. When, however, guilt calls into question the moral or religious integrity of the person as such, i.e., when the *actor* rather than the *act* becomes the primary target of condemnation, then guilt becomes a shattering and paralyzing experience. [37]

Maimonides' aim in the epistle was to limit the guilt felt by the Moroccan community and to prevent that guilt from turning into a paralyzing, destructive form of self-recrimination. In order to sustain the community's strength to practice Judaism even minimally, their guilt must not be exacerbated by feelings of divine rejection. Given the relational context of Jewish ethics and norms, if the Moroccan Jews were to believe that they were excluded from these frameworks of meanings then all would be lost. The relational background of Jewish thought and practice can mitigate the psychological effects of sin and failure so long as the covenantal relationship with God is not called into question. If, however, the individual is led to believe that, in addition to having acted sinfully, he has also jeopardized this relational framework, then the effects can be permanently devastating. Parents who use expressions of love and affection as weapons against their children, systematically withdrawing their love as a punishment for disobedience, place an unbearable burden upon their children. Such severe stress may immobilize a person or lead to cynicism and moral indifference.

In the concluding section of the epistle, Maimonides does not, as Soloveitchik suggests, try to minimize the community's sense of guilt.

Rather, he tries to channel guilt in a way that does not crush a person's integrity or lead to the disintegration of his personality. Maimonides argues against the notion of irredeemable guilt, of feeling condemned to a total sense of worthlessness. He affirms that failure to act heroically during singular dramatic moments of oppression is not a sign of irredeemable moral decadence. The aggadic material that he cites shows that a person always remains accountable for his actions and is never permanently cast aside by God. The example of Jeroboam ben Nebat, who was held accountable not only for having erected the calves, but also for violating the comparatively minor commandment of *eruv tavshilim*, is not introduced simply in order to note a difference between divine "bookkeeping" and the accepted procedures of human courts. Rather, Maimonides leads his readers to understand that they should not view their relationship to God only in terms of the formal rules of halakhic jurisprudence. In the eyes of God a person remains accountable no matter the circumstances. One must be morally vigilant and awake to the divine command even in the most compromising of situations.

The fact that a person is guilty of major transgressions does not free him from responsibility for minor ones. While the framework in which the Jew relates to God is in certain respects analogous to legal frameworks, there are fundamental differences between the concepts of legal accountability and accountability before God. In the eyes of God, a person is responsible for each and every act he does every moment of his life. In addition, God, unlike a judge, may forgive a person and cancel the punishment he deserves for past transgressions.[38] *Teshuvah* is a standing option available to every sinner. The divine call to *teshuvah* is a distinctive feature of Judaism's conception of a person's relationship to God.[39]

Judaism is not a set of mechanistic legal rules. Every *mitzvah* a person performs may awaken within him a deep love for God. A living relationship always allows for "surprise," for unanticipated opportunities for renewal. God is not a judge who rules once and for all "guilty!" or "not guilty!" Maimonides' treatment of *kiddush ha-Shem* and *ḥillul ha-Shem* conveys this understanding of the broad relational framework of Halakhah. His aim was not to assuage the sense of guilt felt by the forced converts, but to deepen and broaden the community's conception of Halakhah. He sought to make the community aware of the richness and breadth of a religious system that provided opportunities for heroism even under the difficult circumstances of its plight.

Maimonides does not minimize the gravity of the sin of *ḥillul ha-Shem*. On the contrary, he emphasizes that it is a terrible transgression in Judaism precisely because it is not an ordinary legal violation, but rather a sin that touches upon the totality of a person's relationship to God. If there are particular *mitzvot* that preserve Halakhah from legalism, they are *kiddush ha-Shem* and *ḥillul ha-Shem*. As Maimonides' elaboration of these notions shows, Judaism aims at producing a person who will bear witness to the sanctifying power of his relationship to God in all facets of his life. He therefore includes every Jew, and not only exceptional pious scholars, within his expanded application of *kiddush ha-Shem* and *ḥillul ha-Shem*. Rather than restrict the scope of heroism, he expands it.

In expanding the framework of heroic demands, Maimonides added to the burden the community had to bear. Yet even when discussing the heroic sacrifices that one is expected to make for the sake of Judaism, he writes with compassion and warmth.

> What I counsel myself, and what I should like to suggest to all my friends and everyone that consults me, is to leave these places and go to where he can practice his religion and fulfill the Law without compulsion or fear. Let him leave his family and his home and all he has, because the divine Law that He bequeathed to us is more valuable than the ephemeral, worthless incidentals that the intellectuals scorn; they are transient, whereas the fear of God is eternal. (p. 31)

Maimonides "counsels" his readers as friends. The advice he gives is not meant to soothe them or placate their feelings of guilt but, on the contrary, to heighten their awareness of the heroic commitment that Judaism demands of its adherents. Nothing in the world—be it family, economic well-being, or social relationships—should be valued more than the worship of God.

> . . . The appeal of the person who pleads his duties to his family and his household is really no excuse. *A brother cannot redeem a man, or pay his ransom to God* [Ps. 49:8]. I do not think it is right to make this plea in order to avoid the obligation and not flee to a reasonable place. He must under no circumstance continue to reside in the land of persecution. If he does, he is a transgressor, profanes God's name, and is almost a presumptuous sinner. (p. 32)

Here Maimonides is asking every member of the Jewish community to follow in the path of Abraham—to break ties to family and soil and become a lonely wanderer. He is told to leave his familiar environment and become a homeless refugee in search of a framework wherein he can worship his God freely and fully. This demand to be like Abraham is not a simple one. Abraham's heroism was not only manifest in the *akedah,* the binding of Isaac, where a human life was to be sacrificed, but also in his willingness to become a wanderer as a result of his love for God. In the epistle Maimonides appeals to this latter model of heroism.

Maimonides places a heavy burden upon the shoulders of his readers. All the same, while heightening their sense of guilt for remaining under the Almohads, he does so in the context of a letter that fortifies them against a paralyzing form of guilt that destroys a person's self-respect. Judaism, claims Maimonides, demands that a person's loyalty to God takes precedence over all his other loyalties and interests. Each Jew is personally accountable for his performance of the commandments. There is no justifiable excuse for passivity in the face of religious persecution.[40] God's claim upon man is absolute. Nevertheless, if one fails to live up to this exalted standard of religious commitment, one is guilty, but not rejected.

The following passage from the epistle is one of the most revealing and profound statements in all of Maimonides' writings:

> . . . Anyone who cannot leave because of his attachments, or because of the dangers of a sea voyage, and stays where he is, must look upon himself as one who profanes God's name, not exactly willingly, but almost so. At the same time he must bear in mind that if he fulfills a precept, God will reward him doubly, because he acted so for God only, and not to show off or be accepted as an observant individual. The reward is much greater for a person who fulfills the Law and knows that if he is caught, he and all he has will perish. It is he who is meant in God's qualification: *If only you seek Him with all your heart and soul* [Deut. 4:29]. Nevertheless, no one should stop to plan to leave the provinces that God is wroth with, and to exert every effort to achieve it. (p. 33)

Even though a person who does not leave his home should regard himself as "one who profanes God's name, not exactly willingly but almost so," he should be awake to every opportunity to express love of God. Maimonides makes his reader aware of the rich complexity of the situation of one who fails to follow in the path of Abraham. He can be guilty of desecration of God's name, yet be capable of acting out of genuine love for God. Maimonides raises Judaism above the level of pure legalism by allowing for such rich complexity within the framework of Halakhah. Halakhah, in the hands of Maimonides, is sensitive to the ambiguities, fragility, and multiple opportunities present in the human condition for expressing heroic love for God.

Toward the end of the epistle, Maimonides cites the *tosefta* stating that one must welcome a person who comes to synagogue even though he be a desecrator of the Sabbath.

It is not right to alienate, scorn, and hate people who desecrate the Sabbath. It is our duty to befriend them, and encourage them to fulfill the commandments. The rabbis regulate explicitly that when an evildoer who sinned by choice comes to the synagogue, he is to be welcomed and not insulted. In this ruling they relied on Solomon's counsel: *A thief should not be despised for stealing to appease his hunger* [Prov. 6:30]. It means do not despise the evildoer in Israel when he comes secretly to "steal" some observance. (p. 33)

Even though Maimonides equates the desecration of the Sabbath with the sin of idolatry, one must treat the desecrator of the Sabbath with compassion.[41] By focusing upon the permanent possibility for change and renewal in Judaism, Maimonides raises Halakhah above the level of legalism and uncovers the living relationship with God at the heart of halakhic Judaism.

As a halakhic leader, Maimonides sought a way of sustaining the community's live interest in *teshuvah* despite the tragic conditions it was compelled to endure. He taught them to live in a state of perpetual conflict so as to sustain the tension between their public and private selves. In public, affirm the faith formula of those who claim that Judaism has been superseded, but in private and in your hearts, know that you are eternally bound by the *mitzvot*. Do not fall victims to an all-or-nothing attitude in order to escape the trying task of living with dissonance. Maimonides tells the Moroccan Jews: If you cannot escape your tragic predicament, turn your attention to doing any *mitzvah* that will keep alive the tension between your covenantal self-image and your self-negating public behavior.

By emphasizing the value of partial behavior, Maimonides sought to implant the seeds of *teshuvah* in the hearts of those who knowingly agreed to compromise. He often used the language of *yirah* ("God will reward you for each and every *mitzvah* you perform"), because he realized that he was addressing people forced to live in an historical "foxhole." His audience did not consist of leisurely intellectuals free to pursue the virtues of self-transcending love of God, but rather of an oppressed, worry-laden community whose most elementary human needs remained unsatisfied. Rather than preach to them about the virtues of selfless devotion to God, he struggled to buttress their self-image so that they could withstand the disintegrating effects of the social reality in which they were compelled to live.

The *Epistle on Martyrdom* sets into motion a dynamic for change by protecting that small nucleus of self-regard that may contain the seeds for the future flowering of an oppressed and discouraged person's true religious identity. So long as that person feels the dissonance between the mask he is compelled to wear in public and the image he unveils when not under the scrutiny of the outsiders, so long as he resists adopting the self-definition implicit in the role he is compelled to assume in public—the gates of *teshuvah* remain open.

CONCLUSION

The *Epistle on Martyrdom* may prove unsatisfying to those seeking clear and sharp guidelines for acting under crisis conditions. Maimonides addresses people compelled to live within the moral penumbra of compromise. His difficult task is that of sustaining a community's will to persevere despite social and cultural dissonance and fragmentation. Instead of promising solutions that would lessen the tension and foster peace of mind, Maimonides heightens his readers' awareness of what living with dissonance involves.

It would appear that Maimonides was fully awake to the psychological propensity to resolve inner conflict by adopting one belief or pattern of behavior at the expense of its discordant rivals. The modern psychological theory of cognitive dissonance bears out Maimonides' evaluation of the stresses felt by those who are forced to live in the shadow of compromise. His final statements concerning "how a person should regard himself in this persecution" are strikingly ambiguous. They reveal the agonizing uncertainty that tears at the heart of a leader who tries to instill a sense of tension in the minds of those who feel compelled to compromise.

The *Epistle on Martyrdom* is a classic example of the complex array of considerations that the halakhic jurist must take into account in cases involving compromise. As Maimonides clearly states, Judaism is a comprehensive way of life that demands total allegiance, unconditional love of God, heroism, and the readiness to bear enormous hardships on its behalf. If, however, a Jew chooses not to make the supreme sacrifice and if he cannot realistically escape the oppressive conditions of religious persecution, he may still be capable of discovering modes of religious authenticity despite the partial nature of his fulfillment of Halakhah.

In this epistle, Maimonides gathers a wide assortment of sources from the Jewish tradition that would be helpful to a person forced to live under stressful, imperfect conditions. Halakhah in the hands of

Maimonides regulates behavior not only before but also after and in the midst of failure.

If the principles and judgments discussed in this epistle do not all qualify as strictly legal considerations, it is because Halakhah is not a pure legal system. The material that influences the halakhic jurist's decisions is not exhausted by the stock of legal rules and definitions narrowly referred to as "Halakhah." In rendering a decision, the halakhist must consider all those factors that may be relevant to the realization of the ultimate goal of Halakhah, i.e., the passionate love of God. The jurist (*posek*) must keep in mind the covenantal relationship with God when he deals with the formal instruments that give substance and form to this relationship. Halakhic norms flow from the relationship with God and are not autonomous. Halakhic categories must be transparent and not opaque; they must always mirror their covenantal experiential ground. Maimonides therefore began his code of Jewish law, the *Mishneh Torah*, with an exposition of the theological foundations of Judaism. By beginning his code with themes touching on the reality of God and the philosophic path to love of God, he placed Halakhah within a context where the yearning to know and love God infuses halakhic rules with covenantal passion.

The halakhic jurist who is not awake to this dimension of Halakhah only fools himself if he believes he can avoid the painful uncertainty of decisions based on inconclusive data by appealing to formal rules and definitions. Those who subscribe to the theory of halakhic formalism tend to overlook the vast array of psychological, social, and historical considerations that play an essential role in responsible decision making. The halakhist should not retreat to the safe, sharply defined world of formal jurisprudence; he should not ignore the exasperating complexity of rendering halakhic decisions for societies capable of realizing only fragments of the ideal whole. How behavior affects a person's character and how rulings affect the social fabric of community are not extraneous to halakhic jurisprudence.

The halakhic judge who feels responsible for the community must be prepared to accept judgments that preclude certainty. Do present circumstances warrant compromise? What historical and psychological forces will be unleashed if I legitimate compromise? Are there sufficient reasons to believe that permitting compromise under existing circumstances will not destroy the willingness to revert to earlier behavior patterns when conditions change? In the *Epistle on Martyrdom*, Maimonides seriously confronted such agonizing questions and, in presenting his view in such vivid detail, he laid bare the often hidden workings of the greatest halakhic mind of all time.

NOTES

1. It is not accidental that *kiddush ha-Shem* and *ḥillul ha-Shem* form the first purely halakhic theme discussed in detail in the *Mishneh Torah*. The *Mishneh Torah* begins with the "Laws of the Foundation of the Torah" (*Hilkhot Yesodei ha-Torah*), of which the first four chapters deal with philosophical theology, e.g., the existence, unity, and noncorporeality of God, and love and fear of God. These chapters are concerned with the themes of *ma'aseh merkavah* (metaphysics) and *ma'aseh bereshit* (natural philosophy) or what the rabbis call *pardes*. The fifth chapter, devoted to *kiddush ha-Shem* and *ḥillul ha-Shem*, is then the beginning of Maimonides' codification of what are commonly considered halakhic themes. The laws of *kiddush ha-Shem* may thus be considered to constitute an organizing framework for the halakhic system.

L. Strauss in "Notes on Maimonides' Book of Knowledge," in *Studies in Mysticism and Religion Presented to Gershom G. Scholem* (Jerusalem: Magnes, 1967), relates chapter 5 to Maimonides' discussion of the divine attributes: "The highest theme of the first four chapters is God and His attributes. From God's attributes one is easily led to His names." (pp. 273–74) But chapter 5 can also be understood in terms of the distinction between philosophy and Halakhah that concludes chapter 4:

> Therefore, I say that it is not proper to dally in *pardes* till one has first filled oneself with bread and meat; by which I mean knowledge of what is permitted and what forbidden, and similar distinctions in other classes of precepts. Although these last subjects were called by the sages "a small thing" (when they say "A great thing, *ma'aseh merkavah*; a small thing, the discussions of Abaye and Rava"), still they should have precedence. For the knowledge of these things gives primarily composure to the mind. They are the precious boon bestowed by God, to promote social well-being on earth, and enable men to obtain bliss in the life hereafter. Moreover, the knowledge of them is within the reach of all, young and old, men and women; those gifted with great intellectual capacity as well as those whose intelligence is limited.

See D. Hartman, *Maimonides: Torah and Philosophic Quest* (Philadelphia: Jewish Publication Society, 1976) pp. 233–35, n. 68; S. Rawidowicz, *Iyyunim be-maḥshevet Yisrael*, ed. B.C.I. Ravid (Jerusalem: Rubin Mass, 1969), pp. 415–18.

2. See Maimonides' *The Commandments: Sefer ha-Mitzvot*, trans. C. B. Chavel (London, Soncino, 1967), positive commandment 9:

> By this injunction we are commanded to sanctify God's Name. It is contained in His words, "But I will be hallowed among the children of Israel." The purport of this commandment is that we are in duty bound to proclaim this true religion to the world, undeterred by fear of injury from any source. Even if a tyrant tries to compel us by force to deny Him, we must not obey, but must positively rather submit to death; and we must not even mislead the tyrant into supposing that we have denied Him while in our hearts we continue to believe in Him (exalted be He).
> This is the commandment concerning the Sanctification of the Name which is laid upon every son of Israel; that we must be ready to die at

the tyrant's hands for our love of Him (exalted be He), and for our faith in His Unity, even as Hananiah, Mishael, and Azariah did in the time of the wicked Nebuchadnezzar, when he forced people to prostrate themselves before the idol, and all did so, the Israelites included, and there was none there to sanctify the Name of Heaven, all being in terror. This was a sore disgrace to Israel, in that this commandment was disregarded by them all, and there was none to fulfill it, all being afraid.

This commandment applies only in circumstances such as those of that great occasion, when the whole world was in terror, and it was a duty to declare His Unity publicly at that time.

There are several distinctive features in Maimonides' treatment of *kiddush ha-Shem* in *Sefer ha-Mitzvot*. 1) He does not elaborate upon the halakhic conditions for the applicability of *kiddush ha-Shem*. He does this only when discussing *ḥillul ha-Shem* in negative commandment 63. 2) There is a universal thrust to "proclaim this true religion to the world." It would thus appear that the realization of *kiddush ha-Shem* is not limited to actions in the presence of ten Israelites. *Kiddush ha-Shem* here is directed against idolatry and all attempts at undermining the sovereignty of God in the world. All of the world and not only the community of Israel are in need of the heroic actions constituting *kiddush ha-Shem*. 3) Nebuchadnezzar is not described simply as an oppressor of Israel, but as a tyrant before whom all were in terror. Furthermore, Maimonides make *kiddush ha-Shem*, as understood in this context, dependent upon sociopolitical conditions like those that prevailed during the time of Nebuchadnezzar. See Rawidowicz, *Iyyunim*, pp. 359–62; M. Kadushin, *Worship and Ethics* (Evanston, Ill.: Northwestern University Press, 1964), pp. 131–35, 231–32.

3. See Sifra, Lev. 22:32.

4. H. Soloveitchik, "Maimonides' *Iggeret ha-Shemad:* Law and Rhetoric," in *Rabbi Joseph H. Lookstein Memorial Volume*, ed. L. Landman (New York: Ktav, 1980), p. 306.

5. Ibid, p. 313.

6. See the profound and sensitive work of P. Van Buren, *Discerning the Way* (New York: Seabury, 1980), which attempts to rethink the relationship between Judaism and Christianity and the modern possibilities for religious pluralism.

7. See M. Perlmann, "The Medieval Polemics between Islam and Judaism," in *Religion in a Religious Age*, ed. S. D. Goitein (Cambridge, Mass.: Association for Jewish Studies, 1974), pp. 103–38.

8. See BT Sanhedrin 74; JT Shevi'it 4:2.

9. See the comments of Rashi and the Ran to Sanhedrin 74a on "even with respect to a minor commandment one ought to suffer death rather than transgress." When considering the question of martyrdom, one may consider what specific actions are demanded by the oppressor, the overall religiosociopolitical situation (*she'at ha-shemad*), the context (private/public) and the oppressor's intention (his personal satisfaction/his desire to overthrow Judaism). The subtle distinctions discussed by different *rishonim* regarding

this issue call into question any attempt at understanding Halakhah in purely behavioristic terms.

10. The Torah spoke only with respect to human passions [*yetzer ha-ra*]; it is better that Israel eat flesh of animals about to die yet ritually slaughtered than flesh of dying animals that have died without ritual slaughter. [BT Kiddushin 21b–22a]

R. Ilai the Elder said: "If a man sees that his evil desire is conquering him, let him go to a place where he is unknown, don black and cover himself with black and do as his heart desires, but let him not publicly profane God's name." [BT Kiddushin 40a]

See the comments of Rashi and Tosafot on this text and those of Rabbenu Hananel in BT Ḥagigah 16a. Halakhah tries to salvage whatever it can from morally imperfect circumstances. It does not allow one to adopt an either/or attitude, even under conditions of sin and compromise. Halakhah tries to retain some degree of moral responsibility even when one submits to the *yetzer ha-ra*. It is in this light that one should understand the serious discussion between Rashi and Tosafot in Kiddushin 21b regarding the time when sexual intercourse was permitted with a captive woman.

11. See remarks of Rabbi Moshe Ha-Cohen on *Hilkhot Yesodei ha-Torah*, in *Hassagot Ha-Ramakh al Ha-Rambam*, ed. S. Atlas (Cincinnati: *Hebrew Union College Annual*, vol. 27, 1956; vol. 34, 1963).

12. Cf. Soloveitchik, "Maimonides' *Iggeret ha-Shemad*," pp. 290–92. Soloveitchik's interpretation fails to explain why Maimonides also mentions the story involving R. Meir. Lieberman shows that R. Eliezer was arrested for *minut*—Christianity—and that the context of the story involves the persecution of Christians. Rashi and Maimonides understand it as referring to the religious persecution of Jews. See S. Lieberman, "Roman Legal Institutions in Early Rabbinics and in the Acta Martyrum," *Jewish Quarterly Review*, n.s. 35 (1944):20–24.

13. See G. D. Cohen's Leo Baeck memorial lecture, *Messianic Postures of Ashkenazim and Sephardim* (New York: Leo Baeck Institute, 1967), pp. 33–42.

14. Soloveitchik, "Maimonides' *Iggeret ha-Shemud*," pp. 294–95.

15. Ibid., p. 295.

16. Ibid., pp. 312–13.

17. Ibid., pp. 295–96.

18. Lamentations Rabbah, introd. 2; JT Ḥagigah 1:7.

19. See D. Hartman, "Risk and Uncertainty" and "Halakhah as a Ground for Creating a Shared Spiritual Language," in *Joy and Responsibility* (Jerusalem: Ben-Zvi Posner, 1978), pp. 116ff, 140–50, 160, nn. 43–45.

20. See Cohen, *Messianic Postures*, p. 37, n. 48; also the moving treatment of the *akedah* model in Jewish history by S. Spiegel, *The Last Trial*, trans. J. Goldin (New York: Schocken, 1969).

21. Cf. Soloveitchik, "Maimonides' *Iggeret ha-Shemad*," pp. 285–93.

22. Cf. *Iggerot*, translation into Hebrew and commentary by J. Kafiḥ (Jerusalem: Mossad Harav Kook, 1972), p. 118, n. 87. Kafiḥ believes that this

view is the same as that stated by Tosafot in BT Avodah Zarah 27b, according to which one is permitted to choose death even when Halakhah does not require it. He maintains that Maimonides changed his position in the *Mishneh Torah*. Contrary to this interpretation, it can be maintained that Maimonides' position remained unchanged and the differences are due to the particular cases in question. In the epistle, Maimonides addresses a specific borderline case and regarding *this* case he states that one is permitted though not required to suffer martyrdom. See Cohen, *Messianic Postures*, pp. 40–41.

23. J. O. Urmson, "Saints and Heroes," in *Essays in Moral Philosophy*, ed. A. I. Melden (London and Seattle: University of Washington Press, 1958), pp. 198–216.

24. See BT Sanhedrin 74b–75a; JT Shevi'it 4:2. In Sanhedrin the question whether Noahides are obligated to fulfill the laws of *kiddush ha-Shem* appears to remain unresolved. In JT Shevi'it, however, it is clearly stated that they are not. Rashi claims that even if Noahides are obligated to fulfill *kiddush ha-Shem*, the concept of "in public" (*be-farhesya*) would refer only to ten Jews. The Ran argues that if the Noahides are required to fulfill *kiddush ha-Shem*, then they also constitute the community before whom one must sanctify God's name.

See *MT Hilkhot Melakhim* 10:2 and comments of *Mishneh Lemelekh* regarding the distinction between murder and idolatry.

To commit murder to save one's life is prohibited not only because of the principle of *kiddush ha-Shem*, but because of the talmudic statement regarding the intrinsic worth of every human being: "Who knows whether your blood is redder. Perhaps his blood is redder." (BT Sanhedrin 74a).

Nahmanides in *Milhamot ha-Shem* claims that the requirement of martyrdom for idolatry, incestuous or adulterous relations and murder is not because of the *mitzvah* of *kiddush ha-Shem*, but because of their intrinsic gravity. See the comments of R. Zerahya Halevi, who places idolatry and incestuous or adulterous relations within the framework of *kiddush ha-Shem*. Maimonides' opening statement in chapter 5 of *MT Hilkhot Yesodei ha-Torah*, with which he introduces the laws of martyrdom, seems to suggest that he does not share Nahmanides' views. See the complex analysis of Meiri. Cf. J. Faur, *Studies in the Mishneh Torah, Book of Knowledge* (Hebrew) (Jerusalem: Mossad Harav Kook, 1978), p. 161.

25. See *MT Hilkhot Yesodei ha-Torah* 5:10; *Sefer Ha-Mitzvot*, negative commandment 63.

26. See *MT Hilkhot Yesodei ha-Torah* 2:1–2; 4:12 (in 2:1–2 awe results from one's awareness of the difference between human beings and God, whereas in 4:12 awe is related to the difference between human beings and the Intelligences); *Guide* 3:52. Also Hartman, *Maimonides*, p. 221, n. 56; p. 265, n. 61. The experience of shame in *yirat ha-romemut* should not be identified with guilt. It is rather an expression of one's full awareness and acceptance of human finitude, which is never overcome even during moments of intense and passionate love for God. See G. Scholem, "Devekut or Communion with God," in *The Messianic Idea in Judaism* (New York: Schocken, 1971), p. 227.

27. See *MT Hilkhot Lulav* 8:13–15. Note the emphasis on joy that accompanies knowledge and love of God in *Sefer ha-Mitzvot*, positive commandment 3, and *Guide* 3:51, See David Hartman, "The Joy of Torah," in *Joy and Responsibility*, pp. 24–26.

28. See *MT Hilkhot Yesodei ha-Torah* 5:11; also Hartman, *Maimonides*, pp. 90–98.

29. See N. J. Coulson, *Conflicts and Tensions in Islamic Jurisprudence* (Chicago: University of Chicago Press, 1969), pp. 77–95, for a similar point regarding Islamic law, and compare with L. L. Fuller, *The Morality of Law* (New Haven: Yale University Press, 1964), and H. L. A. Hart, *The Concept of Law* (Oxford: Oxford University Press, 1961).

30. See BT Bava Meẓia 30b.

31. See Naḥmanides' commentary on Lev. 19:2.

32. Soloveitchik, "Maimonides' *Iggeret ha-Shemad*," p. 319.

33. Ibid., p. 309.

34. *Commentary to the Mishnah*, Makkot 23a. The whole drift of the discussion in Makkot 23b–24a supports Maimonides' appreciation of the value of performing one *mitzvah*. The fact that there are 613 commandments should not paralyze anyone from beginning the religious process. The talmudic discussion regarding the essential principles of Judaism seems to be concerned with enabling one to find an orienting "handle" on the tradition.

35. See BT Sanhedrin 25b regarding the moral and religious rehabilitation of those who have been disqualified from bearing testimony in courts of law; *MT Hilkhot Edut* 12:4–10, *Hilkhot Shabbat* 2:3, *Hilkhot Teshuvah* 2:10, *Hilkhot Tzedakah* 10:1–3, the end of *Hilkhot Avadim*. See J. B. Soloveitchik, *On Repentance*, ed. P. Peli (Jerusalem: Oroth, 1980), pp. 57–68, for an illustration of how one's philosophic (aggadic) understanding of *teshuvah* influences the halakhic process.

36. It is interesting to note that *MT Hilkhot De'ot* gives expression to what Maimonides mentions briefly in the epistle. After the fifth and sixth chapters of *MT Hilkhot Yesodei ha-Torah*, which deal with halakhic themes, the next treatment of halakhic themes rather than foundational dogmatic principles is in *Hilkhot De'ot*. This may suggest that there is an intimate connection between *kiddush ha-Shem* and the development of one's total religious character (*Hilkhot De'ot*). The fact that Maimonides dealt with love of God and the way of life of the *ḥasid* within the context of *kiddush ha-Shem* also points to a comprehensive approach to Halakhah. See Hartman, *Maimonides*, Chapter 2.

37. Compare *The Midrash on Psalms*, trans. W. G. Braude (New Haven: Yale University Press, 1959), vol. 2, book 4, pp. 178–79:

R. Meir had living in his neighborhood a certain sectarian who so vexed him with quotations from scripture that R. Meir was about to pray that the sectarian should die. But R. Meir's wife, Beruria, said to him: "How would you justify your praying thus? Because you think that Scripture says, 'Sinners shall cease' [Ps. 104:35]? But does the verse actually say, 'Sinners shall cease'? It says, in fact, 'Sins shall cease out of the earth!' That is, as soon as sins cease, 'The wicked are no more.' " Whereupon R. Meir prayed that the sectarian would repent and his prayer justified his saying "Bless the Lord, O my soul." See also BT Berakhot 10a.

38. See Makkot 13b–14a regarding Ravena's explanation of R. Akiva's statement that *teshuvah* can cancel the divine punishment of *karet*. For Ravena the permanent possibility of *teshuvah* implies that there is never in fact a final judgment of *karet*. Maimonides was aware of the fact that the principles guiding human judgments and their consequences do not affect how the Halakhah understands God's loving response to the sinner. Compare *MT Hilkhot Teshuvah* 3:14 with *Hilkhot Avodah Zarah* 2:5 and *Responsa* of Maimonides, ed. J. Blau, 3 vols. (Jerusalem: Mekitze Nirdamim, 1957–61), resp. 264, for an interesting distinction between divine and human judgment.

39. Note the contrast between how the Torah, the prophets, and God (the source of both the Torah and prophecy) respond to the sinner in the following midrash from *Pesikta de-Rab Kahana*, trans. W. G. Braude and I. J. Kapstein (Philadelphia: Jewish Publication Society, 1975), *piska* 24:7, p. 369:

Good and upright is the Lord, because He doth instruct sinners in the way (Ps. 25:8). When Wisdom was asked, "The sinner—what is to be his punishment," Wisdom answers: *Evil which pursueth sinners* (Prov. 13:2). When Prophecy is asked, "The sinner—what is to be his punishment?" Prophecy replies: *The soul that sinneth, it shall die* (Ezek. 18:4). When Torah is asked, "The sinner—what is to be his punishment?" Torah replies: "Let him bring a guilt offering in expiation and his sin shall be forgiven him." When the Holy One is asked, "The sinner—what is to be his punishment?" the Holy One replies: "In penitence let him mend his ways, and his sin shall be forgiven him."

The fact that the Torah and the prophets demand different things than God Himself has important implications for one's theology of Halakhah. It has rich possibilities for a contemporary theory of revelation. See also *The Midrash on Psalms*, Ps. 120.

40. Maimonides was harshly critical of those who take comfort in the ultimate coming of the Messiah and who consequently make little effort to escape from their oppressive situation. He knew that an exclusive reliance on miraculous divine intervention in history would sap the community of the strength necessary for survival under the existing circumstances. Passive hope for messianic deliverance can destroy a community if its members are deluded into believing that their survival is guaranteed whether or not they master the brutal game of survival.

Those who delude themselves to think that they will remain where they are until the king Messiah appears in the Maghreb, and they will then leave for Jerusalem—I simply do not know how they will rid themselves of the present difficulties. They are transgressors, and they lead others to sin. The prophet Jeremiah's criticism: *They offer healing offhand for the wounds of My people, saying, "all is well, all is well," when nothing is well* [Jer. 6:14 and 8:11], fits them and others like them very well. There is no set time for the arrival of the Messiah that they can count on and decide that it is close or distant. The incumbency of the commandments does not depend on the appearance of the Messiah. We are required to apply ourselves to study and the fulfillment of the precepts, and we must strive for perfection in both. If we do what we have to, we or our children or grandchildren may be privileged by God to witness the coming of the Messiah, and life will be more pleasant. If he does not come we have not lost anything; on the contrary we have gained by doing what we had to do. But it is wicked and hopeless and a renunciation of the faith for anyone to stay on in these places and see the study of Torah cease, the Jewish population perishing after some time, he himself unable to live as a Jew, but continue to say: "I will stay here until the Messiah appears and then I shall be relieved of the situation I am in." (pp. 32–33)

See also the beginning of Maimonides' *Letter on Astrology*. Cf. Cohen, *Messianic Postures*, pp. 39–40.

41. See *MT Hilkhot Shabbat* 30:14.

THE EPISTLE
TO YEMEN

Not long after his arrival in Egypt in 1167 C.E., Maimonides was appointed physician to the ruler of the country and his entourage. Maimonides was sought out by the Jewish community not only for medical treatment, but also for guidance and help in its private and communal affairs. Such was his reputation that a request for advice soon came to him from Jacob ben Nathanel al-Fayyumi on behalf of the Jews of Yemen. There too a fanatical Muslim movement was threatening the existence of the Jewish community. The movement had been started in 1150 by the Shiʿite Ali ibn Mahdi and was now attempting to force the conversion of all non-Moslems under his son ʿAbd al-Nabiʾ ibn Mahdi.

Jacob raised several issues in his request for advice. What was the significance of the community's suffering? How should they respond to a convert who had become a missionary for Islam and claimed that the Torah itself confirmed the prophethood of Muhammad? What should they make of the claim of another individual to be the Messiah, come to rescue them from their persecutors? Could the date of the Messiah's coming be predicted by astrology?

Maimonides gave his ruling on all these questions in his *Epistle to Yemen* of 1172, so phrasing his answers that the community might be encouraged to avoid succumbing either to the oppressor or to messianic delusions.

I

To the honored, great, and holy master and teacher, Jacob,[1] wise and genial, dear and revered sage, son of the honored, great, and holy master and teacher, Nathanel Fayyumi, distinguished prince of Yemen, president of its congregations, leader of its communities, may the spirit of God rest upon him, and to all his associates and to all the scholars of the communities of Yemen, may the Lord keep and protect them. From a loving friend who never saw him but knows him only by reputation, Moses ben Maimon ben Joseph ben Isaac ben Obadiah[2] of blessed memory.

Just as plants bear testimony to the existence of roots, and waters are evidence of the excellence of the springs, so has the firm shoot developed from the roots of truth and righteousness, and a huge river has gushed forth from the spring of mercy in the land of Yemen, to water therewith all gardens and to make flowers blossom.[3] It flows gently on to satisfy the needs of the weary and thirsty in the arid places; wayfarers and folks from the isles of the sea satisfy their needs with it. Consequently, it has been proclaimed from Spain to Babylonia, from one end of heaven to the other: *Ho, all who are thirsty, come for water* [Isa. 55:1].[4] Men of business and traffic unanimously declare to all inquirers that they have found in the land of Yemen a beautiful and delightful plantation and a rich pasture with faithful shepherds wherein every lean one shall wax fat. They strengthen the indigent with bread and greet the opulent with hospitality and generosity; even the Sabean caravans look forward to their benevolence.[5] Their hands are stretched out to every passerby, and their homes are wide open to every traveler. With them all find tranquillity; sorrow and sighing flee. They continually study the Law of Moses, walk in the way of R. Ashi,[6] pursue justice, repair the breach, uphold the principles of Torah, bring back the stray people of God with encouraging words, observe the religious ceremonies punctiliously in their communities. *There is no breaching and no sortie, and no wailing in our streets* [Ps. 144:14].

Blessed be the Lord, that He has suffered Jews to remain who observe the Torah and obey its injunctions in the most distant peninsulas, as we were graciously assured through Isaiah, His servant, for it is to you people of Yemen he was alluding when he prophesied: *From the end of the earth we hear singing* [Isa. 24:16].[7]

When we departed from the West *to gaze upon the beauty of the Lord, to frequent His temple* [Ps. 27:4],[8] I learned that he[9] passed away. May God bestow His justice and goodness upon him. May he enter unto peace and rest upon his bed. May He send him angels of mercy. May he rest and rise up for his reward at the end of days. This, my dearly beloved friend, is proof that God was pleased with his deeds, and that He will compensate him doubly and grant him peace, that you are his son, and have risen in his place to promote religion and observance, to further justice and righteousness, to obey His precepts and laws, and to abide by His covenant. May the Lord your God be with you as He was with your fathers. May He not forsake nor abandon you. May He give you deep understanding to judge His people. *May His words never depart from your mouth, nor the mouth of your children* [Isa. 59:21], as He declared. May you follow your father as leader of His people, and may God grant that your fame be greater than his.

When your letter, my dearly beloved friend, arrived in Egypt, all were pleased to hear of it and delighted to look at it. It bore witness that you are one of the ministers of the Lord who dwell in His domain and are pitched at His standard, that you pursue the study of the Torah, love its laws, and watch at its gates. May the Lord divulge its secrets unto you, and stock you abundantly with the knowledge of its treasures, make its crown your chief crown, place its necklace upon your neck. May its words be a lamp unto your feet and a light unto your path, and may you become celebrated through them. *And all the peoples of the earth shall see that the Lord's name is proclaimed over you, and they shall stand in fear of you* [Deut. 28:10].[10]

As for the information in your letter, my dear friend, that you heard some of our coreligionists in the Diaspora—may the Lord keep and protect them—praise and extol me very highly and compare me with the illustrious *geonim*, they have spoken thus about me out of mere tenderness for me, and written about me out of pure goodness.[11] However, listen to a word fitly spoken by me, and give no heed to the sayings of others. I am one of the humblest scholars of Spain whose prestige is low in exile. I am always dedicated to my duties, but have not attained to the learning of my forebears, for evil days and hard times have overtaken us and we have not lived in tranquillity; we have labored without finding rest. How can the Law become lucid to a fugitive from city to city, from country to country? I have everywhere pursued the reapers and gathered ears of grain, both the solid and the full, as well as the shriveled and the thin. Only recently have I found a home.[12] Were it not for the help of God, as we are told by our ancestors, I would not have gathered the little I have, from which I continually draw.[13]

Now, the princely priest R. Shelomo, my friend and disciple,[14] who, as you write, indulges in hyperboles in praise of me and speaks extravagantly in appreciation of me, exaggerates unreasonably because he wants to, and waxes enthusiastic because he loves and cherishes me. May the Lord guard him, so that he is like a blooming vineyard, and may he return to us hale and hearty.

The other matters in your letter that you wish me to speak of, I deem it best to write in the Arabic tongue and idiom,[15] so that all men, women, and children can read it with ease,[16] for it is right that your membership be enabled to understand the contents of the reply.

You write of the affair of the rebel leader in Yemen[17] who decreed forced apostasy of the Jews, and compelled all the Jewish inhabitants in all the places he had subdued to desert their religion, just as the Berbers had obliged them to do in the Maghreb.[18] This report has broken our backs and astounded and dumbfounded the whole of our community, and rightly so. For these are evil tidings, and *both ears of everyone who hears about it will tingle* [1 Sam. 3:11 and 2 Kings 21:12]. Indeed, our hearts are weakened, our minds are confused, and our strength wanes because of the dire misfortunes that have come upon us in the form of the religious persecution in the two ends of the world, the East and West, *so they were in the midst of Israel, some on this side and some on the other side* [Josh. 8:22].[19] It is of the like of this dreadful occasion the prophet prayed and interceded in our behalf: *I said, "Oh, Lord God, refrain! How will Jacob survive? He is so small"* [Amos 7:5].[20] Indeed, this is a subject that no religious person dare take lightly,[21] nor anyone put aside who believes faithfully in Moses. There is no doubt that these are the messianic travails[22] concerning which the sages invoked God that they be spared seeing and experiencing them. The prophets trembled when they envisioned them, as Isaiah reacted: *My heart pants, fearfulness affrights me; the twilight I longed for has been turned into trembling* [Isa. 21:4].[23] And the divine exclamation in the Torah expresses sympathy with those who will experience them, by saying: *Alas, who shall live when God does this!* [Num. 24:23].[24]

When you write that the hearts of some people have turned, uncertainty befalls them, and their beliefs are weakened, while others have not lost faith and not become disquieted, we have a divine premonition of it through Daniel. For he predicted that the long stay of Israel in exile and the continuous persecution would cause many to drift away from our faith, to have misgivings, or go astray, because they were to witness our feebleness and note the triumph of our adversaries and their dominion over us, while still others would neither oscillate in their belief, nor be shaken in their convictions. He states: *Many shall purify themselves, and make themselves white, and be refined; but the wicked shall do wickedly; and none of the wicked shall understand* [Dan. 12:10].[25] Further, he explains that even men of understanding and intelligence, who would have brooked milder misfortunes and remained firm in their belief in God and in His servant Moses, will yield to distrust and will err when they are visited by sterner and harsher afflictions. Only a few will remain pure in faith, for he adds: *And some of them that are wise shall stumble* [Dan. 11:35].[26]

And now, brethren, it is essential that all of you give attention and consideration to what I am going to point out to you.[27] Teach it to your women and children, so that their faith, to the extent that it has become enfeebled and impaired, may be strengthened, and that enduring certainty may be reestablished in their hearts. It is—may the Lord deliver you and me—that ours is the true and divine religion, revealed to us through Moses, chief of the former as well as of the later prophets.[28] By means of it God has distinguished us from the rest of mankind, as He declares: *Yet it was to your fathers that the Lord was drawn in His love for them, so that He chose you, their lineal descendants, from among all the peoples* [Deut. 10:15]. This choice was not made thanks to our merits, but was rather an act of grace, on account of our ancestors who were cognizant of God and obedient to Him, as He states: *It is not because you are the most numerous of peoples that the Lord set His heart on you and chose you—indeed, you are the smallest of peoples* [Deut. 7:7].[29]

Since God has singled us out by His laws and precepts, and our preeminence over the others was manifested in His rules and statutes, as Scripture says in narrating God's mercies to us: *What great nation has laws and rules as perfect as all this Teaching that I set before you this day?* [Deut. 4:8];[30] all the nations, instigated by envy and impiety, rose up against us in anger, and all the kings of the earth, motivated by injustice and enmity, applied themselves to persecute us. They wanted to thwart God, but He will not be thwarted. Ever since the time of revelation[31] every despot or rebel ruler, be he violent or ignoble, has made it his first aim and his final purpose to destroy our Law, and to vitiate our religion by means of the sword, by violence, or by brute force. Such were Amalek, Sisera, Sennacherib, Nebuchadnezzar, Titus, Hadrian,[32] and others like them.

The second class consists of the most intelligent and educated among the nations, like the Syrians, Persians, and Greeks.[33] They also endeavor to demolish our Law and to abrogate it by means of arguments that they invent and controversies that they institute. They seek to render the Law ineffectual and to wipe out every trace of it with their compositions, just as the despots try to do with their swords. But neither the one nor the other shall succeed. For a long time ago the assurance was given us through Isaiah that every tyrant who seeks to triumph over our Law and annihilate it by weapons of war will be demolished by the Lord so that they will have no effect. This is a metaphorical way of saying that his efforts will be of no avail. Likewise every disputant who will attempt to demonstrate the falsity of our Law, the Lord will shatter his arguments and prove them absurd, untenable, and ineffective. This is the divine promise: *No weapon formed against you shall succeed, and every tongue that contends with you at law you shall defeat* [Isa. 54:17].[34] Although both of these persuade themselves that this is a structure that can be demolished and lay plans to undermine its firmly established foundations, they only increase their pain and toil. The structure remains as firm as ever, while the Constant[35] mocks and derides them because they endeavor with their feeble intelligence to achieve something no human being can undertake. The prophet,[36] describing their efforts and God's scorn of them, says: *Let us break the cords of their yoke, shake off their ropes from us! He who is enthroned in heaven laughs; the Lord mocks at them* [Ps. 2:3–4].[37] We have been incessantly distressed and harassed by these two parties all through the epoch of our political independence, and in part during the period of our dispersion.[38]

After that a new class arose that combined the two methods, namely, conquest, controversy, and dispute[39] into one, because it believed that this procedure would be more effective in wiping out every trace of the community. It therefore resolved to lay claim to prophecy and to found a new Law, contrary to our divine religion, and to contend that it also came from God, like the true claim. Thus doubts will be generated and confusion will be created, since one is opposed to the other and both supposedly emanated from one god, and it will lead to the destruction of both religions. This is a remarkable plan contrived by a person who is envious and malicious, who will strive to kill his enemy and remain alive, and if he cannot achieve this, he will devise a scheme whereby they both will be slain.[40]

The first to institute this plan was Jesus the Nazarene,[41] may his bones be ground to dust. He was Jewish because his mother was a Jewess although his father was a gentile, and our principle is that a child born of a Jewess and a gentile or a slave, is legitimate.[42] Only figuratively do we call him an illegitimate child.[43] He impelled people to believe that he was sent by God to clarify perplexities in the Torah, and that he was the Messiah predicted by each and every prophet. His purpose was to interpret the Torah in a fashion that would lead to its total annulment, to the abolition of its commandments, and to the violation of all its prohibitions. The sages of blessed memory, aware of his objective before his reputation spread among our people, meted out a fitting punishment.[44] Daniel had already alluded to him when he presaged the downfall of a wicked and heretical Jew who would endeavor to destroy the Law, claim prophecy for himself, make pretense to miracles, and allege that he was the Messiah, as is written: *The children of the impudent among your people shall make bold to claim prophecy, but they shall fall* [Dan. 11:14].[45]

Quite some time later, a religion, which is traced to him by the descendants of Esau, gained popularity.[46] Although this was the aim he hoped to realize, he had no impact on Israel, as neither groups nor individuals became unsettled in their beliefs. His inconsistencies were transparent to everyone, as was also his failure and disappointment when he fell into our hands with the well-known end.[47] After him the Madman[48] arose, who emulated the precursor who had paved the way for him. But he added the further objective of procuring rule and obedience,[49] and he invented his notorious religion.

All of these men wish to liken themselves to the divine religion.[50] But only a simpleton who lacks knowledge of both establishments will liken the divine institutions to human contrivances. The difference between our religion and the other denominations that liken themselves to us is like the difference between the living, rational individual and the statue skillfully molded out of marble, wood, silver, or gold that looks like a man.[51] A person ignorant of divine wisdom or of God's work, when he sees the statue that superficially resembles a man in its contours, form, features, and color, believes that its structure is like the constitution of a man, because he lacks the knowledge of the inner organization of both. But the informed person who knows the interior of both, knows that the internal composition of the statue betrays no skillful workmanship at all, whereas the inward parts of man are truly marvelously made, a testimony to the wisdom of the Creator. The prolongation of the nerves in the muscles and their ramifications, the branching out of the sinews and their intersections, and the network of their ligaments and their manner of growth, the articulations of the bones and the joints, the pulsating and nonpulsating blood vessels and their ramifications, the setting of the limbs into one another, the uncovered and covered parts, every one of them is in proportion, in form, and in its proper place.

Likewise a person ignorant of the secrets of the revealed books and the inner significance of our Law will be led to believe that our religion has something in common with the established confession if he makes a comparison between the two. For he will find that in the Torah there are prohibitions and commandments, and there are prohibitions and commandments in the others; the Torah contains positive and negative precepts, rewards, and punishments, and the others contain negative and positive commandments, rewards, and punishments. Yet if he could only fathom the inner meanings, he would realize that the essence of the Torah lies in the deeper meaning of its positive and negative precepts, every one of which will aid man in his striving after perfection and remove every impediment to the attainment of excellence. They will enable the masses and the elite to acquire moral and intellectual qualities, each according to his ability. Thus, the godly community becomes preeminent, reaching a twofold perfection.[52] By the first I mean man's leading his life in this world under the most agreeable and congenial conditions. The second will constitute the gain of the intelligibles,[53] each in accordance with his native powers. The pretentious religions contain matters that have no inner meaning, only imitations, simulations, and copies by which the inventors aimed to glorify themselves and indulge in the fancy that they are similar to so-and-so. However, their shameful action is an open secret to the learned. They became an object of derision and ridicule,[54] just as one laughs and scoffs at a monkey when it tries to imitate the actions of human beings.

This was predicted by the divinely inspired prophet Daniel, according to whom, in some future time, it would happen.[55] Sometime later a person will appear with a religion similar to the true one, with a book and oral communications, who will arrogantly pretend that God has vouchsafed him a revelation, and that he held converse with Him, and other extravagant claims. In his description of the rise of the Arab kingdom after the Byzantine Empire, he compared the appearance of the Madman and his victories over the Byzantines, Persians, and Greeks with a horn that grew and became long and strong. This is clearly indicated in a verse that can be understood by the masses as well as by the select few. Since this interpretation is borne out by the facts of history, no other meaning can be given to the following verse: *I considered the horns, and, behold, another little horn came among them before which three of the first horns were plucked up by the roots; and, behold, in this horn were eyes like the eyes of a human, and a mouth speaking big things* [Dan. 7:8]. Now consider how remarkably apt the symbolism is. He says that he saw a small horn that was going up. When it became longer, even marvelously longer, it cast three horns down before it, and behold, the horn had two eyes similar to the eyes of a human, and a mouth speaking big things. This obviously alludes to the person who will found a new religion similar to the divine religion and make claim to a revelation and to prophecy. He will produce much talk and will endeavor to alter this Torah and abolish it, as He states: *And he shall seek to change the seasons and the law* [Dan. 7:25].

But God informed him that He would destroy this person, notwithstanding his greatness and his long endurance, together with the remaining adherents of his predecessors. For the three parties that warred against us will ultimately perish: the one that sought to overpower us with the sword, the second that claimed it had arguments against us, and the third that claims to have a religion similar to ours. Though they shall appear to be triumphant for a while, and be in the ascendancy for a longer or shorter period of time, they shall neither last nor endure. We have a continuous divine assurance that whenever a decree of apostasy is passed against us and wrath breaks out, God will ultimately terminate it. When King David, inspired by the Holy Spirit and speaking in the name of the community, reflected on how many peoples ruled over it in the past, and how many trials and tribulations they had undergone from the beginning of their history, and nevertheless were not exterminated, he exclaimed: *Since my youth they have often assailed me, but they have never overcome me* [Ps. 129:2].

My brethren, you know that in the time of the wicked Nebuchadnezzar the Jews were compelled to worship idols, and none was spared save Hananiah, Mishael, and Azariah.[56] Ultimately God destroyed him, and put an end to his laws, and the religion of truth came back into its own. Similarly, during the Second Commonwealth, when the wicked Greek rulers gained control, they instituted severe persecution against Israel in order to abolish the Torah. The Jews were compelled to profane the Sabbath and forbidden to practice circumcision. Every Jew was forced to write on his garment, "I do not have a portion in the Lord God of Israel," and also to engrave these words on the horns of his ox and then to plow with it.[57] Finally, God simultaneously brought their empire and their laws to an end, after a lapse of fifty-two years.[58] The sages of blessed memory frequently allude to persecutions in the following manner: "Once the wicked government passed such and such a decree of persecution,"[59] or "they decreed thus and so."[60] After a while God would make the decree null and void by destroying the power that issued it. It was this observation that led the rabbis of blessed memory to affirm that persecutions are of short duration.[61]

Indeed God assured our father Jacob that although his children would be humbled and overcome by the nations, they and not the nations would survive and would endure. He declares: *Your descendants shall be as the dust of the earth* [Gen. 28:14],[62] that is to say, although they will be abased like the dust that is trodden under foot, they will ultimately emerge triumphant and victorious. And, as the simile implies, just as the dust settles finally upon him who tramples upon it and remains after him, so will Israel outlive its oppressors.[63] The prophet Isaiah predicted that during its exile various peoples will succeed in their endeavor to vanquish Israel and lord over them, but that ultimately God will come to Israel's assistance and put a stop to their woes and afflictions. He says: *A harsh prophecy has been announced to me: "The betrayer is betraying, the ravager ravaging. Advance Elam! Lay siege, Media! I have put an end to all her sighing"* [Isa. 21:2].[64] The Lord has given us assurance through His prophets that we are indestructible and imperishable, and we will always continue to be a preeminent community. As it is impossible for God to cease to exist, so is our destruction and disappearance from the world unthinkable. He declares: *For I am the Lord—I have not changed; and you are the children of Jacob—you have not ceased to be* [Mal. 3:6]. Similarly, He has avowed and assured us that it is unimaginable that He will reject us entirely even if we disobey Him and disregard His behests, as He avers: *If the heavens above could be measured, and the foundations of the earth below could be fathomed, only then would I reject all the offspring of Israel for all that they have done—declares the Lord* [Jer. 31:37].[65] In fact, this very promise was previously given through Moses our Teacher in the Torah. It reads: *Yet, even then, when they are in the land of their enemies, I will not reject or spurn them so as to destroy them, annulling My covenant with them: for I the Lord am their God* [Lev. 26:44].[66]

Put your trust in these true texts of Scripture, brethren, and be not dismayed by the succession of persecutions or the enemy's ascendancy over us, or the weakness of our people. These trials are designed to test and purify us, so that only the saints and the pious men of the pure and undefiled lineage of Jacob will adhere to our religion and remain within the fold, as has been stated: *Anyone who invokes the name of Lord shall be among the survivors* [Joel 3:5].[67] This statement makes it clear that they are not numerous, and that they are the descendants of those who were present at Mount Sinai,[68] witnessed the divine revelation, entered into the covenant of God, and took upon themselves to do and obey, declaring, *we will do, and obey* [Exod. 24:7].[69] They obligated themselves and their descendants, by saying: *for us and our children* [for]*ever* [Deut. 29:28].[70] God has given assurance—He is an adequate guarantor—and informed them that not only did all the persons who were present at the Sinaitic revelation believe in the prophecy of Moses and in his Law, but that their descendants would likewise do so until the end of time. He declares: *I will come to you in a thick cloud, in order that the people may hear when I speak with you and so trust you ever after* [Exod. 19:9]. Consequently, let everyone know who spurns the religion that was revealed at that theophany that he is not an offspring of the folk that witnessed it. This is what the sages of Israel of blessed memory said of those who entertain scruples concerning the divine message: They are not the scions of the race that was present at Mount Sinai.[71] May God guard me and you from doubt, and banish from our midst confusion and suspicion that lead to it and ensnare in it.

Now, all my fellow countrymen in the Diaspora, it behooves you to hearten one another, the elders to guide the youth, and the leaders to direct the masses. Gain the assent of your community[72] to the Truth that is immutable and unchangeable, and to the following postulates of the true faith that shall never fail.[73] God is one in a unique sense of the term.[74] And Moses, His prophet and spokesman,[75] is the greatest and most perfect of all the seers. To him was vouchsafed the knowledge of God, what has never been vouchsafed to any prophet before him, nor will it be in the future. The entire Torah from beginning to end[76] was spoken by God to Moses, of whom it is said: *With him I speak mouth to mouth* [Num. 12:8].[77] It will never be abrogated or superseded, neither supplemented nor abridged. Never shall it be supplanted by another divine law containing positive or negative duties. Keep the revelation at Mount Sinai well in mind in accordance with the divine precept to perpetuate the memory and not to forget this occasion. He enjoined us to teach it to our children so that they grow up knowing it, as He—exalted be the Speaker—says: *But take utmost care and watch yourselves scrupulously, so that you do not forget the things that you saw with your own eyes and so that they do not fade from your mind so long as you live. And make them known to your children and to your children's children: The day you stood before the Lord your God at Horeb* [Deut. 4:9–10].[78]

It is imperative, my fellow Jews, that you make this great spectacle of the revelation appeal to the imagination of your children. Proclaim at public gatherings its nobility and its momentousness. For it is the pivot of our religion and the proof that demonstrates its veracity. Evaluate this phenomenon in its true importance, as God pointed out its significance in the verse: *You have but to inquire about bygone ages that came before you, ever since God created man on earth, from one end of heaven to the other: has anything as grand as this ever happened, or has its like ever been known? Has any people heard the voice of a god speaking out of a fire?* [Deut. 4:32–33]. Remember, brethren, that this great, incomparable, and unique covenant and faith is attested by the best of evidence. For never before or since has a whole nation heard the speech of God or beheld His splendor. This was done only to confirm us in the faith, so that nothing can change it, and to reach a degree of certainty that will sustain us in these trying times of fierce persecution and absolute tyranny, as He says: *For God has come only in order to test you* [Exod. 20:17].[79] It means that God has revealed Himself thus to give you strength to withstand all future trials. Now, brethren, do not slip or err, be steadfast in your religion and persevere in your faith and its duties.

Long ago Solomon[80] compared our community with a beautiful woman having a perfect figure, marred by no defect, in the verse: *Every part of you is fair, my darling; there is no blemish in you* [Song of Songs 4:7].[81] He further depicted the adherents of other religions and faiths, who strive to entice us and win us over to their convictions as beguiling seducers who lure virtuous women for their lewd purposes. Similarly they seek devices to trap us into embracing their religions, and subscribing to their doctrines. To those who endeavor to decoy her into avowing the superiority of their creed, he in his wisdom answered in the name of the community: "Why do you take hold of me, can you confer upon me something like the felicity of the two companies?" She challenges them, saying: "If you can furnish me with something like the theophany at Sinai, in which the camp of Israel faced the camp of the divine presence, then I shall espouse your doctrine."[82] This is metaphorically expressed in the verse: *Turn back, turn back, O maid of Shulem! Turn back, turn back, that we may gaze upon you. "Why will you gaze at the Shulammite in the Mahanaim dance?"* [Song of Songs 7:1][83] *Shulammite* signifies the perfect one; the *Mahanaim dance* the joy of the revelation at Mt. Sinai that was shared by the camp[84] of Israel, as He states: *Moses led the people out of the camp toward God* [Exod. 19:17],[85] and the camp of God, as He explained saying: *God's chariots are myriads upon myriads, thousands upon thousands* [Ps. 68:18].[86]

Note well the wisdom and the deep significance of the verse. The fourfold occurrence of the word *return* is an allusion to the four empires, each of which has endeavored to coerce us to abandon our faith and to join it. Now we are living under the last of them.[87] God has warned us in the Torah that they would draw us to accept their faith, for He says: *There you will serve man-made gods of wood and stone* [Deut. 4:28].[88] However, even then it will not be general throughout the world,[89] and God will never deprive us of His Law, as He assured us: *Since it will never be lost from the mouth of their offspring* [Deut. 31:21].[90] Indeed, Isaiah, the herald of national redemption, has explained that the sign between us and Him, and the token that proves that we are indestructible lies in the perpetuation of God's Torah and His words among us: *And this shall be My covenant with them, said the Lord: My spirit which is upon you, and the words which I have placed in your mouth shall not be absent from your mouth, nor from the mouth of your children, nor from the mouth of your children's children—said the Lord—from now on, for all time* [Isa. 59:21]. Our nation speaks with pride of the persecutions it has suffered, and the sore tribulations it has endured, as he states: *It is for Your sake that we are slain all day long, that we are regarded as sheep to be slaughtered* [Ps. 44:23].[91] The rabbis remark in Midrash Ḥazita[92] that the expression *it is for Your sake* alludes to the generations that undergo persecution. Let these persons exult who suffer dire misfortunes, are deprived of their riches, are forced into exile, and lose their belongings. For the bearing of these hardships is a source of glory and a great achievement in the sight of God. Whoever is visited by these calamities is like a burnt offering upon the altar.[93] It is said to them: *Dedicate yourselves to the Lord this day . . . that He may bestow a blessing upon you today* [Exod. 32:29].[94]

It therefore behooves the victims of this persecution to escape and flee to the desert and wilderness, and not to consider separation from family or loss of wealth.[95] For they are a slight sacrifice and a paltry offering due to God, King of kings, possessor of all things, *this honored and awesome Name, the Lord your God* [Deut. 28:58].[96] God may be trusted to compensate you well in this world and in the world-to-come. Thus we have found that the godly and pious folk who are animated by a desire to get acquainted with the truth and those who are engaged in its pursuit, rush to the divine religion, and wend their way from the most distant parts to the homes of scholars.[97] They seek to gain increased insight into the Law, that they may gain reward from God. How much more is it one's duty to run for the entire Torah! We know that when a man finds it arduous to gain a livelihood in one country, he emigrates to another. It is all the more incumbent upon one who is restricted in the practice of the divine religion to depart for another place. If he finds it impossible to leave that locality for the time being, he must not become careless and indulge in the desecration of the Sabbath and the dietary laws on the assumption that he is exempt from all religious obligations.[98] It is the eternally inescapable duty of everyone belonging to the stock of Jacob to abide by the Law. Nay, he exposes himself to punishment for the violation of each and every positive or negative precept. Let no one conclude that he may freely disregard the less important ceremonies without liability to penalty because he has under duress committed some major sins.[99] For Jeroboam son of Nebat, may his bones be ground to dust,[100] was chastised not only for the sin of worshiping the calves and inciting the Israelites to do the same, but also for his failure to construct a booth on the Feast of Tabernacles.[101] This is one of the fundamentals of our religion. Understand it aright, teach it, and apply the principle widely.

II

You mention that the apostate[102] has misled people to believe that
bm'd m'd is the Madman,[103] or that in the same way *He appeared from
Mount Paran* [Deut. 33:2][104] alludes to him, or similarly, that *a prophet
from among your own people* [Deut. 18:15][105] refers to him, or likewise
his promise to Ishmael: *I will make of him a great nation* [Gen. 17:20].[106]
These arguments have been rehearsed so often that they have become
nauseating. It is not enough to declare that they are altogether feeble;
nay, to cite them as proofs is ridiculous and absurd in the extreme.
Neither the untutored multitudes, nor the apostates themselves who
delude others with them, believe in them or entertain any illusions
about them. Their sole purpose in citing these verses is to win favor
in the eyes of the gentiles by demonstrating that they believe the
statement of the Koran that Muhammad was mentioned in the Torah.
But the Muslims themselves do not accept these arguments; they do
not admit them nor cite them, because they are manifestly fallacious.
Inasmuch as the Muslims could not find a single proof in the entire
Bible, nor a reference, or possible allusion to their prophet that they
could utilize, they are compelled to accuse us, saying: "You have
altered the text of the Torah, and expunged every trace of the name
of Muhammad therefrom."[107] They could find nothing stronger than
this ignominious argument, the falsity of which is easily demonstrated
to one and all by the fact that the Torah had been translated into
Syriac, Greek, Persian, and Latin hundreds of years before the appearance of the "preapostle,"[108] and by the fact that it is an unbroken
tradition[109] in the East and the West, with the result that no differences
in the text exist at all, not even in the vocalization, for they are all
correct. Nor do any differences affecting the meaning exist.[110] Only
the absence of any allusion to him in the Torah compelled them to
rely on these weak proofs.

The phrase *a great nation* implies neither prophecy nor a Law, but
merely large numbers and no more,[111] just as He says of the idolaters
nations greater and more numerous than you [Deut. 11:23].[112] Similarly, the phrase *bm'd m'd* simply signifies *exceedingly*. If the allusion
in the phrase were intended to *that one*, it would read *and I shall bless
him bm'd m'd*,[113] so that whoever likes to hang on a spider's web might

then declare that it means: "I shall bless him that that one may be his seed." But since *bm'd m'd* follows *I will make him numerous*, it can only denote an extravagant increase in numbers.[114]

When God spoke to Abraham He made it amply clear that all the blessings that He promised and all his children to whom He will reveal the Law and whom He will make the Chosen People—all this is meant only for the seed of Isaac.[115] Ishmael is regarded as an adjunct and appendage in the blessings of Isaac, for He says: *As for the son of the slave-woman, I will make a nation of him, too, for he is your seed* [Gen. 21:13].[116] He clearly explains in this verse that Isaac holds a primary position and Ishmael a subordinate place.[117] He announces: *For it is through Isaac that offspring shall be continued for you* [Gen. 21:12] and He ignores Ishmael entirely. The meaning is that although the seed of Ishmael will be vast in numbers, it will be neither preeminent nor the object of divine favor, nor distinguished by the attainment of excellence by which one may become famed or celebrated. Nay, your merit will become known by your illustrious offspring, the seed that will issue from Isaac. The literal meaning of *shall be continued* is *shall be called*, as in the verse: *in them may my name be recalled, and the names of my fathers Abraham and Isaac* [Gen. 48:16];[118] the sense is "you will become famed and celebrated through them." He further stated regarding Isaac that one of the blessings of which He assured Abraham would be that God's Torah and religion would be vouchsafed to his children, as He promised: *I will be their God* [Gen. 17:8].[119] Thus He singled out Isaac to the exclusion of Ishmael in all these blessings. He singled out him and not Ishmael in the religion, as He states: *But My covenant I will maintain with Isaac* [Gen. 17:21],[120] after saying regarding Ishmael: *I hereby bless him* [Gen. 17:20]. He made it clear through Isaac that Jacob was singled out in all this to the exclusion of Esau, for Isaac said to him: *May He grant the blessing of Abraham to you* [Gen. 28:4].[121] In a word, it is clear from the verses in the Torah that the divine covenant made with Abraham to grant the sublime Law to his descendants referred exclusively to those who belonged to the stock of both Isaac and Jacob. Hence the prophet[122] expresses his gratitude to God for the covenant *that He made with Abraham, swore to Isaac, and confirmed in a decree for Jacob, for Israel, as an eternal covenant* [Ps. 105:9–10 and 1 Chron. 16:16–17].

It is also important that you know that the name of the prophet that the Ishmaelites think is written in the Torah, *bm'd m'd*, to which the apostates cling,[123] is not *MHMD* but *AHMD*. So it is explicitly stated: "They find him mentioned in the Torah and the Gospels;"[124] "his name is *AHMD*."[125] The numerical value of *bm'd m'd* is not equal to this name, which is supposed to be written in the Torah.[126]

His argument from the phrase *he appeared from Mount Paran* is not valid. *Appeared* is past tense. Had it employed the future tense "he will appear from Mount Paran," the impostors might have had something to hang onto. However, the use of the past tense indicates that it is an event that has taken place, namely, it describes the revelation at Mount Sinai: It did not descend suddenly like a thunderbolt, but came down gently, manifesting itself gradually first from the top of one mountain, then from another, until it came to rest on Sinai. Hence He says: *The Lord came from Sinai; He shone upon them from Seir; He appeared from Mount Paran* [Deut. 33:2]. Mark well the expression *upon them*, i.e., Israel. Note that with Paran, which is further removed from Sinai, He says *appeared;* of Seir, which is nearer, *He shone;* and of the revelation, of the full splendor of God on Sinai, which was the goal of the theophany (as is related): *The Presence of the Lord abode on Mount Sinai* [Exod. 24:16],[127] He says *came from Sinai.*

Similarly, the idea that the Light descended gradually from mountain to mountain is conveyed in Deborah's description of the grandeur of Israel at the revelation at Sinai, when she exclaimed: *O Lord, when You came forth from Seir, advanced from the country of Edom, . . .* [Judg. 5:4].[128] Basing themselves on this verse, our sages relate that God sent a messenger before the time of Moses to go to the Romans, and another to go to the Arabs with the purpose of presenting them with the Torah,[129] but each of them in turn spurned it. When Moses was sent to us we signified our acceptance in the words: *All that the Lord has spoken we will do and obey* [Exod. 24:7].[130] The aforementioned event happened before the giving of the Torah, consequently the verbs in it come in the past: *He came, He shone, He appeared;* they are not predictions of what will be.

You write in your letter that some people were duped by the apostate's argument that Muhammad is alluded to in the verse: *The Lord your God will raise up for you a prophet from among your own people,*

like myself [Deut. 18:15],[131] while others remained unconvinced because of the phrase *from among your own people*.[132] It is most aston-
ishing that some folks should be duped by this, while others were
almost persuaded, were it not for the phrase *from among your own
people*. Under these circumstances it is incumbent upon you to con-
centrate and understand what I am about to say. Remember that it is
not right to take a passage out of its context and argue from it. Before
making any deduction, it is imperative to take into account the preceding and following contents in order to comprehend the meaning and
fathom the writer's aim.[133] If it were permissible for anyone to draw
proof from passages out of context, someone would have the right to
say that God has forbidden us in the Torah to obey any prophet, and
interdicted belief in miracles, for he could cite the passage: *Do not
heed the words of that prophet* [Deut. 13:4].[134] He could also maintain
that God commands us to worship idols, for He says: *There you will
serve man-made gods* [Deut. 4:28].[135] Other illustrations could be mul-
tiplied *ad libitum*. But this is absolutely vicious. No text can possibly
be cited as evidence before the aim of the author and its context are
grasped.

In order to comprehend the verse under discussion unequivocally:
*The Lord your God will raise up for you a prophet from among your
own people like myself*, it is necessary to ascertain its context. In the
beginning of the paragraph from which this verse is taken, He forbids
us to engage in acts of augury, divination, astrology, witchcraft, spells,
and the like. The gentiles believe that through these practices they
can predict the future course of events and take the necessary precautions to forestall them. The interdiction of these occult proceedings
is accompanied by the explication that the gentiles believe they can
depend upon them to determine future happenings. But you may not
follow this method in order to know what will happen. Nay, you will
know it from a prophet that I will send among you, who will truthfully
inform you of what is going to be and it will not fail. You will arrive
at a foreknowledge of the future from him, without recourse to augury,
divination, astrology, and the like. Matters will be facilitated for you
by the fact that every prophet whom I will send to foretell what will
happen will live in your midst. You will not be compelled to go in

search of him from country to country, nor to travel to distant parts. This is the sense of *in your midst*.

Moreover, He conveys another notion, namely, that in addition to being near you and living in your midst, he will also be one of you, an Israelite. The obvious deduction is that you shall be distinguished above all others by the sole possession of prophecy. The words *like myself* were specifically added to indicate that only the descendants of Jacob are meant. For the phrase *from among your own people* might have been misunderstood and taken to refer also to Esau and Ishmael, since we do find Israel addressing Esau as brother, in the verse: *Thus says your brother Israel* [Num. 20:14].[136] The words *like myself* cannot mean like me in rank and achievement, for He had indeed stated: *Never again did there arise in Israel a prophet like Moses* [Deut. 34:10].[137] The general drift of the chapter points to the correctness of our interpretation and will be confirmed by the succession of verses, to wit: *Let no one be found among you who consigns his son or daughter to the fire* [Deut. 18:10]; *one who casts spells* [Deut. 18:11]; *you must be wholehearted* [Deut. 18:13]; *to you, however, the Lord your God has not assigned the like* [Deut. 18:14]; *a prophet from among your own people* [Deut. 18:15].[138] It is obvious that the prophet alluded to here will not be a person who will produce a new Law or found a new religion. He will merely enable us to dispense with diviners and astrologers, and will be available for consultation concerning anything that may befall us, just as the gentiles consult soothsayers and prognosticators. Thus we find Saul inquiring of Samuel regarding a loss that he sustained, as is stated: *For the prophet of today was formerly called a seer* [1 Sam. 9:9].[139]

Our disbelief in the prophecies of Omar and Zeid[140] is not due to the fact that they are non-Jews, as the unlettered folk imagine, and in consequence of it are compelled to establish their stand from the biblical phrase *from among your own people*. For Job, Zophar, Bildad, Eliphaz, and Elihu are all considered prophets by us although they are not Israelites.[141] On the other hand, although Hananiah the son of Azzur was a Jew, he was deemed an accursed and false prophet.[142] But we give credence to a prophet or we disbelieve him because of what he preaches, not because of his descent, as I shall explain. This prophet Moses our Master, foremost among all the prophets, whose colloquy with God we heard, and in whom we reposed implicit faith when we said to him, *you go closer and hear* [Deut. 5:24],[143] assured us that no other Law remained in heaven that would be subsequently revealed, nor would there be another divine dispensation, as He says: *It is not in the heavens* [Deut. 30:12].[144] For this reason we have been forbidden to make any additions to the Law or to eliminate anything, for He said: *Neither add to it nor take away from it* [Deut. 13:1].[145] We pledged and obligated ourselves to God to abide by His Law, we, our children, and our children's children, until the end of time. This is the content of his statement: *Concealed acts concern the Lord our God; but with overt acts, it is for us and our children ever to apply all the provisions of this Teaching* [Deut. 29:28]. Any prophet, therefore, no matter what his pedigree is, be he priest, Levite, or Amalekite, is perfidious even if he asserts that only one of the precepts of the Torah is void, for he denies our Master Moses who said: *for us and our children ever*. We would declare such a one a false prophet and would execute him if we had jurisdiction over him.[146] We would take no notice of the miracles that he might perform, just as we disregard the wonder-working of one who seeks to lure people to idolatry, as He says: *Even if the sign or portent that he named to you comes true, do not heed the words of that prophet* [Deut. 13:3–4].[147] Since Moses, of blessed memory, has prohibited idol worship for all time, we know that the miracles of a would-be seducer to idolatry are wrought by trickery and sorcery. Similarly, since Moses has taught us that the Law is eternal, we definitely stamp as a prevaricator anyone who argues that it was destined to be in force for a fixed period of time, because he contravenes Moses.[148] Consequently, we do not ask him for a sign and we pay no attention to supernatural performances, which impress us as such when he performs them. Inasmuch as we believe in Moses not because of his miracles, we are under no obligation to make comparisons between his miracles and those of others. Our everlastingly firm trust and steadfast faith in him is due to the fact that we as well as he heard the divine discourse at Sinai, as He states: *And they will trust you forever* [Exod. 19:9].

This event is analogous to the situation of two witnesses who observed a certain act simultaneously. Each of them saw what his fellow saw, and each of them is sure of the truth of his fellow's statement as well as of his own, and does not require proof or demonstration, whereas other people, to whom they would report their testimony, would not be absolutely convinced without confirmation or certification to everybody's satisfaction. Similarly, we of the Jewish faith are convinced of the truth of the prophecy of Moses, not simply because of his wonders, but because we, like him, witnessed the theophany on Mount Sinai. He performed all of the miracles only as the occasion demanded, as is recorded in Scripture. We do not give credence to the tenets of a miracle worker in the same way we trust in the truth of Moses our Teacher, nor does any analogy exist between them. This distinction is a fundamental principle of our religion, but seems to have fallen into oblivion, and has been disregarded by many of our coreligionists.[149] It is because of this reality that Solomon addressed the gentile nations on behalf of Israel: *Why will you gaze at the Shulammite in the Mahanaim dance?* [Song of Songs 7:1]. The verse means to say: "If you can produce anything like the Revelation at Sinai, then we shall concede some misgivings concerning Moses."

Now, if a Jewish or gentile prophet urges and encourages people to follow the religion of Moses without adding thereto or diminishing therefrom, like Isaiah, Jeremiah, and the others, we demand a miracle from him.[150] If he performs it we recognize him and bestow upon him the honor due to a prophet, but if he fails to do so he is put to death.[151] We require only a miracle as his credentials, although it may be wrought by stratagem or magic, just as we accept the evidence of witnesses although there is a possibility of perjury. It is because we are divinely commanded through Moses to render judgment in a suit of law in accordance with the testimony of two witnesses whom we believe, the possibility of false swearing notwithstanding.[152] Similarly we are enjoined to act in accordance with the declaration of one who asserts that he is a prophet provided he can substantiate his claim by miracle or proof, although there is a possibility that he is an impostor. However, He has also controlled us by teaching that if the would-be prophet gives a sign or a portent that appears credible, but he teaches tenets that negate the doctrine of Moses, we must repudiate him. This theme was made abundantly clear in the Introduction to our extensive commentary on the Mishnah, where you will find some useful information concerning principles that form the foundation of our religion and the pillars of our faith. [153]

It is incumbent upon you to know that the rule that nothing may be added to or diminished from the laws of Moses applies equally to the Oral Law, that is, to the traditional interpretation transmitted through the sages of blessed memory. Be cautious and on your guard lest any of the heretics, may they speedily perish, mingle among you, for they are worse than apostates. [154] For, although this country as you know is a place of scholars, students, and schools, [155] they indulge in bombastic talk, but we warn our people against their occasional errors, heresies, and mistakes. [156] As for you in this distant country, although you are scholars, learned in the Law, and pious, you are few in number, may God increase your numbers and hasten the day of gathering you with the entire religious community. [157] If any of the heretics mingles among you and undertakes to corrupt the people, he will undermine the faith of the young and they will not find a savior. Beware of them, and know that it is permitted to slay them in our opinion, [158] for they repudiate the statement in the prophecy of Moses who commanded us to act *in accordance with the instructions given you and the ruling handed down to you* [Deut. 17:11]. [159] In wicked defiance they assert that they believe most firmly in the prophecy of Moses, as the Muslims and Christians claim to believe, [160] yet they destroy and nullify His law and kill the adherents thereof. Whoever joins them is just like his seducer. I deem it imperative to call your attention to these facts, and to raise the young generation on these tenets, because they are a pillar of our faith.

III

You have adverted to the computations of the date of the redemption, [161] and Rabbi Saadiah's opinion on the subject. [162] First of all, it devolves upon you to know that no human being will ever be able to determine it precisely, as Daniel has intimated: *For these words are secret and sealed* [Dan. 12:9]. Indeed many hypotheses were advanced by scholars who fancied they had discovered the date. This was anticipated in his declaration: *Many will run to and fro, and opinions will be multiple* [Dan. 12:4], that is, there will be numerous views concerning it. Furthermore, God has communicated through His prophets that many people will calculate the time of the advent of the Messiah, but they will be disappointed and fail.[163] He also cautioned us against giving way to doubt and distrust because of these miscalculations. The longer the delay the more fervently we hope, as He states: *For there is a prophecy for a set term, a truthful witness for a time, that will come. Even if it tarries, wait for it still; for it will surely come, without delay* [Hab. 2:3].

Remember that even the date of the termination of the Egyptian exile was not precisely known and gave rise to differences of opinion. Although God fixed its duration in Scripture, where He says: *And they shall be enslaved and oppressed four hundred years* [Gen. 15:13],[164] some reckoned the period of four hundred years from the time of Jacob's arrival in Egypt, others dated it from the beginning of Israel's bondage, which happened seventy years later, and still others computed it from the time of the Covenant of the Pieces[165] when this matter was divinely predicted to Abraham. At the expiration of four hundred years after this event, and thirty years before the appearance of Moses,[166] a band of Israelites left Egypt because they believed that their exile had ended.[167] The Egyptians slew and destroyed them, and the subjugation of the Israelites who remained was consequently aggravated, as we learn from our sages, the teachers of our national traditions. David, in fact, alluded to the vanquished Israelites who miscalculated the date of the redemption in the verse: *The Ephraimite bowmen turned back in the day of battle* [Ps. 78:9].[168]

In truth, the period of four hundred years commenced with the birth of Isaac, the true seed of Abraham as God declared: *For it is through Isaac that offspring shall be continued for you* [Gen. 21:12].[169] This is the sense of the verse: *Know well that your offspring shall be strangers in a land not theirs, and they shall be enslaved and oppressed four hundred years* [Gen. 15:13].[170] The four hundred years mentioned in this forecast refer to the duration of the exile and not solely to the Egyptian bondage. This fact was misunderstood until the great prophet Moses came, when it was realized that the four hundred years dated back precisely to the birth of Isaac.[171] Now if such uncertainty prevailed in regard to the date of emancipation from the Egyptian bondage, the term of which was fixed, it is much more so with respect to the date of the final redemption, the prolonged and protracted duration of which appalled and dismayed our inspired seers. One of them exclaimed in the form of a question: *Will You be angry with us forever, prolong Your wrath for all generations?* [Ps. 85:6].[172] Isaiah, too, alluded to the long, drawn-out exile when he said: *They shall be gathered in a dungeon as captives are gathered; and shall be locked up in a prison. But after many days they shall be remembered* [Isa. 24:22]. Inasmuch as Daniel has proclaimed the matter a deep secret, our sages have interdicted the calculation of the time of the future redemption, or the reckoning of the period of the advent of the Messiah, because the masses might be mystified and bewildered should the Messiah fail to appear as forecast. The rabbis invoked God to frustrate and destroy those who seek to determine precisely the advent of the messianic era, because they are a stumbling block to the people, and that is why they uttered the imprecation, "May the calculators of the final redemption come to grief."[173]

As for Rabbi Saadiah's calculations, there are extenuating circumstances for them though he knew they were disallowed.[174] For the Jews of his time were perplexed and misguided. The divine religion might have disappeared had he not encouraged the pusillanimous, and diffused, disseminated, and propagated by word of mouth and the pen a knowledge of its underlying principles. He believed, in all earnestness, that by means of the messianic calculations he would inspire the masses with hope to the Truth.[175] Verily all his deeds were for the sake of heaven.[176] Consequently, in view of the probity of his motives, which we have disclosed, one must not decry him for his messianic computations.[177]

I note that you are inclined to believe in astrology and the influence of the past and future conjunctions of the planets upon human affairs.[178] Dismiss such notions from your mind. Cleanse your mind of them as one cleanses dirty clothes. Accomplished gentile and certainly Jewish scholars refuse to believe in the truth of this science. Its postulates can be refuted by real proofs on rational grounds, but this is not the place to enter into a discussion of them.[179] Mark well, however, what Scripture has to say about the astrologers. At the time when Moses rose to leadership, the astrologers had unanimously predicted that our nation would never be freed from bondage, nor gain its independence.

But fortune smiled upon Israel, for the most exquisite of human beings[180] appeared and redeemed them at the very time that was supposedly most inauspicious for them. Furthermore, Egypt was smitten with the plagues at the very time for which the astrologers had foretold an epoch of wholesome climate, abundance, and prosperity for the inhabitants. To the failure of their vaticinations, Isaiah alludes when he says: *Where, indeed, are your sages? Let them tell you, let them discover what the Lord of Hosts has planned against Egypt* [Isa. 19:12].[181]

Similarly, the pundits, astrologers, and prognosticators were all of one mind that the administration of Nebuchadnezzar the wicked marked the beginning of an era of enduring prosperity. Forsooth, his dynasty was extinguished and destroyed, as was divinely forecast by Isaiah. He derided them for pretending to foreknowledge, and held up to scorn the state that fancied itself in possession of sapient folk versed in futurity. He says: *Let them stand up and help you now, the scanners of heaven, the star-gazers, who announce, month by month, whatever will come upon you* [Isa. 47:13].[182]

This is how matters stand regarding the era of the Messiah, may he speedily come. For while the gentiles believe that our nation will never constitute an independent state, nor will it ever rise above its present condition,[183] and all the astrologers, diviners, and augurs concur in this opinion, God will prove their views and beliefs false, and will order the advent of the Messiah. Isaiah makes reference to this event in the verse: *I who annul the omens of the diviners, and make fools of the augurs, who turn sages back and make nonsense of their knowledge; but confirm the word of My servant and fulfill the prediction of My messenger. It is I who say of Jerusalem, "It shall be inhabited," and of the towns of Judah, "They shall be rebuilt; and I will restore their ruined places"* [Isa. 44:25–26].[184] This is the correct view that every Israelite should hold, without paying any attention to the conjunctions of the stars, of greater and smaller magnitude.[185]

I have observed your statement that in your country science is little cultivated, and that learning does not flourish, and you attribute it to the influence of the conjunction in the earthly trigon.[186] Remember that this low state of learning and science is not peculiar to your country, but is widely prevalent in Israel today. Indeed a divine premonition of such a state of affairs through Isaiah says: *Truly, I shall further baffle that people with bafflement upon bafflement; and the wisdom of its wise shall fail, and the prudence of its prudent shall vanish* [Isa. 29:14].[187]

This condition is not due to the earthly or fiery trigon, as is proved by the fact that Solomon, king of Israel, lived during the earthly trigon,[188] and yet Scripture testifies that *he was the wisest of all men* [1 Kings 5:11].[189] So did Abraham of blessed memory, who was designated the Pillar of the World,[190] discover the First Cause of the entire universe and demonstrate the central importance of the principle of the unity of God for all mankind.[191] He, Isaac, and Jacob, all three of them, carry the throne of the glory in their hearts; to make use of a rabbinical metaphor "the patriarchs are the chariot,"[192] which in turn was suggested by the verse *God rose up over him* [Gen. 35:13]. The meaning is that they have attained a true conception of the deity, yet the three patriarchs lived during the earthly trigon.

This matter will become clear if the following facts are borne in mind. There is first the smaller conjunction, that is, the meeting of Saturn with Jupiter, which occurs once in approximately twenty years. These conjunctions continue to take place twelve times within the same trigon, covering a period of two hundred and forty years. Then conjunctions take place in the second trigon; the change from one trigon to another is known as the medium conjunction. It is the conjunction of change, which occurs every two hundred and forty solar years. According to this calculation an interval of nine hundred and sixty years will elapse between the first and second meeting of two planets in the same point on the zodiac. This is termed the great conjunction, and occurs once in nine hundred and sixty years. This is the time that must elapse between the first and second meeting of Saturn and Jupiter in the same degree of Aries. If you calculate back, you will understand my statement above that Abraham, Isaac, and Jacob, as well as David and Solomon, lived during the earthly trigon. My purpose in going into detail was to dispel any of your suspicions that the trigon exercises any influence upon human affairs.[193]

Furthermore you write that some people have figured out the forthcoming conjunction and have determined that all of the seven planets will meet in one of the constellations of the zodiac. This is an untrue forecast by the one who told you this.[194] There will simply not be a seven-planet conjunction, either in the next meeting or in the following ones. Such an event will not happen even in ten thousand years, as is well known to those who are familiar with the astronomical law of equation. Verily, this is the calculation of an ignorant person, as is evinced by another remark of his, quoted by you, to the effect that there will be a deluge of air and dust.[195] It is essential for you to know that these and similar assertions are fabricated and mendacious. Do not consider a statement true only because you find it in a book, for the prevaricator is as little restrained with his pen as with his tongue.[196] The untutored and the uninstructed are convinced of the veracity of a statement by the mere fact that it is written; nevertheless, its accuracy must be demonstrated in another manner.

Remember that a blind person submits to an individual having power of sight for intelligent direction, knowing that he lacks the vision to guide himself safely; and an ailing person, unskilled in the art of medicine and uninformed as to matters detrimental or beneficial to his health, defers to a physician for guidance and obeys him implicitly. Just so, it is indispensable for the laity to yield unswervingly to the prophets, who were men of insight, and to limit themselves to what they teach them regarding the truth or error of any given matter. Next in importance are the sages who have studied the dogmas, doctrines, and views of our faith day and night, and have learned to distinguish between the genuine and the spurious.

After this exposition you may trust me that the statements you have previously quoted are inaccurate, and this applies equally to similar views that you heard expressed in conversation or have met in books. For the author of such sayings is either ignorant, a mountebank, or seeks to destroy the Law and demolish its bulwarks. Do you not realize the brazenness of these people who assert that there will be a deluge of air, and dust, and fire, in order to deceive and delude others to believe that the Deluge was merely due to a concentration of water,[197] and was not brought on by God to punish the immorality of the time, as is explicitly related in Scripture, which guides us against error and fallacy?[198] Similarly Sodom and the other cities were not destroyed because of their unbelief and the wickedness of their inhabitants, in direct contradiction to the Bible, which says: *I will go down to see whether they have acted altogether according to the outcry that has come to Me; if not, I will take note* [Gen. 18:21].[199] So whatever happens in this world that has its source in God, they say it is the inescapable consequences of planetary conjunctions.

They have affirmed the truth of their propositions in order to undermine the principles of our religion, and to give free rein to their animal instincts and passions as do the beasts and the ostriches. We have been admonished by God against those views in Scripture to the following effect: "If you rebel against Me so that I bring disaster upon you as a punishment of your misdeeds, but you ascribe your reverses to chance rather than to your guilt, I shall increase your afflictions and make them more grievous."[200] This is the intent of His words in the Chapter of Admonitions: *If you remain* be-keri *toward Me, I too will remain* be-keri *to you* [Lev. 26:27–28]. Now *keri* signifies chance, hazard. It means to say: "If you regard My chastisement as a fortuitous event, I shall bring the most severe calamities upon you, *sevenfold for your sins*" [Lev. 26:21].[201] These foregoing remarks have made it abundantly clear that the advent of the Messiah is in no way subject to the influence of the stars.

Indeed one of our keen minds in the province of Andalusia calculated by means of astrology the date of the final redemption, and predicted the coming of the Messiah in a particular year.[202] Every one of our distinguished scholars made little of his declaration, discounted what he did, and censured him sharply for it. But grim fate dealt more sternly with him than we could have. For at the very time the Messiah was supposed to arrive, a rebel leader rose in the Maghreb who issued an order of conversion. As you are well aware, the event proved to be a great debacle for the partisans of this prognosticator. Indeed, the hardships experienced by our people in the Diaspora are responsible for these extravagances, for a drowning man catches at a straw.[203]

Now, my coreligionists, you *be strong and of good courage, all you who wait for the Lord* [Ps. 31:25]. Strengthen one another, affirm your faith in the Expected One, may he speedily appear in your midst. *Strengthen the hands that are slack, make firm the tottering knees* [Isa. 35:3]. Remember, God has informed us through Isaiah, the herald of the nation, that the prolongation of the adversities of exile will impel many of our people to believe that God has relinquished and abandoned us—far be it from Him—but He assured us that He would not abandon and would not relinquish us for He declared: *Zion says, "The Lord has forsaken me, my Lord has forgotten me." Can a woman forget her baby, or disown the child of her womb? Though she might forget, I never could forget you* [Isa. 49:14–15]. God had already divulged this through the First Prophet, saying: *For the Lord your God is a compassionate God: He will not fail you nor will He let you perish* [Deut. 4:31], and also: *Then the Lord your God, will restore your fortunes and take you back in love* [Deut. 30:3].

It is, my coreligionists, one of the fundamental articles of the Jewish faith that most surely the future redeemer of Israel will spring only from the stock of Solomon son of David.[204] He will gather our nation, assemble our exile, redeem us from our degradation, propagate the true religion, and exterminate his opponents, as God promised us in the Torah: *What I see for them is not yet, what I behold will not be soon: a star rises from Jacob, a meteor comes forth from Israel; it smashes the brow of Moab, the foundation of all children of Seth. Edom becomes a possession* [Num. 24:17–18].[205] The hour of his arrival will be at a time of great catastrophe and dire misfortune for Israel, as was predicted in the verse: *And neither bond nor free is left* [Deut. 32:36].[206] Then God will bring him forth and he will fulfill the promises made in his behalf. A later prophet too was alluding to the messianic tribulations when he declared: *But who can endure the day of his coming?* [Mal. 3:2].[207] This is the proper belief that one must hold.

From the prophecies of Daniel and Isaiah and from the statements of our sages it is clear that the advent of the Messiah will take place some time subsequent to the universal expansion of the Roman and Arab empires, which is an actuality today. This fact is true beyond question or doubt. Daniel is the last prophet to portray the kingdom of the Arabs, the rise of Muhammad, and then the arrival of the Messiah.[208] Similarly, Isaiah intimated that the coming of the Messiah will occur after the rise of the Madman, for he says: *Riders on asses, riders on camels, horsemen in pairs* [Isa. 21:7,9].[209] Now the rider on ass is the Messiah, as is evident from the verse, which describes him as *humble, riding on an ass* [Zech. 9:9].[210] He will follow the man riding a camel, that is the Arab kingdom.[211] The statement *horsemen in pairs* refers to the two empires Edom and Ishmael. A similar interpretation of Daniel's vision concerning the image and the beasts[212] is correct beyond doubt. They are conclusions drawn from the plain meaning of the text.

The precise date of the messianic advent cannot be known. But I am in possession of an extraordinary tradition that I received from my father, who in turn received it from his father,[213] going back to our early ancestors who were exiled from Jerusalem, as the prophet testified: *and the exiles of Jerusalem that are in Spain* [Obad. 1:20].[214] The tradition is that a covert indication lies in the prediction of Balaam to the future restoration of prophecy in Israel. Incidentally,[215] it may be stated that there are other verses in the Torah that contain cryptic indications in addition to their simple meaning. For example, the word *rdu* in the remark of Jacob to his sons: *go down . . . there (rdu shamah)* [Gen. 42:2] has the numerical value of 210 and contains a hint as to the length of Israel's stay in Egypt.[216] Likewise, the statement of Moses our teacher: *Should you, when you have begotten children and children's children and are long established in the land . . .* [Deut. 4:25] [217] embodies a reference to the duration of Israel's stay in the land of Israel, from the time of their arrival to the exile in the time of Yehoiakin, that is, 840 years, corresponding to the numerical value of the word *vnoshantem*[218] (and are long established). We find many others like them.[219] By this method of cryptic allusion it was transmitted to me that Balaam's statement: *Jacob is told at once (ka'et), yea Israel, what God has planned* [Num. 23:23],[220] contains a veiled hint as to the date of the restoration of prophecy to Israel. The sentence means that after the lapse of an interval equal to the time that passed from the six days of creation to Balaam's day, seers will again tell Israel what God has planned. Now Balaam uttered his prediction in the thirty-eighth year after the Exodus, which corresponds to the year 2485 after the creation of the world, for the Exodus took place in the beginning of the year 2448.[221] It is doubtless true that the reappearance of prophecy in Israel is one of the signs betokening the approach of the messianic era, as is stated: *After that I will pour out My spirit upon all flesh; your sons and daughters shall prophesy. . .* [Joel 3:1].[222] This is the most reliable tradition concerning the advent of the Messiah. I call it reliable, although I have admonished against it, and strictly prohibited blazoning it abroad, lest some people deem it unduly postponed. I have already apprised you concerning it, but God best knows what is true.[223]

Your statement that the time of the advent of the Messiah is indicated by Jeremiah, who said: *It is a time of trouble for Jacob, but he shall be delivered from it* [Jer. 30:7],[224] is incorrect. For it must refer to the war of Gog and Magog, which will take place some time after the oncoming of the Messiah.[225] Some of the supposed signs, such as the Gate of Gerson and others, are very doubtful.[226] Some are wrongly ascribed to the sages, while others owe their origin to figures of speech and enigmatic sayings which should not be literally taken.

IV

You write that a certain man in one of the cities of Yemen pretends that he is the Messiah.[227] As I live, I am not surprised at him or at his followers, for I have no doubt that he is mad, and a sick person should not be rebuked or reproved for an illness brought on by no fault of his own. Neither am I surprised at his votaries, because they were persuaded by him owing to their sorry plight, their ignorance of the importance and high rank of the Messiah, and their mistaken comparison of the Messiah with ibn Mahdi,[228] whose rise they are witnessing. But I am astonished that you, a scholar who has carefully studied the doctrine of the rabbis, are inclined to repose faith in him.[229] Do you not know, my brother, that the Messiah is a very eminent prophet, more illustrious than all the prophets after Moses? Do you not know that a false pretender to prophecy is to suffer capital punishment for having arrogated to himself unwarranted distinction, just as the person who prophesied in the name of the idols is put to death? For God says: *But any prophet who presumes to speak in My name an oracle which I did not command him to utter, or who speaks in the name of other gods—that prophet shall die* [Deut. 18:20].[230] What stronger evidence exists than his very pretensions to be the Messiah that he is a liar?

How odd is your remark about this man, that he is renowned for his meekness and a little wisdom. Do these characteristics make him a Messiah? You were beguiled by him because you have not considered the preeminence of the Messiah, the manner and place of his appearance, and the marks by which he is to be identified. The Messiah indeed ranks above all prophets after Moses in eminence and distinction, and God has bestowed some gifts upon him that he did not bestow upon Moses, as may be gathered from the following verses: *He shall sense the truth by his reverence for the Lord* [Isa. 11:3]; *The spirit of the Lord shall alight upon him* [Isa. 11:2]; *Justice shall be the girdle of his loins* [Isa. 11:5].[231] God has conferred upon him six appellations in the verse: *For a child has been born to us, a son has been given us. And authority has settled on his shoulders. He has been named "the Mighty God is planning grace; the Eternal Father, a peaceable ruler" (Pele, Yoetz, El, Gibbor, Aviad, Sar-shalom)* [Isa. 9:5].[232] He continues to magnify him, and declares: *You are My son; I have fathered you this day* [Ps. 2:7].[233] All these statements demonstrate the superiority of the Messiah to all the descendants of Adam.

Transcendent wisdom is a *sine qua non* for inspiration. It is an article of our faith that the gift of prophecy is vouchsafed only to the wise, the strong, and the rich. Strong is defined as the ability to control one's passions.[234] Rich signifies wealthy in knowledge. Now if we dare not put trust in a man's pretensions to prophecy if he does not excel in wisdom, how much less must we take seriously the claims of an ignoramus that he is the Messiah. That the man in question is untutored is evident from the order he issued to the people to give away, as you state, all their possessions for eleemosynary purposes. They did right in disobeying him, and he was wrong inasmuch as he disregarded the Jewish law concerning almsgiving. Scripture says: *But of all that a man owns, be it man or beast or land of his holding, nothing that he has proscribed for the Lord may be sold or redeemed* [Lev. 27:28]. The rabbis explain, in their comment on this verse, "part of all that he owns, but not all that he has."[235] The sages accordingly set bounds to the bounty of the beneficent in an explicit ruling, which reads: "He who is inclined to be liberal with the poor, may not part with more than a fifth of his possessions."[236] There is no doubt that the reasoning that led him to claim that he is the Messiah induced him to issue a command to his fellowmen to give away their property and distribute it to the poor. But then the affluent would become destitute and vice versa. According to his ordinance it would be necessary for the *nouveaux riches* to return their recently acquired property to the newly impoverished. Such a regulation, which would keep property moving in a circle, is the peak of folly.

As to the place where the Messiah will make his first appearance, He informs us that he will first present himself only in the land of Israel as is stated: *He will suddenly come to His temple* [Mal. 3:1].[237] As to the how of his advent, nothing at all will be known about it before it occurs. The Messiah is not a person concerning whom it may be predicted that he will be the son of so-and-so, or of the family of so-and-so. On the contrary, he will be unknown before his coming, but he will prove by means of miracles and wonders that he is the true Messiah. In allusion to his mysterious lineage, God says: *Behold a man whose name is the Shoot, and who shall shoot up* [Zech. 6:12].[238] Similarly Isaiah, referring to his arrival, implies that neither his father nor mother, nor his kith and kin will be known, for he will grow, by his favor, like a sapling, like a root out of arid ground [Isa. 53:2].[239] After his manifestation in Palestine, Israel will be gathered in Jerusalem and the other cities of Palestine. Then the tidings will spread to the East and to the West until it will reach Yemen and those beyond you in India, as we learn from Isaiah: *Go, swift messengers, to a nation far and remote, to a people thrust forth and away . . . which sends out envoys by sea, in papyrus vessels upon the water* [Isa. 18:2].[240] The redemption will not be reversed so that it will appear in distant lands first, and ultimately reach Palestine.[241]

What the great powers are that all the prophets from Moses to Malachi ascribe to the Messiah may be inferred from various statements in the twenty-four books of Scripture. The most significant of them is that the report of his advent will strike terror into the hearts of all the kings of the earth, and their kingdoms will fall; neither will they be able to war or revolt against him. They will neither defame nor calumniate him, for the miracles he will perform will frighten them into complete silence. Isaiah refers to the submission of the kings to him in the verse: *Kings shall be silenced because of him* [Isa. 52:15].[242] He will slay whom he will by the word of his mouth, none will escape or be saved, as is written: *He shall strike down a land with the rod of his mouth* [Isa. 11:4].[243] Revolution and war in the entire world, from East to West, will not cease at the beginning of the messianic era, but only after the wars of Gog and Magog, as was indicated by Ezekiel.[244] I do not believe that this man who has appeared among you possesses these powers. You know that the Christians falsely ascribe marvelous powers to Jesus the Nazarene, may his bones be ground to dust, such as the resurrection of the dead and other miracles. Even if we granted this for the sake of argument, we should not be convinced by their reasoning that Jesus is the Messiah. For we can bring a thousand proofs from Scripture that it is not so even from their point of view.[245] Indeed, will anyone arrogate this rank to himself unless he wishes to make himself a laughing stock?

In sum, had this man acted presumptuously or disdainfully, I would deem him worthy of death.[246] The truth seems to be that he became melancholy and lost his mind. In my opinion, it is most advisable, both for your good and for his, that you put him in iron chains for a while, until the gentiles learn that he is demented. After you have blazoned and bruited abroad the intelligence concerning this man among them, you may release him without endangering his safety. If the gentiles gain knowledge about him after he has been locked up by you, they will taunt him and pronounce him irrational, and you will remain unmolested by him. If you procrastinate until they learn of this affair of their own accord, you will most likely incur their wrath. Remember, my coreligionists, that on account of the vast number of our sins God has hurled us into the midst of this people, the Arabs, who have persecuted us severely, and passed baneful and discriminatory legislation against us, as God has forewarned us: *Our enemies themselves shall judge us* [Deut. 32:31].[247] Never did a nation molest, degrade, debase, and hate us as much as they.[248] Therefore, when David king of Israel of blessed memory, inspired by the Holy Spirit, envisaged the future tribulations of Israel, he bewailed and lamented their lot only in the kingdom of Ishmael, and prayed on their behalf for their deliverance in the verse: *Woe is me, that I live with Meshekh, that I dwell among the clans of Kedar* [Ps. 120:5].[249] Note the distinction between Kedar and the children of Ishmael, for the Madman is of the lineage of the children of Kedar, as they readily admit.[250] Daniel also alludes to our humiliation and degradation *like the dust in threshing* [2 Kings 13:7],[251] suffered only at the hands of the Arabs, may they be speedily vanquished, when he says: *And it made fall to the earth some of the host, yea of the stars, some of which it trampled* [Dan. 8:10].[252] Although we are dishonored by them beyond human endurance, and have to put up with their fabrications, we yet behave like him of whom the prophet said: *But I am like a deaf man, unhearing, like a dumb man who cannot speak up* [Ps. 38:14].[253] Similarly, our sages instructed us to bear the prevarications and lies of Ishmael in silence. They found it in a cryptic allusion to this attitude in the names of his sons, Mishma, Dumah, and Massa,[254] which have been interpreted to mean *listen, be silent,* and *endure.* We have acquiesced, both young and old, to inure ourselves to humiliation, as Isaiah instructed us: *I offered my back to the floggers, and my cheeks to those who tore out my hair* [Isa. 50:6].[255] All this notwithstanding, we do not escape this continued maltreatment and pressure, which well-nigh crush us. No matter how much we suffer and elect to remain at peace with them, they stir up strife and sedition, as David describes: *I am all peace; but when I speak, they are for war* [Ps. 120:7].[256] Most certainly therefore if we start trouble, and claim power from them absurdly and preposterously, we surely give ourselves up to destruction.

I shall now succinctly narrate several episodes to you, subsequent to the rise of the Arab kingdom, from which you will derive some benefit.[257] One of these is the exodus of a multitude of Jews, numbering hundreds of thousands from the East beyond Isfahan, led by an individual who pretended to be the Messiah.[258] They were accoutred with military equipment and drawn swords, and slew all those that encountered them. According to the information I received, they reached the vicinity of Baghdad. This happened in the beginning of the reign of the Omayyads.[259]

The king then said to all the Jews of his kingdom: "Let your scholars go out to meet this multitude and ascertain whether their pretensions are true, and he is unmistakably your expected one. If so, we shall conclude peace with you under any conditions you may prefer. But if it is dissimulation, I shall wage war against them." When the sages met these Jews, the latter declared: "We belong to the children of the district beyond the River."[260] Then they asked them: "Who instigated you to make this uprising?" Thereupon they replied: "This man here, one of the descendants of David, whom we know to be pious and virtuous, this man whom we knew to be a leper at night, arose the following morning healthy and sound." They believed that leprosy was one of the characteristics of the Messiah, to which they found an allusion in the verse: *plagued, smitten and afflicted by God* [Isa. 53:4],[261] that is, by leprosy. The sages explained to them that this interpretation was incorrect, and that he lacked even one of the traits of the Messiah, let alone all of them. Furthermore, they advised them as follows: "O brethren, you are still near your native country and have the possibility of returning there. If you remain in this land you will not only perish, but also undermine the teachings of Moses, by misleading the people to believe that the Messiah has appeared, and has been vanquished, whereas you have neither a prophet in your midst, nor an omen betokening his oncoming." They were persuaded by these arguments. The sultan turned over to them so-and-so thousands of dinars by way of hospitality in order that they should leave his country. But after they returned home he had a change of heart with respect to the Jews, upon whom he imposed a fine for his expenditures. He ordered them to make a special mark on their garments,[262] the writing of the word *cursed,* and to attach one iron bar in the back and one in the front. Ever since then the communities of Khurasan and Isfahan have experienced the tribulations of the Diaspora. This episode we have learned from oral records.[263]

The following incident we have verified and know to be true, because it occurred in recent times.[264] About fifty years ago or less, a pious and virtuous man by the name of Moses al-Darri came from Darra[265] to the province of Andalusia to study under Rabbi Joseph ha-Levi ibn Migash,[266] of blessed memory, of whom you have very likely heard. Later he left for Fez, the center of the Maghreb. People flocked to him because of his piety, virtue, and learning. He informed them that the Messiah was about to come, as was divinely revealed to him in a dream. Yet he did not pretend on the basis of a divine communication, as did the former lunatic, that he was the Messiah. He merely affirmed that the Messiah would appear. Many people became his adherents and put their faith in him. My father and master, of blessed memory, endeavored to dissuade and discourage people frcm following him. However, only a few were influenced by my father, while most, nay, nearly all clung to R. Moses. Finally he predicted events that would come true no matter what was going to occur. He would say: "I was informed yesterday that this and this would happen," and it did happen exactly as he predicted. Once he foretold a vehement rain for the coming Friday and that the falling drops would be blood. This was considered a sign of the approaching advent of the Messiah, of which the text says: "*I will set portents in the sky and on·earth, blood and fire and pillars of smoke*" [Joel 3:3].²⁶⁷ This episode took place in the month of Marḥeshvan.²⁶⁸ A very heavy rain fell that Friday and the fluids that descended were red and viscous as if mixed with clay. This miracle convinced all the people that he was undoubtedly a prophet. In itself it is not inconsistent with the tenets of the Torah, for prophecy, as I have explained, will return to Israel before the messianic advent. When the majority of the people put their trust in him, he predicted that the Messiah would come that very year on Passover eve. He advised the people to sell their property and contract debts to the Muslims with the promise to pay back ten dinars for one, in order to observe the precepts of the Torah in connection with the Passover festival, for they would never see them again, and so they did. When Passover came and nothing transpired, the people were ruined, as most of them had disposed of their property for a trifling sum, and were overwhelmed with debt. When the gentiles in the vicinity and their serfs learned of this hoax they were minded to do away with him, were they to locate him. As this Muslim country no longer offered him protection, he left for Palestine where he died, may his memory be blessed. When he left he made predictions, as I was told by those who saw him, concerning events both great and small in the Maghreb, which were later fulfilled.²⁶⁹

My father of blessed memory told me that about fifteen or twenty years before that episode, some respectable people in Cordova, the center of Andalusia, among whom a number were given to the cult of astrology, were all of one mind that the Messiah would appear that year. They sought a revelation in a dream night after night,²⁷⁰ and ascertained that the Messiah was a man of the city. They picked a pious and virtuous person by the name of ibn Arieh, who had been instructing the people. They wrought miracles and made predictions just as al-Darri did, until they won over the hearts of all the people. When the influential and learned men of our community heard of this, they assembled in the synagogue, had ibn Arieh brought there, and had him flogged in public. Furthermore, they imposed a fine on him and put him under the ban, because by his silence he gave assent to the professions of his adherents, instead of restraining them and pointing out to them that they were contradicting our religion. They did the same thing to the persons who assembled about him. The Jews escaped the wrath of the gentiles only with the greatest difficulty.[271]

About forty years preceding the affair of ibn Arieh in Andalusia, a man of Linon,[272] a large center in the heart of France, which numbered ten thousand Jews, pretended that he was the Messiah. He was supposed to have performed the following miracle. On moonlit nights he would go out and climb to the top of high trees in the field and glide from tree to tree like a bird. He cited a verse from Daniel to prove that such a miracle was within the power of the Messiah: *And, behold, there came with the clouds of heaven one like . . . a man . . . and there was given him dominion, and glory, and a kingdom* [Dan. 7:13–14].[273] Many who witnessed the miracle became his votaries. The French discovered this, pillaged, and put many of his followers to death, together with the pretender. Some of them maintain however that he is still in hiding until this very day.[274]

The prophets have predicted and instructed us, as I have told you, that pretenders and simulators will appear in great numbers at the time when the advent of the true Messiah will draw nigh, but they will not be able to make good their claim. They will perish with many of their partisans. Solomon of blessed memory, inspired by the Holy Spirit, foresaw that the prolonged duration of the exile would incite some of our people to seek to terminate it before the appointed time, and as a consequence they would perish or meet with disaster. Therefore he admonished them and adjured them in metaphorical language to desist, as we read: *I adjure you, O maidens of Jerusalem, by gazelles or by hinds of the field: do not wake or rouse love until it please* [Song of Songs 2:7].[275] Now, brethren and friends, abide by the oath, and stir not up love until it pleases.

May God, who created the world with the attribute of mercy,[276]

grant us to behold the ingathering of the exiles to the portion of His
inheritance, to contemplate the graciousness of the Lord, and to visit
early in His temple.[277] May He take us out from the Valley of the
Shadow of Death wherein He put us. May He remove darkness from
our eyes and gloom from our hearts. May He fulfill in our days as well
as in yours the contents of the verse: *The people that walked in darkness
have seen a brilliant light* [Isa. 9:1].[278] May He darken our opponents
in His anger and wrath, may He illuminate our obscurity, as He promised us: *Behold! Darkness shall cover the earth, and thick clouds the
peoples; but upon you the Lord will shine* [Isa. 60:2].[279]

Greetings unto you, my dear friend, master of the sciences, and
paragon of learning, and unto our erudite colleagues, and unto all the
rest of the people.[280] Peace, peace, as the light shines, and much
peace until the moon be no more.[281] Amen.

I beg you to send a copy of this missive to every community in the
cities and hamlets, in order to strengthen the people in their faith and
put them on their feet. Read it at public gatherings and in private,
and you will thus become a public benefactor. Take adequate precautions lest its contents be divulged by an evil person and mishap overtake us. (God spare us therefrom.)[282] When I began writing this letter
I had some misgivings about it, but they were overruled by my conviction that the public welfare takes precedence over one's personal
safety. Moreover, I am sending it to a personage such as you: *The
counsel of the Lord is for those who fear Him* [Ps. 25:14].[283] Our sages,
the successors of the prophets,[284] assured us that persons engaged in
a religious mission will meet with no disaster.[285] What more important
religious mission is there than this! Peace be unto all Israel. Amen.

NOTES

1. Jacob, the head of the Jewish community in Yemen, is an unknown
figure except for what Maimonides tells of him in this epistle. In this epistle,
sent to Jacob, Maimonides praises him for scholarship and leadership. Jacob's
father, Nathanel, leader of the community before him, wrote the *Garden of
Intelligences*, a philosophic and theological tract. More on Nathanel can be
found in J. Kafiḥ, *Iggerot* (Jerusalem: Mossad Harav Kook, 1972), pp. 11–15.
2. This is one of the few instances where a long genealogy of the ancestry

of the celebrated Maimonides is found, and tradition maintains that it goes
back to R. Judah ha-Nasi (second and third centuries C.E.), who compiled
the Mishnah. Maimonides himself usually signed his own name and his father's name.

3. In this sentence, Maimonides succeeded in heaping praises on both
father and son.

4. In rabbinic literature water is a metaphor for Torah, e.g., in BT Ta'anit
7a, and the implication is that Jewish learning is stored with Jacob and his
father.

5. Based on Job 6:20, referring to the paucity of water, a problem faced
by caravans.

6. R. Ashi (335–427/28 C.E.) is accepted as the compiler and editor of
the Babylonian Talmud.

7. Traditional writers usually find support in the Bible for declarations
they make from verses that are, in fact, out of context. Yemen, however, is
in *the end of the earth*.

8. Maimonides may be referring to his brief stay in Palestine on his way
to Egypt in 1165–66.

9. Nathanel, Jacob's father, whose death can be dated approximately to
1165.

10. One of the blessings on Israel when it is obedient to God.

11. Note Maimonides' humility, even if it is *pro forma*.

12. Maimonides expresses graphically how he wandered from his native
Spain to Fez, to Palestine, and finally to Egypt. One wonders whether his
allusion to Ps. 27:4 indicates that he entertained thoughts of settling in Palestine or only visiting it.

13. It is instructive to bear in mind that by the time he composed this
epistle he had to his credit the masterly commentary to the Mishnah, which,
as he informs us at the end of the work, he began at the age of twenty-three
and completed when he was thirty (in 1168).

14. It is not possible to identify this friend and disciple. In his collected
responsa the name "Shelomo" appears a few times.

15. The epistle thus far is phrased in florid Hebrew.

16. One may legitimately ask what the degree of literacy was in Yemen.

17. He is 'Abd al-Nabi' ibn Mahdi who c. 1170 conquered most of
Yemen. He was defeated in a battle in 1173, and had to fortify himself in
his castle in Zabid. During his years in power he was highly honored (one
of the historians of Yemen reports that he was paid more honor than Muhammad). He tended toward extremism, which explains his decree against
non-Muslims.

18. Maimonides refers to the religious persecution in Morocco initiated
by the Berber Almohads, which was in force from the 1150s to 1180s. It was
there that the *Epistle on Martyrdom* was composed. In the Hebrew and Arabic
the Berbers are designated Canaanites.

19. The capture of Ai is described in this passage.

20. This is Amos's reaction to the second of the five visions of disaster
he was shown.

21. It is too serious an event to be considered one of many.

22. The rise of the Messiah will be preceded by dreadful woes, called by this term in the BT Sanhedrin 97a–98b, where the reaction of a few rabbis to the miserable situation is: "May I not see them come."

23. Part of the description of the overthrow of the Babylonians by the Medes.

24. One of the concluding verses in Balaam's predictions of the future.

25. In the last admonition of the angel to Daniel.

26. In the account of the outrages by the wicked ruler.

27. Maimonides is about to present his view of the situation, ways to cope with it, and a sober understanding of what is wrong and what is right, what true and what false. This is the reason he urges them to read this epistle attentively and to convey its contents to their families.

28. Moses is the master of all the prophets, both those who preceded him, like Adam and Abraham, and those who followed him, down to Malachi. In the *Guide* 2:45 Maimonides, who classifies all the prophets into eleven groups, specifically excludes Moses from any group. Maimonides regarded Moses as qualitatively different because he was endowed with characteristics unique to him (also see *MT Hilkhot Yesodei ha-Torah* 7:6).

29. The Biblical text continues: *but it was because the Lord loved you and kept the oath He made to your fathers . . .* [Deut. 7:8].

30. This is part of the introduction to the description of the theophany.

31. The rabbis related the name *Sinai* to the word *sin'ah*—hatred (BT Shabbat 89a–b). They date the hostility to the gentiles from the time of Revelation. Maimonides argues that the tension between Israel and the larger world became a factor from the time of the Revelation.

32. Amalek: Exod. 17:8–13; Sisera: Judg. 4–5; Sennacherib: 2 Kings 18:13–19:37; Nebuchadnezzar: 2 Kings chaps. 24–25; Titus: BT Gittin 56bf.; Hadrian: Genesis Rabbah 63:7.

33. Maimonides correctly differentiates between those who resorted to the sword, and those who employed other means. He refers to the anti-Jewish decrees of Antiochus IV. It is doubtful that he knew the anti-Jewish writings by Greek and Roman authors, such as Manetho or Cicero (cf. Stern, *Greek and Latin Authors on Jews and Judaism* I, 62ff. and 193ff.) But he was acquainted with Galen's disparagement of Moses, as can be learned from his refutation of him in his monograph *Pirkei Moshe* (see Kafiḥ l.c., 152ff.).

34. The conclusion of one of the predictions of comfort by the prophet Isaiah.

35. Literally, the *Truth*. For its use in the Koran as an appellation of God see *Encyclopedia of Islam*[2], III, s.v. "Hakk," and *Lexicon of Islam,* s.v. "Hakk."

36. David, the traditionally accepted author of Psalms, is not ordinarily called a prophet (in *Guide* 2:45, Maimonides does not classify him as a full-fledged prophet), but a saint.

37. The first verse is the call of the enemies, and God's retort follows.

38. Of the first type of antagonists, all but the last two oppressed the Jews

in their homeland, while Titus and Hadrian were Roman emperors in whose days there were diasporas. There were also activities of literary anti-Semites.

39. Both Christians and Muslims, of whom we are about to read, engaged in polemics with the Jews and also in persecution and forced conversion.

40. This is an interesting psychological observation.

41. This word in Hebrew is the ordinary term for Christian. In this place, however, in view of Maimonides' reasoning, the rendering *Nazarene* is more appropriate. The following malediction is rabbinic, and can be used for any individual condemned by tradition.

42. BT Yevamot 45a and Kiddushin 68b.

43. I.e., it is a popular term, not a tradition. It appears in the medieval biography of Jesus as told by Jews. See S. Krauss, ed., *Das Leben Jesu nach jüdischen Quellen* (Berlin: S. Calvery, 1902), p. 39.

44. They condemned him to death. In BT Sanhedrin, in a passage censored by Christian officials, it is reported that he was hanged on the day before Passover. See Kafih 22, note 31. This is confirmed by John's Gospel, but the other gospels date it on the first day of Passover.

45. In *MT Hilkhot Melakhim* 11:5 (originally censored), Maimonides likewise states that the verse refers to him. This was the consensus of rabbinic, and even of Karaite commentators to Daniel.

46. The assertion is explicit. Jesus was called the founder of a new religion some centuries after his death by "the descendants of Esau," i.e., the Romans, but he had nothing to do with it, and never considered it; and what he did was not a source of harm to Israel. This history of the rise of Christianity was current among Jewish writers in medieval times.

47. The fact seems to be that he was convicted by the Jewish court, but the Romans executed him by crucifixion.

48. It has been pointed out that in the Bible true prophets and others are sometimes called "mad" (see Hos. 9:7 and 2 Kings 9:11). But the nickname attached to Muhammad is either an expression of disparagement, or is based on the general view in ancient Arabia that a poet was a madman, and hence the prophet's nickname. In fact Muhammad challenges this epithet (cf. Koran, Surah 15:6, 44:13ff., 52:29ff., etc.). Jews probably seized on it for their own purposes. However, it may be that Maimonides did not use this term and it was introduced by a copyist who was accustomed to this appellation. The title of the sacred book of Islam, the Koran, was likewise perverted to *Kalon* ("disgrace").

49. Maimonides correctly links this ambition for power as a motive with his religious fervor, especially after his flight from Mecca to Medina in 622 with hundreds of his followers.

50. The most interesting explanation of the similarities between the fundamentals of the Jewish faith and those of its two daughters, which Maimonides is about to develop, was adumbrated by a Palestinian sage in the fourth century and expanded by an eleventh-century scholar, Judah ben Barzillai. He interprets Hos. 8:12: *The many teachings I wrote for him have been treated as something alien,* to mean that the Christians have taken the Torah and claim that it is their own, since they maintain they are the true Israel. And

God wonders: Shall I write down the hidden meanings (the Oral Law), which the Christians might get to know as well, and claim that they also are for them? Let these laws be treated as strange, so that they will not appropriate them. Cf. his commentary to *Sefer Yetzirah* 5–6.

51. This differentiation between the real and the artificial was also made by the poet and thinker Judah Halevi in *Kuzari* 3:9 and by Maimonides' son Abraham in his commentary to the Torah on Exodus 19:6.

52. Note should be taken of this distinction made by the Jewish Law.

53. The doctrines of the philosophers in the Middle Ages was that immortality was limited to the mind to the extent that it was actualized through the acquirement of intelligibles, i.e., knowledge of the theoretical and the practical.

54. It is important to remember that the derision and ridicule could be indulged in by Jews only privately, or they would suffer physical punishment. But the adherents of each of the other faiths takes its own very seriously and hurls attacks at the other and at Judaism.

55. In Dan. 2 and 7 the subject is the four kingdoms that will rise successively, followed by the triumph of the Law of God and of His people. Before the rise of Islam, the four kingdoms were identified as Babylonia, Persia, Macedonia (Greece), and Rome. Jews who lived in the Islamic domain counted it as the fourth kingdom, either by including it with Rome or by joining Greece and Rome as the third. It is not easy to determine from the passage cited and interpreted by Maimonides which of the two approaches he adopted, unless his comment that the state that the heavenly King will overthrow consists of Rome, Byzantium, and Persia suggests his understanding of the verse. It may be that he is guided by the existence of these empires in his time.

56. The story is narrated in Dan. 3 that an edict ordered the people to bow down to an idol at a given time, and the three Jews disobeyed. They were thrown into a red-hot furnace, but came out unscathed.

57. See *Bet ha-Midrash*, ed. A. Jellinek (Leipzig, 1853; reprint ed. Jerusalem: Wahrmann, 1947), 133, 137, 139, 143; Genesis Rabbah 2:5. The *Scroll of Antiochus* speaks only of the Sabbath, new moon, and circumcision.

58. The number fifty-two is a frequent approximation in the Bible (2 Kings 15:2,27; Ezra 2:29) and in postbiblical compilations. Actually, Greek control lasted fifty-seven years.

59. E.g., BT Berakhot 61b; BT Ketubbot 50b.

60. E.g., BT Berakhot 61b.

61. E.g., BT Ketubbot 3b.

62. In God's revelation to Jacob when Jacob dreamt he saw a ladder.

63. Genesis Rabbah 41:12 and 49:3.

64. Although the theme of the vision is the fall of Babylon to the Elamites and Medes, Maimonides unhesitatingly reads into it a forecast of the fate of enemies of the Jews at all times.

65. It is the second of the predictions that begins with *See, a time is coming*.

66. The consoling conclusion to the long list of maledictions in this chapter.

67. The same verse is used by Maimonides in *Guide* 1:34, for the few who are not theologically confused.

68. Literally, "heard the words from the Almighty." According to tradition, the first two of the Ten Commandments were heard directly from God, and the others reached them through the mediation of Moses.

69. The rabbis were impressed by their haste in answering *we will do* before *we will obey* (lit. *listen*).

70. The context of the quoted verse is *but with overt acts, it is for us and our children ever to apply all the provisions of this Teaching*.

71. BT Nedarim 20a. This talmudic statement (also in JT Kiddushin chapter 4, Halakhah 1) is directed against those who know no shame. Since bashfulness is one of the characteristics of the Jew, Maimonides probably counts in this group people who entertain doubts regarding the religion that came to us through the mediation of Moses.

72. The Arabic reads *your word* (the same word is also in the preceding paragraph), but two medieval translations treated it as a mistake for the word that means *your community*, and this appears to be correct.

73. Particular attention should be paid to the fundamentals of Judaism that Maimonides spells out: the uniqueness of Moses and the eternal validity of the Torah. They are included in the thirteen articles of faith that Maimonides appended to his introduction to chapter 10 in the Mishnah Sanhedrin.

74. We speak of *one* book, when there are many, or of *one* as the first number. Neither is appropriate to God, who is One, incomparable, alone.

75. The Arabic term *kalim allah* is also the epithet of Moses in the Koran.

76. Maimonides marks the beginning and end by giving the first word of the Torah and the last three.

77. In his differentiation between the sources of other prophets and the position of Moses. Cf. *Guide* 2:35, 39.

78. The verse continues: *when the Lord said to Me: "Gather the people to Me that I may let them hear My words, in order that they may learn to revere Me as long as they live on earth, and may so teach their children."* In the tradition, Horeb is a synonym for Sinai.

79. Maimonides does not mean to suggest that the Revelation and the theophany were for the sole purpose of giving them the strength to remain steadfast, but that this was given them along with the faith to which they cling despite all adversity.

80. Jewish tradition ascribes Song of Songs, as well as Proverbs and Ecclesiastes, to King Solomon, who is named here as the father of the verse.

81. Maimonides offers the interpretation of verses in Song of Songs before he quotes them. Like the Midrash he uses as his source, he finds in them much more than the simple meaning.

82. The explanation comes from Song of Songs Rabbah 7:1. The application of the sentence is likewise there, and also the sense of the Mahanaim dance. Several implications of the word *Shulammite* are recorded there.

83. This is the verse he divides between the nations and her questioning reply.

84. The Hebrew word, a dual, means two camps.

85. In the verse after the account of the great vision and before the Ten Commandments were pronounced.

86. This is part of an enigmatic series of verses that may refer to the theophany at Sinai.

87. Regarding the four empires see note 55 above. The reference to them is found in Song of Songs Rabbah 7:1. The two empires in Maimonides' time were Christendom and Islam.

88. In its context the verse does not imply compulsion or even suasion, but that it will be a consequence of their exile and dispersion.

89. Maimonides knew firsthand that persecutions and forced conversions do not affect the entire Jewish population, but are limited to certain areas.

90. The complete verse reads: *And the many evils and troubles befall them—then this poem shall confront them as a witness, since it will never be lost from the mouth of their offspring. For I know what plans they are devising even now, before I bring them into the land that I promised on oath.*

91. After opening with a recitation of God's wonders to His people, which they heard from their parents, the chapter deals with the grave distress that afflicts the nation, emphasizes their steadfastness, and wonders why God allows them to be harassed.

92. Song of Songs Rabbah 2:7. It is called *Midrash Ḥazita* because it opens with this word (Prov. 22:20). Maimonides' rabbinic source is also BT Gittin 57b.

93. This and the preceding sentence are directed at the contemporaries in Yemen who are victims of the forced conversion. The treatment of this sacrifice is said to be *an offering by fire of pleasing odor to the Lord* [Lev. 1:9].

94. In context the verse is Moses' call to the Levites to punish the worshipers of the golden calf.

95. The same behavior is urged by Maimonides on the victims of the Almohad persecution. See the *Epistle on Martyrdom*, p. 32.

96. Deut. 28:58 reads: *If you fail to observe faithfully all the terms of this Teaching that are written in this book, to reverence this honored and awesome Name, the Lord your God.*

97. He has in mind the practice of scholars in the Middle Ages who wandered from home to centers of study and discussion of Torah, and showed readiness to endure discomfort for this. It should be remembered that Christian and Muslim students also followed this practice.

98. This is a commonly held view, which is also mentioned in BT Gittin 52b, 53a. This was also the judgment of the man who aroused Maimonides' anger in the *Epistle on Martyrdom*.

99. The reasoning of this sort is summed up in the principle that "he suffers a severer penalty" [BT Gittin 53a], i.e., since he is punished for the grave sin of forsaking the Torah, it makes little difference that he disregards a single prescription.

100. He is the archsinner in Jewish tradition, cf. *Epistle on Martyrdom*, p. 28.

101. Maimonides may have selected this example because it is considered a "light act," i.e., not of major significance. See BT Avodah Zarah 3a.

102. His identity is not known. As an apostate to Islam he evidently undertook to spread the new faith among his former coreligionists.

103. The numerical value of the letters of these two words (Gen. 17:20) is ninety-two, and so is the value of the letters MḤMD, Muhammad.

104. Deut. 33:2 reads: *He said: The Lord came from Sinai; He shone upon them from Seir; He appeared from Mount Paran, and approached from Ribeboth-kodesh, lightning flashed at them from His right.* This is a brief summary of the theophany.

105. Deut. 18:15 reads: *The Lord your God will raise up for you a prophet from among your own people, like myself; him you shall heed.*

106. In response to Abraham's plea: *Oh that Ishmael may live by Your favor!* God speaks: *As for Ishmael, I have heeded you. I hereby bless him. I will make him fertile and exceedingly numerous. He shall be the father of twelve chieftains, and I will make of him a great nation* [Gen. 17:18,20].

107. This accusation is found in the Koran (e.g., 2:73), and it was taken up and expanded later by Muslim critics of Jews and Judaism. Cf. article by Ignaz Goldziher (1850–1921), the outstanding student of Islam, in *Zeitschrift der morgenländischen Gesellschaft* 32 (1878): 341–67 and by Martin Schreiner (1863–1926), in ibid., 42:591–675.

108. This word was coined to reflect the play on words Maimonides utilizes. The Arabic term for *apostle* is *rasul;* the Hebrew word is *pasul,* which sounds like it means unfit, disqualified.

109. Literally, "a tradition from everybody to everybody." In the Islamic world a statement handed down in an unbroken chain from generation to generation by the whole community is unchallengeably true.

110. Modern examination of the Greek, Latin, and Syriac versions of the Bible have revealed a great many variations.

111. I.e., the phrase implies only numerical strength, with no suggestion of prophethood.

112. In this phrase also the root *rb* is used to denote a large population.

113. If the verb *I shall bless him* stood before the words *I will make him numerous,* it might be understood by people desperately looking for proof to refer to their prophet.

114. The two words *bm'd m'd* come right after the phrase *I shall make him numerous,* not after the earlier verb *I shall bless him.*

115. Maimonides stresses this point to exclude any other claimant, just as earlier Judah Halevi developed the idea in *Kuzari* 2:14.

116. The context of the verse is the incident of Sarah's demand that her husband cast out Ishmael and his mother. Since Abraham hesitated, God assures him of Isaac's privileged status.

117. The use of the particle *gam* (too) proves that Ishmael is an addition, a concession to Abraham's concern for this son (see Gen. 21:10–13).

118. Part of Jacob's blessing of his two grandchildren, the sons of Joseph.

119. At the point where the patriarch's name is changed from Abram to Abraham.

120. It follows the consolation to Abraham regarding Ishmael.

121. In Isaac's blessing to Jacob when the latter is about to leave for Haran.

122. The reference is to David, the traditional author of Psalms. He is not generally known by the epithet *prophet*. In the *Guide* 2:45 Maimonides categorizes him as a prophet of the second class (out of eleven). In Islam David is taken to be a prophet; see *EI²*, 2:182.

123. Koran 7:156.

124. Koran 61:6. Maimonides cites these two passages to substantiate his challenge. Muhammad asserts he is mentioned in the Torah, but elsewhere he declares his name is Ahmed.

125. The Koranic verse is "And when Jesus son of Mary said, O children of Israel, verily I am the apostle of God sent unto you, confirming the law which was delivered before me, and bringing good tidings of an apostle who shall come after me, and whose name shall be Ahmad."

126. The Hebrew words equal ninety-two and the name AHMD, fifty-three.

127. Exod. 24:16 reads: *The Presence of the Lord abode on Mount Sinai, and the cloud hid it for six days. On the seventh day He called to Moses from the midst of the cloud.*

128. Judg. 5:4 continues: *the earth trembled; the heavens dripped, yea, the clouds dripped water.* This is Deborah's ode in celebration of the victory over the Canaanites.

129. *Sifrei* (ed. Finkelstein), 396 (section 343); the story of the offer of Torah to the gentiles is linked to this verse.

130. The rabbis humorously criticize the Israelites for being in such haste to receive the Torah that they said they would *do* before they would *obey* (literally: "we will listen").

131. This verse is a stock argument among Muslim polemicists. The literal translation of the text in the Torah is: *from among you, from your brethren, like me.* See Samau'al al-Maghribi, *Silencing the Jews*, 45.

132. Samau'al argues that the words *Your brethren* may well apply to an Arab, supporting himself by the phrase: *Your brethren the children of Esau* (Deut. 2:4).

133. No one can doubt that this is a most reasonable requirement. Nor can Maimonides be challenged that he takes passages out of context. If it is for the purpose of edification, bolstering the faith, or any other purpose consonant with tradition, it is legitimate. But it cannot be done if it is misused to undermine the tradition.

134. The context of the verse is the attempt by a false prophet to seduce the people to worship idols.

135. Part of God's admonition not to be seduced to worship idols. Deut. 11:16 reads: *Take care not to be lured away to serve other gods and bow to them.*

136. Num. 20:14 continues: *You know all the hardships that have befallen us.* See note 132 above.

137. Maimonides consistently teaches that Moses was unique among the prophets; in fact, he should not be regarded as a prophet.

138. Deut. 18:9–16 reads: *When you enter the land that the Lord your*

*God is giving you, you shall not learn to imitate the abhorrent practices of
those nations. Let no one be found among you who consigns his son or
daughter to the fire, or who is an augur, a soothsayer, a diviner, a sorcerer,
one who casts spells, or one who consults ghosts or familiar spirits, or one
who inquires of the dead. For anyone who does such things is abhorrent to
the Lord, and it is because of these abhorrent things that the Lord your God
is dispossessing them before you. You must be wholehearted with the Lord
your God. Those nations that you are about to dispossess do indeed resort to
soothsayers and augurs; to you however, the Lord your God has not assigned
the like.*

*The Lord your God will raise up for you a prophet from among your own
people, like myself; him you shall heed.*

139. The loss was the asses of his father, which led to his being anointed
king over Israel.

140. Two random common names.

141. Of the characters of Job, save the last, it is generally assumed they
were gentiles (BT Bava Batra 14b). Elihu ben Berakh'el ha-Buzi is said to
have been Jewish. However, a number of sages hold Job also to have been
Jewish. In fact, a summary seems to conclude that only some regard him a
non-Jew. And in BT Avodah Zarah 3a only the first three friends are taken
to be non-Jews.

142. He was challenged by the prophet Jeremiah, and was proved to have
delivered a false prediction; see Jer. 28.

143. Deut. 5:24, the last sentence of the story of their fear to listen to
God directly lest they die, reads: *You go closer and hear all that the Lord
our God says, and then you tell us everything that the Lord our God tells you,
and we willingly do it.*

144. Continuing the assertion that the fulfillment of the Torah is not much
of a strain, Deut. 30:12 emphasizes: *It is not in the heavens, that you should
say, "Who among us can go up to the heavens and get it for us and impart it
to us, that we may observe it?"*

145. Deut. 13:1 reads in full: *Be careful to observe only that which I enjoin
upon you: neither add to it nor take away from it.*

146. I.e., if we were an independent state, and not subject to other gov-
ernments with their legal systems. It is to be noted how emphatic Maimonides
is in his insistence that first and foremost is the content of the pretender's
message rather than the skills he may display.

147. Deut. 13:4 reads: *Do not heed the words of that prophet or that dream-
diviner. For the Lord your God is testing you. . . .*

148. Once again Maimonides states his basic thesis: nothing about the role
of Moses, his person, or his miracles bears any resemblance to any other prophet.

149. Since his discourse is beyond criticism, we ask him to perform a
miracle to verify that he is indeed a prophet.

150. The miracle is parallel to the testimony of two witnesses who may
be sure of what they wish to testify and we accept their statements as valid
without their feeling of certainty.

151. See note 146 above.

152. Deut. 17:6 rules: *A person shall be put to death only on the testimony of two or more witnesses; he must not be put to death on the testimony of a single witness.* This is the basis of the faith put in two witnesses.

153. A full exposition of the subject will be found in the Introduction (ed. Kafih), 4–11.

154. In this admonition Maimonides warns his readers against the wiles of anti-Talmudic Jewish groups, such as the Karaites or the Samaritans, who protest their absolute faith in the Torah, but do not accept the oral tradition.

155. In Maimonides' time Egypt was the home of many Karaites and Samaritans, and many were influential in their group or in government circles.

156. In one of his responsa (ed. Blau, no. 242/II, 434ff.), Maimonides refers several times to the pernicious influence of "the heretics," and the duty to contravene them.

157. This is the traditional wish for an early restoration of political independence and the ingathering of the exiles to their homeland, the land of Israel.

158. This is not a legal decision to be implemented, but a definition of the extent of their rejection.

159. Deut. 17:11 continues: *you must not deviate from the verdict that they announce to you either to the right or to the left.* The rabbis explain the last phrase to mean that even if in your judgment they were to call the right left and left right. See *Sifrei* 207 (section 154).

160. The Christians have almost always considered the Jewish Scriptures as part of their divine heritage. The Muslims have not incorporated the Bible into their sacred literature, but they admit its divine origin. Curiously, they, on the one hand, accuse the Jews of altering and of falsifying it, yet at the same time they seek to find in it proof of their claims.

161. In Daniel (7:24, 8:14, 25; 9:24–6; 12:7, 11, 12) numbers appear that tradition has recognized as mystifying calculations predicting the end of the travail and the beginning of the glorious era (in Hebrew: *ketz*). Many Jewish writers have attempted to figure out when the change will come.

162. Saadiah Gaon (882–942) devotes chapter 8 of his philosophic work, *The Book of Beliefs and Opinions,* to the establishment of the date. See Rosenblatt's translation (New Haven: Yale University Press, 1948), pp. 290–322 and especially 295–98.

163. In his work *A History of Messianic Speculations in Israel* (New York: Macmillan, 1927), A.H. Silver summarizes the conclusions of the various students who attempted to fix the date. See in particular chapter 1 on the eleventh and twelfth centuries (pp. 58–80).

164. The passage from which this verse comes is a declaration of God to Abraham: *Know well that your offspring shall be strangers in a land not theirs, and they shall be enslaved and oppressed four hundred years.*

165. This is the name of the vision in Gen. 15:8–21, where the covenant was made in a ceremony involving passage between the pieces of the beasts that Abraham had cut.

166. Evidently Maimonides has Exod. 12:40–41 in mind. The first of the

two verses reads: *The time the Israelites lived in Egypt was four hundred and thirty years*. It was then that Moses was sent by God to free the Israelites from bondage in Egypt.

167. This incident is an old tradition, cf. *Mekhilta* 13:17 (ed. Rabin, p. 76) and 15:14 (p. 147).

168. Cf. 1 Chron. 7:21.

169. Gen. 21:12 reads: *But God said to Abraham, "Do not be distressed over the boy or your slave; whatever Sarah tells you, do as she says, for it is through Isaac . . ."* This is the accepted calculation, since, as we read elsewhere, their actual bondage lasted 210 years.

170. The commentator Naḥmanides (1194–1270) suggests that the correct order of the phrases is different, i.e., *your offspring shall be strangers in a land not theirs four hundred years and they shall be enslaved and oppressed*.

171. Maimonides makes this statement in view of the premature move of the tribe of Ephraim.

172. It is obvious that in its context this verse (and the next) deals with a much more immediate difficulty. But Maimonides does not hesitate to read another meaning into it since it does not violate the spirit of the religious outlook.

173. BT Sanhedrin 97b. Maimonides' reasoning has its origin in the Talmud, which continues with this explanation: for they (the calculators), when their prediction time arrives and the redemption is not in sight, conclude that it is not going to happen. No, you have to wait, as the prophet says: *Even if it tarries, wait for it still* [Hab. 2:3].

174. The excuse he offers for Saadiah's efforts to fix the date of the redemption can be offered for the other attempts to calculate it. The masses were probably at all times not firm believers in the ultimate change for the better, so anything more definite might bolster their faith.

175. See note 35 above.

176. This phrase is taken from Mishnah Avot 2:15, and offered as counsel to the members of the community.

177. Maimonides follows the commendable Jewish tradition of maintaining an attitude of respect and acceptance of the words and acts of the ancient sages.

178. Maimonides was one of the few in the Middle Ages, Jews or non-Jews, who rejected astrology, and he tried hard to disprove it.

179. In his three major Jewish compositions, the *Commentary to the Mishnah*, the *Code*, and the *Guide*, Maimonides gave voice to his strong repudiation of astrology. In his response to the sages of France, who wished to learn his opinion, he took the same stand, and even blamed the fall of Jerusalem to the Romans on the Jewish neglect of preparedness, owing to their reliance on astrology.

180. An epithet of Moses. Maimonides' appreciation of the uniqueness of Moses traditionally and philosophically very naturally led him to designate the prophet in these terms; Jewish tradition likewise regards him this way. It must also be remembered that when the other dominant faiths glorified their

founders and objects of worship (cf. Tor Andrae, *Die Person Mohammads*), Jews realized they had to emphasize the superiority of Moses.
181. In Isaiah's "lament" over the calamity that will overwhelm Egypt.
182. From Isaiah's satire on Babylonia.
183. Maimonides summarizes the doctrine that Judaism was replaced by Christianity and that no improvement would come in the fate of the Jews before they confessed the beliefs of the dominant faiths.
184. One of the numerous verses of consolation, which begin with Isaiah 40.
185. Although Maimonides rejects astrology, he demonstrates his knowledge of it by the certainty with which he makes his assertions.
186. The imaginary zodiac can be divided by two axes, one vertical, the other horizontal, into four quarters called trigons, and three of the twelve constellations are located in each. The earthly trigon (the others are the watery, airy, and fiery), according to the astrologers, is the period when culture is at an ebb.
187. Here is another argument against the inclination to believe in the effects of the heavenly bodies.
188. With the aid of astronomy it was possible to work out the relation between events and the movements of the stars and planets.
189. This chapter recites the impressiveness of Solomon and his accomplishments.
190. Exodus Rabbah 2:13. Maimonides calls Abraham by this title in *MT Hilkhot Akum* 1:2 and in the *Guide* 3:29.
191. This is the honor of Abraham, that by his reasoning he arrived at the correct recognition of the God of the universe. It is the basis of the legend that he was thrown into the hot furnace by the idolatrous Babylonian king.
192. The statement (based on Gen. 35:13) is found in Genesis Rabbah 47 and 82. Note that by the insertion of the phrase *in their hearts* Maimonides converts the rabbinic explanation into a psychological experience. This rabbinic assertion was also explained theosophically. See Encyclopedia Judaica, vol. 10, 505 (in the article "Kabbala").
193. Abraham bar Hiyya (twelfth century), who believed in astrology, also states in his *Megillat ha-Megalleh*, pp. 119–33, that the events enumerated here occurred during the earthly trigon. But he involves the course of the other planets and their locations within the zodiac, and does not call the earthly trigon unlucky. His figures are exact, unlike the round figures of Maimonides.
194. "Professional" astrologers in medieval times predicted that it would happen. See Boll, *Sternglaube und Sterndeutung*, p. 111.
195. For the source of this belief see L. Ginzberg, "A deluge of fire and water" (in Hebrew), in *ha-Goren*, VIII. It is reported by Syrian and Arab historians that in 1095 the caliph Mustazhir in Baghdad was informed that the deluge in Noah's time was caused by a conjunction of the seven planets, and in this ruler's time six planets met and a heavy rain fell elsewhere.
196. Maimonides repeats this true adage in his letter to the French sages.

197. That is, a calamity in nature resulting from the unusual position of the planets.

198. Maimonides recalls what the Bible records of the sins of mankind and God's sending the deluge to *blot out from the earth the men whom I created—men together with beasts, creeping things, and birds of the sky; for I regret that I made them* [Gen. 6:7].

199. The destruction of Sodom and Gomorrah, in punishment of *the outrage . . . that is so great, and their sin so grave* [Gen. 18:20], is related in the remainder of Gen. 18 and 19.

200. Whenever Maimonides challenges the belief in astrology as sinful, he utilizes the same verses from Lev. 26 as proof that *sin only* is the cause of calamity for Israel, as in *Hilkhot Ta'aniyyot* 1:3, the *Guide* 3:37, his letter to the French sages, and the *Essay on Resurrection*, pp. 230ff.

201. Maimonides paraphrases Lev. 26:21 and then he quotes from it. The context of the quoted phrase is: *I will go on smiting you sevenfold for your sins*.

202. Maimonides does not reveal the name of the individual who made the forecast. Since he finds that the Almohad persecution came when he predicted the appearance of the Messiah, it can be concluded that he expected him about 1150. Ibn Ezra, in his commentary on Dan. 11:30, counts several who made computations but were all disappointed, and calls their efforts "futile and pursuit of wind," arguing that even Daniel himself did not know the date.

203. This is a psychological truth and shows understanding of the mood of the Yemenite leader, who was ready to believe anything in the hope that it would bring relief.

204. Maimonides' specification that the Messiah is to be a scion of David through Solomon made here, in his commentary to Mishnah Sanhedrin ch. 10, in *Sefer ha-Mitzvot*, negative commands 362, and in his *Epistle on Martyrdom* is meant to combat a tradition that traced the genealogy to Nathan son of David (cf. 2 Sam. 5:14), and confused him with the prophet Nathan. Cf. Rashi's comment to Zech. 12:12.

205. Part of Balaam's last predictions to the Moabite king Balak.

206. In the last song by Moses, a review of the history of God's relation with Israel, and a demonstration of the futility of idolatry.

207. Describing the imminence of the messenger.

208. Some commentators on the Book of Daniel in Muslim lands found reference to Muhammad in the second half of Dan. 11 and 12. Ibn Ezra is a notable exception. But in his interpretation of Nebuchadnezzar's dream in Dan. 2 he identifies the iron with the Muslims, unlike the usual trend of seeing Rome in the iron. He calls Byzantium Rome, yet it is Greece. He likewise finds the Muslims in Daniel's vision in 7.

209. Rashi and Radak correctly apply the vision to the Elamites and the Medes, who were about to overthrow Babylonia. But Maimonides, not bound by the context, sees in it a reference to the Messiah.

210. It is a traditional interpretation. Although Radak brings it in the name of some who differ whether it is the Davidic Messiah or the Ephraimite,

he himself is inclined to find in it a reference to Judah the Maccabee, and he further reports that Moses ben Gikatilla thought it spoke about Nehemiah.

211. This too is the traditional view. The traveler ibn Sapir in the nineteenth century wrote that in the city of Alexandria a statue of a camel and its rider was erected to serve as a seat of judgment.

212. Maimonides has Dan. 2 and 7 in mind. See note 208.

213. Maimonides brings in the authorities backing the tradition.

214. Basing themselves on this phrase, the Jews in Muslim Spain generally believed they were descended from the exiles of Jerusalem, and arrogated to themselves the distinction of being the most eloquent in Hebrew. See Moses ibn Ezra, *Book of Examination and Discussion* (ed. Halkin) pp. 54–55, and ibn Daud, *Sefer ha-Qabbalah* (ed. Cohen, Philadelphia: Jewish Publication Society, 1967), p. 97, line 94ff.

215. Maimonides digresses at this point to offer illustrations of how biblical allusions aided the rabbis. His purpose is to inspire more faith in the tradition of his family.

216. The implication is in Genesis Rabbah 91:2. The number 210 is the total years of bondage from the death of Joseph.

217. The remainder of Deut. 4:25 reads: . . . *act wickedly and make for yourselves a sculptured image in any likeness, causing the Lord your God displeasure and vexation*.

218. In the Hebrew word the two *vavs* are not included in the computation.

219. For example, in Hab. 3:2, the phrase *in Your anger remember to have mercy* has the Hebrew word *rhm*, which is said to hint at Abraham (both equal 248).

220. The argument is based on the word *ka'et*, "like the present time."

221. For the year 2448 for the Exodus, see Rashi's computation in BT Sanhedrin 9a.

222. The remainder of this section of Joel 3 predicts great cosmic upheavals, wars, and refuge in Zion.

223. The report of this tradition raises several questions. What Maimonides calls "a family secret" is in fact a statement in JT Shabbat ch. 6, Hal. 9 (43a). Despite his awareness of acting contrary to his own admonitions and availing himself of the excuse that people were falling into despair, some scholars have suggested that this section is not part of the original epistle, but was interpolated by an outside hand. However, he does not actually predict the arrival of the Messiah, but only the renewal of prophecy. Above all, it is important that younger contemporaries or immediate successors of his speak of this family tradition, and the first translator into Hebrew corresponded with the Master. Further, it cannot be reasonably maintained that after 1216 (when prophecy did not return) someone would insert a forecast that it would return. Possibly Maimonides, who robbed his friend of the hope that the community was at the threshold of the final Redemption, felt that he had to provide him with some comfort.

224. Maimonides' explanation of the verse agrees with Rashi and Radak.

225. It is a bit surprising that Maimonides, who so readily takes verses out of context to confirm his arguments, challenges another person's action.

Possibly he felt that since JT Ta'anit 1:1 suggests the Messiah's age, the sense he finds in this text is more appropriate.

226. It is one of the gates of Damascus. In a pseudepigraph (Zerubabel), it is connected with the emergence of the Messiah.

227. Nothing is known of this pretender.

228. The wicked ruler who initiated the persecution.

229. For an earlier, similar reaction to R. Jacob's belief see p. 116.

230. Maimonides evidently classes the pretender as a false prophet with unfounded claims, and therefore subject to capital punishment.

231. The verses come from the chapter that has been taken to be a sketch of the Messiah.

232. The first six verses of Isa. 9 are explained by some as references to Hezekiah and the expected victory over Assyria. Maimonides' treatment of this text is in the tradition voiced in Deuteronomy Rabbah 1:20.

233. This verse has been viewed by many as a vindication of the Messiah, see BT Sukkah 52a.

234. This assertion is a restatement of BT Shabbat 82a at greater length. Maimonides develops this view in the *Guide* 2:32 and also in his other two major works, the *Mishneh Torah* and the commentary to the Mishnah.

235. The rabbis derive from this biblical verse the rule that a person must not spend on charitable needs more than a fifth of his possessions (BT Ketubbot 50a and Arakhin 28a).

236. In *MT Hilkhot Arakhin* 8:1, Maimonides explains: "This giving more is not piety but silliness, since he will lose his money and will require help."

237. The emphasis on the land of Israel's being the Messiah's locale, also made in the *Epistle on Martyrdom*, is further proof that the pretender's claim is unfounded.

238. The Aramaic Targum of the Prophets (*Targum Jonathan*) says of this text: "This is the King Messiah, whose name is destined to be revealed." Bible commentators find a reference to Zerubabel in it.

239. This chapter, which is the essential one in linking Jesus to the Bible in the Christian view, has been regarded by many Jewish scholars as referring to the Messiah. Others find Israel depicted in it, and still others Jeremiah. See Neubauer, *The Fifty-Third Chapter of Isaiah* (Oxford: J. Parker, 1876–77), vol. 1 (texts), vol. 2 (translations).

240. See Rashi and Radak ad loc. who read of the Messianic age in this chapter, as Saadiah Gaon did before them.

241. Like other arguments, this one also aims to undo hopes pinned on the pretender.

242. Notwithstanding the chapter division at the end of this verse, it and the preceding sentence belong with ch. 53, and are treated so by commentators.

243. From the messianic chapter; see note 231.

244. The grave threat and the divine role in the triumph of the Israelites over the combined hostile forces are graphically sketched by Ezekiel in chapters 38–39.

245. It is of interest that Maimonides chooses his proof against the

pretender from the story of Jesus, as he lived in the Muslim world all his life, and Muhammad also had a chain of miracles credited to him and a spiritualization of his person that continued to grow (cf. Tor Andrae, *Die Person Muhammads*, pp. 26–91 and 285–89). The wonders of Jesus are much more fundamental in Christian theology than the miracles of Muhammad in Islam.

246. As a deliberate impostor who arrogates to himself powers granted by God to the Messiah, he would be guilty of a grave sin. But this individual was not a presumptuous liar.

247. The verse begins: *For their rock is not like our Rock.* This quotation is part of Moses' farewell address to the people at the eastern bank of the Jordan.

248. This judgment indicates that Maimonides probably did not know enough of the difficult situation of the Jews in the Christian lands from the time of the Crusades (1096 and after), which was far more irksome and physically painful than under the Muslims.

249. Ibn Ezra and Radak cite the *History of ben Gorion* to the effect that Meshekh is Tuscany, an application of metonymy. But Radak prefers to translate the *meshekh* as *continuous*, and to explain that the cry is against Islam, "because the majority of the Jews live there."

250. Maimonides evidently equates *Kedar* with *Kuraish*, the tribe of Muhammad and the caliphs, as does Radak.

251. The verse describes the sad condition of the northern Israelites under Aramaic rule.

252. Dan. 8:10, with changes. See the comment of pseudo-Saadiah.

253. In the Middle Ages the Jews under Christendom and Islam were forbidden to criticize those religions publicly.

254. Gen. 25:14. Three names from the list of the "children of Ishmael." The meanings he assigns to the names conform to the meanings of the roots on which the names are built.

255. This is one of the few instances where Isaiah speaks of himself in the first person.

256. Notwithstanding note 248 above, the depth of suffering experienced by Maimonides and his generation from the humiliation, degradation, and false charges heaped on them by the Muslims, particularly at the time of the Almohad persecution, is not to be minimized.

257. The examples of the four Messiahs are available in two versions. Although weighty reasons support the belief that the succinct account is the original in the epistle, the longer one is offered here in translation.

258. For some reason Maimonides does not mention his name. He seems to have been Abu 'Isa Obadiah al-Isfahani, active during the eighth or ninth century, and the spiritual father of the Isawiyya, a sect treated by Jewish, Karaite, and Islamic historians.

259. This dynasty ruled the Islamic empire from 661 to 750 and vastly expanded its extent.

260. This is the name in Arabic of the land beyond the Oxus river, the province of Khurasan.

261. In the description of the individual who suffered, yet was destined to be acknowledged as the sufferer for the many. One of the epithets can be translated *leprous*.

262. This is distinctly anachronistic. It was only some hundred years after his fall that a caliph of another family issued such an edict against the Jews.

263. It is surprising that Maimonides did not consult the available written sources.

264. The implication is clear: Maimonides is not at all certain of the story he related regarding the first pretender.

265. This man is not to be confused with Moses ben Abraham Dar'i, a twelfth-thirteenth-century Karaite poet, whose father moved from Dar'a to Alexandria. See *Encyclopedia Judaica*, 5:1302.

266. An important rabbinic scholar (1077–1141), with whom Maimon, Maimonides' father, studied Torah.

267. It is interesting that this prophecy speaks of the inspiration that will be bestowed on old and young, men and women.

268. Consistent with his views, Maimonides accepts without demur the prophetic endowment of this man.

269. The restraint and respect with which Maimonides relates this incident are impressive. He stresses his virtues, despite the illusions under which he labored. Maimonides cites him in one of his responsa in the matter of *tefillin*, cf. Blau's ed. no. 289.

270. The Hebrew phrase usually signifies the question regarding a dream asked of an interpreter. In our text it means finding something out by a dream.

271. Maimonides relates this story on the authority of his father, who lived in Cordova with his family before they set out on their wanderings. It is an incident for which he can vouch.

272. A likely misspelling of Lyon, an old city in France, but hardly containing the population of Jews mentioned here.

273. These verses do not suggest flying, only appearance in the clouds.

274. The loyalty of followers to a disappointing, disappointed redeemer, and the continued belief that he will come back and realize his predictions is common in the annals of the Shi'ite sects.

275. This is one of three times repeated in Song of Songs, and on that basis the rabbis stated that God adjured Israel in a threefold oath: that they not force the final redemption, not rebel against their rulers, and that the gentiles not oppress them too harshly (BT Ketubbot 111a). It is of interest that this talmudic statement serves as the main reason for many people's opposition to the Zionist movement and to the State of Israel.

276. This characterization of the manner of creation is found in rabbinic sources, cf. BT Ḥagigah 12a and Genesis Rabbah 12:15. Interestingly, Gen. 1, the story of creation, carries the name *Elohim*, which indicates divine justice. In Gen. 2 this name is used jointly with the tetragrammaton (the four-letter name), which stands for divine mercy, and therefore the tradition has included it in the story of creation.

277. Phrases from Ps. 27:4, which are very easily fashioned into a prayer for an early return to the land of Israel.

278. Isa. 9:1 continues: *On those who dwelt in a land of gloom, light has dawned.*

279. Isa. 60:2 continues: *And His Presence be seen over you.*

280. The customary conclusion of the letter, addressed to R. Jacob ben Nathanel Fayummi, begins at this point.

281. The phrase is from Ps. 72:7, which opens with: *That the righteous may flourish in his time.*

282. On the one hand Maimonides urges the recipient to circulate the epistle among the members of the community. At the same time he cautions him against letting it fall into the hands of a non-Jew. If there was contact between Jews and Muslims in Yemen, it is difficult to assume that it could be arranged both to have Jews read it and to avoid communication of it to non-Jews.

283. A phrase usually invoked when privacy or secrecy is recommended.

284. This is the traditional succession as traced in rabbinic sources. Maimonides mentions it because he wishes to endow their statement with authority.

285. BT Pesaḥim 8a. As he comments, the epistle certainly falls within the category of a religious mission.

DISCUSSION OF
THE' EPISTLE TO YEMEN

I beg you to send a copy of this missive to every community in the cities and hamlets, in order to strengthen the people in their faith and put them on their feet. Read it at public gatherings and in private, and you will thus become a public benefactor. Take adequate precautions lest its contents be divulged by an evil person and mishap overtake us. (God spare us therefrom.) When I began writing this letter I had some misgivings about it, but they were overruled by my conviction that the public welfare takes precedence over one's personal safety. Moreover, I am sending it to a personage such as you: *The counsel of the Lord is for those who fear Him.* [Ps. 25:14]. Our sages, the successors of the prophets, assured us that persons engaged in a religious mission will meet with no disaster. What more important religious mission is there than this! Peace be unto all Israel. Amen. (p. 131)

These concluding words of the *Epistle to Yemen* speak volumes for Maimonides' heroic commitment to and concern for the community. The philosopher-halakhist may not remain silent while his community is in a state of confusion and desperation. He may not dissociate himself from a community that is being crushed by religious persecution and endangered by apostasy.

The *Epistle to Yemen* should be read as Maimonides' response to the tragic predicament of a community struggling to retain faith in the eternal covenant of the Torah despite the prevailing conditions of history. Because of the Jewish community's powerlessness and vulnerability relative to the growing strength of Islam, many Jews despaired of holding out against their religious adversaries who claimed that Islam was the authentic expression of biblical monotheism. How can a community maintain its self-image as God's covenant-elect when the events of history show no signs of divine love and concern? How can one believe in God's eternal promise to Israel when one's lived reality seems to support those who argue that God's covenant with Israel has been abrogated?

The plight of the Jewish community in Yemen revealed the problematic nature of *galut* (exile) in general. Judaism's credibility was strained by the discrepancy between biblical descriptions of history and the conditions that prevailed during the long dark years of exile. God's apparent silence stood in sharp contrast to the biblical account of God's intimate providential relationship with Israel and His overt involvement in its history (e.g., the liberation from Egypt). The gap between the community's lived and sacred histories was a disruptive feature of Jewish consciousness throughout history. [1]

Maimonides was fully aware of the desperate predicament of the community in Yemen and therefore felt compelled to write this epistle. Despite the danger in which he placed himself by writing it, he insisted that it be read publicly in every city and hamlet. The *Epistle to Yemen* is not a dispassionate philosophic treatise on history; it is a letter written with the express purpose of strengthening a community in its battle against hostile surrounding forces. The tone and substance of the epistle express the anger and bitterness of a leader who felt called upon to support a community that was disillusioned and shattered by the world in which it lived.

As a committed halakhist, Maimonides could not choose the path of the isolated philosopher who seeks personal perfection in a Plotinian type of leap of the alone to the Alone. The philosopher-halakhist is firmly implanted within the matrix of the community. He is barred from escaping into his self so long as his community is endangered. His personal security and quest for self-realization are of secondary importance when the people of Israel are suffering and endangered.

The singular individual who follows the lonely and tortuous path to love of God charted by Maimonides in his *Guide of the Perplexed* cannot remain satisfied with his quest for philosophical love of God if his community is in shock because of a loss of trust in the biblical promise. Like the philosopher of Plato's *Republic*, he must return to the cave. To use a midrashic metaphor, he must descend from the mountaintop as God told Moses to do when the people were engaged in worshiping the golden calf: "Go down. All the greatness that I have given you is for the sake of Israel! And now that they have sinned, what need do I have of you?" (BT Berakhot 32a).

Maimonides could not turn his back on the community in moments of crisis because the community constituted an essential component of his self-consciousness. While scholars may debate whether commitment to the community is a necessary component of the Platonic or Aristotelian conceptions of human perfection, i.e., whether, according to these philosophers, the ultimate state of human realization includes morality and political responsibility, there is no doubt where Maimonides stood on this issue.[2] Maimonides exposed himself to great danger in order to aid the oppressed community in Yemen to regain a sense of purpose and direction. He returned to the darkened cave of history because, in addition to being a philosopher, he was a halakhic Jew. The language in which he spoke and thought, the language of *mitzvot* (commandments), is fundamentally a collective medium of discourse.[3] His consciousness was defined by his membership in the community.

Maimonides' life bears testimony to what he wrote in his *Mishneh Torah* concerning the individual's identification with the community.

> One who separates himself from the community, even if he does not commit a transgression but only holds aloof from the congregation of Israel, does not fulfill religious precepts in common with his people, shows himself indifferent when they are in distress, does not observe their fast, but goes his own way, as if he were one of the gentiles and did not belong to the Jewish people—such a person has no portion in the world to come. [*MT Hilkhot Teshuvah* 3:20]

Maimonides' empathic identification with the community was expressed not only in the act of writing the epistle and in insisting that it be read in public, but also in the substance of the epistle itself. The nature of the arguments presented exemplify what may be called the "logic of the sufferer" as opposed to the "logic of action" found in his legal works. Whereas in his legal works, Maimonides sought to alter the community's understanding of religious life, in the *Epistle to Yemen* he sought to comfort and encourage the community to persevere. Maimonides' treatment of Christianity and Islam, his interpretation of Israel's suffering, his use of messianic categories to explain existing historical conditions, his description of the future Messiah, his mention of his family's tradition concerning the return of prophecy, and his frequent references to biblical sources that allegedly anticipated all the hardships that the community underwent—all these features are explicable in terms of Maimonides' overriding concern to communicate with a suffering community in the grip of despair and hopelessness.

The *Epistle to Yemen* ought not to be used to reconstruct Maimonides' overall theory of history and messianism or his general approach to Christianity and Islam. It treats such themes from a specific point of view, namely, through the eyes of the sufferer. It is no wonder, therefore, that Maimonides' treatment of these themes in his major legal works differs in important respects from his treatment here.

The following comments show the importance of considering the intended audiences of Maimonides' writings.[4] The logic that characterizes legal writings addressed to a community of action differs from the logic that characterizes a treatise addressed to a community of sufferers. In the former, Maimonides writes as a philosopher-educator; in the latter, as an empathetic leader of a broken community.

THE AUDIENCE OF THE *EPISTLE TO YEMEN*

At the outset of the epistle, Maimonides mentions the religious doubt that was undermining the community's faith: "The hearts of some people have turned, uncertainty befalls them, and their beliefs are weakened. . . ." Because of its historical predicament, the community was beginning to question the validity of the binding covenant between God and Israel. This mood of uncertainty was reinforced by the apparent similarity between Judaism and Islam.

> . . . a person ignorant of the secrets of the revealed books and the inner significance of our Law will be led to believe that our religion has something in common with the established confession if he makes a comparison between the two. For he will find that in the Torah there are prohibitions and commandments, and there are prohibitions and commandments in the others; the Torah contains positive and negative precepts, rewards, and punishments, and the others contain negative and positive commandments, rewards, and punishments. (p. 99)

The community was unsure of its ability to defend Judaism against the seductive arguments presented by other monotheistic faith communities. The conflict was not between Judaism and paganism, but between Judaism and another monotheistic faith. In addition, the great successes of such rival religions led some Jews to wonder whether it made sense to suffer for the sake of Judaism if the differences between the major monotheistic faiths were only superficial.

The polemical context in which the epistle was written is manifest in Maimonides' allusions to some of the standard arguments that were used against the Jewish community.

Put your trust in these true texts of Scripture, brethren, and be not dismayed by the succession of persecutions or the enemy's ascendancy over us, or the weakness of our people. (p. 102)

A great deal of polemical literature was based directly on scriptural arguments.

You mention that the apostate has misled people to believe that *bm'd m'd* is the Madman, or that in the same way *He appeared from Mount Paran* [Deut. 33:2] alludes to him, or, similarly, that *a prophet from among your own people* [Deut. 18:15] refers to him, or likewise his promise to Ishmael: *I will make of him a great nation* [Gen. 17:20]. These arguments have been rehearsed so often that they have become nauseating. (p. 107)

Jewish scripture was being used as a weapon against the integrity of traditional Judaism. Enthusiastic converts to Islam mouthing classical Islamic polemics tried to show that Islam is the genuine embodiment of the covenant with Abraham. Jews were accused of falsifying scripture by expunging all references to Muhammad from it. Such polemical arguments were difficult to ignore because they emerged from within the frameworks of monotheism and the biblical tradition.[5]

The audience of the *Epistle to Yemen* was in many respects similar to the audience of the *Epistle on Martyrdom*. The psychologically corrosive effects of compromise had undermined belief in the significance of partial fulfillment of the *mitzvot*. The sense of guilt that grips a person who knowingly compromises his principles under duress can lead to an all-or-nothing attitude to religious observance. Maimonides therefore felt compelled to reiterate arguments showing the validity of partial fulfillment of *mitzvot* in compromise situations.

Let no one conclude that he may freely disregard the less important ceremonies without liability to penalty because he has under duress committed some major sins. For Jeroboam son of Nebat, may his bones be ground to dust, was chastised not only for the sin of worshiping the calves and inciting the Israelites to do the same, but also for his failure to construct a booth on the Feast of Tabernacles. (p. 106)

The community was gripped by a paralyzing sense of guilt and doubt about its ability to withstand the seductive offers to abandon Judaism and join the ranks of the powerful majority. While recognizing the need to bolster the community's faith in its own tradition, Maimonides also had to confront the destructive "extravagances" to which this community had turned in its desperation.

. . . Indeed, the hardships experienced by our people in the Diaspora are responsible for these extravagances, for a drowning man catches at a straw. (p. 120)

The "extravagances" Maimonides had in mind were messianic movements and the popular belief in astrology. With respect to those who used astrology to calculate the coming of the Messiah, Maimonides argued that "the advent of the Messiah is in no way subject to the influence of the stars." Nevertheless, Maimonides could not ignore the community's deep need for external "proofs" of their imminent redemption. In reaction to the dire predictions of astrologers claiming that their fate was unalterable, many among the community turned to messianic prognosticators who presented evidence that the end of days (ketz) was fixed and rapidly approaching. The mood engendered by astrological speculation created an insatiable hunger for counterarguments that would show that the astrologers' interpretation of the blueprint of history was mistaken. The community required necessitarian beliefs that could counteract the necessitarian beliefs of the astrologers.

Maimonides mentions Saadiah's computations of the date of redemption. While acknowledging that all such computations are expressly prohibited by the rabbis, he refrained from criticizing Saadiah, who "believed in all earnestness that by means of the messianic calculations he would inspire the masses with hope in the Truth."

The community's preoccupation with messianism was not focused only upon arguments and calculations, but also upon charismatic personalities claiming to be the Messiah. Maimonides was well aware of this propensity and of its causes. When mentioning an incident concerning a messianic pretender, he writes,

Neither am I surprised at his votaries, because they were persuaded by him owing to their sorry plight, their ignorance of the importance and high rank of the Messiah, and their mistaken comparison of the Messiah with ibn Mahdi, whose rise they are witnessing. (p. 123)

Furthermore, the community Maimonides addressed was volatile and potentially impetuous. When people live in a prolonged state of persecution and deprivation, they become prone to take great risks in the belief that they have little to lose.

. . . Solomon of blessed memory, inspired by the Holy Spirit, foresaw that the prolonged duration of the exile would incite some

of our people to seek to terminate it before the appointed time,
and as a consequence they would perish or meet with disaster.
(p. 130)

This then was the audience of the *Epistle to Yemen*. It was comprised
of a people torn apart by contradictory claims. Astrologers claimed
that their fate was sealed and nothing could effectively alter their
miserable condition, while others, such as Saadiah, presented esoteric
calculations predicting an imminent messianic upheaval in history.
The community was continually bombarded by polemical attacks on
the integrity of Judaism aimed at showing that the ascendancy of Islam
proved that the Mosaic covenant had been abrogated and the Jewish
version of Scripture was a forgery. While some were feeling grave
doubts about God's providential involvement in Jewish history, others
were swayed by charismatics claiming to be Messiahs.

THE CONTENT OF THE EPISTLE

When reading the *Epistle to Yemen*, it is important to keep in mind
its intended audience, just described. Both the style and the content
of the work reveal Maimonides' concern to establish rapport with that
audience and to help them make sense of their suffering. The following
sections will indicate how the "logic of the sufferer" influenced both
what Maimonides wrote in the epistle and how he expressed himself.

In order to communicate effectively with a suffering person, we must
convince him that we understand his pain and agony. Words of consolation seem empty if they fail to convince the hearer that the speaker
shares some of the bitterness and anguish that he experiences. Maimonides conveys this sense of identification with his audience's suffering in two ways. First, he cites numerous prophetic texts that ostensibly contain references to the community's situation and express
the prophet's shock about such terrible suffering. Maimonides thus
informs his audience that they are not alone; the great biblical prophets
were aware of and disturbed by what this community would suffer at
the hands of its Islamic rulers. By marshaling a wide array of sources
from biblical literature, Maimonides made the plight of the community
in Yemen into a focal point of all of Jewish history. His readers could
feel that not only he but also many other great leaders in Jewish history
understood their pain and anguish.

Second, by his harsh and abusive description of Islam and Christianity, Maimonides offers the sufferer an outlet for his anger toward
his oppressor. In contrast to his usual controlled and unemotional style
of writing, Maimonides inveighs against Christianity and Islam with

bitterness and derision. His unrestrained attacks on Jesus ("may his bones be ground to dust") and Muhammad ("the Madman") enable the sufferer to identify with the author. Before trying to inspire hope in his readers, he joins them in venting their deep feelings of anger and frustration.

Because of the specific audience-oriented nature of the *Epistle to Yemen*, one must be careful not to take Maimonides' remarks on Christianity and Islam out of context. They are not the pronouncements of a philosopher reflecting on the meaning of Jewish history as a neutral observer. His comments on the relationship between Judaism, Christianity, and Islam should not be read as Maimonides' definitive views on comparative religion. Likewise, his vehement description of the Islamic persecution ("Never did a nation molest, degrade, debase and hate us as much as they") is more an expression of anger than an objective judgment on history.

The author of the epistle is not writing as a dispassionate philosopher of history or of religion, but as a philosopher-halakhist who feels compelled to speak out in response to an immediate crisis situation.

THE UNIQUENESS OF THE TORAH

> *See, I have imparted to you laws and rules, as the Lord my God has commanded me, for you to abide by in the land which you are about to invade and occupy. Observe them faithfully, for that will be proof of your wisdom and discernment to other peoples, who on hearing of all these laws will say, "Surely, that great nation is a wise and discerning people." For what great nation is there that has a god so close at hand as is the Lord our God whenever we call upon Him? Or what great nation has laws and rules as perfect as all this Teaching that I set before you this day?*
>
> *But take utmost care and watch yourselves scrupulously, so that you do not forget the things that you saw with your own eyes and so that they do not fade from your mind as long as you live. And make them known to your children and to your children's children: The day you stood before the Lord your God at Horeb, when the Lord said to me, "Gather the people to Me that I may let them hear My words, in order that they may learn to revere Me as long as they live on earth, and may so teach their children."* [Deut. 4:5–10]

While Maimonides often refers to this biblical text describing the election of Israel and the unique nature of its Torah, his use of it in the *Epistle to Yemen* differs markedly from that in the *Guide of the Perplexed*. In the latter it serves as a proof text for interpreting Jewish law in terms of universal criteria of intelligibility, whereas in the *Epis-

tle to Yemen it is introduced to explain the animosity of the nations of
the world toward Israel.

In the *Guide of the Perplexed* 3:31, Maimonides quotes the text in
support of his attempt to offer reasons for all the commandments,
including the statutes (*ḥukkim*). According to Maimonides, all the
commandments are accessible to human reason. Unlike those who
made blind obedience the supreme religious virtue and accordingly
insisted on the nonrational nature of the commandments, Maimonides
argues that only our ignorance of history prevents us from discovering
reasons for all the commandments. The commandments do not constitute a private language intelligible only to the faithful, but rather
they are intelligible to a universal audience. It is precisely because of
this that the Torah characterizes the commandments as *proof of your
wisdom and discernment to other peoples, who on hearing of all these
laws will say, "Surely, that great nation is a wise and discerning people."*

> Now if there is a thing for which no reason is known and that
> does not either procure something useful or ward off something
> harmful, why should one say of one who believes in it or practices
> it that he is "wise and discerning" and of great worth? And why
> should the religious communities think it a wonder? (Guide 3:31)

Because the text concerned places the commandments within a universal framework of rationality, it serves as a proof text against non-
rationalistic interpretations of Judaism. The appreciative response of
the nations of the world to the Torah inspires the Jewish philosopher
to go beyond the conception of the *mitzvot* as a private language limited
to a particular community and to explicate Jewish law in terms of
universal canons of rationality.[6]

In the *Epistle to Yemen*, however, the text is given a strikingly
different interpretation. The response of the nations of the world is not
described as a positive and spontaneous expression of admiration that
encourages the Jew to participate in a universal framework of rationality, but rather as a negative reaction of anger and animosity leading
to Israel's tragic isolation.

> Since God has singled us out by His laws and precepts, and our
> preeminence over the others was manifested in His rules and
> statutes, as Scripture says in narrating God's mercies to us: *What
> great nation has laws and rules as perfect as all this Teaching
> that I set before you this day?* [Deut. 4:8]; all the nations, insti-
> gated by envy and impiety, rose up against us in anger, and all
> the kings of the earth, motivated by injustice and enmity, applied

themselves to persecute us. They wanted to thwart God, but He will not be thwarted. (p. 97)

Israel's election as manifest in this, the most perfect of legal systems, unleashed diabolic forces seeking to undermine God's love for Israel and Israel's loyalty to the Torah. Israel's suffering in history is a direct result of the envy felt toward this people for its having been singled out by God. The real object of the nations' hatred is thus not Israel but rather God Himself.

This relentless battle against Israel cannot succeed, for it is a battle aimed at thwarting God's will. Israel's destiny among the nations is inseparably connected with God's plan in history. And, as Maimonides writes repeatedly, "Just as God cannot be destroyed, so Israel cannot be destroyed."

The struggle against God's will in history has assumed various forms. Amalek, Nebuchadnezzar, and Titus sought to destroy Israel and its Torah by brute force. The Syrians, Persians, and Greeks used arguments as means to undermine the Torah intellectually. The third form of the universal conspiracy against Torah was the establishment of monotheistic faiths to compete with Judaism. The devious strategy behind the latter scheme is that rival claims to divine revelation tend to cancel each other out, thereby neutralizing the claims of all revealed religions including Judaism.

. . . Thus doubts will be generated and confusion will be created, since one is opposed to the other and both supposedly emanated from one god, and it will lead to the destruction of both religions. This is a remarkable plan contrived by a person who is envious and malicious, who will strive to kill his enemy and remain alive, and if he cannot achieve this, he will devise a scheme whereby they both will be slain. (p. 98)

The hatred of God is so intense that the enemy will stop short of nothing to realize his diabolical plan, even should it entail his own destruction.

In response to the seemingly overwhelming forces aimed at Israel's destruction, Maimonides tells his readers to make the revelation at Sinai into a vivid and dramatic image that could capture the imagination of the entire community. The key to sustaining the community's loyalty and determination during dark periods of history is the internalization of the account of the Sinai revelation. The dramatic imagery of the theophany at Sinai must be inscribed on the heart of each and every member of the community.

It is imperative, my fellow Jews, that you make this great spectacle of the Revelation appeal to the imagination of your children. Proclaim at public gatherings its nobility and its momentousness. For it is the pivot of our religion and the proof that demonstrates its veracity. (p. 104)

Maimonides singles out the story of revelation as the central event around which Jewish consciousness must revolve. In order to withstand the onslaughts of history, the Sinai revelation must be transformed into a compelling image deeply engrained in the minds of all members of the community. By dramatically reliving this founding event of Jewish history, the community will recover the unassailable certainty felt by those who personally witnessed the unique moment of revelation.

In the *Epistle to Yemen*, Maimonides focuses on the collective nature of the Sinai revelation.[7] The fact that the entire community participated in the theophany at Sinai becomes a source of strength enabling the community to defy the spurious claims of rival monotheistic religions regardless of their historical triumphs and successes.

Remember, brethren, that this great, incomparable, and unique covenant and faith is attested by the best of evidence. For never before or since has a whole nation heard the speech of God or beheld His splendor. This was done only to confirm us in the faith, so that nothing can change it, and to reach a degree of certainty that will sustain us in these trying times of fierce persecution and absolute tyranny. (p. 104)

What is more, lack of belief in the veracity of the Sinai revelation is treated as a sign of not being a genuine descendant of those who participated in that event.

God has given assurance—He is an adequate guarantor—and informed them that not only did all the persons who were present at the Sinaitic revelation believe in the prophecy of Moses and in his Law, but that their descendants would likewise do so until the end of time. . . . Consequently, let everyone know who spurns the religion that was revealed at that theophany that he is not an offspring of the folk that witnessed it. (p. 103)

The certainty felt by the generation of Sinai is a permanent inheritance for their children. Jewish history is thus interpreted in terms of "the survival of the spiritually fittest"—the fittest being those who continue to believe in Mosaic prophecy. History purifies the community of foreign elements by exposing their lack of belief in the permanence of the Torah. Those who abandon the community in moments of crisis should not be considered as losses to the community, since their very decision to forsake Judaism shows them not to have been genuine members of the historical people of Israel. In taking this view, Maimonides was undoubtedly aware of talmudic precedents that ascribed character traits to those descended from the Sinai generation.

> No man who experiences shame (i.e., who is not callous and impudent in wrongdoing) will easily sin: and he who is not shamefaced—it is certain that his ancestors were not present at Mount Sinai.[8]

The sense of certainty inspired by the Sinai revelation, moreover, is justified by the unique way Mosaic prophecy was validated. Unlike other prophets and the founders of other religions, Moses did not rely on miracles to prove the genuineness of his prophecy.

> We do not give credence to the tenets of a miracle worker in the same way we trust in the truth of Moses our Teacher, nor does any analogy exist between them. (p. 113)

Indeed, Maimonides argues, the legitimacy of using miracles to authenticate prophetic claims logically presupposes the acceptance of Mosaic prophecy. Miracles can never serve as incontrovertible signs of an authentic prophet, since there are no reliable independent criteria for distinguishing between a genuine miracle and trickery. If miracles are nonetheless used to authenticate claims to prophecy, it is only because this procedure is legitimized in the Torah revealed at Sinai. We accept miracles in such cases for the same type of reasons (i.e., legal reasons) that we accept the testimony of witnesses in a court of law despite the possibility of lying.[9]

Unlike ordinary prophecy, Mosaic prophecy is corroborated by the participation of the entire community in the revelation at Sinai.[10]

> Inasmuch as we believe in Moses not because of his miracles, we are under no obligation to make comparisons between his miracles and those of others. Our everlastingly firm trust and steadfast faith in him is due to the fact that we as well as he heard the divine discourse at Sinai, as He states: *And they will trust you forever* [Exod. 19:9].
>   This event is analogous to the situation of two witnesses who observed a certain act simultaneously. Each of them saw what his fellow saw, and each of them is sure of the truth of his fellow's statement as well as of his own, and does not require proof or

demonstration, whereas other people, to whom they would report
their testimony, would not be absolutely convinced without confirmation or certification to everybody's satisfaction. Similarly,
we of the Jewish faith are convinced of the truth of the prophecy
of Moses, not simply because of his wonders, but because we,
like him, witnessed the theophany on Mount Sinai. (pp. 112–113)

Apart from answering challenges to the genuineness of Mosaic
prophecy, Maimonides had to counter the claim of rival monotheistic
faiths that the covenant with Israel, though binding during an earlier
period of history, had been abrogated in favor of a new covenant.
Consequently, Maimonides adds the notion of unconditionality to his
characterization of the Sinai covenant.

Similarly, He has avowed and assured us that it is unimaginable
that He will reject us entirely even if we disobey Him and disregard His behests, as He avers: *If the heavens above could be
measured, and the foundations of the earth below could be fathomed, only then would I reject all the offspring of Israel for all
that they have done—declares the Lord* [Jer. 31:37]. In fact, this
very promise was previously given through Moses our Teacher in
the Torah. It reads: *Yet, even then, when they are in the land of
their enemies, I will not reject or spurn them so as to destroy them,
annulling My covenant with them: for I the Lord am their God*
[Lev. 26:44]. (p. 102)

The covenant between God and Israel is not conditional on Israel's
merit. Failure to fulfill the commandments does not nullify God's eternal promise to His people. The community is thus fortified in the
knowledge that the fundamental framework of its relationship with God
is permanent and unchanging. Nothing short of another Sinai theophany could challenge Moses' authority as a prophet.

The source of hope in the *Epistle to Yemen* is the belief in the
eternal normative force of the Torah rather than the memory of the
miraculous liberation from Egypt.[11] Maimonides believed that in order
to survive the cruel vicissitudes of history, Jews must perennially reen-
act the dramatic story of Sinai so as to sustain their vital belief in the
validity of Mosaic prophecy and in the eternity of God's covenant with
Israel.

SUFFERING IN A MEANINGFUL CONTEXT

One of the dimensions of suffering that often makes it unbearable is
its arbitrariness. Suffering may involve not only physical pain, but also
the disorienting terror resulting from the sufferer's belief that he is the

victim of blind and irrational forces. A person can withstand this terrifying aspect of suffering if he is convinced of some underlying purpose that gives meaning and order to his world.

One way of achieving this is to locate a person's immediate experience within a broader framework, such as a grand plan or dramatic story spanning all of history. Maimonides does precisely this in the *Epistle to Yemen* by linking Israel's suffering to its being God's elect. The community's suffering is not the result of arbitrary factors, but rather is implicit in its very identity and faithfulness to the Sinai covenant. Maimonides redeems the community's suffering from its seeming arbitrariness and contingency by showing its relationship to the choice to remain committed to the Torah.

In this epistle, Maimonides concentrates on providing explanations of suffering that would support the community's strength to preserve. He does not mention *teshuvah* (repentance) or the relationship between suffering and repentance as he often does in his legal writings, because now his primary concern is to fortify the community against despair and disillusionment. Israel's suffering is interpreted as a heroic sacrifice in behalf of God. Like the *olah* sacrifice that is completely consumed by fire, Israel is wholly consumed because of its love for God and faithfulness to His covenant. It is in this context that Maimonides invokes the Song of Songs. Although elsewhere he makes this great love poem into an allegory of the philosophic love of God that is the highest goal of Judaism, here he interprets it as an allegory of Israel's unyielding commitment to God and Torah despite relentless persecution and suffering.[12]

Maimonides also strengthens the community's resolve to persevere by introducing the theme of God's explicit assurance that Israel will remain steadfast in its loyalty to the Torah throughout history. The phrase *trust you* [Moses] *ever after* (Exod. 19:9) is interpreted as an assurance of Israel's undying loyalty to the Torah of Moses throughout history. Whereas in his *Mishneh Torah* Maimonides had made the Sinai revelation a founding principle and a basis for legislative authority, in the *Epistle to Yemen* it becomes also a source of belief in Israel's ability to withstand its numerous enemies throughout history.[13]

Sinai creates a nation with a particular character. Apart from its doctrinal significance, this revelation inspires a people to uphold the Torah with courage and tenacity under all circumstances. Mosaic prophecy is thus confirmed by Israel's unwavering loyalty to the Torah in spite of the emergence of Islam and Christianity and in spite of the brutality of its enemies. Maimonides recalls in this context the biblical affirmation that the covenant concluded between God and Israel includes not only those who were actually present at the foot of the mountain of Sinai, but also those who were not present (i.e., later generations). Instead of treating this affirmation as merely a legal notion extending the authority of Torah to later generations, Maimonides transforms it into a divine promise that later generations will feel the same certainty and conviction as the generation that witnessed the public theophany at Sinai.[14]

In addressing the sufferer, one must be sensitive to the specific needs of the person in question. Because Maimonides is trying to comfort and encourage a suffering community, he uses multiple models and suggestions directed at the different types of people comprising his audience. Consequently, the epistle shifts from calls for heroic defiance to comforting words of encouragement and advice. As in the *Epistle on Martyrdom*, Maimonides encourages people to abandon their homes and possessions and flee to foreign lands in order to escape religious persecution. In the same breath, however, he comforts those who, for whatever reason, refuse to leave their homes by telling them that each and every halakhic act they perform is significant in the eyes of God. Even if forced to compromise and acquiesce in ignoble demands such as public apostasy, a Jew should continue to perform as many *mitzvot* as he can. Compromise does not vitiate the validity and value of however few *mitzvot* he feels capable of fulfilling.

In addition, Maimonides seeks to comfort the less heroic members of the community by assuring them that the end of their suffering is not far off. At the very outset of the epistle, he characterizes their present suffering as *ḥevlei mashiaḥ*, the birth pangs of the Messiah, implying that it is a sign of the approach of redemption.

> Indeed, our hearts are weakened, our minds are confused, and our strength wanes because of the dire misfortunes that have come upon us in the form of the religious persecution in the two ends of the world, the East and the West, *so they were in the midst of Israel, some on this side and some on the other side* [Josh. 8:22]. It is of the like of this dreadful occasion the prophet prayed and interceded in our behalf: *I said, "Oh, Lord God, refrain! How will Jacob survive? He is so small"* [Amos 7:5]. Indeed, this is a subject that no religious person dare take lightly, nor anyone put aside who believes faithfully in Moses. There is no doubt that these are the messianic travails concerning which the sages invoked God that they be spared seeing and experiencing them. The prophets trembled when they envisioned them, as Isaiah reacted: *My heart pants, fearfulness affrights me; the twilight I have longed for has been turned into trembling* [Isa 21:4]. And the divine exclamation in the Torah expresses sympathy with

those who will experience them, by saying: *Alas, who shall live when God does this!* [Num 24:23]. (pp. 95–96)

Maimonides repeatedly adduces evidence from Scripture to support the claim that what the community was undergoing was not a unique and unanticipated historical aberration, but rather was a part of a grand scheme of history known to the ancient prophets. Because Israel's suffering was a direct consequence of its election, the prophets predicted that future generations would suffer terrible persecutions. The *Epistle to Yemen* is filled with references to prophetic premonitions of the community's present circumstances. Maimonides thereby tries to make his readers aware of the prophets' empathic involvement with their suffering. Through listening to the prophetic anguish, the painful isolation and loneliness of the Jews of Yemen is in some way alleviated.

In addition, he cites numerous precedents from Jewish history of communities that underwent and survived similar persecutions. He refers, for example, to the period during the Second Commonwealth when Jews were compelled to profane the Sabbath, abstain from practicing circumcision, and write upon their garments: "I do not have a portion in the Lord God of Israel." Many scholars have questioned the source of Maimonides' claim that this persecution lasted fifty-two years.[15] From the context, however, it seems clear that Maimonides mentioned a definite length of time in order to reinforce the rabbinic observation that "persecutions are of short duration." Such observations could have an important impact on the minds of his readers by encouraging them to persevere just a short while longer.

As if to counteract the sufferer's feeling that his condition is permanent and hopeless, Maimonides refers to the changing fortunes of Jewish history. Periods of darkness were succeeded by periods of prosperity and cultural flourishing. At the same time, however, he tempers his message of hope with caution. While belief in the possibility of change would clearly have a salutary effect on the community's attitude toward its condition, the belief that its suffering heralded the coming of the Messiah could have dangerous consequences. Maimonides realized that by introducing the concept of *hevlei mashiah* he risked opening up a Pandora's box of historical fantasies and reckless behavior.

Maimonides mentions the community's interest in Saadiah's computations and the excitement surrounding other predictions concerning the *ketz*, the commencement of the end of days. While he understands the reasons behind the interest in messianic speculations, his attitude on this issue is ambivalent and cautionary. On the one hand he states that "no human being will ever be able to determine it [the date of redemption] precisely, as Daniel has intimated: *For the words are secret and sealed*." On the other hand, however, he intimates—by this and other statements from Daniel—that the date of redemption is fixed and predetermined. The analogy he draws between the uncertainty that prevailed prior to Moses with respect to the date of the liberation from Egypt and the unpredictability of the date of the final redemption suggests that, like the period of enslavement in Egypt, the period of exile prior to the advent of the Messiah is of a fixed but incompletely known duration.

Maimonides shifts back and forth between intimating that the outbreak of the messianic redemption is imminent and cautioning the community against acting recklessly on the basis of such expectations. While he mentions the birth pangs of the Messiah and refers repeatedly to the apocalyptic book of Daniel, he warns against turning belief in the promised end into a program of political action.

> Remember that even the date of the termination of the Egyptian exile was not precisely known and gave rise to differences of opinion. Although God fixed its duration in Scripture, where He says: *And they shall be enslaved and oppressed four hundred years* [Gen. 15:13], some reckoned the period of four hundred years from the time of Jacob's arrival in Egypt, others dated it from the beginning of Israel's bondage, which happened seventy years later, and still others computed it from the time of the Covenant of the Pieces when this matter was divinely predicted to Abraham. At the expiration of four hundred years after this event, and thirty years before the appearance of Moses, a band of Israelites left Egypt because they believed that their exile had ended. The Egyptians slew and destroyed them, and the subjugation of the Israelites who remained was consequently aggravated, as we learn from our sages, the teachers of our national traditions. David, in fact, alluded to the vanquished Israelites who miscalculated the date of the redemption in the verse: *The Ephraimite bowmen turned back in the day of battle* [Ps. 78:9]. (p. 115)

The promised four-hundred-year period of enslavement was indeed the duration of Israel's bondage in Egypt. Yet, prior to Moses' appearance as the great liberator, no one could ascertain the starting point of the four-hundred-year period. All attempts at translating the promised liberation into a program of political action, like the premature uprising of the tribe of Ephraim, resulted in catastrophe and aggravated the nation's already terrible condition.

The implications of this account of the events preceding the liberation from Egypt were clearly relevant to the situation of the community
in Yemen.

> . . . Now if such uncertainty prevailed in regard to the date of
> emancipation from the Egyptian bondage, the term of which was
> fixed, it is much more so with respect to the date of the final
> redemption, the prolonged and protracted duration of which ap-
> palled and dismayed our inspired seers. (pp. 115–116)

The promise of redemption that Maimonides imparts to his audience
conveys a sense of immediacy coupled with a warning to desist from
action. Belief in a predetermined scheme of redemption is a legitimate
basis of hope, but not of political action. On the one hand, Maimonides
adduces a host of facts to support the contention that the community
in Yemen was in fact living in premessianic times.

> . . . The hour of his [the Messiah's] arrival will be at a time of
> great catastrophe and dire misfortune for Israel, as was predicted
> in the verse: *And neither bond nor free is left* [Deut. 32:36]. Then
> God will bring him forth and he will fulfill the promises made in
> his behalf. A later prophet too was alluding to the messianic
> tribulations when he declared: *But who can endure the day of his
> coming?* [Mal. 3:2]. This is the proper belief that one must hold.
> From the prophecies of Daniel and Isaiah and from the state-
> ments of our sages it is clear that the advent of the Messiah will
> take place some time subsequent to the universal expansion of
> the Roman and Arab empires, which is an actuality today. This
> fact is true beyond question or doubt. (p. 121)

Yet, while pointing to such compelling signs of the messianic fulfillment, he immediately adds that "the precise date of the messianic
advent cannot be known."

Toward the conclusion of the epistle, Maimonides mentions a further
sign of the coming, namely, the proliferation of messianic pretenders,
and again he quickly adds words of caution.

> The prophets have predicted and instructed us, as I have told
> you, that pretenders and simulators will appear in great numbers
> at the time when the advent of the true Messiah will draw nigh,
> but they will not be able to make good their claim. They will
> perish with many of their partisans. Solomon of blessed memory,
> inspired by the Holy Spirit, foresaw that the prolonged duration
> of the exile would incite some of our people to seek to terminate

it before the appointed time, and as a consequence they would
perish or meet with disaster. Therefore he admonished them and
adjured them in metaphorical language to desist, as we read: *I
adjure you, O maidens of Jerusalem, by gazelles or by hinds of
the field: do not to wake or rouse love until it please* [Song of Songs
2:7]. Now, brethren and friends, abide by the oath, and stir not
up love until it pleases. (p. 130)

In quoting the latter passage from the Song of Songs, Maimonides
alludes to the following talmudic passage:

What was the purpose of those three adjurations [Song of Songs
2:7, 3:5, 5:8]? One, that Israel shall not go up [all together as
if surrounded] by a wall; the second, that whereby the Holy One,
blessed be He, adjured Israel that they shall not rebel against
the nations of the world; and the third is that whereby the Holy
One, blessed be He, adjured the idolators that they shall not
oppress Israel too much. (BT Ketubbot 111a)

Despite the disgrace and oppression suffered at the hands of their
enemies, the people of Israel are sworn to silence and forbearance.

Although we are dishonored by them beyond human endurance,
and have to put up with their fabrications, we yet behave like
him of whom the prophet said: *But I am like a deaf man, unhearing, like a dumb man who cannot speak up* [Ps. 38:14].
Similarly, our sages instructed us to bear the prevarications and
lies of Ishmael in silence. They found it in a cryptic allusion to
this attitude in the names of his sons, Mishma, Dumah, and
Massa, which have been interpreted to mean *listen, be silent,* and
endure. We have acquiesced, both young and old, to inure ourselves to humiliation, as Isaiah instructed us: *I offered my back
to the floggers, and my cheeks to those who tore out my hair* [Isa.
50:6]. All this notwithstanding, we do not escape this continued
maltreatment and pressure, which well-nigh crush us. No matter
how much we suffer and elect to remain at peace with them, they
stir up strife and sedition, as David describes: *I am all peace;
but when I speak, they are for war* [Ps. 120:7]. Most certainly
therefore if we start trouble, and claim power from them absurdly
and preposterously, we surely give ourselves up to destruction.
(p. 127)

Israel's response to persecution must be expressed in dignified restraint and hope for the promised redemption. While the consequences
of such forbearance are continued suffering and degradation, the con-

sequences of active revolt are far worse. The theology of redemption implicit in the liberation from Egypt justifies hope and perseverence; it may not be translated into a political manifesto calling for immediate action.

Notwithstanding his words of caution, Maimonides offers the community many reasons for believing that the end to its suffering was near. Israel's very suffering points to redemption. Also many of the prevalent conditions of history seem to correspond to events that, according to tradition, signal the advent of the messianic redemption. While certainty as to the date of redemption is impossible, Israel's terrible suffering, the appearance of messianic pretenders, the emergence of the Arabic empire, and other events alluded to in the book of Daniel—all these signs reinforce the belief that the final redemption is ever so close.

As if not content with the imprecision of such proofs that messianic times were approaching, Maimonides goes a step further and divulges a secret "extraordinary tradition" that comes as close as possible to being a precise prediction of the onset of the messianic era. The tradition that Maimonides received from his father "who in turn received it from his father, going back to our early ancestors who were exiled from Jerusalem," sets the time of the return of prophecy at 1210 C.E., roughly forty-five years from the time he wrote the epistle.[16]

Lest one object that this tradition predicts merely the return of prophecy and not the commencement of the messianic era, Maimonides adds,

> It is doubtless true that the reappearance of prophecy in Israel is one of the signs betokening the approach of the messianic era, as is stated: *After that I will pour out My spirit upon all flesh; your sons and daughters shall prophesy* . . . [Joel 3:1]. This is the most reliable tradition concerning the advent of the Messiah. I call it reliable, although I have admonished against it, and strictly prohibited blazoning it abroad, lest some people deem it unduly postponed. I have already apprised you concerning it, but God best knows what is true. (pp. 122–123)

The claim that the return of prophecy betokens the commencement of the messianic era is related to the fact that in the *Epistle to Yemen* the Messiah is portrayed as a prophetic figure. By describing the Messiah as a great prophet ("The Messiah indeed ranks above all prophets after Moses in eminence and distinction") Maimonides in effect neutralizes the appeal of messianic pretenders who could not but lack the extraordinary characteristics of the true Messiah.

The description of the messianic figure in the *Epistle to Yemen* serves as a paradigm by which to evaluate critically the claims of false Messiahs. First, the Messiah must perform miracles that prove beyond any shadow of doubt that he is the true Messiah.

> What the great powers are that all the prophets from Moses to Malachi ascribe to the Messiah may be inferred from various statements in the twenty-four books of Scripture. The most significant of them is that the report of his advent will strike terror into the hearts of all the kings of the earth, and their kingdoms will fall; neither will they be able to war or revolt against him. They will neither defame nor calumniate him, for the miracles he will perform will frighten them into complete silence. (p. 125)

Second, the Messiah must possess great wisdom and knowledge. Maimonides castigates the rabbi addressed in the epistle for not dismissing out of hand the claim of a certain messianic pretender by virtue of his ignorance.

> But I am astonished that you, a scholar who has carefully studied the doctrine of the rabbis, are inclined to repose faith in him. Do you not know, my brother, that the Messiah is a very eminent prophet, more illustrious than all the prophets after Moses? . . .
> Now if we dare not put trust in a man's pretensions to prophecy if he does not excel in wisdom, how much less must we take seriously the claims of an ignoramus that he is the Messiah. (pp. 123–124)

Furthermore, the Messiah must first appear in the land of Israel and not in Yemen or other places in the Diaspora.

> After his manifestation in Palestine, Israel will be gathered in Jerusalem and the other cities of Palestine. Then the tidings will spread to the East and to the West until it will reach Yemen and those beyond you in India, as we learn from Isaiah: *Go, swift messengers, to a nation far and remote, to a people thrust forth and away. . . which sends out envoys by sea, in papyrus vessels upon the water* [Isa. 18:2]. The redemption will not be reversed so that it will appear in distant lands first, and ultimately reach Palestine. (p. 125)

Although the readers of the epistle are told to expect the Messiah's arrival in the near future, they are presented with a description of the messianic figure that destroys the credibility of existing messianic pretenders. Maimonides once again drives a wedge between hopeful expectancy of the Messiah and political behavior predicated on such hope. While building up the community's hope in the approaching return of prophecy and by implication in the advent of the true Messiah, Maimonides protects the community against being duped by charismatic messianic pretenders by portraying the Messiah as an idealized prophetic figure.

MESSIANISM IN THE WORKS OF MAIMONIDES

Maimonides' approach to messianism in the *Epistle to Yemen* is closely linked to a predeterministic and necessitarian concept of history, unlike his treatment of messianism in particular and history in general in other works. This difference further confirms the thesis that the *Epistle to Yemen* reflects the particular audience that Maimonides was addressing.

In contrast to this thesis, Amos Funkenstein's article "Maimonides' Political Theory and Realistic Messianism" uses the *Epistle to Yemen* as a frame of reference for understanding Maimonides' overall philosophy of history.[17] Funkenstein states explicitly: "We shall rather treat all of Maimonides' assertions in the matter as part of one comprehensive theory."[18] In this connection, he cites the theory of the "divine ruse" that Maimonides used in the *Guide of the Perplexed* to explain why the Torah contains many commandments whose rational basis is not evident at first sight. Their purpose, according to the *Guide*, was to wean the original Israelite community away from idolatrous worship. God knew that the Sinai generation would not accept a radical break with the religious practices of the time. He therefore adapted those practices to the worship of Himself, with the intention of leading the community on to higher forms of worship gradually in the course of history. Funkenstein discerns a similar historical "divine ruse" in the *Epistle to Yemen:* just as God used existing forms of worship as means to further the realization of higher forms of worship, God promotes the emergence of Christianity and Islam as vehicles for preparing the world for the eventual triumph of monotheism in the form of Judaism.[19]

Given Maimonides' rejection of the eternal rule of necessity as an explanatory principle in natural science and metaphysics and his consequent commitment to a type of indeterminacy in being, he was able, according to Funkenstein, to subscribe to a theory of history that was in certain respects similar to Hegel's notion of the cunning of reason.

> Just as Hegel's "objektiver Geist" uses the subjective, egotistic freedom of man to further the objective goals of history (for otherwise history would cease to be "Fortschritt im Bewusstsein der

Freiheit"), so also Maimonides' God fights polytheism with its
own weapons and uses elements of its worship as a fruitful deceit.
Maimonides spoke of the "cunning of God" (" 'ormat hasem ute-
bunato; talattuf fi'allahu") where Hegel will speak of the "cunning
of reason" ("List der Vernunft"). . . . Maimonides, as all other
medieval versions of the divine economy, allows at best a relative
autonomy to the collective evolution of man. [20]

Without going into the reasons why this analogy between Maimonides and Hegel is questionable,[21] an attempt will be made to show
that the *Epistle to Yemen* cannot be treated as a paradigm of Maimonides' theory of messianism or history. Maimonides did not espouse a
comprehensive theory of history. On the contrary, a careful analysis
of the *Guide of the Perplexed* would show that a predeterministic theory
of history based on the notions of divine cunning and an end to history
is foreign to Maimonidean thought.[22] Such an analysis, however, is
beyond the scope of this discussion, which is restricted to the dispar-
ities between Maimonides' theory of messianism and of human autonomy as presented in the *Epistle to Yemen* and his treatment of the same
themes in his commentary to the tenth chapter of Sanhedrin (*Ḥelek*)
and in sections of the *Mishneh Torah*. It will be seen that Maimonides
argues differently depending on whether he writes within a context of
suffering or whether he writes in order to move his audience toward a
higher level of worship of God.

MESSIANISM IN *ḤELEK*

The central issue Maimonides deals with in *Ḥelek* is that of the meaning
and purpose of commitment to the Torah. At the very beginning of
Ḥelek, he points to a general confusion regarding the true purpose of
fulfilling the commandments.

> I have thought fit to speak here concerning many principles be-
> longing to fundamental articles of faith which are of very great
> importance. Know that the theologians are divided in opinion as
> to the good which man reaps from the performance of these pre-
> cepts which God enjoined upon us by the hand of Moses our
> teacher; and that they also differ among themselves with regard
> to the evil which will overtake us if we transgress them. Their
> differences on these questions are very great and in proportion
> to the differences between their respective intellects. As a con-
> sequence, people's opinions have fallen into such great confusion
> that you can scarcely in any way find any one possessing clear
> and certain ideas on this subject; neither can you alight upon
> any portion of it which has been transmitted to any person without
> abundant error.[23]

He then proceeds to discuss various classes of thinkers who base their eschatological expectations on literal interpretations of biblical and rabbinic texts. One class "holds that the hoped-for good will be the Garden of Eden, a place where people eat and drink without toil or faintness." They imagine "houses of costly stones . . . couches of silk and rivers flowing with wine and perfumed oil."

A second class

> . . . firmly believes and imagines that the hoped-for good will be the days of the Messiah . . . They think that when that time comes all men will be kings for ever. Their bodily frames will be mighty and they will inhabit the whole earth unto eternity. According to their imagination, that Messiah will live as long as the Creator . . . and at that epoch the earth will bring forth garments ready woven and bread ready baked, and many other impossible things like these.

A third class believes that the ultimate good is the resurrection of the dead: "that man will live after his death; that in the company of his family and relatives he will once again eat and drink and never more die."

A fourth class consists of those who believe that

> the good which we shall reap from obedience to the Law will consist in the repose of the body and the attainment in this world of all worldly wishes, as, for example, the fertility of lands, abundant wealth, abundance of children, long life, bodily health and security, enjoying the sway of a king, and prevailing over the oppressor.[24]

The common feature of all these views is their focusing on material gratification as the ultimate goal of religious observance. The popular notion of messianism was but one instance of this preoccupation with gratifying one's need for power, wealth, or sensual pleasure. It was a collective fantasy born of repression and deprivation.

Maimonides then states that the ultimate purpose of the Torah, ignored by all the aforementioned views, is the world to come, i.e., the immortality of the soul. As shown in the analysis of the *Essay on Resurrection*, the world to come, *olam ha-ba*, was for him the embodiment of the ideals of knowledge and love of God, since then the soul will eternally know and love God.

Maimonides' goal in *Ḥelek* was to reeducate the community to regard disinterested worship of God as the ultimate goal of Judaism. To achieve this, he had to break the hold of literalism on the minds of the majority of the community. In order to convince them that knowledge and love of God for their own sakes constituted the ultimate purpose of the commandments, he offered his readers a new perspective on the material benefits promised in the Bible and rabbinic literature. After elaborating on the meaning of the world to come and of worship for its own sake (li-shmah), Maimonides explains the biblical promises of material rewards as follows:

> As regards the promises and threats alluded to in the Torah, their interpretation is that which I shall now tell you. It says to you, "If you obey these precepts, I will help you to a further obedience of them and perfection in the performance of them. And I shall remove all hindrances from you." For it is impossible for man to do the service of God when sick or hungry or thirsty or in trouble, and this is why the Torah promises the removal of all these disabilities and gives man also the promise of health and quietude until such a time as he shall have attained perfection of knowledge and be worthy of the life of the world to come. The final aim of the Torah is not that the earth should be fertile, that people should live long, and that bodies should be healthy. It simply helps us to the performance of its precepts by holding out the promise of all these things.[25]

Maimonides tried to accomplish two tasks in Helek. First and foremost, he sought to alter the community's attitude to Judaism by making disinterested worship—knowledge and love of God—the ultimate goal. He tried to make olam ha-ba the highest good in the hierarchy of "rewards" that Judaism promises to its adherents and to make all other goods, including those of the messianic age, subservient to it. He therefore ascribes instrumental value to messianism. Messianism offers a community conditions that free its members of mundane worries and distractions so that they can devote themselves to the single-minded pursuit of knowledge of God.

> The days of the Messiah are not ardently longed for on account of the plentiful vegetation, and the riches which they will bring in their train, nor in order that we may ride on horses, nor that we may drink to the accompaniment of various kinds of musical instruments, as is thought by those people who are confused in their ideas on such things. No! the prophets and saints wished and ardently desired [the days of the Messiah] because it implies the coming together of the virtuous, with choice deeds of goodness and knowledge, and the justice of the king, the greatness of his wisdom and his nearness to his Creator, as it is said: "The Lord said unto me, thou art my son; this day have I begotten

thee." And because it implies obedience to all the laws of Moses, without ennui or disquietude or constraint, as it is promised in the words, "And they shall teach no more every man his neighbour and every man his brother saying, Know the Lord; for they shall all know me from the least of them unto the greatest of them." "And I will take away the stony heart from your flesh." And there are many more similar verses on like themes.

It is under conditions like these that one will obtain a firm hold upon the world to come. The final goal is the attaining to the world to come, and it is to it that the effort must be directed.[26]

Second, he strove to neutralize religious fantasy. He tried to counteract the exaggerated expectations fostered by biblical and midrashic literature and naturalize the concept of messianism by interpreting it in terms of the regular patterns of nature. Wherever possible, he made the content of messianic beliefs consistent with the order of nature by allegorizing prophetic and rabbinic statements that in their literal sense placed messianism beyond the natural order.

Maimonides states expressly that the Messiah himself will be mortal and that the longevity that people will enjoy in the messianic era will be a perfectly natural consequence of the conditions that will then obtain.

But the Messiah will die, and his son and son's son will reign in his stead. God has clearly declared his death in the words, "He shall not fail nor be discouraged, till he have set judgment in the earth." His kingdom will endure a very long time and the lives of men will be long also, because longevity is a consequence of the removal of sorrows and cares. Let not the fact of the duration of his kingdom for thousands of years seem strange to you, for the sages have said that when a number of good things come together it is not an easy thing for them to separate again.[27]

The length of days that people will enjoy during the messianic era need not imply a miraculous change in the natural order. When human society is free of violence, when people are not burdened psychologically by anxieties resulting from scarcity and the struggle for survival, and when people become conscious of their true human purpose, i.e., to know God, then that society will be stable and ordered and its members will enjoy lengthy and satisfying lives.

Although in *Ḥelek* Maimonides naturalized the messianic era to a great extent, he did not altogether allegorize the powers traditionally ascribed to the messianic figure.

His [the Messiah's] name will be great and fill the earth to its uttermost bounds. It will be a greater name than that of King Solomon and mightier. The nations will make peace with him and lands will obey him by reason of his great rectitude and the wonders that will come to light by his means. Any one that rises up against him God will destroy and make him fall into his hand.[28]

Maimonides is vague with respect to the "wonders that will come to light by his means." Although he alludes to this miraculous aspect of the Messiah's influence over the nations of the world, he immediately adds:

So far as existing things are concerned there will be no difference whatever between now and then, except that Israel will possess the kingdom. And this is the sense of the rabbis' statement: "There is no difference between this world and the days of the Messiah except the subjugation of the kingdoms alone." In his days there will be both the strong and the weak in their relations to others. But verily in those days the gaining of their livelihood will be so very easy to men that they will do the lightest possible labor and reap great benefit. It is this that is meant by the remark of the rabbis, "The land of Israel will one day produce cakes ready baked, and garments of fine silk." For when one finds a thing easily and without labor, people are in the habit of saying, "So and so found bread ready baked, and a meal ready cooked."[29]

The net result of the argument presented in *Ḥelek* is that the messianic age is not the ultimate good promised by Judaism, but rather an instrument serving the true purpose of the commandments: the world to come. The latter is to be attained through worship of God grounded in love and not in fear of punishment or anticipation of reward, a level of worship to which it will be easier for the people to rise in the messianic age. Messianism is thus a worthwhile inspiration insofar as it enables man to realize his nature. By emptying messianism of miraculous connotations as much as he could and by reevaluating its importance in terms of the true end of Judaism, Maimonides sought to alter the community's orientation to Judaism by setting knowlege and disinterested worship of God at the center of their religious world view.

MESSIANISM IN THE *MISHNEH TORAH*

Hilkhot Teshuvah   The final chapters of *Hilkhot Teshuvah* have some relevance to the theme of messianism, starting with a brief reference in chapter seven. The context is a forceful description of the importance of *teshuvah*, repentance. "Since every human being . . . has free will," writes Maimonides, "a person should strive to repent." Everyone should imagine that death is imminent and thus be impelled to repent immediately. *Teshuvah* is not restricted to actions, but includes character traits and dispositions that are often graver and more resistant to change than sinful acts; it involves the transformation of a total personality. A person who does *teshuvah* is not inferior to a person who never sinned: "The sages say: 'Where penitents stand, the completely righteous cannot stand' " (BT Berakhot 34b).

In the midst of this elaboration on the value and urgency of *teshuvah*, Maimonides adduces the biblical calls for repentance.

> All the prophets charged the people concerning repentance. Only through repentance will Israel be redeemed, and the Torah already offered the assurance that Israel will, in the closing period of his exile, finally repent and thereupon be immediately redeemed. (*MT Hilkhot Teshuvah* 7:5)

The chapter then continues with an impassioned description of the power of *teshuvah* to restore a person from being abhorred and estranged from God to being "beloved, desirable, near to God, a friend."

The force of this chapter is clearly persuasive, to inspire and rouse people to appreciate the importance of *teshuvah*. It would therefore be mistaken to infer from Maimonides' brief remark on the divine promise that in the end of its exile Israel will repent and thereupon be redeemed, that Maimonides held an eschatological view of history or, as Gershom Scholem claims, that he believed that: "It is not Israel's repentance which brings about the redemption; rather because the eruption of redemption is to occur by divine decree, at the last moment there also erupts a movement of repentance in Israel itself."[30] The dominant focus of this chapter is upon the individual's everyday struggle with the destructive influence of sin and the possibilities for personal renewal through *teshuvah*. Maimonides is not here dealing independently with the theme of Israel's historical redemption. In the midst of his impassioned description of the greatness of *teshuvah* for the individual sinner, he invokes the prophetic call to *teshuvah* and the inseparable connection between redemption and repentance. In invoking the authority of the Torah and the prophets, he reinforces his exhortation to personal repentance.

In the eighth chapter, Maimonides states that life in the world to come is the ultimate goal of Judaism. Then the soul will exist forever in an immaterial state. Since it is rather material rewards and punishments that are emphasized in the biblical promises, the ninth chapter explains that such promises are only a means of encouraging people to achieve the ultimate goal. In chapter ten, Maimonides discusses the notions of love and fear of God and concludes the "Book of Knowledge" with what might be considered its central motif: "One only loves God with the knowledge with which one knows Him. According to the knowledge, will be the love."

In the discussions of these three chapters, the context in which the theme of messianism is introduced is the ninth chapter, where Maimonides is seeking to show that the material rewards promised in the Torah are of instrumental value alone. Accordingly, the purpose ascribed to the messianic age is basically the same as in *Ḥelek:* to make it easier for the people to know and love God.

> Hence all Israelites, their prophets and sages, longed for the advent of messianic times, that they might have relief from the wicked tyranny that does not permit them properly to occupy themselves with the study of the Torah and the observance of the commandments; that they might have ease, devote themselves to getting wisdom, and thus attain to life in the world to come. For in those days, knowledge, wisdom and truth will increase, as it is said, *For the earth will be full of the knowledge of the Lord* [Isa. 11:9], and it is said, *They will no more teach everyone his brother and everyone his neighbor* [Jer. 31:34], and further, *I will remove the heart of stone from your flesh* [Ezek. 36:26].
>
> Because the king who will arise from the seed of David will possess more wisdom than Solomon and will be a great prophet, approaching Moses, our teacher, he will teach the whole of the Jewish people and instruct them in the way of God; and all nations will come to hear him, as it is said, *And at the end of days it shall come to pass that the Mount of the Lord's house shall be established as the top of the mountains* [Mic. 4:1, Isa. 2:2]. (*MT Hilkhot Teshuvah* 9:8–10)

Maimonides does not mention the terror that the Messiah will strike into the hearts of the nations of the world, as he does in the *Epistle to Yemen*. Nor does he mention the Messiah's producing great miracles, as he does in *Ḥelek* as well as the epistle. Because this treatment of messianism is aimed at showing its instrumental value, Maimonides stresses the teaching role of the messianic figure. Rather than being terrified by his miracles, the nations of the world will be drawn to him by virtue of his great wisdom: "all nations will come to hear him."

The main point is thus that whenever material well-being is promised or hoped for in Judaism, it is not regarded as an end in itself, but rather as a means for furthering knowledge and love of God. Messianic times are desired because the conditions that will obtain then will be conducive to becoming worthy of life in the world to come. It is realism and not materialism that accounts for Judaism's concern for material well-being; human beings cannot devote themselves to the pursuit of knowledge or disinterested worship of God when they are overburdened with physical and psychological concerns.

One may conclude, therefore, that Maimonides' description of the Messiah in the ninth chapter was dictated by the central theme of chapters eight through ten. Rather than expound a theory of messianism as such, Maimonides states only its relationship to the ultimate purpose of Judaism.

"Kings and Wars"   Maimonides' most elaborate treatment of messianism is in "Kings and Wars," a part of the "Book of Judges." He devotes two entire chapters to a detailed description of the messianic figure and his basic task: the establishment of a society conducive to the attainment of "an understanding of their Creator to the utmost capacity of the human mind." The only miraculous power ascribed to the Messiah is that, by virtue of possessing *ruah ha-kodesh*, the Holy Spirit, he will be able to determine who among the descendants of the tribe of Levi are priests and who are ordinary Levites. Then the temple can be rebuilt and the sacrificial cult reinstituted. The miraculous aspect of the messianic figure is thus confined to an internal halakhic requirement, namely, the determination of the members of the priestly class for the sake of restoring a traditional Jewish kingdom. The contrast with the external focus of the miraculous powers ascribed to the Messiah in the *Epistle to Yemen* is striking: there the Messiah's miracles are directed at terrifying and subduing the nations of the world.

In order to place Maimonides' description of the messianic figure in "Kings and Wars" in its proper perspective, one must consider the implications of his treatment of the Messiah as a king figure. Although only the two final chapters of "Kings and Wars" deal exclusively with the messianic period, the preceeding ten contain features that bear upon the Messiah's role as a king. Already in the first chapter, Maimonides distinguishes between kings of the House of David and those selected from the rest of Israel, e.g., "the kings of the House of David will endure forever" (1:9). This distinction underlies the halakhic requirement that *melekh ha-mashiah*, the king Messiah, be a descendant of David.

Whether or not the king is Davidic, his primary functions are both temporal and spiritual. He must provide social and political stability and security, but also establish the sovereignty of the Torah over his entire kingdom. Because he is an instrument for extending the rule of

the Torah, he may not use his power for the sake of personal aggrandizement. This limitation on the king's accumulation of wealth and
power is a recurrent theme in Maimonides' discussion of monarchy.[31]
While according the king considerable freedom in using the power
at his disposal, Maimonides tries to set limits to his use of that power
by educating the king to view himself as a messenger of God sent to
establish a community spiritually committed to the way of the Torah.

> Just as Scripture accords great honor to the king and bids all pay
> him honor, so it bids him cultivate a humble and lowly spirit, as
> it is written: *And my heart is humbled within me* [Ps. 109:22].
> He must not exercise his authority in a supercilious manner, as
> it is said: *that his heart be not lifted up above his brethren* [Deut.
> 17:20]. He should deal graciously and compassionately with the
> small and the great, conduct their affairs in their best interests,
> be wary of the honor of even the lowliest. When he addresses
> the public collectively, he shall use gentle language, as did David
> when he said: *Hear me, my brethren, and my people* [1 Chron.
> 28:2]. It is also written: *If thou wilt be a servant unto this people
> this day . . . then they will be thy servants forever* [1 Kings 12:7].
> At all times, his conduct should be marked by a spirit of great
> humility. None was greater than Moses, our teacher; yet he said:
> *And what are we? Your murmurings are not against us* [Exod.
> 16:8]. He should put up with the cumbrances, burdens, grum-
> blings, and anger of the people as a nursing father puts up with
> a suckling child. The Bible styles the king "shepherd," [as it is
> written] *to be shepherd over Jacob His people* [Ps. 78:71]. The
> way in which a shepherd acts is explicitly stated in the prophetic
> text: *Even as a shepherd that feedeth his flock, that gathereth the
> lambs in his arms, and carrieth them in his bosom and gently
> leadeth those that give suck* [Isa. 40:11]. ("Kings and Wars" 2:6)

In the fourth chapter, Maimonides discusses the king's right to levy
taxes, to conscript an army and wage war, to take wives and concubines
from among the captives, to confiscate property, and so on. The Messiah, he adds, will have a further prerogative.

> The king Messiah will receive one-thirteenth of all the provinces
> to be conquered by Israel. This is the share that will be assigned
> to him and his descendants forever. ("Kings and Wars" 4:8)

The chapter then continues with other laws pertaining to kings in
general. The incidental mention of the Messiah in the midst of a
chapter on the prerogatives of any ruling monarch indicates that the
concept of Messiah is but one form of the general halakhic concept of

kingship. While the king Messiah has special rights and privileges, he is nonetheless a member of the halakhically defined class of kings.[32]
The fifth chapter deals with the legal status of the wars waged by the king. A war is said to be "obligatory" (milḥemet mitzvah) if it is waged against Amalek, or against the seven nations inhabiting the Promised Land in the time of Moses, or if it is waged in order to deliver Israel from attacking enemies. The king may also engage in an "optional war" (milḥemet reshut) in order to "extend the borders of Israel and to enhance his greatness and prestige." According to the sixth chapter, the following condition pertains to all declarations of war:

> No war is declared against any nation before peace offers are made to it. This obtains both in an optional war and a war for a religious cause. . . . If the inhabitants make peace and accept the seven commandments enjoined upon the descendants of Noah, none of them is slain. . . . ("Kings and Wars" 6:1)

The Rabad questioned Maimonides' requirement that the seven commandments of Noah (the fundamental principles incumbent upon all human beings according to Halakhah) be imposed upon nations as a result of an optional war waged beyond the immediate borders of Israel.[33] Whatever the sources of Maimonides' decision, his extending the imposition of the Noahidic commandment to optional wars shows that he regarded the promotion of monotheism as a universal norm. The Noahidic commandments, which prohibit idolatry and enjoin certain fundamental norms of social justice, comprised what Maimonides believed to be the essential conditions necessary for a universal monotheistic world order. The obligation to enforce them was unconditional and thus could not be confined to the geographical borders of Israel and its surroundings.[34]
In the ninth chapter, Maimonides expounds his understanding of the twofold framework of norms—the Torah and the seven commandments of Noah—that must govern a monotheistic kingdom under Judaism.

> Moses, our teacher, bequeathed the law and commandments to Israel, as it is said: an inheritance of the congregation of Jacob [Deut. 33:4], and to those of other nations who are willing to be converted [to Judaism], as it is said: One Law and one ordinance shall be both for you, and for the resident alien [Num. 15:16]. But no coercion to accept the Law and commandments is practiced on those who are unwilling to do so. Moreover Moses, our teacher, was commanded by God to compel all human beings to

accept the commandments enjoined upon the descendants of Noah. Anyone who does not accept them is put to death. ("Kings and Wars" 8:10)

Mosaic prophecy not only enjoins a code of laws upon a particular community but also obligates that community to rid the entire world of idolatry and to establish the universal sovereignty of God as mediated through Moses and Israel. There is possibly a polemical aspect to this position insofar as it recognizes only Sinaitic revelation as the exclusive source for validating obedience to the Noahidic laws.[35]

A heathen who accepts the seven commandments and observes them scrupulously is a "righteous heathen," and will have a portion in the world to come, provided that he accepts them and performs them because the Holy One, blessed be He, commanded them in the Law and made known through Moses, our teacher, that the observance thereof had been enjoined upon the descendants of Noah even before the Law was given. But if his observance thereof is based upon a reasoned conclusion he is not deemed a resident alien, or one of the pious of the gentiles, but one of their wise men. ("Kings and Wars" 8:11)

We turn now to Maimonides' description of the king Messiah in the eleventh and twelfth chapters of "Kings and Wars." Messianism is here placed within the framework of the general concept of kingship expounded in the previous chapters. While it is the task of every Jewish king to promote the rule of the Torah within the borders of Israel and the Noahidic commandments among the gentiles, the messianic age will be characterized by the complete achievement of those goals. Just as Maimonides earlier cautioned the king against misusing his power, so too does he caution the community against viewing that age in self-serving material terms alone.

The sages and prophets did not long for the days of the Messiah that Israel might exercise dominion over the world, or rule over the heathens, or be exalted by the nations, or that it might eat and drink and rejoice. Their aspiration was that Israel be free to devote itself to the Law and its wisdom, with no one to oppress or disturb it, and thus be worthy of life in the world to come.
In that era, there will be neither famine nor war, neither jealousy nor strife. Blessings will be abundant, comforts within the reach of all. The one preoccupation of the whole world will be to know the Lord. Hence Israelites will be very wise, they will know the things that are now concealed and will attain an understanding of their Creator to the utmost capacity of the human

mind, as it is written: *For the earth shall be full of the knowledge of the Lord, as the waters cover the sea* [Isa. 11:9]. ("Kings and Wars" 12:4–5)

By attaching a transcendent purpose to the community's dream for national rebirth, Maimonides in effect undermines the legitimacy of triumphal nationalism. He neutralizes the natural longing for wealth, power, and supremacy over other nations by making the self-transcending ideal of knowledge of God the focal point of messianic hope. As love on the individual level signifies a person's ability to transcend egocentric drives and interests, so messianism on the national level signifies a people's ability to transcend collective egotism by establishing a society conducive to the unfolding of a person's human essence through the knowledge and love of God.[36]

Maimonides allows for the possibility that new Jewish kings may arise in the land of Israel before the coming of the Messiah himself. The Messiah is thus not pictured as a prophetic figure performing spectacular miracles as in the *Epistle to Yemen*, but rather as one among a series of kings who will follow him and perhaps also precede him. What distinguishes him is his success in restoring Jewish national life in all its aspects and abolishing idolatry throughout the world.

The king Messiah will arise and restore the kingdom of David to its former state and original sovereignty. He will rebuild the sanctuary and gather the dispersed of Israel. All the ancient laws will be reinstituted in his days; sacrifices will again be offered; the sabbatical and jubilee years will again be observed in accordance with the commandments set forth in the Law. ("Kings and Wars" 11:1)

The king Messiah is meant to realize the full scope of Mosaic prophecy including sacrifices and the temple cult. He is not a messenger announcing a new revelation or radical change in the natural order. Nor is he the harbinger of an end to history. He is simply the ideal embodiment of the halakhic conception of the king, who will fulfill the essential purpose of all kings by reestablishing a national kingdom governed by the Law of Moses. Maimonides' description of the Messiah thus parallels his conception of messianism as the means of an ideal fulfillment (i.e., implementation) of the Torah. He therefore emphasizes that the Law will in no way be abrogated during the messianic age, but indeed will be restored in its entirety.

Messianism is the fulfillment of the biblical promise that Israel will be given the historical opportunity to observe the entire Torah. This promise, as interpreted by Maimonides, does not presuppose an eschatological end to history as we know it.

> Do not think that the king Messiah will have to perform signs and wonders, bring anything new into being, revive the dead, or do similar things. It is not so. Rabbi Akiva was a great sage, a teacher of the Mishnah, yet he was also the armor-bearer of Ben Kozba. He affirmed that the latter was the king Messiah; he and all the wise men of his generation shared this belief until Ben Kozba was slain in [his] iniquity, when it became known that he was not [the Messiah]. Yet the rabbis had not asked him for a sign or token. The general principle is: this Law of ours with its statutes and ordinances [is not subject to change]. It is forever and all eternity; it is not to be added to or to be taken away from. ("Kings and Wars" 11:3)

In stating that miracles are not a necessary condition for identifying someone as the true Messiah, Maimonides is not merely engaging in polemics (e.g., to circumvent Christian claims that Jesus performed miracles), but seeking to naturalize the transition between premessianic and messianic history.[37] He also upholds the attitude of those sages who considered Bar Kokhba (Ben Kozba) to be the Messiah. Since the king Messiah does not inaugurate a radically changed history, Rabbi Akiva initially may have had grounds for concluding that Bar Kokhba was the Messiah. There is a perennial obligation to support legitimate attempts to restore Israel's national independence, because a national political framework is indispensable for the fulfillment of the Torah. Hence, Maimonides' statement about the eternity and unalterability of the Torah ("The general principle is: this law of ours . . . is not subject to change") summarizes the fundamental principle underlying his conception of messianism: Jews are obligated to try to establish a national framework in which the total corpus of Torah Law can be concretely implemented in the world.[38]

The difference from a halakhic point of view between an ordinary king of the House of David and the king Messiah depends to a great extent on the latter's success at fulfilling the tasks imposed on all kings. Maimonides enumerates various conditions that a king must fulfill in order to be regarded as a prima facie candidate for being the Messiah.

> If there arise a king from the House of David who mediates on the Torah, occupies himself with the commandments, as did his ancestor David, observes the precepts prescribed in the Written and the Oral Law, prevails upon Israel to walk in the way of the

Lord, it may be assumed that he is the Messiah. ("Kings and Wars" 11:4)

The criteria for concluding that the king in question is unquestionably the Messiah mirror the functions that the Halakhah ascribes to all kings. Like an ordinary king, the king Messiah will seek to provide Israel with political security, inspire the community to observe the Torah, and "fight the battles of the Lord" by abolishing idolatry wherever his power extends. He will differ from ordinary kings in his success at realizing these goals in a convincing manner.

If he does these things and succeeds, rebuilds the sanctuary on its site, and gathers the dispersed of Israel, he is beyond all doubt the Messiah. He will prepare the whole world to serve the Lord with one accord, as it is written: *For then will I turn to the peoples a pure language, that they may all call upon the name of the Lord to serve Him with one consent* [Zeph. 3:9]. ("Kings and Wars" 11:4)

What if he fails to pass some of these tests? The answer of Maimonides is given in a passage found in only a few manuscripts of "Kings and Wars."

But if he does not meet with full success, or is slain, it is obvious that he is not the Messiah promised in the Torah. He is to be regarded like all the other wholehearted and worthy kings of the House of David who died and whom the Holy One, blessed be He, raised up to test the multitude, as it is written: *And some of them that are wise shall stumble, to refine among them, and to purify, and to make white, even to the time of the end; for it is yet for the time appointed* [Dan. 11:35].[39]

Accordingly, one must await the verdict of history to know whether a successful king from the House of David is the true Messiah. If the person in question ultimately fails, he remains a king figure though not a messianic figure. It is clear, therefore, why Maimonides did not censure Rabbi Akiva for presuming that Bar Kokhba was the Messiah. The restoration of political independence to Israel is a perennial normative ideal that gives expression to the ultimate goals of Judaism. This ideal must be acted upon whenever historical conditions allow. Failure is not a sign that the presumed Messiah is a false Messiah in the pejorative sense. The verse quoted by Maimonides from Daniel does not condemn the presumed messianic king for this failure, but rather explains such failures against the background of the messianic promise. Since Daniel predicted such failures, one ought not to be disillusioned or feel divinely rejected when such well-meaning attempts at restoring Israel's independence do not meet with success.

In his philosophic and legal writings Maimonides makes the rabbinic statement: "The world conforms to its usual course," the cornerstone of his philosophy of history and nature. He dispenses almost entirely with miracles in explaining natural phenomena and chooses instead to merge the notion of divine will with the notion of the natural order. Divine love and concern are built into the belief in God's creation of an ordered universe.[40]

Accordingly, messianism does not involve a rupture in nature or history. The messianic kingdom endures not because of a radical transformation of man, but rather as a natural consequence of a just and peaceful organization of society. A messianic society does not eliminate uncertainty and contingency. While it provides a framework conducive to the fulfillment of the goals of Judaism, it does not guarantee their fulfillment nor does it limit the potential misuse of freedom. Although a potential messianic figure may begin a process that appears to lead towards the messianic fulfillment, he may fail at a later stage. A Maimonidean halakhist is willing to participate in such exciting historical opportunities because of his overriding concern and commitment to realize his normative obligations.

Messianism in the *Mishneh Torah* is explained primarily in terms of the meaning of a halakhic society rather than as the supernatural fulfillment of a predetermined divine plan. The commitment to the 613 commandments creates the need for an autonomous political commonwealth, i.e., messianism.

Maimonides mentions the restoration of the temple and the sacrificial cult during the messianic age not only because of their religious significance per se, but because they constitute parts of the total system of Halakhah that provides the rationale for messianism. (The sacrificial cult and the laws of the sabbatical and Jubilee years are not operative during exile and dispersion of the community.) For Maimonides, messianism grows out of the conceptual matrix of normative Judaism and not necessarily out of an eschatological aspiration for a new creation that would eliminate the possibility of evil in history.

The Role of Christianity and Islam   The passage last quoted was generally expurgated, because it goes on to discuss Jesus and Muhammad as examples of false Messiahs.

Even of Jesus of Nazareth, who imagined that he was the Messiah, but was put to death by the court, Daniel had prophesied, as it is written: *And the children of the violent among thy people shall lift themselves up to establish the vision; but they shall stumble* [Dan. 11:14]. For has there ever been a greater stumbling than this? All the prophets affirmed that the Messiah would redeem Israel, save them, gather their dispersed, and confirm the commandments. But he caused Israel to be destroyed by the sword, their remnant to be dispersed and humiliated. He was instrumental in changing the Torah and causing the world to err and serve another beside God.

But it is beyond the human mind to fathom the designs of the Creator; for our ways are not His ways, neither are our thoughts His thoughts. All these matters relating to Jesus of Nazareth and the Ishmaelite [Muhammad] who came after him, only served to clear the way for King Messiah, to prepare the whole world to worship God with one accord, as it is written: *For then will I turn to the peoples a pure language, that they may all call upon the name of the Lord to serve Him with one consent* [Zeph. 3:9]. Thus the messianic hope, the Torah, and the commandments have become familiar topics—topics of conversation [among the inhabitants] of the far isles and many peoples, uncircumcised of heart and flesh. They are discussing these matters and the commandments of the Torah. Some say: "Those commandments were true, but have lost their validity and are no longer binding." Others declare that they had an esoteric meaning and were not intended to be taken literally, that the Messiah has already come and revealed their occult significance. But when the true King Messiah will appear and succeed, be exalted and lifted up, they will forthwith recant and realize that they have inherited naught but lies from their fathers, that their prophets and forbears led them astray.[41]

Maimonides' treatment of Christianity and Islam here deserves special attention, particularly because it differs so strikingly from what he says in the *Epistle to Yemen*.[42] One can only offer conjectures about what Maimonides intended in this passage. He himself makes it clear that his interpretation of the emergence of the two religions is based more on speculation than on knowledge. The limitations of human understanding preclude the possibility of acquiring knowledge of God's ways in history: "But it is beyond the human mind to fathom the designs of the Creator; for our ways are not His ways, neither are our thoughts His thoughts."

After introducing this note of caution, Maimonides presents an account of Christianity and Islam that presupposes, as Funkenstein interprets it, a divine cunning manipulating the surface occurrences of history. Yet if Maimonides had intended to convey the notion of a divine cunning in history, as Funkenstein believes, one would have to conclude that God was immoral and diabolic. It would be sheer perversity for God to elect Israel and then deliberately unleash forces in history to inflict suffering upon Israel in order to bring about Israel's eventual triumph. According to this alleged scheme, Israel is chosen and then persecuted by God for the sake of realizing the divine goal in history. It is unlikely that Maimonides would accept a conception of history that was indifferent to moral considerations.[43] All of Maimonides' statements, moreover, are compatible with the view that God had not preordained the activities of Jesus and Muhammad, but was simply committed to frustrating their attempts to frustrate the divine promises to Israel. Their successes might seem irreversible, yet even those successes could turn to the benefit of this chosen people.

Rather than offering a theology of history, Maimonides was making two important points. First, he was cautioning his audience against misconstruing Christianity's and Islam's strength and expansion as signs of their truth. Since he had just spoken of the duty of Jews to promote the worldwide rule of monotheism, and since Christianity and Islam were by then so much more powerful and widespread than Judaism, some of his readers might ask themselves whether one of those two religions was meant to serve as the carrier of monotheism toward its universal triumph. The universal dimension of biblical monotheism and the realities of medieval history together added weight to the claim that God had replaced Israel with one of the two new universal faiths: Christianity or Islam.

Maimonides therefore cautioned his readers against confusing the universal triumph of monotheism with the abolition of Jewish particularity. The triumph of monotheism during the messianic era will not involve the abrogation of Israel's ancient covenant with God. On the contrary, Israel's national political restoration is a necessary condition for the realization of the messianic promise.

The choice of universality at the expense of Jewish particularity negates the messianic ideal. Maimonides cites Christianity as an example of this. While the failures of certain presumed messianic figures can be viewed positively, Maimonides singles out Jesus for condemnation because "he was instrumental in changing the Torah and causing the world to err and serve another beside God." A messianic ideal that is at the expense of Israel and its Torah is, claims Maimonides, fraudulent and destructive.

The second point Maimonides makes in this passage concerns the plausibility of the belief in the actualization of the messianic hope. It might appear that, given the conditions of medieval history, the messianic triumph of monotheism with Israel as its carrier would henceforth be impossible without the miraculous intervention of God. If that were the case, then how could one retain belief in messianism without reverting to fantasy or exaggerated miracle claims?'

Maimonides therefore sought to provide an interpretation of history that would make messianism plausible without recourse to belief in miracles. His interpretation of the important roles played by Christianity and Islam in furthering the spread of monotheism makes the triumph of monotheism—and hence messianism—empirically plausible. Maimonides was thus able to safeguard his naturalistic conception of messianism. The triumphs of Christianity and Islam are not presented as proofs that history is governed according to a divine blueprint, but rather, in order to show that the messianic reality may be realized without any radical changes in the natural order of things.

The crux of Maimonides' argument is that the eventual triumph of Judaism is built into the conceptual fabrics of Christianity and Islam. Although they persecute Israel and claim that its weakness and vulnerability are proof of divine rejection, nevertheless they are conceptually within the framework of the Torah. By their own account, Israel was the precursor of the other monotheistic faiths. When a king emerges to restore Israel's sovereignty and change its historical condition from weakness and vulnerability to strength and self-reliance, the central argument against Israel's election will be demolished. A reborn Israel will constitute a compelling refutation of those religions insofar as they base their claims to authenticity on Israel's suffering. A nonsuffering Israel would force Christians and Muslims to rethink their respective theologies. And in revising their picture of Israel as the rejected people of God, they will feel impelled to acknowledge that Israel is the true carrier of the universal triumph of monotheism.

Maimonides' treatment of Christianity and Islam in "Kings and Wars" is not part of a general theory of history, but rather a *post facto* explanation of existing conditions. His argument was not meant to show that the emergence of these two religions was inevitable. Christianity and Islam are treated as given facts of history; they are introduced not to show that divine cunning operates in history, but rather to explain the connection between the restoration of Israel's sovereignty and the universal triumph of monotheism. Since the two religions have exposed vast numbers of people to the biblical world of concepts and ideas, they have created a plausible framework for Judaism's reemergence in history as the dominant monotheistic religion.[44]

Maimonides did not propound a theology of history in the *Mishneh Torah*.[45] This work is a comprehensive codification of law—a framework for organizing one's personal, family, and communal affairs according to the *mitzvot*. When discussing the purpose of the Jewish people's national political restoration in messianic times, Maimonides strove to neutralize collective fantasy and religious triumphalism. In "Kings and Wars," as throughout the *Mishneh Torah*, Maimonides placed the ideal of knowledge and love of God at the center of halakhic life. Since the collective fantasies of national hegemony and supernaturalism were obstacles to developing a religious orientation based on that ideal, Maimonides sought to naturalize the community's conception of messianism and make love of God the focal point of its historical hopes and aspirations.

MESSIANISM IN THE *EPISTLE TO YEMEN*

We are now in a position to appreciate the striking differences between Maimonides' treatment of messianism in his other works and in the *Epistle to Yemen*. Above all, the latter totally ignores the instrumental interpretation of messianism expounded in *Ḥelek* and the *Mishneh Torah*. The theme of that interpretation was that messianism is not an end in itself, but a good desired insofar as it constitutes a set of socioeconomic conditions conducive to achieving the ultimate goal of Judaism: the world to come, which is attained through knowledge and love of God. Nothing of this is recalled in the epistle.

This difference can be characterized as follows: in those other works Maimonides used messianism to explain the meaning of Judaism, while in the *Epistle to Yemen* he used it to provide a community with hope. The focal point of his treatment of messianism in his legal works was what transpires *after* rather than *before* the coming of the Messiah. Since messianism in the epistle served as a category of hope, the events preceding and leading to the advent of the Messiah were deemed all-important. This is also why, conversely, the concept of the birth pangs of the Messiah is introduced in the epistle, though it is notably absent from his other works.

The problem facing Maimonides in the *Epistle to Yemen* was not materialism or disregard for the spiritual goals of Judaism, but a community sinking into despair and disillusionment because of its suffering. Messianism, therefore, was not introduced in order to draw the community's attention to the sublime purposes of Judaism, but simply to counteract hopelessness by interpreting suffering as evidence of approaching redemption.

The messianic figure as described in the *Epistle to Yemen* is not primarily a teacher who moves the nations of the world by virtue of his wisdom. He is a prophetic figure who crushes opposition by performing remarkable miracles. When Maimonides mentions the Messiah's wisdom, it is only in order to debunk the claims of messianic pretenders, i.e., to provide his readers with criteria for rejecting false

Messiahs. The picture of the true Messiah presented in the *Epistle to Yemen* preserves hope in the community by neutralizing the potentially disruptive effects of charismatic pretenders. Maimonides treats the Messiah as a weapon with which to fight false Messiahs, and by and large ignores the Messiah's positive role in awakening the community to love of God.

The community addressed in the *Epistle to Yemen* may be distinguished from the general audience of Maimonides' legal works by virtue of its suffering condition. A suffering community differs from a community of action. It perceives itself as a passive victim of external forces. When this sense of vulnerability grips a community, it loses confidence in its own ability to effect changes in its condition. Consequently, the motif of redemption through miracles recurs throughout the *Epistle to Yemen*. The Messiah, therefore, is primarily a performer of miracles. What is more, the epistle's picture of history is dominated by the principle of unilateral divine action. The notion of the *ketz*, the predetermined time of redemption, is a key notion in the epistle, for it makes redemption independent of the community's own efforts and deserts. Messianism is thus unrelated to human action or initiative; it is not a process that human beings can influence, but rather a preordained state of affairs that miraculously erupts in history according to a fixed divine scheme.

In "Kings and Wars," Maimonides' description of unsuccessful messianic "experiments" creates the impression that there can never be absolute certainty that the messianic age has come about. The example of Rabbi Akiva believing that Bar Kokhba was the Messiah shows that there are various stages in ascertaining whether the messianic era has commenced and that in fact failure is always a possibility. Because miracles play a minor role both in validating the credentials of the Messiah and in determining whether messianic conditions obtain, one can never be absolutely certain that what seem to be messianic conditions will endure. In addressing a community of action in the *Mishneh Torah*, Maimonides is less concerned with providing guarantees as to the final redemption than with pointing out the spiritual implications of the concept of messianism for a full appreciation of Judaism.

Maimonides, who fashions his philosophy of *mitzvot* on the basis of the imperative: "See, I set before you this day life and good, death and evil. . . . Choose life" (Deut. 30:15, 19), does not require a predeterministic view of history in order to sustain his religious commitment. The crucial belief that underlies his religious orientation is that human actions have significance because the *mitzvot* are eternally binding.

The aim of the *Epistle to Yemen* is to create hope and not necessarily to influence action. Maimonides was content with gaining time by encouraging the community to persevere for an additional thirty to forty years. The figures he mentions for the duration of previous periods of persecution, such as fifty-two years, were short enough to encourage the community to "hold on" a little longer. Even the date of the predicted return of prophecy was close enough to inspire hope, yet distant enough to gain time to allow conditions to change.

The *Epistle to Yemen* was aimed at instilling within the community a capacity to wait without being disillusioned. The courage and tenacity required for such an historical attitude was to be nurtured by the vivid image of the covenant at Sinai. In order to withstand the challenges of its enemies, the community had to be convinced of its unique place in history. This victimized, suffering community would be able to bear its degradation if it could retain belief in its singularity in the eyes of God.

The treatment of Christianity and Islam in the *Epistle to Yemen* also answers to this fundamental need. In the *Mishneh Torah*, where the goal is to educate a community of action to strive to implement the values implicit in the messianic ideal, Christianity and Islam are placed in a relatively positive light. They are viewed as instruments serving the realization of messianism and, therefore, their ascendancy in history lends plausibility to the belief in the ultimate triumph of Judaism. The epistle, in contrast, seeks merely to denigrate them as vain schemes to undermine Judaism.

In the *Epistle to Yemen* the emphasis on action is absent. The theme of *teshuvah*, which encourages action and heightens a person's sense of responsibility,[46] is hardly mentioned. The logic here is not one that promises action, but rather one that explains suffering. The perspective on history conveyed in the epistle is centered on the unique and envied place of Israel in the divine scheme of history. The nations of the world, driven by resentment for not having been elected by God, try repeatedly to thwart the divine will.

This Israel-centered picture of history has particular significance for a suffering Jewish community. Because of his pain, the sufferer tends to focus on his personal needs and to assume a self-centered attitude to the world. Suffering may imprison a person within the limited circle of his subjective needs and interests. Maimonides therefore realized the pointlessness of speaking to a suffering community about such ideals as love and knowledge of God, i.e., about ideals that presuppose a person's ability to transcend egocentricity in order to appreciate that which has intrinsic worth. The sufferer is not open to hear the virtues of knowledge and worship of God for their own sakes.

Because of the traumatic and disillusioning events it was forced to undergo, the community in Yemen was preoccupied with its own needs and interests. At this moment in time, its perception of history was no longer objective and dispassionate. The *Epistle to Yemen* reflects this suffering community's outlook on reality. Christianity and Islam, as seen through the eyes of the sufferer, have no positive significance; their sole objective is to subvert God's plan by destroying the people of Israel and Judaism. All of history reveals this conspiracy against Israel. Whether it be through the sword, sophistical arguments, or the invention of rival religions, the central preoccupation of the great nations of history is to weaken and destroy the people of Israel.

While a suffering community is not an active community, there is a danger of its being driven out of desperation to act impetuously and irrationally. Maimonides uses the text from the tractate Ketubbot concerning the oath not to rebel in anticipation of the advent of the Messiah to caution the community against translating hope into political action. This text, which reflects the traumatic aftermath of the Bar Kokhba uprising, does not appear in any of Maimonides' other writings. In chapter five of "Kings and Wars," Maimonides deals with themes contained in the section of Ketubbot where this text appears, yet he never once mentions the oath binding Israel to remain passive and not act to restore its political independence. On the contrary, in a later chapter of "Kings and Wars," he goes on, as we saw, to imply approval of Rabbi Akiva's decision to support Bar Kokhba.

In the *Epistle to Yemen* the community is told to bear its suffering with dignity. Its suffering is a burnt offering unto God; its heroic refusal to succumb to its enemies expresses the profound love of God described allegorically in the Song of Songs. Redemption is dissociated entirely from human initiative. It is guaranteed by a predetermined divine plan and the community's suffering is deemed to be a sure sign of its approach.

NECESSITY AND FREEDOM

A related difference between the *Epistle to Yemen* and Maimonides' legal writings is that the latter place a much greater stress on the extent of human freedom. Whereas the picture of history that dominates the epistle is necessitarian, the picture given in the legal writings is more action-oriented and open-ended.

To begin with, there are several places in his legal works where the belief in human freedom is made a cornerstone of the Torah and Halakhah. An example is the *Eight Chapters*.

If a man's actions were done under compulsion, the commandments and prohibitions of the Law would be nullified and they would all be absolutely in vain, since man would have no choice in what he does. . . .

The truth about which there is no doubt is that all of man's actions are given over to him. If he wishes to act he does so, and if he does not wish to act he does not; there is no compulsion whatsoever upon him. Hence it necessarily follows that commands can be given.[47]

A theology that would negate the significance of human freedom would in turn undermine Halakhah. Consequently, in the *Eight Chapters* Maimonides interprets the rabbinic statement "Everything is in the hands of heaven except fear of heaven" in a way that emphasizes human freedom.[48] He expands the scope of "fear of heaven" to include all human actions and restricts the class of things "in the hands of heaven" to natural and biological conditions that are not subject to human choices. Thus "fear of heaven" includes all of human behavior and not only behavior governed explicitly by the commandments. Whereas the rabbinic statement in question seems to constrict the scope of human freedom by describing "fear of heaven" as the exception and "in the hands of God" as the rule, Maimonides packs all of human behavior into "fear of heaven" and thereby turns the statement into a rabbinic affirmation of free will.

There are, however, certain biblical texts that seem to contradict Maimonides' radical approach to human freedom. While the law presupposes an open universe which human beings can shape, certain biblical texts suggest a theology of history that is incompatible with this world view. God's revelation to Abraham that his descendants would be enslaved and oppressed (Gen. 15:13) is an example of "verses that lead people to fancy that God preordained and compels disobedience." If the enslavement in Egypt was preordained by God and if, consequently, the Egyptians necessarily oppressed Abraham's descendants, then God's punishment of the Egyptians not only violates our basic intuitions about justice, but also contradicts Maimonides' claim that freedom is a necessary presupposition of the Torah. According to Maimonides, a predictive, necessitarian theory of history would destroy the normative framework of the Sinai covenant.

Maimonides resolves this apparent contradiction in the Bible by arguing that none of the predictions mentioned in the Torah entailed the necessity of actions predicted.[49] No individual was compelled to act in a particular way as a result of any of these predictions. While they are expressed as unconditional statements about what will inevitably occur in the future, they are logically no different from correct predictions based upon the moral habits of human beings.

The answer is that this is like the Exalted saying that some people born in the future will be sinful, some will be obedient, some virtuous, and some bad. Now this is correct, but it does not necessarily follow from this statement that a given bad man is bad without fail, nor that a given virtuous man is virtuous without fail. Rather, whoever is bad is so by his own choice. If he wishes to be virtuous, he can be so; there is nothing preventing him. Similarly, if any virtuous man wishes to, he can be bad; there is nothing preventing him. The prediction is not about a particular individual, so that he could say: "It has been preordained for me." Rather, it is stated in a general way, and each individual remains able to exercise his choice upon his original inborn disposition. Similarly, if any individual Egyptian who oppressed them and treated them unjustly had not wanted to oppress them, he had choice about that; for it was not preordained that a given individual would oppress them.

This answer is the same as the answer to the problem posed by His saying: "Behold, you are about to sleep with your fathers, and this people will rise up and go astray after the foreign gods of the land." There is no difference between this and His saying: "Thus we shall act toward and deal with whoever worships idols." If there were never anyone who committed a transgression, then the threats, all of the curses, and likewise all of the punishments which are in the Law would be futile. The existence of the judgment of death by stoning in the Torah does not make us say that the man who profaned the Sabbath is compelled to profane it, nor do the curses force us to say that those idol worshipers upon whom the curses fell were preordained to idol worship. Rather, everyone who worshiped [idols] did so by choice and punishment befell him. "Just as they have chosen their ways . . . I too shall choose, etc."[50]

Maimonides lumps God's prediction to Abraham that Israel would be enslaved and oppressed in Egypt together with legal judgments conditional upon the violation of specific norms. Just as in the latter case there is no presumption that violations of the laws in question must occur necessarily, so too in the cases involving divine predictions there is no presumption that particular individuals must necessarily act in predetermined ways.

The crucial point of this argument is that predictive judgments concerning human behavior and divine predictions concerning the future course of history share a common logic. In neither case does necessity replace contingency. Regardless of the accuracy of the divine predictions related in the Torah, history remains within the domain of freedom and not "in the hands of heaven." Maimonides *qua* halakhist was

disturbed by biblical allusions to a divinely predetermined course of
history;[51] he was repelled by any theology of history that reduces
freedom to an illusion and undermines human effort and initiative.
In the light of his consistent opposition to any necessitarian theological doctrine, it is clear why Maimonides makes the redemption of
Israel dependent upon *teshuvah* in *Hilkhot Teshuvah*. This part of the
Mishneh Torah reveals the same approach to freedom as is reflected
in the *Eight Chapters*. Since the primary focus of *teshuvah* is upon a
person's freedom to effect meaningful changes in his life, Maimonides
deals with various problematic biblical texts and ideas that prima facie
contradict the belief in human freedom. For example, he discusses the
biblical text concerning God's hardening pharaoh's heart and the general problem of whether divine foreknowledge implies necessity.[52] As
in the *Eight Chapters*, Maimonides neutralizes the necessitarian implications of biblical predictive statements.

In addition to arguing against theological determinism, he presents
a remarkably naturalistic interpretation of divine grace.

What is meant by David's utterance: *Good and upright is the
Lord; therefore He will teach sinners in the way; He will guide the
meek in judgment and will teach the meek His way* [Ps. 25:8]? It
refers to the fact that God sent them prophets to teach them the
ways of the Lord and bring them back in repentance; furthermore,
that He endowed them with the capacity of learning and understanding. For it is characteristic of every human being that, when
his interest is engaged in the ways of wisdom and righteousness,
he longs for these ways and is eager to follow them. Thus the
sages say: "Whoever comes to purify himself receives aid"; that
is, he will find himself helped in his endeavor. (*MT Hilkhot
Teshuvah* 6:10)

The aid one receives when praying for divine grace consists in one's
inclination to proceed along the paths of righteousness and wisdom
after having become engaged in these pursuits. Divine grace is implicit
in human rationality and in the joy derived from intellectual and moral
activities. Grace is not a supernatural act of divine beneficence that
delivers a person from responsibility for his condition. Grace is not
antithetical to human freedom, but rather is expressed in the free
unfolding of a person's rational nature. This is perhaps the most revealing statement of a philosopher-halakhist opposed to any theology
that would minimize the importance of human freedom and initiative
in a person's encounter with God.

Very different is the approach of the *Epistle to Yemen*. Here Maimonides emphasizes the necessitarian aspects of God's involvement in

human history. In contrast to the approach in his legal writings, he makes repeated references to biblical predictions and allusions to the unalterable course of events in order to convey a necessitarian picture of history. The difference of approach is also evident in his discussion of astrology.[53]

Maimonides viewed astrology as a pseudoscience whose "postulates can be refuted by real proofs on rational grounds." The most disturbing aspect of astrology was not its falsity but the harm that belief in it could cause to the community. For one thing, astrologers predicted that Israel would never be redeemed.

> This is how matters stand regarding the era of the Messiah, may he speedily come. For while the gentiles believe that our nation will never constitute an independent state, nor will it ever rise above its present condition, and all the astrologers, diviners, and augurs concur in this opinion, God will prove their views and beliefs false, and will order the advent of the Messiah. (p. 117)

Without going into a discussion of the rational proofs that show astrology to be a pseudoscience, Maimonides cites authoritative texts as evidence for the unreliability of astrological predictions.

> . . . Mark well, however, what Scripture has to say about the astrologers. At the time when Moses rose to leadership, the astrologers had unanimously predicted that our nation would never be freed from bondage, nor gain its independence. But fortune smiled upon Israel, for the most exquisite of human beings appeared and redeemed them at the very time that was supposedly most inauspicious for them. Furthermore, Egypt was smitten with the plagues at the very time for which the astrologers had foretold an epoch of wholesome climate, abundance, and prosperity for the inhabitants. . . . Similarly, the pundits, astrologers, and prognosticators were all of one mind that the administration of Nebuchadnezzar the wicked marked the beginning of an era of enduring prosperity. Forsooth, his dynasty was extinguished and destroyed, as was divinely forecast by Isaiah. (pp. 116–117)

Maimonides' main attack on astrology centers on the incompatibility of believing in a moral Judge of history and believing that events on earth are causally determined by planetary or stellar configurations. While the Torah explains the Flood and the destruction of Sodom and Gomorrah in terms of the wickedness of the generations in question, the astrologers insist that these events were the result of amoral causes.

. . . So whatever happens in this world that has its source in
God, they say it is the inescapable consequences of planetary
conjunctions.

They have affirmed the truth of their propositions in order to
undermine the principles of our religion, and to give free rein to
their animal instincts and passions as do the beasts and the
ostriches. (p. 120)

Maimonides then cites a passage from Leviticus, which he repeats
in the *Guide*, in the *Mishneh Torah*'s "Laws of Fasting," and in the
Letter to the Rabbis of Marseilles on Astrology:

. . . We have been admonished by God against those views in
Scripture to the following effect: "If you rebel against Me so that
I bring disaster upon you as a punishment of your misdeeds, but
you ascribe your reverses to chance rather than to your guilt, I
shall increase your afflictions and make them more grievous."
This is the intent of His words in the Chapter of Admonitions: *If
you remain* be-keri *toward Me, I too will remain* be-keri *to you*
[Lev. 26:27–28]. Now *keri* signifies chance, hazard. It means to
say: "If you regard My chastisement as a fortuitous event, I shall
bring the most severe calamities upon you, *sevenfold for your
sins*" [Lev. 26:21]. These foregoing remarks have made it abundantly clear that the advent of the Messiah is in no way subject
to the influence of the stars. (p. 120)

What Maimonides fails to mention here is that Israel's destiny is
determined by *teshuvah*, i.e., the observance of the commandments.
In his legal works, his attack on astrology is aimed at fortifying belief
in the efficacy of human action; astrology has to be refuted because
Judaism affirms human freedom and the ability to effect changes both
individually and collectively through moral action. In contrast, the
themes of *teshuvah* and human freedom are notably absent from the
Epistle to Yemen. Here his discussion of astrology is motivated by the
need to show that the "advent of the Messiah is in no way subject to
the influence of the stars." Astrology is attacked primarily because it
creates disillusionment and despair in the community. Maimonides
assails the belief in astrology in order to safeguard belief in the divine
promise to redeem Israel at the preordained time. The crucial conflict
of beliefs is not between necessitarian astrology and human freedom,
but rather between a necessitarian conception of history implied by
astrology and a necessitarian conception of history based on the biblical promises.

Astrology is viewed as a rival to the Jewish belief in the inevitable
coming of the Messiah. It is an enemy of hope. Even when Jews use

astrology to prove the coming of the Messiah at a particular time, the results are disastrous for invariably these prognostications fail to materialize. Nevertheless, people fall victim to such "extravagances, for a drowning man catches at a straw." The epistle is addressed to such drowning people. It is pointless to tell a drowning person to trust in his ability to alter his environment through moral action. When a person's world seems to be collapsing, he turns outward in search of redemption. In the epistle, redemption is not a challenge but a promise. Belief in historical necessity is a source of comfort and hope.

The *Epistle to Yemen* thus differs from the bulk of Maimonides' legal writings also by virtue of its emphasis on necessity rather than on freedom. In it Maimonides chose the way of the concerned and compassionate leader. Rather than preach the need for *teshuvah* and disinterested worship of God, Maimonides responded to the community in terms of its particular needs. He did not attempt to destroy its fantasies or to point out its weaknesses.

The compassionate leader does not focus on the meaning of messianism in terms of the ideals of love and knowledge of God when the community he addresses is being brutalized. His primary goal is to fortify its will to survive. Rather than picture messianism in terms of the universal triumph of monotheism, he talks of a universal conspiracy against God because of His election of Israel. In the *Epistle to Yemen*, Maimonides provides the lonely and distraught sufferer with a theology of grace. He addresses the confused and frightened victim who feels drawn toward charismatics and false messiahs—who catches at straws— and tries to provide him with the strength to persevere in heroic silence in his belief in and commitment to Judaism.

In the *Mishneh Torah*, Maimonides argues for the uniqueness and inviolability of Mosaic prophecy in order to support the belief in the eternity of the commandments. In the *Epistle to Yemen*, however, these notions are used to give meaning to the community's suffering and degradation. By establishing the eternal validity of Mosaic prophecy in the epistle, Maimonides provides the framework wherein the community can perceive its anguish and pain as expressions of an all-consuming love for God. The focal point of the *Mishneh Torah* is the meaningfulness of human action; the focal point of the *Epistle to Yemen* is the meaningfulness of suffering.

The person who feels powerless to act is comforted and strengthened by a vision of history dominated by necessity. Maimonides turns to a community that is trapped within its own terrors and feeling of futility and he tells them: I have a tradition from my father, who received it from his father, that prophecy will be restored in the near future and we shall then witness the promised triumph of Judaism. Necessity is the message of hope for a person who has lost faith in his ability to act.

NOTES

1. See BT Kiddushin 39b, Yoma 69b, Gittin 56b. Also D. Hartman, *Joy and Responsibility* (Jerusalem: Ben Zvi-Posner, 1978), pp. 1–4, 181–87, 225–28.

2. See D. Hartman, *Maimonides: Torah and Philosophic Quest* (Philadelphia: Jewish Publication Society, 1976), p. 246, n. 10; p. 261, n. 39.

3. See D. Hartman, "The Joy of Torah," and "Halakhah as a Ground for Creating a Shared Spiritual Language," in *Joy and Responsibility*, pp. 28–29, 150–54.

4. See L. Strauss, *Persecution and the Art of Writing* (Glencoe, Ill.: The Free Press, 1952), Chapter 2; and D. Hartman, *Maimonides*, Chapter 1. According to Strauss, the importance of considering audiences grows out of the philosopher's quest to survive in a world that feels threatened by the philosopher (e.g., Socrates). Our concern with audiences in Maimonides' writings focuses on the logic of the educator who speaks only after he understands his audience. See Maimonides' description of the logic of the educator in his introduction to *Ḥelek* and in the *Guide* 3:32; and in the discussion of the *Essay on Resurrection* in this volume.

5. See the introduction to A. S. Halkin's edition of *Moses Maimonides' Epistle to Yemen*, trans. B. Cohen (New York: American Academy for Jewish Research, 1952), pp. xiii–xxi; M. Perlmann, "The Medieval Polemics between Islam and Judaism," in *Religion in a Religious Age*, ed. S. D. Goitein (Cambridge, Mass.: Association for Jewish Studies, 1974), pp. 103–38.

6. See I. Twersky, *Introduction to the Code of Maimonides (Mishneh Torah)* (New Haven and London: Yale University Press, 1980), pp. 380–87; Y. Ben-Sasson, "Le-ḥeker mishnat ta'amei mitzvot," *Tarbiz* 29 (1960): 268–82. Rabbi J. B. Soloveitchik follows in the spirit of Maimonides with his psychological and existential interpretation of *mitzvot*. The universal dimensions of the human condition serve as the ground upon which he explicates his philosophy of Judaism. Yeshayahu Leibowitz, though influenced by Maimonides, considers this aspect of Maimonides as a preliminary stage in one's religious growth (*she-lo li-shmah*), which should be superseded by an approach to *mitzvot* that has no bearing upon the human condition. See Y. Leibowitz, *The Faith of Maimonides* (Hebrew) (Tel Aviv: Ministry of Defense, 1980), pp. 78–85.

7. In *Guide* 2:33, Maimonides is somewhat embarrassed by the biblical account of the collective nature of revelation because it conflicts with his treatment of the intellectual and moral qualities necessary for prophecy. Compare Maimonides' exegesis of Joel 3:1 at the end of this epistle and in *Guide* 2:32.

8. BT Nedarim 20a. See BT Yevamot 79a; *MT Hilkhot Issurei Bi'ah* 12:24, 19:17, *Hilkhot Teshuvah* 2:10, *Hilkhot Avadim* 8:9. These halakhot are interesting examples of the integration of Aggadah and Halakhah. It is also

important to distinguish between a normative use of the character traits of the covenantal Jew and Judah Halevi's understanding of Israel's unique spiritual talents. For Maimonides the description of character traits serves a moral purpose; it does not endow the community with unique spiritual and intellectual powers. Unlike Judah Halevi, Maimonides does not restrict the spiritual capacity to achieve prophecy to Jews. See Hartman, *Maimonides*, p. 267, n. 73.

9. See Hartman, *Maimonides*, pp. 105–9; *MT Hilkhot Yesodei ha-Torah* 8:2.

10. See *MT Hilkhot Yesodei ha-Torah* 8; Judah Halevi, *Kuzari* 1:87, 4:11; Halkin, ed., *Epistle to Yemen*, pp. xix–xx.

11. See D. Hartman, "Maimonides' Approach to Messianism and Its Contemporary Implications," *Daat* 2–3(1978–79): 5–33.

12. See *MT Hilkhot Teshuvah* 10:5; *Guide* 3:51, 54; G. D. Cohen, "The Song of Songs and the Jewish Religious Mentality," in *The Samuel Friedland Lectures 1960–61* (New York: Jewish Theological Seminary, 1966), pp. 1–21; Hartman, *Maimonides*, p. 52.

13. See *Commentary to the Mishnah*, trans. J. Kafih (Jerusalem: Mossad Harav Kook, 1963–68), Intro., p. 4; *MT Hilkhot Yesodei ha-Torah* 8:1.

14. See BT Shevu'ot 39a.

15. See Halkin, ed., *Epistle to Yemen*, p. 22, n. 26. There is an interesting connection between the following facts: the persecution of the community in Yemen began around 1165; the return of prophecy, according to Maimonides' extraordinary tradition, was to begin around 1210 or 1216; and Maimonides' claim that the persecution during the Second Jewish Commonwealth lasted fifty-two years.

16. See A. J. Heschel, "Ha-he'emin ha-Rambam she-zakhah la-nevu'ah?" in *Louis Ginzberg Jubilee Volume*, ed. A. Marx et al. (New York: American Academy for Jewish Research, 1945), Hebrew section, pp. 159–88. Heschel claims that Maimonides seriously believed in this tradition. For Heschel, this fact adds weight to his overall thesis concerning Maimonides' striving for prophecy. See G. D. Cohen's Leo Baeck memorial lecture, *Messianic Postures of Ashkenazim and Sephardim* (New York: Leo Baeck Institute, 1967), pp. 22–29. Cohen's attempt to link the messianic speculations of Sephardic thinkers such as Maimonides with the "rationalism, science, philosophy, and Hebrew classicism that were the hallmarks of this group" (p. 22) is farfetched. He claims:

> Hence, they would have little truck with apocalyptic fantasy. Accordingly, it is not surprising to discern in their writings an effort to calculate the end by the movements of the stars or by rhythmic periodizations of history. Having been trained in philosophy, they regarded the universe and human history as mechanisms or organisms, the functioning of which had been committed by the Creator to immutable laws. Built into these mechanisms as part of the law of their operation they postulated laws of time which would—in the fullness of time—catapult the elect segment of the cosmos—indeed, the world at large—into a happier and more harmonious course. Since it was all a question of a particular

manifestation of the laws of nature, fixed by God, to be sure, but capable of rational analysis nonetheless, if one could but permeate the complex secrets of the essential part of the machine or organism, one could determine when its course would change.

Cohen's interpretation of Judah Halevi's departure for Palestine as "not a logical conclusion of Andalusian messianism but a total rejection of it" (p. 24) is similarly unconvincing. In the light of what has been shown in this essay concerning Maimonides' rejection of the doctrine of a fixed, predetermined scheme of history, Cohen's argument is highly implausible.

Halkin describes Maimonides' extraordinary tradition as one that negates present delusions without destroying hope for the future (*Epistle to Yemen*, p. xiii), but this view does not necessarily reflect Maimonides' personal beliefs. Maimonides' exoneration of Saadiah may be viewed as a veiled justification of his own decision to engage in speculation concerning the return of prophecy and by implication, the commencement of the messianic era.

17. A. Funkenstein, "Maimonides' Political Theory and Realistic Messianism," in *Miscellanea Mediaevalia* 11 (1977): 81–103.

18. Ibid., p. 84, n. 10.

19. Ibid., pp. 98–100. See the analysis of *Guide* 3:32 in the discussion of the *Essay on Resurrection* in this volume.

20. Funkenstein, "Maimonides Political Theory," pp. 92–93.

21. The imminent necessity for the Absolute Spirit to realize itself in history, which is the lifeblood of Hegel's notion of the cunning of reason, has no basis in Maimonidean thought. There is no inner compulsion for the monotheistic idea to be realized in history. The triumph of monotheism is a normative ideal for the complete realization of Torah in the life of the community and not a dialectical force working itself out in history. The model for understanding the divine patience and use of ruse is, as S. Pines has shown, nature and not history. Pines, in introducing his translation of the *Guide of the Perplexed* (Chicago: University of Chicago Press, 1963) by no means equates Hegel with Maimonides; he simply points out that Maimonides' use of the expression *talattuf* "calls to mind Hegel's expression: 'the ruse of reason'—'List der Vernunft.'"

For Maimonides, the normative ideal of history—knowledge and love of God—is in principle realizable for individuals outside of a messianic society; see G. Scholem, *The Messianic Idea in Judaism* (New York: Schocken, 1971), p. 25. It is for this reason that messianism does not play a central role in the *Guide of the Perplexed*. Even in the *Mishneh Torah*, *olam ha-ba* (an ahistorical category) is the culmination of the religious aspiration.

Maimonides' opening statement in *MT Hilkhot Yesodei ha-Torah* is totally incompatible with Hegel's theology and undermines the dynamic necessitarian picture of history behind Hegel's philosophy of history.

> The basic principle of all basic principles and the pillar of all sciences is to realize that there is a First Being who brought every existing thing into being. All existing things, whether celestial, terrestrial, or belonging to an intermediate class, exist only through His true existence.

If it could be supposed that He did not exist, it would follow that nothing else could possibly exist.

If, however, it were supposed that all other beings were nonexistent, He alone would still exist. Their nonexistence would not involve His nonexistence. For all beings are in need of Him; but He, blessed be He, is not in need of them nor of any one of them. Hence, His real essence is unlike that of any of them. (*MT Hilkhot Yesodei ha-Torah* 1:1–3)

It is worthwhile comparing Maimonides' treatment of the problem of evil and human suffering in the *Guide* 3:17–24 with Hegel's necessitarian conception of history that serves as a rational theodicy. Not only is there a radical difference in their theologies, but there are crucial differences in their anthropologies. A person who philosophizes in the spirit of Maimonides moves from history to nature and finally realizes his own insignificance and the radical difference between divine and human knowledge (see *MT Hilkhot Yesodei ha-Torah* 2:2). As distinct from Hegel's anthropology, Maimonidean man never oversteps the bounds of finitude. On the contrary, it is the philosopher who is filled with awe and humility when he fully understands his finitude in relationship to God's infinity. Also, Maimonidean man never discovers the necessity of suffering, but only ways of transcending its paralyzing effects (*Guide* 3:24).

In any discussion of Maimonides' philosophy of history, and specifically regarding the notion of progress in history, one should bear in mind the parenthetical remark in his chapter on the Sabean background of biblical culture (*Guide* 3:29):

If the belief in the existence of the deity were not generally accepted at present to such an extent in the religious communities, our days in these times would be even darker than that epoch. However, their darkness is of different kinds.

As a believing Jew who took Halakhah and the community seriously, Maimonides surely believed in messianism and in the importance of the fulfillment of the prophetic promise of the eradication of idolatry in history. This is a far cry from claiming that he believed, like Hegel, that he could penetrate into the secrets of the divine mind and decipher the strange and mysterious workings of the divine cunning in history.

See G. Scholem, *The Messianic Idea*, pp. 24–33; S. Avineri, *Hegel's Theory of the Modern State* (Cambridge: Cambridge University Press, 1972), pp. 230–34; C. Taylor, *Hegel and Modern Society* (Cambridge: Cambridge University Press, 1979), pp. 37–38, 95–100; R. Tucker, *Philosophy and Myth in Karl Marx* (Cambridge: Cambridge University Press, 1961), pp. 45–56; W. Kaufmann, *Hegel: A Reinterpretation* (Garden City, N.Y.: Anchor, 1966), pp. 249–75; E. Fackenheim, *The Religious Dimension in Hegel's Thought* (Boston: Beacon, 1967), pp. 116–59.

22. See *Guide* 2:27–29 regarding the question of an end to history; *Guide* 2:48, regarding how causality mediates the will of God; and Hartman, "Maimonides' Approach to Messianism," pp. 9–24.

23. Introduction to *Ḥelek*, trans. J. Abelson in his "Maimonides on the Jewish Creed," *Jewish Quarterly Review* 19(1906–7): 29.
24. Ibid., pp. 29, 30.
25. Ibid., p. 40.
26. Ibid., p. 44.
27. Ibid., p. 44.
28. Ibid., p. 42.
29. Ibid., pp. 42–43.
30. Scholem, "Toward an Understanding of the Messianic Idea in Judaism," in *The Messianic Idea*, p. 31. Rabbi J. B. Soloveitchik makes the point that since, according to Maimonides, historical redemption depends upon Israel's freely choosing to do *teshuvah*, absolute certainty regarding messianism requires a dogmatic belief in the eternal spiritual power of Israel that will one day express itself in the redemptive act of *teshuvah*. According to Soloveitchik, one cannot believe in messianism without believing in Israel. See J. B. Soloveitchik, *On Repentance*, ed. P.H. Peli (Jerusalem: Oroth, 1980), pp. 132–36.
   For an analysis of the talmudic discussion on the relationship between redemption and repentance, see E. E. Urbach, *The Sages: Their Concepts and Beliefs* (Jerusalem: Magnes, 1975), pp. 668–73, and "Redemption and Repentance in Talmudic Judaism," in *Types of Redemption*, ed. Z. Werblowsky and J. Blecker (Leiden: Brill, 1970), pp. 190–206.
31. See "Kings and Wars" 2:6, 3:3. Note how 3:8 and 3:9 balance each other and how the tenth Halakhah of chapter 4 balances the rest of that chapter. For further halakhic examples of how Maimonides attempts to mitigate the misuse of authority and power, see *MT Hilkhot Sanhedrin* 24:4–10, 25:1–2. See Twersky, *Code of Maimonides*, pp. 271–72.
   For the way the pursuit of philosophic knowledge of God can act as a corrective against the corrupting influence of power, see *Guide* 2:36 and compare with Plato, *Republic* 520–21a. Also see Hartman, *Maimonides*, pp. 197–200.
32. See R. Lerner, "Moses Maimonides," in *History of Political Philosophy*, ed. L. Strauss and J. Cropsey (Chicago: Rand McNally, 1963), p. 217.
33. See "Kings and Wars" 6:1,4, and the comments of Rabad.
34. "Kings and Wars" 8:10.
35. Cf. "Kings and Wars" 9:1; *Commentary to the Mishnah*, Hullin 7:6; *Guide* 2:39. Note the repeated references to the biblical patriarchs as educators rather than as legislators in *MT Hilkhot Avodah Zarah* 1. See S. Atlas, *Pathways in Jewish Law* (Hebrew) (New York: American Academy for Jewish Research, 1978), pp. 23–30. Also S. S. Schwarzschild, "Do Noachites Have to Believe in Revelation?" *Jewish Quarterly Review*, n.s. 72 (1962): 297–365; Spinoza's *Theologico-Political Treatise*, trans. R. H. M. Elwes (New York: Dover, 1951), p. 80, and L. Strauss, *Spinoza's Critique of Religion* (New York: Schocken, 1965), pp. 23, 273, n. 58; Hartman, *Maimonides*, p. 222, n. 62.
36. See *Guide* 3:11.
37. See S. Pines, "Histabrut ha-tekumah me-ḥadash shel medinah yehudit

le-fi Yoseph ibn Kaspi u-le-fi Spinoza," in *Studies in the History of Jewish Philosophy* (Hebrew) (Jerusalem: Bialik Institute, 1977), p. 294; also Hartman, *Maimonides*, p. 249, nn. 33–35.

38. Cf. A. M. Hershman, "Textual Problems of Book Fourteen of the *Mishneh Torah*," *Jewish Quarterly Review*, n.s. 40 (1950): 401–12.

> It can be readily seen that the "general principle" enunciated in this section has no bearing on what precedes it. The first part of the section rejects the popular notion that the Messiah will be endowed with superhuman gifts which will enable him to perform signs and wonders; the second part stresses belief in the immutability of the Law. There is obviously a missing link between the two parts. (p. 410)

Hershman suggests that "the general principle" of the immutability of the Law originally must have followed the expurgated passage concerning Jesus of Nazareth and the roles of Christianity and Islam quoted further on in this essay. In the light of the logical connection between Maimonides' conceptions of messianism and of the purpose of the Law, as explained in this essay, section 11:3 is perfectly coherent and thus Hershman's reconstruction is unnecessary.

39. *The Code of Maimonides, Book Fourteen: The Book of Judges*, trans. A. M. Hershman, Yale Judaica Series, vol. 3 (New Haven: Yale University Press, 1949), p. xxiii.

40. Maimonides counters those who would argue that such a radical approach to human freedom is more in keeping with a secular than a religious conception of the world, by arguing that one ought to ascribe religious significance to the fixed structures of nature and not only to miraclelike interventions. One need not picture natural regularities as the cumulative effect of innumerable particular divine acts. Just as it is pointless to speak of particular divine volitions to account for an object's falling to the earth as the result of the force of gravity, so too it is pointless to speak of particular divine volitions to account for each and every act of human freedom. Every occurrence of the law of gravity expresses divine will only insofar as God is the Creator of the universe; thus He is the ultimate cause of all the forces and laws found in nature.

Similarly, Maimonides argues that divine will is expressed in voluntary human actions because free will is part of the very nature of a human being. Freedom is an essential condition of human nature and therefore every voluntary act may be regarded as an expression of divine will simply by virtue of its being an act of free will. In this respect, human freedom and divine will coincide. See *Eight Chapters*, chapter 8; *MT Hilkhot Teshuvah* 5 (especially 5:4); *Guide* 2:48. For an understanding of the religious sensibility of the halakhist who conceives of divine action in this way, see Hartman, *Maimonides*, chapter 4.

41. *The Book of Judges*, trans. A. M. Hershman, pp. xxiii–xxiv.

42. See *Responsa of Maimonides*, ed. J. Blau, 3 vols, (Jerusalem: Mekitze Nirdamin, 1957–61), Resp. 149, 448; *MT Hilkhot Avodah Zarah* 9:4, text as in *Sefer ha-Mada*, ed. S. Lieberman (Jerusalem: Mossad Harav Kook,

1964); *MT Hilkhot Ma'akhalot Assurot* 11:7; H. A. Wolfson, "Maimonides on the Unity and Incorporeality of God," *Jewish Quarterly Review*, n.s. 56 (1965): 112–36; Pines, "Histabrut ha-tekumah me-hadash," p. 292, n. 16; J. Katz, *Exclusiveness and Tolerance* (Oxford: Oxford University Press, 1961), ch. 10; H. H. Ben-Sasson, "Jewish Reflections on Nationhood in the Twelfth Century," *P'raqim* 2 (1969–74): 178–95.

43. See *Guide* 3:17.

44. See Judah Halevi, *Kuzari* 4:11–23; Ben-Sasson, "Jewish Reflections on Nationhood," pp. 181–83. Ben-Sasson's attempt at integrating Maimonides' overall appreciation of reason, choice, and freedom with his attitude toward Christianity and Islam as instruments serving the ideal of messianism warrants serious consideration. Funkenstein's position was greatly influenced by Ben-Sasson's. See Twersky, *The Code of Maimonides*, pp. 452–53.

45. Cf. Twersky, *The Code of Maimonides*, pp. 225–28; L. Kaplan, "Maimonides on the Singularity of the Jewish People" (unpublished); Funkenstein, "Maimonides," pp. 98–9.

In contrast to those who treat the first chapter of *MT Hilkhot Avodah Zarah* as the initial stage of a historical process culminating in messianism (i.e., as a chapter in Maimonides' philosophy of history), Maimonides' construction of the transition from monotheism to paganism, and the transition from Abraham's community of faith based on knowledge to Moses' covenantal community based on *mitzvah* can also be construed as an introduction to the laws of idolatry. The first chapter provides an explanation of why Judaism rejects mediative or intermediary worship regardless of whether the worshipers' belief framework is monotheistic. In showing how the loss of monotheism was caused by mistaken forms of worship (a halakhic rather than a philosophic error; see *Guide* 1:36), Maimonides enables the reader to appreciate Judaism's serious preoccupation with how one worships God.

Furthermore, the first chapter deals not only with the transition from monotheism to paganism and Abraham's struggle to reestablish monotheism, but also with the failure of Abraham's efforts once the community of faith based on knowledge was exposed to the cultural influences of Egypt. Maimonides shows that only a remnant, i.e., the tribe of Levi, could survive as monotheists without some counterpart to the disciplined structure of idolatry. Only through the efforts of Moses was Israel able to realize the monotheistic ideal. (Note the analogy Maimonides draws between the tribe of Levi and singular individuals who worship God on the basis of philosophic knowledge at the end of *MT Hilkhot Shemitah ve-Yovel*.)

Maimonides' chapters on Abraham and on messianism serve normative and educational purposes; they are not meant to convey a philosophy of history culminating in the eschatological triumph of Judaism in the messianic era. The notion of an imminent, necessary process in history is foreign to Maimonidean thinking. Messianism is a guiding normative ideal of the community and not a prediction of an inevitable process. See Hartman, *Maimonides*, pp. 54–61, and Hartman, "The God of Abraham and the God of the Philosophers," in *Joy and Responsibility*, pp. 162–97.

46. See *Guide* 3:36 and *MT Hilkhot Ta'anit* 1:1–3.
47. *Eight Chapters,* in *Ethical Writings of Maimonides,* trans. R. L. Weiss with C. E. Butterworth (New York: New York University Press, 1975), pp. 84–5.
48. See BT Niddah 16b (the comments of Rashi and Tosafot are far removed from Maimonides' interpretation); BT Megillah 25a; BT Berakhot 33b; *Responsa,* ed Blau, Resp. 436, pp. 714–16.
49. Cf. the comments of Naḥmanides to Gen. 15:13. See G. Von Rad, *Genesis: A Commentary,* trans. J. H. Marks (Philadelphia: Westminster, 1961) on this verse.
50. *Eight Chapters,* pp. 88–9.
51. See A. Altmann, "The Religion of the Thinkers: Free Will and Predestination in Saadia, Bahya, and Maimonides," in *Religion in a Religious Age,* ed. S. D. Goitein (Cambridge, Mass.: Association for Jewish Studies, 1974), pp. 35–45; L. Strauss, "Notes on Maimonides' Book of Knowledge," in *Studies in Mysticism and Religion Presented to Gershom G. Scholem* (Jerusalem: Magnes, 1967), pp. 280–83.
52. See the comments of Rabad to *MT Hilkhot Teshuvah* 5; I. Twersky, *Rabad of Posquières* (Cambridge: Harvard University Press, 1962), pp. 280–81. For contemporary discussions on determinism and freedom, see P. F. Strawson, "Freedom and Resentment," in *Freedom and Resentment and Other Essays* (London: Methuen, 1974), pp. 1–25; I. Berlin, "Historical Inevitability," in *Four Essays on Liberty* (Oxford: Oxford University Press, 1969), pp. 41–117, and Berlin's interesting discussion with his critics in the introduction, pp. ix–xxxvii.

It would be fruitful to compare Maimonides' comments on coercion and freedom in *MT Hilkhot Gerushin* 2:20 with Berlin's distinction between positive and negative freedom in his essay, "Two Concepts of Liberty."
53. See "The Correspondence between the Rabbis of Southern France and Maimonides about Astrology," ed. A. Marx, *Hebrew Union College Annual* 3 (1926): 311–58; Halkin, ed., *Epistle to Yemen,* pp. xxi–xxvi.

THE ESSAY
ON RESURRECTION

During his lifetime, Maimonides achieved fame throughout Jewish communites as well as in the non-Jewish community. Not only was he the recognized leader of Egyptian Jewry but also he was widely known for his extensive correspondence and his major works. Yet fame also brought him controversy and opposition. In particular, some Jews who denied the resurrection of the dead claimed to base their beliefs on the teachings of Maimonides. Eventually, Samuel ben Ali, the head of the talmudic academy in Baghdad, openly accused him of rejecting this cardinal belief of Judaism. In 1191, late in a long life of devoted service to the Jewish people, Maimonides wrote his *Essay on Resurrection* in order to defend himself against the charge of heresy. Even in this circumstance, however, he did not write solely for personal reasons.

I n the name of the Lord, the Everlasting God.[1]
Sincere are all the words of my mouth, there is nothing tortuous
or perverse in them; they are all of them straightforward to the man
of understanding, and right to those who find knowledge [Prov. 8:8–9].
A man of sense conceals what he knows, but fools proclaim their folly
[Prov. 12:23].[2]

It is not rare that a person aims to expound the intent of some
conclusions clearly and explicitly, makes an effort to reject doubts and
eliminate far-fetched interpretations, and yet the unbalanced will draw
the reverse judgment of the conclusion he sought to clarify. Some such
thing occurred even to one of God's declarations. When the chief of
the prophets[3] wished by order of God to teach us that He is One,
without associates, and to remove from our hearts those wrong doctrines that the Dualists[4] propound, he proclaimed this fundamental:
The Lord is our God, the Lord alone [Deut. 6:4].[5] But the Christians
utilized this verse to prove that God is one of three, teaching that *Lord,*
our God, the Lord makes three names, all followed by One,[6] which
indicates that they are three and that the three are one. Far be God
from what they say in their ignorance.[7] If this is what happened to
God's proclamation, it is much more likely and to be expected to
happen to statements by humans.

The same thing came to pass when some in our religious community
challenged my understanding of one of the fundamentals of the Torah.
I sought to call people's attention to the sorely neglected basic tenet
that they doubted, notwithstanding the fact that it is a plain and explicit
dogma of the faith and leaves no uncertainty about it. This is what
happened. When I concentrated on a compilation of the law of the
Torah and an exposition of its statutes, my object was to find favor
with God, not to look forward to honor or reward from people.[8] I wished
to the best of my ability to provide guidance, understanding, and
comprehension to whomever is not qualified to grasp the teachings of

the scholars of the Law who lived before me. I was persuaded that I had smoothed remote and difficult matters, and collected, and joined scattered and disarranged items. I knew that I would profit from it in either of two possibilities. If, as I thought, I smoothed, collected, and put within reach of people what was never done before me, I succeeded in bringing aid to people and in gaining reward from God. If it is not so, and my compilation has not resulted in better understanding and greater simplicity than was gained from the writings of any of my predecessors, I at least earned reward from God. My intentions were good, and God takes cognizance of intentions.[9] It was this calculation that impelled my tongue to speak and my hand to write on every subject in which I hoped to succeed, as I stated, in its compilation and clarification.

When I applied myself to this task, I realized that it was not correct to strive to explain the ramifications of the religious law, and to leave its roots neglected, unexplained, and its essentials undiscussed,[10] providing no guidance. This is especially urgent since I have met some who think they are among the sages of Israel—by God, they indeed know the way of the Law ever since childhood, and they battle in legal discussions[11]—but they are not certain if God is corporeal, with eyes, hands, and feet, as the Bible says, or if He has not a body.[12] Others, whom I have met in some lands, assert positively that He is corporeal and call anyone who thinks differently a nonbeliever,[13] name him a heretic and Epicurean.[14] They explain the homilies of Berakhot literally.[15] I have received similar reports of some whom I have not met.

When I learned of these exceedingly deficient folk and their doubts, who, although they consider themselves sages in Israel, are in fact the most ignorant, and more seriously astray than beasts, their minds filled with the senseless prattle of old women and noxious fantasies, like children and women, I concluded that it was necessary that I clearly elucidate religious fundamentals in my works on law.[16] I determined not to teach these basic truths in the idiom of inquiry, since examination of these roots requires skills in many fields, of which, as I pointed out in the *Guide*,[17] the learned in Torah know nothing.[18] More than anything else I preferred to have the truths accepted by the masses.[19] I therefore published principles that need to be acknowledged in the introduction to the commentary on the Mishnah[20] regarding prophecy and the roots of tradition and what every Rabbanite had to believe concerning the Oral Law.[21] In chapter 10 of Sanhedrin[22] I expounded fundamentals connected with the beginning and the end, i.e., what pertains to God's unity and the world-to-come and the other tenets of the Torah. I acted the same way in my major work, which I called *Mishneh Torah*, a work whose worth only people of integrity will appreciate, scholars in religion and science, products of sound reliable training, who can evaluate the methods pursued in my work, and discern how I collected and compiled material that was dispersed and scattered.[23] I also listed all of the religious and legal roots, my objective being that those who are called disciples of the wise, or *geonim*, or whatever you choose to name them, build their legal details on legal foundations, so that their learning will be organized and their knowledge systematically arranged.[24] I wish to have all this established on religious dogmas. They will no longer cast the knowledge of God behind their backs,[25] but will exert themselves to the limit of their power to attain what will perfect them and bring them nearer to their Creator, not to what the general public imagines to be perfection.[26]

Among the dogmas that demand our attention is the world-to-come. I undertook to relate its essence, emphasized and extended my remarks, and fortified them with proofs from relevant biblical verses and from pertinent words of the sages of blessed memory. I interpreted what was suitable in the view of the men of science.[27] I wrote an exposition of my views in chapter 10 of Sanhedrin, and disclosed why I set as my objective the elaboration of the belief in the world-to-come rather than in the Resurrection. I explained that we find men concerned only with resurrection; asking if the dead will rise naked or in their garments, and other such problems.[28] But the world-to-come is entirely overlooked.

I thereupon announced very clearly that the Resurrection is a fundamental of the Torah of Moses our master,[29] but that it was not the ultimate goal, and that the ultimate goal is the life in the world-to-come. I engaged in this long discussion so that I dispelled the serious skepticism that contends that the Torah knows of no reward that is not in this world, and that it makes no mention of reward or punishment in the afterlife. I quoted verses from the Torah, as explained to us by tradition, to demonstrate that it contemplated the world-to-come as the ultimate goal of recompense and of punishment, which is rejection from the afterlife. These are the same concepts I expounded at length in my major work in the section on repentance.[30]

After a protracted analysis of the world-to-come in chapter 10 of Sanhedrin, as all who look for it will find, I stated that the Resurrection was a biblical dogma, and that whoever did not accept it had neither religion nor any connection with the Torah of our master Moses,[31] but that it was not the ultimate goal. Similarly, when I enumerated in my major work those who would not share in the world-to-come, I gave their number, specifying they were twenty-four, all this because of my fear that a copyist might omit one and someone would claim that I did not list it. Included in the twenty-four is "he who denies the Resurrection."[32] In connection with the world-to-come, to which I referred there, I clearly stressed that it was the ultimate goal. To quote myself: "This is the reward with none greater, and the good with nothing better."[33]

There I further explained that in the world-to-come no bodies would exist, in conformity with the talmudic description: In it there will be no food, nor drink, nor sexual intercourse.[34] It is absurd to assume that these organs will exist in vain; far be God from producing in vain! If it is a person with mouth, stomach, liver, and other food mechanisms, but he does not eat, and with genitals but he does not reproduce, the existence of the organs is absolutely futile.[35] It is not correct to parallel these strong, rationally established proofs of mine with homilies that more appropriately belong to women in their condolence calls.[36]

It happens that someone contradicted this judgment of mine by arguing that Moses and Elijah survived for some time without food or drink, yet they had their bodies, and that this will be the condition of the members of the world-to-come.[37] *May it never befall you, all who pass along the road! Look about and see* [Lam. 1:12]. The organs of Moses and Elijah were not in vain, because they lived before the miracle and after it. What sort of analogy can be drawn from that to the extended, eternal existence in a world that is, as they describe it, "all good, all lasting"?[38] How then can it be a place for bodily organs in vain? It is well known that the body as a whole is only the carrier of the soul, which performs all its acts with it. Not a single one of these acts is ever performed by the members in the world-to-come. But these fellows are not aware how necessarily disgraceful it is of anyone to ascribe to God creation in vain and the fashioning of organs from which purposeless purpose is expected.

However, all this is an inescapable consequence of premature misconceptions in the minds of the masses. They do not recognize true existence other than in a body.[39] They also admit that if something that is in a body but is not itself a body, like the accidents, is in existence, it is not as real as the body.[40] But what is neither a body nor an accident in a body is deemed nonexistent by the ignorant who, despite the hoariness of their bodies, are undoubtedly *weaned from milk, just taken away from the breast* [Isa. 28:9].[41] For this reason, most of them believe that God is corporeal, because in their judgment He would not be in existence if He were not. Those, however, who can be called learned, not metaphorically but literally, have concluded by incontrovertible reasoning that everything separated from matter is more firmly existent than anything material, nay, not only more so; this is actual existence, since it is not affected by any of the variety of change.[42] These know most certainly that God is neither a body nor a faculty within a body. Hence the level of His existence is the most absolute.

In the same way, every separated creature,[43] namely, the angels and the intellect, is firmer and more stable than any body. Hence, I believe that the angels are not bodies, and that the members of the world-to-come are separated souls, namely, intellects. In my work that I named *Guide of the Perplexed* I have culled proofs of this from the Torah.[44] If one of the simpletons does not care to accept this, and prefers to believe that the angels are bodies and even eat—because the text of the Bible reads *they ate* [Gen. 18:8][45]—and that the members of the world-to-come are also bodies, I do not mind.[46] I would this were the extent of the ignorance of any of them. I hope their view of the Creator is free from any acceptance of corporeality. There is no harm in their assuming it for the separated beings.[47]

If a boor is not content with having his doubts about this, so that neither view prevails, but chooses to adhere to the popular opinion, and finds fault with my view and damns me for thinking that the angels and the members of the world-to-come are separated from matter and free of it, I hold no grievance against him. I forgive him and freely admit my "fault." There is no limit to the number of homilies that serve as refutations of my opinion, and I am not surprised. There are just as many biblical verses and even prophetic passages that refute me, since their simple meaning teaches that God is a body with eyes and ears. However, since the intellectual proofs and the incontrovertible deductions that rule this out are valid, it becomes clear, as the sages say, that "the Torah speaks in the style of people."[48] But the anthropomorphist can neither grasp nor understand these unshakable conclusions or the intellectual proofs that teach that angels and the members of the world-to-come are divested of anything corporeal, so much so that I am compelled to assume that the passages that suggest corporeality are metaphorical. Those who presume that they are corporeal cannot appreciate these proofs. How then can it be imagined that they will concede that they are bare of matter? These conjecture that their very existence, I mean the angels and the souls, that is, the members of the world-to-come, cannot be known save by tradition rooted in the Torah, and there is no speculative approach that can teach that the angels exist and the souls are immortal. Such are the assertions of those who think that they have attained knowledge of the essential truths by leisurely living, by these vague notions, by relaxed study, by the lack of all the sciences, and by limiting themselves to the literal meaning of what has come down to us by tradition.[49] It is as though the sages of blessed memory never stated so many times in the Talmud that the words of the Torah carry an outer and an inner meaning[50]—for this reason the hidden is called the inner meaning of the Torah—and as though they never breathed a word about the secrets of Torah. But these pathetic folk are much too distracted to know anything of all this. In the *Guide* I dealt with all these matters to an extent sufficient for the people of understanding, spoke of all the evidence from the sages regarding this, and called attention to where this evidence is located, so that the texts that serve me as proof are revealed and their true sense becomes known.[51]

After this book of mine, I mean my major work, was published and spread to the far corners, word reached me that a student in Damascus asserted there would be no resurrection, and the soul would not return to the body after they separated. All of the people present questioned him: "How can you say so?" He took to citing what I wrote in my book, that the ultimate goal was the world-to-come, where there were no bodies.[52] When his disputants brought proof from what the community believed and from what the sages repeated many times, his reply was that it was all metaphorical. Their discussion was long. But when the report reached me I paid no attention to it. I assumed it was an isolated incident, because no one else would speak with such ignorance, or find it so difficult to understand what I taught.

In the course of 1185 a letter reached me from Yemen inquiring about various matters. It also related that some among them decided that the body would decompose after death, the soul would not return to the body after separation, and reward and punishment would be reserved only for the soul. They relied on what I had written about the members of the world-to-come. When the clear and explicit statements of the sages were brought to their attention as well as some verses from the prophets they disposed of them by maintaining they were metaphorical and required interpretation. My correspondents further informed me that this view was popular among them and they discarded other beliefs. In my answer to their request for my position, I wrote very plainly that resurrection was a biblical fundamental, which means that the soul will return to the corpse, and that it was not to be explained away. Life in the world-to-come follows the Resurrection,[53] as I stated explicitly in chapter 10 of Sanhedrin.[54] I reckoned this was sufficient.

But this year, 1191, a letter arrived from some of my colleagues in Baghdad, in which they wrote that an individual from Yemen inquired regarding these selfsame issues of Samuel ha-Levi, the incumbent head of the Academy—may God protect him—who at present resides in Baghdad.[55] He composed an essay on resurrection, and in it he calls some of my views an error and a sin, and others defensible. His judgment of me is moderate, and he is somewhat reserved in his wording. Following this correspondence, I received a copy of the essay that the Gaon wrote.[56] I found it was a collection of the homilies and legends that he had gathered. Everyone knows that scholars are not expected to rehearse the homilies and the curious tales,[57] of the sort that women tell one another in their condolence calls. What is wanted is their interpretation, and an exposition of their implied meaning, so that they conform to a rational position, or at least approximate it.

It is remarkable that he asserts that those amazing views he espouses are the doctrines of the philosophers on the soul. This clearly suggests that in his opinion what the *mutakallimun*[58] and others propose, and their wrong ideas, are philosophic theories. The strangest in this essay—it is all very strange!—is his contention that the wise philosophers do not deem the return of the soul to the body after separation absurd; no, it is rationally of the class of the possible. This is exactly what he writes. These statements of his indicate that in his estimate the *mutakallimun* are the wise philosophers and that he does not have the slightest notion of the methods by which the philosophers discern the necessary, the impossible, and the contingent.[59] He also includes matters taken from that tract on the afterlife by ibn Sina,[60] and from the *al-Mu'tabar*,[61] which one of theirs in Baghdad wrote, and Samuel considers decidedly philosophic. I also discover that the Gaon decided that the immortality of the soul has not been validated by the philosophers, and that their judgments differ. Would I knew who those philosophers are whom he designates by this name.[62] Still another surprise: the Gaon does not define the intellect. We do not know whether in his philosophy the soul and the intellect are the same, or the soul is immortal while the intellect perishes, or if it is the intellect that survives and the soul that perishes.[63] This is the soul that he says the philosophers do not know, and one of their theories is that it is the blood.[64] Perhaps in his judgment the intellect is an accident, which is what the *mutakallimun* assert, and in his opinion they are the wise philosophers. In that case it will undoubtedly perish.[65]

It would have been far more attractive and preferable if a man like the Gaon had confined himself to a compilation of these homilies and tales and to the interpretation of the verses that prove midrashically that the Resurrection is clearly affirmed in the Torah. On the whole, all he wrote, or most of it, has been said in more or less the same manner. But my aim and purpose in this essay is the benefit that can result to the learner, not the defense and admiration of a person nor the disapproval and disparagement of another. The way of contention and repudiation are open to whomever chooses to walk it. But may God close this road and the likes of it.

I shall now turn to the discussion of the objective of the treatise. You must realize, O inquirer, that in this tract I intend to elucidate what I believe regarding this fundamental, the Resurrection, which has become a subject of disagreement among students. There is absolutely nothing more in it about this theme than what I wrote down in the commentary on the Mishnah or in my major work.[66] It is nothing other than a repetition and a general elaboration, and some further comment, which even women and ignorant folk will understand.

The meaning of resurrection, I declare, which is popular and well known in our community, and all our sects agree on it, is the return of the soul to the body after separation. It is very frequently recalled in the prayers, sermons, and supplications that the prophets and the outstanding sages composed, and in the contents of the Talmud and the midrashim. Nothing contradicting it has been heard of in our community, nor any kind of reinterpretation. It is not right to suppose that anyone of our religion believes something contrary to that.[67] In this essay I shall clarify to you why these texts are not to be explained away, as I have done with many others in the Torah and abandoned their plain sense.[68] In the same way, this resurrection, the return of the soul to the body after death, is affirmed by Daniel in a form that does not allow for reinterpretation, for the verses read: *Many of those that sleep in the dust of the earth will awake, some to eternal life, others to reproaches, to everlasting abhorrence* [Dan. 12:2]. And the angel adds: *But you, go on to the end; you shall rest and rise to your destiny at the end of the days* [Dan. 12:13].

Now, when it is reported of me that I maintain that the Resurrection in the Torah is metaphorical, this is a downright lie and a pure invention. My writings are in circulation; let them be perused, and let someone show where I say this. I did state that the sages of Israel disagree about the assertion of some of them regarding the dead in Ezekiel,[69] for example. But every issue that does not involve practice, on which opinions differ, cannot be resolved in favor of one over the other. This was pointed out several times in my commentary on the Mishnah.[70] These remarks make obvious to me that the individuals who will return to their bodies will eat, drink, marry, and procreate, and they will die after a long life, like those who will live during the messianic age.

The life, however, that is not followed by death, is life in the world-to-come, since it will be bodiless. It is my view, a valid assumption with every intelligent person, that the world-to-come is made up of souls without bodies, like the angels.[71] The reason for it is that the body is an aggregate of limbs and organs solely for the actions of the soul, as has been definitely established. The constituents of the body are of three parts: vegetative, by which nourishment is procured, like the mouth, the stomach, the liver, the intestines, in a word, all that is in the lower belly; generative, like the genital organs, the semen, and the fetus; means of improving the body so that it can supply the soul with all its needs, like the eye and the other senses, the muscles, the veins, and the ligaments by which all movement is accomplished. If it were not for these, the animal could not move toward the food it seeks, nor flee from what opposes it, and may destroy or spoil it. Consequently, since man's nourishment can only be acquired by acts he performs and by many preliminary preparations that require thought and reflection, he has been provided with the rational faculty to control his actions and the natural means with which he performs these acts, I mean hands and feet, because the legs are not only for walking. The details of this summary are known to students.[72]

It thus becomes clear that the existence of the entire body is needed for certain ends, nourishment for its maintenance and reproduction of the like for its continued presence. Now, since these ends are discarded and unneeded in the world-to-come—the reason being, as the sages have all made clear, that there is no eating in it, nor drinking, nor intercourse[73]—it is obvious there is no body. God creates absolutely nothing in vain, makes things only for things. Far, indeed, far be it from Him that His sophisticated acts bear any similarity to the work of the makers of idols. *They have eyes, but cannot see; they have ears, but cannot hear* . . . [Ps. 135:16–17].[74] In the view of these folk God also creates bodies or limbs not to do what they were created for nor for any reason. According to them, maybe the members of the world-to-come do not have limbs but they are unquestionably bodies, perhaps solid spheres, or pillars, or cubes. Really, they are laughable. *If you would only keep quiet it would be considered wisdom* [Job 13:5].[75]

I have already explained what accounts for it all. The masses do not recognize existence except of a body or of what is in a body. What is not a body or in a body does not exist. The more secure they want to make the existence of something, the more they endow it with corporeality, that is, they solidify the substance of its body. I have expressly discussed it on many occasions in the *Guide*.[76] Now, whoever wishes to fault me for this view, it is up to him; if he desires to call it a mistake or an error let him say so. I do not mind. As I established in the *Guide*, I prefer to be followed by the intelligent in accepting the truth, even if it is one individual, and to have thousands from among the ignorant shun me because they believe nonsense.

What I do deny and disown before God is any assertion that the soul will never return to the body, and that it simply cannot happen. This kind of rejection leads to the rejection of all the miracles;[77] the denial of miracles is a denial of God and a defection from the Law. Absolutely nothing in all I have written suggests that I deny the return of the soul to the body. On the contrary, it suggests the opposite.[78] Whoever wishes and chooses to malign me and to attribute to me opinions which I do not hold—like one who suspects the pious of sin—and to invent the most farfetched explanations of what I have written, so that he can prove me guilty, will surely be punished for it,[79] and will be treated like anyone who suspects the innocent.[80]

Following this clear declaration, no one has the right to maintain that I believe every reference in the Bible to the Resurrection to be a metaphor. No, some are valid truths, and some are undoubtedly fables; others raise the question: are they fact or fiction? If you study in depth everything written by the sages and by the Andalusian commentators,[81] and the context of the doubtful passage, it will become clear to you. Considering the purpose of this essay, I do not need to go into it in detail. Ideas are not reinforced by a repetition of their formulation, nor is their validity weakened when they are not repeated.[82] You surely know that the fundamental of God's unity, the Lord is one, is not repeated in the Torah.[83] Since I found a prophetic statement, not susceptible to interpretation, which speaks of the return of the soul to the body,[84] the prophetic announcement is therewith made. This prediction will not increase in validity if you take every word in the Bible meaning *revival* to refer to the return of the soul to the body, nor will it lose its validity if you render some of the relevant verses, or all of them metaphorically. In a word, the prophetic prediction has been made either once or many times,[85] the ancient and more recent sages of Israel have stated it innumerable times, our religious community is unanimously agreed that the soul of man will return to the body. This is what resurrection means wherever a sage or an author speaks of it.[86]

Others were also led astray because of what I wrote at the end of my major work.[87] This is what I said: "Do not think for a moment that the king, the Messiah, will be required to perform miracles and wonders, or that he will inaugurate new things in the world, or will resurrect the dead, or anything like it." I found support of it in what I expounded.[88] Some less than mature minds assumed that this was a repudiation of the Resurrection, and it contradicted what I stated explicitly in my commentary on the Mishnah, to the effect that the Resurrection is one of the fundamentals of the Law. But all this is perfectly clear, free from doubts and contradictions. I said that the Messiah would not be required to do wonders, like miraculously splitting the Red Sea, or resurrecting the dead. He would not be required to perform miracles, seeing that the early prophets, whose predictions are valid, foretold that he would come.[89] But from this analysis it does not follow that God will not revive the dead by His will and wish when He desires and whomever He desires to resurrect. It will happen in the lifetime of the Messiah, or before him, or after he dies. In short, in all I wrote in my compositions, nothing can lead any thinking individual to doubt, except students at the beginning of their studies.

They were likewise puzzled by my statement that Isaiah's forecast: *The wolf shall dwell with the lamb* [Isa. 11:6], is a parable.[90] This is not only my view.[91] In fact I was anticipated by the keen commentators on the meaning of the passage, men like Gikatilla, or ibn Bal'am, and other exegetes.[92] The end of the sentence proves it: *In all of My sacred mount they shall do nothing evil or vile, for the land shall be filled with the knowledge of God. . . .* The reason is provided;[93] they will do nothing vile or evil because they will know God. Just look, all of you people who have a mind! Can you believe that the lion is under God's command? That at present he is disobedient and hence carnivorous, but at that time repentant, learning from his Creator that which is right and that it is not permissible to be hostile, so that he will change and become herbivorous? Indeed, this characterization is confirmed: *So that all prophecy has been to you like the words of a sealed document* [Isa. 29:11].[94] I, for my part, have elucidated the meaning of this in a chapter of the *Guide*,[95] and in my major composition[96] I have expounded my clear proof of their statement that in the messianic age nothing will change of the laws of nature.[97]

You must realize that I am not at all positive that all the promises and the like of them are metaphorical.[98] No revelation from God has come to teach me they are parables. Nor did I find any rabbinic tradition derived from the prophets in which they say categorically that these matters are allegorical. I will only explain to you what impels me to speak this way. My endeavor, and that of the select keen-minded people, differs from the quest of the masses.[99] They like nothing better and, in their silliness, enjoy nothing more, than to set the Law and reason at opposite ends, and to move everything far from the explicable. So they claim it to be a miracle, and they shrink from identifying it as a natural incident, whether it is something that happened in the past and is recorded, or something predicted to happen in the future. But I try to reconcile the Law and reason, and 'wherever possible consider all things as of the natural order. Only when something is explicitly identified as a miracle, and reinterpretation of it cannot be accommodated, only then I feel forced to grant that this is a miracle.[100]

In the *Guide* I construed the plain biblical texts, and also the passages from the sages, to mean there are many fables among the words of the prophets.[101] I went to such lengths in their exposition that none of the contentious boors will find it possible to reject it. For this reason, I, and the excellent commentators who preceded me, assert that these are allegories, as we have interpreted them.[102] It may, however, be argued that as the population grows, and the earth becomes more cultivated, the hostility of the beasts to one another will decrease and they will become mutually amicable.[103] In his book on animals,[104] this is how Aristotle accounts for the decrease of the mutual discord among the beasts of Egypt. But this may also be fantasy, to use the expression of the sages: "The Torah speaks in hyperboles."[105] More-

over, if Isaiah's visions should come to be literally, they will be confined to the Temple Mount, for he adds: *In My holy mountains* [Isa.
11:9].[106] They will then be of a kind with the rabbinic tradition: "Never
did serpent or scorpion do harm in Jerusalem."[107]

To sum up, none of these matters is a fundamental of the Law, and
no one should be concerned how they are regarded.[108] We must simply
wait until the decision falls, may it come speedily, on how they are to
be regarded, and then it will become known whether they are allegory
or miracle.[109] It is recognized that I shun as best I can changes in the
physical order.[110] But everyone, whether he lived before the present
or is not yet born, is mistaken if he does not realize the distinction
between happenings that come as miracles and do not become permanent at all, so that they occur out of necessity or to confirm prophecy, and natural, continuous events that are the way of the world,[111]
and of which our sages say: "The world runs its normal course."[112]
They also rule: "Miracles cannot be used as proof."[113] Solomon declared: *I realized, too, that whatever God has brought to pass will recur
evermore; nothing can be added to it and nothing taken from it* [Eccles.
3:14].[114] From this it becomes clear that natural events always continue regularly. This has also been explained in the *Guide* in my
discussion of this world.[115]

It occurs to me that what has made this people be in error about
my views of the Resurrection is the difference in treatment. When I
dealt with the world-to-come I dwelt at length and in detail on its
description, elucidated its essence, and cited all the statements of the
prophets and the sages that refer to it. But when I wrote of the Resurrection I disposed of it in few words, asserting that it is a valid
fundamental.[116] Two considerations dictated this treatment. In the first
place, all of my compositions are to the point and brief.[117] I do not
seek to enlarge the size of the books, nor to lose time on what yields
no benefit. When I write a commentary, it is only on what requires
exegesis, and only so far as it will help understanding, and when I
write a book, I include only epitomized conclusions. Secondly, elaboration is to be applied only to the comprehension of a hidden matter
so that it is achieved or its verity is proved. This is needed in the
three classes of science: mathematics, physics, and metaphysics. In
them, meaning is frequently obscure and comprehension remote until

their contents are adequately defined. Often the intelligible thesis requires very many arguments, so that the validity it wants is provided.
But with miracles the understanding of what is told is neither hidden
nor difficult. Nor is proof possible of the validity of what has not
happened, or of what has been foretold. They are only witnessed with
the senses or learned from one who saw them. For these reasons I
expound themes of the world-to-come and shed light on its mysteries,
and also because it, I mean the immortality of the soul, is a doctrine
in harmony with the nature of the world order.

The Resurrection, however, is a miraculous event. Its sense is easily
grasped, and nothing more is needed than to believe in it as the
authentic tradition teaches us. It is something outside the nature of
existence,[118] and no rational proof of it exists. It simply follows the
pattern of all miracles; it is to be accepted, and that is that. What can
I say on this subject, or how can I treat it at length? Or do you think
I am expected to provide rational arguments from which resurrection
will necessarily follow? Most probably such folk expect me to indulge
in my works in those homilies that are preached on the theme and
those legends,[119] but this is a procedure suitable to someone other
than myself, in line with the objective of its composition. All of you
who have read my works know well that I always aim to avoid dis-
agreements and challenges. If I could squeeze the entire Law of the
Torah into one chapter, I would not write two chapters for it. How then
can I be expected to speak of homilies and legends, when they can
be found where they are? What advantage lies in their repetition and
in the claim that I produced a book?[120]

After reaching this point in this monograph, which was its objective,
and realizing that it is entirely bereft of benefits, because it contains
nothing more than repetition of what is written in my commentary to
the Mishnah and in my major composition, with some additional explanation for the unintelligent or the skeptic, I think it proper not to
deprive it of some new interest. I shall take up two problems relevant
to this subject.

The first is to clarify the intent of the very many verses in the Bible
that clearly indicate, beyond the possibility of interpretation, the denial of the Resurrection. For example: *If a man dies, can he live again?*
[Job. 14:14], or *As a cloud fades away, so whoever goes down to Sheol*

does not come up [Job 7:9], or *Before I go whence I shall not return, even to the land of darkness and of the shadow of death* [Job. 10:21]. These very numerous verses are in the book of Job. Hezekiah protests: *Nor do they who descend into the Pit hope for Your grace. The living, only the living can give thanks to You as I do this day* [Isa. 38:18–19]. This is proof that the dead are those who go down into the pit. It is also written: *We must all die; we are like water that is poured out on the ground and cannot be gathered up* [2 Sam. 14:14]. Another text says: *Do You work wonders for the dead? Do the shades rise to praise You?* [Ps. 88:11]. *A passing breath that does not return* [Ps. 78:39]. If you follow the verses in the Bible closely you will discover them all generally negating the Resurrection, save some apparently different passages in Isaiah,[121] which upon close examination raise doubts about whether they are literally true or symbolic.[122] There is no conclusive text other than in Daniel and its assertion: *Many of those that sleep in the dust of the earth will awake . . .* [Dan. 12:2] and the sentence: *You shall rest, and arise to your destiny at the end of the days* [Dan. 12:12].[123] But this also creates great perplexity. Some become very skeptical of this fundamental of the Resurrection, and others who confirm this tenet are compelled to reinterpret every one of the explicit passages by explanations too farfetched to be acceptable.[124]

The second problem is that the Torah has not mentioned this fundamental in any way, certainly not plainly, nor even by a hint. True, it has been undoubtedly claimed that the Torah implies this belief, and the matters of which I speak are introduced with the query: What proof of the Resurrection can be found in the Torah?[125] At most, it can be maintained that they are recondite suggestions or references, particularly since the sages disagree regarding them.[126] Accordingly, this second problem is why the Torah has not mentioned it in plain words in a style not susceptible to reinterpretation? If it has spoken of it, as these suppose, it is like one concealing the statement, wishing to keep it secret.[127]

In answer to the first question, it is my opinion that the discourses of the prophets and the texts of the Hagiographa mean only to portray the customary, familiar pattern of existence. It is well known that the natural course is intercourse between male and female, procreation of the like,[128] and the gradual growth of the child until the individual dies. It is not in the course of nature for that individual to return after his death and come into being a second time. The scheme of nature is that when the beasts of the animal world die, they never again return. On the other hand, they slowly disintegrate and decompose until they return to the elements and to the primary matter, to a degree that does not allow for the recovery of a noticeable remnant, of which it might be said it was part of so-and-so. Man alone receives the divine flow that makes for the survival of something that will neither perish nor become corrupted. His body, however, perishes, like the bodies of all the other members of the animal world. Anyone who devotes himself to investigate these profound problems, I mean the survival of the immortal something that the human has been granted, will learn this by speculative reasoning.[129] This is the course of nature, and this is what the prophetic books call by the homonyms soul and spirit.[130] The extinction of the body, and its decomposition into what it was made of in this manner of return, is detailed in the text: *And the dust return-eth to the ground as it was, and the spirit returneth unto God who gave it* [Eccles. 12:7].[131] This is the way of nature, and all the biblical verses are in accord with it.

Actually there is no difference between the question: *If a man dies, can he live again?* [Job. 14:14] and the challenge: *Shall we get water for you out of this rock?* [Num. 20:10].[132] The sense is that naturally it is not so; it is impossible. Yet water did miraculously come out of that rock. Similarly, the Resurrection is simply one of the miracles.[133] There is no difference between the doubt: *Can the Ethiopian change his skin?* [Jer. 13:23] and the question: *Do you work wonders for the dead?* [Ps. 88:11].[134] Indeed the color of the noble hand did turn white.[135]

If a person claimed that the inanimate objects could not possibly move, his contention would be correct in terms of the natural, but it would not disprove the change of the rod to serpent, since that was a miracle.[136] Likewise whatever you find in Scripture that repudiates the return of the dead follows the course of nature and does not contradict the return of the dead whom God will wish to resurrect. Thus the purport of these verses has been explained to you most plausibly, and you do not need to reinterpret any of these phrases with those outland-ish and farfetched explanations that do not provide enlightening proof,[137] but reinforce the contentions of the person who rejects resurrection and supply solid ground to his challenges.

You must understand that the denial of the belief in the return of the soul to the body is positively rooted in one of two reasons. The repudiation may arise because it is contrary to nature. If so, all miracles must be refused because they are contrary to nature. Or the denial comes because it is not stated in the text, and there are no authentic traditions regarding it, as there are for the other miracles. However, I have demonstrated that there are texts, even if few, confirming the return of the dead. If one should object that he reinterprets these passages as he does others, my answer is that what impels you to reinterpret them is that the Resurrection is contrary to nature, so that you will explain the passages and make them conform to the natural phenomena.[138] But for this reason you must reinterpret the change of the rod to a serpent, the falling of the manna,[139] the theophany on Mt. Sinai,[140] and the pillars of cloud and fire.[141] Nay, by this approach you are compelled to explain them all, so they will conform to the natural phenomena.[142]

In my discussion in the *Guide* of the creation of the world, I pointed out that it necessarily follows that once the doctrine of the production of the universe is accepted, all miracles are possible; therefore the Resurrection is also possible.[143] I believe every possible happening that is supported by a prophetic statement and do not strip it of its plain meaning. I fall back on interpreting a statement only when its literal sense is impossible, like the corporeality of God; the possible however remains as stated. Anyone who continually strives to explain resurrection away so that there will not be a return (of the soul to the body) does so not because it is naturally unlikely, but because it is rationally inconceivable. If this is the case, the same is necessarily required with respect to the other miracles. All of them are decidedly impossible only in the light of the affirmation that the world is eternal. But one who affirms the eternity of the world cannot possibly be a member of the community of Moses and Abraham, as I established in the *Guide*.[144] Following these fundamentals, I affirmed the Resurrection literally. I counted it a fundamental of the Torah, and ruled that it would not be right to reinterpret plain texts that clearly establish it and are not susceptible of other explanations.

Now for the answer to the second problem, which is why is the Resurrection not mentioned in the Torah? This is my reply. You must realize that, as is well known, we do not believe that the Torah comes from Moses.[145] No, it is in its entirety the word of the Lord.[146] The problem then becomes a quest of God's wisdom in alerting us to life in the world-to-come and saying nothing to us clearly of the Resurrection.[147] The reason is that, as I explained, this resurrection is of the type of the miraculous, and the belief in what is of this nature comes only from the assertion by a prophet.[148] In those days all the people were Sabeans, who affirmed the eternity of the universe.[149] They used to believe, as I taught in the *Guide*,[150] that the spirit in the spheres is God, and they called the claim a lie that the revelation comes from God to the human species. Following their assumption they have to repudiate miracles and attribute them to magic and chicanery.[151] You know, do you not, that they tried to counter the miracles of Moses with their magic: *each cast down his rod* [Exod. 7:12].[152] You know, do you not, that they marveled: *We have seen this day that man may live though God has spoken to him* [Deut. 5:21].[153] This indicates that they had regarded prophecy to be of the class of the impossible. How can a person who does not believe in prophecy be told a story of which there is no other proof save the faith in the prophet? It is decidedly impossible for those who followed their affirmation of the eternity of the world. Were it not for miracles, we would not regard the Resurrection to be of the class of the possible.[154]

Now, when God willed to give Israel the Torah, and to promulgate His commandments and prohibitions in the entire world through the chief of the prophets[155]—as is written: And . . . *that My fame may resound throughout the world* [Exod. 9:16][156]—He produced the miracles that are recorded in the Torah, to authenticate with them the messages of the prophets and the creation of the world. The genuine miracle is decisive proof of the production of the universe, as I pointed out in the *Guide*.[157] But in the area of reward and punishment He did not go beyond the happenings of this world and the course of nature.[158] This embraces immortality of the soul or its discontinuity, as I explained, that is, the world-to-come or extermination.[159] Beyond this He did not present the innovation of the return (of the soul to the body). Matters continued this way until, in the course of generations, these fundamentals became firm and valid, with no doubts lingering about the veracity of the prophets and the performance of miracles.[160] After that, when the prophets informed us of what they were told of the Resurrection, its acceptance was facilitated.[161]

We encounter exactly this sort of solicitude in God's treatment of Israel. For it is written: *God did not lead them by way of the land of the Philistines because it was nearer; for God said: "The people may have a change of heart when they see war, and return to Egypt"* [Exod. 13:17].[162] True, they had matured to some extent in the affairs of the world, but He anticipated[163] that they would return to Egypt, and would forfeit what was planned for them. Likewise, He also anticipated that they would not accept this principle, I mean the return of the soul to the body, and as a result would forfeit the ultimate goal provided for them. They will surely mature and will accept the doctrines as well, seeing that the Leader and the Developer is the same.[164]

It is known that these masses, in whose time God willed to reveal the Torah, were firm in their wrong ideas. Even forty years later, after they had beheld God's wonders, He said of them: *The Lord has not given you a mind to understand or eyes to see or ears to hear* [Deut. 29:3].[165] He knew that when they were informed of the innovation of the return of the dead, they would consider it impossible and would emphatically shun it. They would indulge in sin, since retribution was greatly delayed.[166] For this reason they were warned and threatened with punishment, of which they were quickly persuaded: if you listen, . . . if you do not listen. . . .[167] Their acceptance of that was more immediate and more beneficial. This too is a great benefit as obedience will make their situation in this world prosper and disobedience will hurt it. The Torah affirms it as a continuous miracle over the generations, that is, success in their activities if they obey God, and failure if they disobey. It is written: *They shall serve as signs and proofs against you and your offspring for all time* [Deut. 28:46].[168]

This is the basis of the rabbinic declaration: "Israel has no star,"[169] meaning that their success and failure are not the result of natural causes or customary existence, but are linked to their obedience and disobedience; this is the most convincing sign.[170] I have already stated that this applies to the community and to every individual.[171] It is clear from that anecdote,[172] which is in harmony with the verse: *and your offspring*, and also from the counsel, well known in the community: When a person feels that he is being afflicted, let him examine his behavior.[173] This same idea is implied in God's assertion regarding the singularity of the community: *These the Lord your God allotted to the other peoples everywhere under heaven, but you the Lord took* [Deut. 4:19–20].[174] The meaning is that their situation does not follow the pattern of the situation of the other communities. No, they are singled out by this great miracle: success or failure in their activities will always be linked to their actions.[175]

What I must clarify at this point, although it is too important for this essay,[176] is that miracles may occur in the realm of the naturally impossible[177]—like the change of the rod into a serpent, or the sinking of the earth in the story of the followers of Korah,[178] or the splitting of the Red Sea[179]—and they may occur in the realm of the naturally possible—like the onset of the locust, the hail, and the pestilence in Egypt.[180] It is the way of these latter happenings to occur at certain times and in certain places.[181] So also is the breaking of the altar of Jeroboam when the man of God announced: *Here is the portent which the Lord has decreed: This altar shall break apart, and the ashes on it shall be spilled* [1 Kings 13:3].[182] For it is the way of structures to fall apart, particularly recently reconstructed buildings. Similarly the rain, so rare in the summer, which Samuel foretold,[183] and also the blessings and curses in the Torah.[184] Every one of them may come at any time in any country. They are all of the class of the possible when you examine them.

However, these possible occurrences become miracles by one of three conditions or by all of them. One: that the possible incident comes when the prophet says it will, as happened to Samuel: *I will pray to the Lord and He will send thunder and rain. . . . Samuel prayed to the Lord, and the Lord sent thunder and rain* [1 Sam. 12:17–18]. This is what happened to the man of God who came from Judah: *The altar broke apart and its ashes were spilled—the very portent which the man of God had announced . . .* [1 Kings 13:5]. Two: that that possible happening is singular and exceptional beyond anything imaginable of its kind. The locust is described: *before it there had been no locust like it, nor will there ever be like it* [Exod. 10:14]. Of the hail it is written: *Such as had not fallen on the entire land of Egypt since it had become a nation* [Exod. 9:24]. Of the pestilence it is stated: *But of the livestock of the Israelites not a beast died* [Exod. 9:6]. The particularity of that possible happening, whether in a class referred to, or some specific place, or some species mentally conceived,[185] is the singularity and the exclusiveness of that possible event. Three: the duration and the persistence of that possible event, like the blessings and the maledictions.[186] For, if it came once or twice, it would not be miraculous; it could be claimed to have been a chance incident. This has been clearly expounded in the Torah: *And if you remain hostile to Me and refuse to obey Me* [Lev. 26:21],[187] that is, if you regard the afflictions that will befall you as accidents and not as punishment, He will protract the violent distress you thought was an accident. He expresses it thus: *And if you remain hostile to Me, I will act against you with wrathful hostility*.

Now that this has been clarified, you must realize that the miracles in the naturally impossible class will not last at all, nor will they tarry or remain with their features. For, if they persisted, they would open the way to suspicion.[188] If the rod remained a serpent, the uncertainty would be entertained that it had been originally a serpent, so that the miracle is achieved by its return to a rod: *And it became a rod in his hand* [Exod. 4:4]. If, in the incident of the followers of Korah, the ground had burst asunder, and stayed open for good, the miracle would be challenged. In fact, the miracle was completed when the ground returned to its former condition: *The earth closed over them* [Num. 16:33]; so also: *And at daybreak the sea returned to its normal state* [Exod. 14:27].[189] Because of this fact, which I have alerted you to, I refuse to accept the duration of an unnatural situation, as I have explained in this essay.

But the miracle in the class of the possible is more wondrous the longer it lasts and endures. This is why I accept the blessings that come from obedience and the maledictions on the community from disobedience unto eternity. For they become a sign and a portent, as I pointed out. If someone should ask why this miracle was performed before them, why not the ultimate wonder, that is, the Resurrection, or the reward and punishment of the soul and body together after death, he may just as well ask regarding any of the miracles of the apostle: Why was the rod changed into a serpent? Why not into a lion? The entire issue is connected with the decision of divine wisdom of which we know nothing. Moreover, I have suggested a sort of sensible explanation of it,[190] but perhaps there is another reason or reasons that His wisdom requires, of which we know nothing.

No intelligent person has the right to blame me for the repetition in this essay, the additions to the main idea, or for the extensive clarification of what does not really require further light.[191] I wrote this tract only for the common people who had begun to doubt what I had stated explicitly, and for those who reproached me for brevity when I spoke of the Resurrection. Those who are truly learned are satisfied with a suggestion; they need neither repetition nor prolonged exegesis; they need only summary statements, as I have done with the profound questions in the *Guide* and in all my works.[192] I followed the method related by the sages: He said to him: Explain it, but he answered: A sage needs no explaining. He said: Repeat it, but he answered: A sage requires no repetition.[193] From this it becomes clear that discourse with the wise stands in need of neither repetition nor elucidation: *Instruct a wise man, and he will grow wiser* [Prov. 9:9]. But the common people need both, *precept after precept, precept after precept, now here, now there* [Isa. 28:13].[194] The sense of it is that they understand but little, they comprehend a bit, a little here, a little there. But the right thing to do is to address each group according to its capacity.[195]

May God lead me in word and deed, may He protect me from mistake and error in His goodness, graciousness, and mercy, blessed be He. Amen. Amen.

The essay is finished with the help of God, blessed be He and blessed be His name.

NOTES

1. This formula appears at the beginning of many of Maimonides' writings, and is also used by Yemenite writers and copyists. See S. Lieberman, *Hilkhot ha-Yerushalmi* (1947) p. 5 and note 7.

2. The purpose of these introductory verses is to create the proper mood for the reader. He is about to read a work that is honest, correct, and clear to him who peruses it, as is its author.

3. A reference to Moses, universally accepted by the Jews as the master, the greatest of all the prophets.

4. A party within the Muslim world; Dualists believe in two gods, good and evil, competing with each other for the management of the world.

5. This phrase is accepted in the Jewish world as the basic affirmation of the oneness of God.

6. Cf. Augustine, *De Fide et Symbolo,* chapter 9. This is essentially the definition of monotheism as Christianity conceives it.

7. This exclamation is a means of removing the guilt that may have been incurred by just uttering the phrase.

8. Maimonides is speaking of his major work, the *Mishneh Torah* (or *Yad ha-Ḥazakah,* since the first word numerically equals 14, the number of books in the compilation), a compendium of the entire Jewish Law: beliefs and doctrines, practices in force at present and those that were in use when a Jewish government administered the land of Israel, and the gifts and offerings that are obligatory only in that land.

9. Maimonides wishes to emphasize that his goal was to help those who needed guidance, not to gain glory or material advantage. This saying is from BT Kiddushin 106b; in that text the term used for God is "the Holy One blessed be He."

10. This judgment of his enterprise allows us a glimpse into the thinking of this philosopher-Jew. Fundamentals are of primary importance when any phenomenon is understood. Most compilations of the laws (those written before as well as after Maimonides) do not include explanations of the roots and essentials of the Law.

11. That is, they are very familiar with the details of the Law and with the methods of analyzing and resolving legal difficulties.

12. The traditional literature includes at least one work in which the immeasurable difference between God and man is the quantity and size of the organs and not in their essence. In the kabbalistic writings, such as the *Zohar* and later works, many allusions to God's limbs and organs are to be found, but they are meant to be figurative.

13. Cf. the study by S. Ravidovicz, "The Problem of the Anthropomorphization of God in Saadia Gaon and Maimonides" (in Hebrew), in his collected works *Iyyunim be-Maḥashavet Yisrael,* ed. B. Ravid (Jerusalem: Reuben Mass, 1969–71), pp. 171–233.

14. Although *Epikoros* is clearly the Greek philosopher Epicurus, its connotation in Hebrew is nonbeliever, synonymous with *min,* a heretic.

15. BT Berakhot and Sanhedrin contain many passages that, if taken literally, are exceedingly anthropomorphic.

16. This expresses the degree of Maimonides' concern with guiding and instructing his fellow Jews who did not know the fundamental truths.

17. The opening sentence of *Guide* 1:34 states that Talmud students do not properly appreciate the philosophic doctrines regarding God. Also in the celebrated parable in *Guide* 3:51 Maimonides describes Talmud students as people who learn their articles of faith from tradition and not from reasoning.

18. Maimonides here says it is more important to have correct beliefs than to learn to reason correctly.

19. Despite the low opinion of the masses that Maimonides expresses, he wants them to believe the correct principles.

20. Here follow some of the themes discussed in Maimonides' lengthy introduction to his commentary on the Mishnah. Other themes in the introduction include the generations of the sages represented in the compilation, "the laws Moses received from Sinai" (that is, laws not provided with a source in the Torah), and the reason for the order of the tractates in the collection.

21. In this statement Maimonides explicitly excludes the Karaites, who do not recognize the Oral Law (although they do have their own Oral Law).

22. This chapter is generally called *Helek*, as in the Arabic, because the first sentence in it reads: "All Israel have their portion (*Helek*) in the world-to-come." In the text of the Mishnah it is chapter 10, followed by 11, but in the printed editions of the Talmud, the eleventh chapter is numbered 10, and the latter is the last in BT Sanhedrin.

23. See note 8 above. Maimonides' own appreciation of what makes this work important can hardly be called vanity.

24. The Hebrew phrases behind this expression ("so that their learning . . .") are found in BT Eruvin 54a and Ta'anit 7b–8a.

25. Maimonides was fully aware of the low esteem in which the talmudists held philosophy and theology and that they applied their energies to legal matters.

26. Maimonides refers here to the deficiencies of popular approval, and recommends what he considers a matter of real value, i.e., coming nearer to the Creator by understanding what must be assumed regarding Him and His work.

27. Statements in the sacred texts not acceptable literally to the men of science were interpreted by Maimonides so that they would conform to the scientists' conclusions.

28. These are examples of their thoughts regarding the Resurrection, not reflections of what is expected to happen.

29. The last of the thirteen articles of faith, all listed in that introduction. At the end of the excursus he urges his fellow Israelites to treat everyone who subscribes to them with consideration and compassion. But he who doubts any of these articles, let alone denies them, has in fact left the faith. He must be hated and rejected.

30. *MT Hilkhot Teshuvah*, chapter 8.

31. The same phrase occurs in the introduction to chapter 10 (ed. Kafih, 206).

32. *MT Hilkhot Teshuvah*, chapter 3, Halakhah 14.

33. Ibid., chapter 8, Halakhah 3.

34. The passage, with variations, is BT Berakhot 17a.

35. In *Guide* 3:25, Maimonides classifies all human activity in four categories, the first of which is in vain if the objective sought by the action is not attained. There he emphasizes that no such activity can be ascribed to God.

36. It has been noted that condolence calls were frequently the occasion for gossip, cf. Finkel's edition of the Arabic and Hebrew texts (New York: American Academy for Jewish Research, 1939), 95, note 11. The implication is that it is futile dialogue.

37. Among writers who lived after Maimonides, Nahmanides (1194–1270), for example, proves the continued existence of bodies in the world-to-come from Moses and Elijah, cf. *Torat ha-Adam* (ed. Chavel) 2:74.

38. BT Kiddushin 39b, in connection with the assertion that there is no reward for good deeds in this world.

39. In *Guide* 1:46, Maimonides also notes this failure of the average person.

40. The "accidents" are the attributes and qualities of substances or creatures.

41. That is, children. Isaiah [28:9] spoke pitifully of his contemporaries who seemed unable to understand.

42. Maimonides stresses that the existence that is said to be God's is perfect because it is not subject to the deterioration that overtakes physical matter.

43. Distinct, different from one another, although they are not corporeal.

44. See the *Guide* 1:49, at the beginning, on the angels, and 1:70, where Maimonides differentiates between the rational soul and the vegetative and animal souls.

45. In the report of the angels that visited Abraham, Rashi, quoting the Talmud, explains that they pretended to eat.

46. Maimonides may be instructing his critics to be more tolerant.

47. Cf. his vigorous argument in support of the belief in the absolute incorporeality of God presented in *Guide* 1:49.

48. The numerous references in the Talmud to this principle are listed by Kafih in his edition of Maimonides' *Epistles*, p. 77 note 88.

49. The implication of this criticism is that truth is attained the hard way, by study, intensive reflection, seriousness of objective, and the avoidance of fruitless pursuits.

50. See BT Pesahim 119a.

51. In the introduction to the *Guide*, toward the end, Maimonides counts seven types of apparent contradictions in his text. The third is that not all statements in question are to be taken in their external sense: some are parables and hence have an inner content. Alternatively, two apparently contradictory propositions may both be parables and when taken in their external sense may contradict one another.

52. Cf. *MT Hilkhot Teshuvah* 8:1–3.

53. See Kafih's edition of Maimonides' commentary to the Mishnah, 4:207–9, where Maimonides states his view of what the messianic age will bring to people.

54. Ibid., 4:208, where Maimonides indicates that the life of study and life in accordance with God's Law during the messianic age will bring the ultimate goal, life in the world-to-come.

55. Samuel ben Ali ha-Levi (d. 1194) was an outstanding leader of the yeshiva in Baghdad. He disagreed with Maimonides on a number of halakhic subjects, including the beliefs about the future. He left behind an interesting, vigorous argument in favor of the authority of the sage rather than the secular head within the Jewish community. It was published (in Hebrew) by S. Asaf in *Tarbiz* 1 (1930).

56. Samuel's essay has not been found. In addition to the refutation by Maimonides in this monograph, part of another writing against the position held by the sage of Baghdad was published by E. Harkavy in *Zeitschrift für hebräische Bibliographie*, 2 (1897): 125–128 and 181–88.

57. The scholars referred to are not learned talmudists such as the head of the academy in Baghdad.

58. Like the Muslim philosophers, Maimonides held the *mutakallimun* (theologians) in low esteem; see his summary and criticism of their principles in *Guide* 1:73–76.

59. It is the doctrine of the philosophers, Muslim and Jewish, that all existence can be classified into three categories: the necessarily existent (God); all the rest of what is in the universe, which may or may not have come to be (the contingent); and what is rationally impossible (it implies no deficiency in God that these are impossible to Him). But this last class does not embrace the naturally unlikely, as Maimonides explains toward the end of this monograph.

60. Abu Ali al-Hussein ibn Sina (980–1037), called Avicenna in Western writings, was a famous physician and an equally celebrated philosopher, particularly in the Islamic world. Evidently Maimonides did not think highly of Avicenna's *al-mabda wal-ma'ad* (the beginning and the return), mentioned above.

61. The book, by Abu al Barakat ben Ali al-Baghdadi Hibat Allah (d. 1134), a Jew who adopted Islam in his old age, deals with logic, physics and metaphysics. Shlomo Pines published studies of his theories on space, time, and the physical world.

62. Maimonides intimates that Samuel makes statements without true knowledge and with no supporting evidence.

63. Samuel ben Ali speaks of the soul without definition or discrimination. The philosophers established that the soul is composed of three faculties: the vegetative, the animal, and the rational. Only the last is considered capable of gaining the afterlife.

64. In Deut. 12:23 we are told that the soul is the blood. Cf. *Guide* 1:73, proposition 5, and its elaboration.

65. As it is a fundamental of Kalam physics that all accidents perish and are constantly recreated, death, or the failure to be recreated, means the end of the soul.

66. See the introduction to chapter 10 of Mishnah Sanhedrin and *MT Hilkhot Teshuvah* 3. But it should be remembered that he makes new points in this essay.

67. Maimonides proceeds to assert that he too holds this belief.

68. Many of the verses in the Bible and of the passages in postbiblical literature containing anthropomorphisms and anthropopathisms have been reinterpreted by Jewish scholars, including Maimonides, so as to render them rationally acceptable.

69. Maimonides refers to the celebrated vision of Ezek. 37:1–14. For the different views held by the rabbis, see BT Sanhedrin 92b.

70. See Maimonides comments on Mishnah Sotah 3:3, Sanhedrin 10:3, and Shevu'ot 1:4.

71. Cf. *MT Hilkhot Yesodei ha-Torah* 4:8–9.

72. This summary of human physiology was common knowledge of the enlightened sector of the Jewish population of the time, who drew it from the works of famous physicians, such as Avicenna.

73. In BT Berakhot 17a.

74. It has been noted that the biblical authors made no references to the symbolic role of the idols, and confined themselves to ridicule of these images serving as gods.

75. This is Job's retort to the judgments of his suffering by his friends.

76. For example, in *Guide* 1:26, 46.

77. Later in this essay Maimonides identifies the Resurrection more fully as a miracle. The brunt of the argument is that a Jew is bound by his faith to recognize that God is the Creator of the universe and the Author of miracles.

78. It is one of the thirteen articles of faith, all cardinal principles of the Law, summarized by Maimonides in the introduction to Chapter 10 of Mishnah Sanhedrin.

79. The two Hebrew phrases Maimonides introduces into the Arabic are from Tosefta Kiddushin 1:14 and BT Avodah Zarah 54b.

80. BT Shabbat 97a. When someone entertains unfounded suspicions of an upright person, he will suffer physically.

81. Maimonides speaks of the sages because there are examples of their decisions to call some miracles resurrection parables, e.g., the vision of Ezek. 37:1–14, cf. note 68 above. The Andalusian commentators are the rationalists who refused to treat some of the stories of the Resurrection as valid facts. Cf. David Kimhi's explanation of Elijah's revival of the lad in his commentary on 1 Kings 17:17, 20.

82. In a similar vein Maimonides declares in *Guide* 2:15 that whatever is demonstrably true will not become truer or more valid if all the learned agree with it; nor will it become less true or valid if all the world disagrees with it.

83. Deut. 6:4 is the only place in which God's unity is stated so clearly and succinctly.

84. I.e., Dan. 12:2, 12.

85. I.e., where the rabbis find references to the Resurrection in biblical verses, cf. BT Sanhedrin 90b.

86. The revival of the dead always means the return of the soul to the body, and this is its sense no matter who writes about it.

87. In the discussion of messianic times, in *MT Hilkhot Melakhim* 11:3.

88. In evidence of the assertion Maimonides cites the case of Bar Kokhba, the leader of the revolt against the Romans in 132–135 whom Rabbi Akiva believed to be the Messiah, although he performed no miracles.

89. In order to persuade the people that he came to inaugurate the messianic age.

90. In Isaiah's prediction of the divinely inspired *shoot . . . out of the stump of Jesse* [Isa. 11:1].

91. Ibn Ezra in his comment *ad locum* explains: "allegorically, of the peace that will prevail in his time."

92. Neither Gikatilla (1248-1325) nor ibn Bal'am (eleventh century) has anything to say regarding the verse. But on Isa. 65:17 (*For behold! I am creating a new heaven and a new earth*), the latter writes that it is a metaphor for the restoration of the government. David Kimḥi in his note on Isa. 11:6 says that some people say that it is allegorical.

93. Kimḥi utilizes this sentence to refute the metaphoric approach.

94. After demonstrating the absurdity of the logical conclusion of their naive belief, Maimonides feels justified in applying Isaiah's condemnatory judgment.

95. In *Guide* 2:29, Maimonides similarly utilizes this verse to criticize those who are unable to comprehend the implications of the prophetic hyperbole. In the phrase *is under God's command,* the word "command" in both Hebrew and Arabic connotes a sense of one on whom God has imposed an obligation. It is found, for example, in the theologically important sentence: "He who acts because he has been commanded to do is of higher rank than he who acts although he has not been commanded." (BT Kiddushin 31a)

96. *MT Hilkhot Melakhim* 12:1-2.

97. Literally, the order set up at creation, cf. BT Shabbat 53b.

98. Note Maimonides' admirable honesty and caution. Since his conclusions are essentially the outcome of his reasoning, he feels he cannot be absolutely sure that he is right. As he continues to explain, he cannot claim certain knowledge as opposed to the certainty of divine revelation.

99. Maimonides points to this basic difference between the intellectual approach and the thinking of the masses in *Guide* 3:31.

100. This position, which is in accord with Maimonides' general tendency to make the biblical text rationally creditable, is well exemplified in the opening statement of *Guide* 2:25: "Know that our shunning the affirmation of the eternity of the world is not due to a text in the Torah, according to which the world has been produced in time. For the texts indicating that the world has been produced in time are not more numerous than those indicating that the Deity is a body. Nor are the gates of figurative interpretation shut in our faces, or impossible of access to us, regarding the subject of the creation of the world in time. For we could interpret them as figurative, as we have done when denying His corporeality." Since as a Jew he must believe the miracles in the Bible, he is not forced to give figurative meaning to Dan. 12:2.

101. In the introduction to the *Guide* and in 2:29, Maimonides engages in a long analysis of speech, parables, and allegories, the differences in their structure, and an interpretation of their sense.

102. "The excellent commentators" are the rationalists who came under the influence of Greek philosophy. In France commentators took the biblical descriptions of the messianic age much more literally.

103. In view of Maimonides' reluctance to claim that his explanation is certain, he suggests a method of accepting the literal sense of Isaiah's vision in Isa. 11.

104. *De Hist. An.* 9:12.

105. BT Ḥullin and Tamid 29a, in both of which the use of hyperboles in the three collections of the Bible and in words of the sages is recognized.

106. David Kimḥi's readiness to believe in the literal meaning of the wonders (see note 92) is justified by him because they will be confined to the Temple Mount.

107. Mishnah Avot 5:4, which lists ten wonders in connection with the Temple Mount.

108. In halakhic matters a clear ruling is necessary in order to know how to act in accordance with the Law, but in subjects classed as Aggadah, like the item under discussion, such definiteness is not required.

109. Maimonides follows the rabbinic policy in matters difficult to decide: let it remain unsettled until Elijah comes (Mishnah Bava Meẓia 3:5), i.e., when the messianic age arrives every puzzling question will be cleared up. In the same spirit, the term *teku* (let it stand), which closes debates that are not clearly resolved, has been explained as the first letters of four words: Tishbi (Elijah) will resolve puzzles and challenges.

110. Maimonides means that he tries hard not to fall back on miracles as the explanation of anything unusual rather than regard it as an explainable phenomenon.

111. The differentiation Maimonides introduces in the next few lines is treated more fully toward the end of this essay; it aims to clarify miracles and to define changes in nature and logically impossible happenings.

112. The rabbinic statement is found BT Avodah Zarah 54b; cf. Finkel's note 31a (p. 97).

113. Maimonides, who apparently cites a fixed phrase, formulates it almost like the text in BT Berakhot 60a and in Bava Meẓia 59b.

114. This verse is fully consonant with the mood of the book.

115. *Guide* 2:28, in the analytical examination of the theory of creation versus the assumption of an eternal world. In it Maimonides provides the meaning of the phrase: *But the earth remains the same forever* [Eccles. 1:4].

116. Maimonides here presents another reason why people are ready to charge that he does not believe in the Resurrection.

117. In his introduction to Mishnah Sanhedrin 10, Maimonides devotes considerable space to the subject of the world-to-come, but disposes of the Resurrection in a short statement.

118. The Hebrew phrase (BT Berakhot 55a) means the practice of the world.

119. Maimonides undoubtedly knew the many tracts and *midrashim* that deal with this theme and draw their authority from their inventiveness.

120. If Maimonides merely retold these legends in his work on the Resurrection, he would have filled another book; however, he feels this is unnecessary.

121. Maimonides has in mind Isa. 26:19: *Thy dead shall live*, which has been utilized by the rabbis to prove the Resurrection; see BT Sanhedrin 90b.

122. Jewish commentators on the Bible generally accept the verse as a reference to the Resurrection. A modern exegete writes: "The reference to a literal resurrection is the more probable meaning," *Interpreters' Bible*, Isaiah, 167.

123. Maimonides states that Daniel speaks explicitly of the Resurrection in these two verses.

124. Maimonides is not impressed by the efforts of Jewish scholars to buttress their belief in the Resurrection with methods of indirect proof.

125. BT Sanhedrin 90bff.

126. The proof is not obvious but has to be deduced. In some of the answers to the question of what proof is in the Torah, the sages disagree and cite another verse in their place.

127. I.e., if we assent to the deductions the rabbis infer from the verses, it may be asked why the Torah informed us of it in this manner. Why did it not plainly say there would be a resurrection?

128. The Torah and the rabbis strictly forbid relations with the animal world, see Lev. 18:23.

129. The immortality of the part of the soul that will not perish with the body (like the vegetative and the animal faculties) can be rationally demonstrated.

130. Maimonides employs the term *homonym* to designate a noun that has two or more senses and none of which is a derivative of another. When the connection between meanings is apparent the use is called *metaphorical*.

131. The first six verses in Eccles. 12 present a graphic sketch of the continuous deterioration of physical man until it comes to its end.

132. This is the challenge that Moses hurls at the community before he draws water from the rock.

133. In both instances the expected answer is no, but the unexpected happened when Moses drew water from the rock, and the unnatural will happen when the souls of the dead return to their bodies.

134. The same parallel exists between the two sets of questions.

135. Maimonides picks a random example. In Exod. 4:6–7, God orders Moses to put his hand into his bosom, and when Moses withdraws it, it is encrusted with snowy scales. Then God tells him to put his hand into his bosom again, and when he withdraws it this time, it has returned to normal.

136. The reference is to the first of the two signs that God gave Moses, with which Moses would establish his credibility (see Exod. 4:1–9).

137. Maimonides dismisses the efforts made by commentators of his age, like Saadiah, ibn Ezra, Radak, and others, because they are farfetched and are incapable of providing enlightening proof.

138. Maimonides confronts the individual who claims belief in what the Bible relates and the rabbinic tradition teaches but who does not believe in the Resurrection for the reason that he does not believe in anything unnatural.

139. Exod. 16:11–36.

140. Exod. 19, 20.

141. Exod. 13:21–22.

142. The person has a defensible right to single out a miracle and resort to interpretation. He can either take the position that miracles do not happen, therefore denying God's words in the Torah, or he must accept all of these occurrences without discrimination.

143. *Guide* 2:25. The fundamental argument is that we cannot deny prophetic statements, and that the incorporeality of God, which is rationally demonstrable, also finds clear proof in the Bible.

144. In *Guide* 2:13, Maimonides affirms that the Jew who believes in the

Torah believes in creation (one of three theories held by thinkers), and in 2:23 he maintains that if Aristotle, who postulated an eternally existent universe, found support of his hypothesis in Sabean tales, the Jewish philosopher can certainly, with better reason, support his acceptance that the universe was created with the words of Abraham and Moses.

145. It is important for him to stress this, since in his writings he speaks many times of the "Torah of Moses."

146. Maimonides repeats what was universally accepted among the Jews. He emphasizes it because the rabbinic view commonly held was that the Israelites heard only the first two commandmants directly from God; all the others, and the bulk of the Torah, were reported to them by Moses, who heard them from God, and it was generally named the Torah of Moses. Cf. BT Makkot 24a.

147. Although it is God who did not include the Resurrection in the Torah, and it is His mystery, attempts were made, in the spirit of sound tradition, to penetrate His secrets. But Maimonides is not sure that his understanding of God's reason for not mentioning the Resurrection is absolutely correct.

148. The prophet, who reports to the people what God tells him, is the source of the doctrine regarding the future.

149. The Sabeans are an ancient people known from records, including the Bible (e.g., 1 Kings 10). Like his Muslim contemporaries, Maimonides knew they believed in the eternal existence of the universe, and he believed their name was held by all the people in the past who adhered to this view.

150. *Guide* 3:29; after opening with the statement that Abraham was born among the Sabeans, Maimonides presents a brief summary of their views.

151. Despite their refusal to lend credence to prophets, they trusted that their teachings came from their founders Adhimun and Hermes. Cf. Shahrastani, *al Milal wal Niha*, 203 (in German), Haarbrucker, *Religionspartheien und Philosophe Schulen*, II, 5.

152. Maimonides assumes that the Egyptian magicians were Sabeans; see *Guide* 3:29.

153. The verse is a statement by the Israelites at the time of the theophany on Mt. Sinai. Maimonides thinks that at the time they were adherents of the Sabean doctrine.

154. That is, we, at the present time, would continue to doubt the truth of the Resurrection if we did not believe in creation and, as a result, in the acceptance of the miracles.

155. Moses, whom Maimonides identifies by this description, rather than naming him.

156. In Moses' warning to Pharaoh that the next plague would be the hail.

157. *Guide* 2:25, where it explicitly states that the belief in the eternity of the universe, which postulates natural law as an eternal factor, excludes the possibility of miracles in the past that are recorded in the Bible and all the promises for the future that are made in it.

158. The rewards and the chastisements in the Torah do not refer to the afterlife, but are blessings and afflictions that occur in this world.

159. Maimonides is faithful to his view that immortality of the soul is

logically demonstrable, so that the Israelites of Moses' time believed in it along with the assurances of reward and punishment in this world. The Arabic word, translated "extermination," is the literal rendering of the Hebrew term *karet*, with the same sense.

160. As the years passed, and the succeeding generations witnessed the miracles performed by prophets, they learned by experience that the prophets were trustworthy messengers of God.

161. Primarily Dan. 12:2, 12, and, with the aid of these specific declarations, less obvious references in other prophetic books, e.g., Isa. 26:19.

162. The phrase beginning with *because* offers the reason that God should have led them *by way of the land of the Philistines*, but did not. The same construction is found in Isa. 14:29: *Rejoice not, all Philistia, because the staff of him that beat you is broken*.

163. Maimonides' choice of the word "anticipate" is to eliminate the possibility that God may not have known how the Israelites would react when they encountered the challenge of the pursuing Egyptians.

164. Realizing that it is God who redeemed them and revealed the Torah to them, they will recognize that He is also the Author of the hopes and promises laid before them.

165. In Moses' last address to the Israelites, he recites all that God had done for them and says they have not drawn the proper lessons from it.

166. A reward that would come much later could not have the force to compel them to obey God's commands, so they would disregard the laws.

167. These phrases open sections in the Torah that present the alternatives to the Israelites, for example: Lev. 26:3 (*If you follow My laws*); Lev. 26:14 (*But if you do not obey Me*); Deut. 28:1 (*Now, if you obey the Lord your God*); and Deut. 28:15 (*But if you do not obey the Lord your God*). In these and others like them the consequences, good or bad, are terrestrial and impending.

168. Maimonides takes this verse as a point of departure for his stand against astrology.

169. BT Shabbat 156a. It is interesting that in the novellae of R. Samuel Edels (1555–1631) to this statement he attempts to reconcile the two contradictory views in the Talmud (one maintains that Israel has a star) by suggesting that the community is governed only by God, but the individual is subject to the stars (ed. Vilna, 38a).

170. Maimonides is quite emphatic. In his epistle to the scholars of France (*Responsa of Maimonides*, Leipzig, 1859, pp. 24b–26b), and in the *Epistle to Yemen*, he voices strong opposition to the practice of astrology and dismisses it as an unreliable pursuit. He teaches the Jews that it is religiously sinful, because the Bible explicitly stresses that their fate is bound to God's judgment of their deeds.

171. See note 167, above. It may be that the discrimination introduced here was made before or in the time of Maimonides. The point is that the text in Deut. 28:46 reads: . . . *against you and your offspring*. This indicates that the reckoning is made with both the individual and the community.

172. In BT Shabbat 156b it is related that an astrologer and the amora

Mar Samuel disagreed regarding the fate of a certain Jew who was about to
be attacked by a snake. Unlike the astrologer, Samuel predicted that he would
be saved, as indeed he was. Another tale deals with Rabbi Akiva's daughter
and has a similar lesson.

173. BT Berakhot 5a. The context of the statement discusses afflictions,
when they seize one, and how to avoid them or to get rid of them. The sentence
cited by Maimonides continues: "But if he did not discover the likely cause
in his behavior, let him understand that he brought the troubles on himself
because he wasted time and did not study Torah. When he realizes that even
this does not account for his difficulties let him assume they are visitations
due to divine love."

174. The verses are part of the conclusion to the pericope that admonishes
the Israelites not to make idols. Deut. 4:19–20 reads in full: *And when you
look up to the sky and behold the sun and the moon and the stars, the whole
heavenly host, you must not be lured into bowing down to them or serving
them. These the Lord your God allotted to other peoples everywhere under
heaven; but you the Lord took and brought out of Egypt, that iron blast furnace,
to be His very own people, as is now the case.*

175. Whereas all other nations utilize the guidance that they believe comes
to them from the heavenly bodies, i.e., from astrology, the people of Israel
are instructed to look upon God, and God only, as the judge who treats them
as they deserve.

176. He bears in mind his contention that this essay was prepared for
simple folk, and they will neither appreciate nor understand what he is about
to explain.

177. See note 110, above, and p. 224.

178. See Num. 16:32.

179. See Exod. 14:21.

180. See Exod. 10:14 and 9:2–6.

181. Unusual or extraordinary occurrences are known in various places
and at different times, such as earthquakes, typhoons, and hurricanes.

182. Among the changes that Jeroboam introduced as head of northern
Israel, which seceded from Judah and its king, Rehoboam, we find that he
set up the golden calves, pushed the Feast of Tabernacles to the eighth month
(instead of the seventh), appointed unauthorized priests (1 Kings 12:26–33).
He himself ascended the altar to offer sacrifices on the Feast of Tabernacles.
Thereupon a man of God appeared and predicted that a time would come
when a ruler (Josiah) would break the altar.

183. See 1 Sam. 12:17–18. These verses are part of Samuel's last address
to the people of Israel. He rebukes them for their ingratitude to God in the
face of all He did, which includes asking for a king. He also admonishes
them henceforth to be true to God, fearing, and obedient. As testimony to
what he tells them, he has the people see rain with lightning and thunder in
the middle of the summer.

184. Both Lev. 26 and Deut. 28 specify the blessings that will be granted
if God's bidding is done, and the curses that will be sent in retribution for
disobedience.

185. The expression in Exod. 10:14: *there had been no locust like it,* which is not based on an actual count or calculation is clearly a product of the mind.

186. Both the blessings and curses are predicted as developments that will endure in their time and place of incidence.

187. The verse is one of the summaries that teaches the direct relationship between disobedience and punishment.

188. This is the difference between naturally possible and naturally impossible happenings. The latter, totally unexpected, occur and do not endure, so as to impress the sense of the miraculous. The former, which are within the realm of possibility, are miracles when they are quantitatively or chronologically extraordinary, or when their imminence is predicted by a prophet.

189. The report of the sea's return to its normal state is followed by: *And when Israel saw the wondrous power which the Lord had wielded against the Eygptians, the people feared the Lord: they had faith in the Lord and in His servant Moses* [Exod. 14:31].

190. Again Maimonides' awareness is manifested in his confession that he may not have divined the reason for the choice of miracles.

191. Maimonides reiterates that the writing of this monograph was unnecessary, and its only purpose was to teach the unintelligent.

192. Maimonides certainly did not expect the average person to study the *Guide.*

193. *Sifra* to Lev. 15:13. It is a conversation conducted between Ben Azzai, who arrived at a certain conclusion dialectically, and Rabbi Yose ha-Gelili, who makes the requests of him.

194. The rendering here is in keeping with Kimḥi's comment on the verse, *ad loc.*

195. Despite Maimonides' low opinion of the capacity of the masses, he is concerned about providing instruction in accordance with their ability.

DISCUSSION OF
THE ESSAY ON RESURRECTION

Throughout his life, Maimonides devoted himself singlemindedly to raising the level of the community's appreciation and understanding of Judaism. He sought to make the intricate legal discussions of the Talmud accessible to the majority of the community by writing the *Mishneh Torah*, a comprehensive codification of the entire corpus of Jewish law. In the *Guide of the Perplexed*, he sought to bridge the alleged gap between the cognitive framework of Judaism and the truths of the science and philosophy of his day. The religious impulse that informed Maimonides' writings was the yearning to transform worship motivated by self-interest into worship motivated by passionate love of God.[1] He drew attention to the wisdom of God manifest in nature in order to cultivate a yearning to know God independently of human needs and wants and to develop a religious personality whose every thought and action would be dominated by the quest to know and love God.[2]

How strange and painful it must have been for this great teacher of Israel, whose *Mishneh Torah* and *Guide of the Perplexed* are landmarks in the cultural-religious history of the Jewish people, to feel compelled to defend himself against the accusation that he did not believe in the doctrine of the resurrection of the dead. There is bitter irony in the fact that this God-intoxicated philosopher, whose writings had deliberately neutralized the importance of the miraculous, wrote a final work in support of the doctrine of miracles.

The *Essay on Resurrection* is prima facie a tragic document, in which one of the great teachers and exemplars of intense faith in God is compelled to write to a confused and frightened community a defense of his being a true believer. In reading the essay, one cannot but sense Maimonides' deep anger and resentment at having to respond publicly to the accusation that he denied resurrection. Maimonides' anger should be explained against the background of his lifelong struggle to make love of God the community's central ideal. The lovesick person he describes in *Hilkhot Teshuvah* exemplifies the passion that informed his attitude to God:

> What is the love of God that is befitting? It is to love the Eternal with a great and exceeding love, so strong that one's soul shall be knit up with the love of God, and one should be continually enraptured by it, like a lovesick individual, whose mind is at no time free from his passion for a particular woman, the thought of her filling his heart at all times, when sitting down or rising up, when he is eating or drinking. Even intenser should be the love of God in the hearts of those who love Him. And this love should continually possess them, even as He commanded us in the phrase: *with all your heart and with all your soul* [Deut. 6:5]. This, Solomon expressed allegorically in the sentence: *for I am sick with love* [Song of Songs 2:5]. The entire Song of Songs is indeed an allegory descriptive of this love.[3]

Maimonides' reluctance to write a treatise expressly devoted to a doctrine such as resurrection, a doctrine that is a material reward pure and simple, should be explained as a particular manifestation of a God-intoxicated individual's general reluctance to concern himself with the whole issue of rewards and punishments. Rather than claim that Maimonides did not believe in rewards and punishments in general and in resurrection in particular, it is more correct to claim that he was embarrassed to talk at length about doctrines used to motivate observance of commandments by appeals to self-interest.

Forcing a person like Maimonides to defend the miracle of resurrection is, to use a Maimonidean metaphor, like drawing a king away from his regal activities in order to play ball in the street:

> For we live in a material world and the only pleasure we can comprehend must be material. But the delights of the spirit are everlasting and uninterrupted, and there is no resemblance in any possible way between spiritual and bodily enjoyments. We are not sanctioned either by the Torah or by the divine philosophers to assert that the angels, the stars, and the spheres enjoy no delights. In truth they have exceeding great delight in respect

of what they comprehend of the Creator (glorified be He!). This to them is an everlasting felicity without a break. They have no bodily pleasures, neither do they comprehend them, because they have no senses like ours, enabling them to have our sense experiences. And likewise will it be with us too. When after death the worthy from among us will reach that exalted stage he will experience no bodily pleasures neither will he have any wish for them, any more than would a king of sovereign power wish to divest himself of his imperial sway and return to his boyhood's games with a ball in the street, although at one time he would without doubt have set a higher worth upon a game with a ball than on kingly dominion, such being the case only when his years were few and he was totally ignorant of the real significance of either pursuit, just as we today rank the delights of the body above those of the soul.[4]

The pettiness of the joy of resurrection relative to the joy of the world-to-come, i.e., the joy of intellectual love of God, was a major reason behind Maimonides' anger. Whereas his whole philosophy of Judaism centered around the lovesickness of one who strives after knowledge of God, he was now compelled to write a defense of the belief that God will miraculously restore our bodily existence so that we can enjoy the material pleasures of this world!

In contrast to most of Maimonides' writings, the *Essay on Resurrection* is decidedly personal. There is anger, sarcasm, and bitterness. The lover feels degraded when he is asked to discuss his relationship to his beloved in gross utilitarian terms. The community's disproportionate interest in resurrection relative to more important aspects of his teachings on Judaism undoubtedly pained Maimonides deeply, for it was a sign that all that he had tried to accomplish as a Jewish leader and educator might have failed.

If the implication is that the *Essay on Resurrection* testifies to the failure of his life's work, then one must read this essay as Maimonides' painful acknowledgment of the futility of the philosopher's "return to the cave." The philosopher, according to the Platonic metaphor, leaves the cave wherein the community is captivated by mere shadows of true reality, ascends the ladder of philosophic knowledge, and beholds Truth. The philosopher may then sever his ties to the community, or he may return to the cave in order to guide the community to follow the path leading to the true reality beyond the life dominated by shadows.[5] Maimonides had chosen the latter path. Although for him the ultimate state of human perfection and happiness consisted in knowledge and love of God, he remained aware that the Halakhah demands from every Jew a commitment to the community. In his earlier writings, he had therefore accepted the challenge of the Torah and sought to make love and knowledge of God not only a personal quest, but an orienting goal for the entire community.

Did Maimonides now regret having "returned to the cave"? Do the irony and bitterness expressed in this essay indicate a profound disgust for and abandonment of a community that required miracles and promises of reward to motivate religious behavior? Does Maimonides' final essay communicate the utter loneliness of the philosopher within the halakhic community? Is the philosopher-halakhist doomed to be a "lonely man of faith," because of the unbridgeable gap separating a religious world view centering on the quest for love of God from a religious outlook dominated by reward and punishment? These are some of the agonizing questions one must consider when pondering Maimonides' subtle and fascinating final work.

Leo Strauss, one of the most meticulous and insightful readers of Maimonides' writings, regards this essay as a most important commentary to the *Guide of the Perplexed*.[6] The *Essay on Resurrection* can be seen as a commentary to the totality of Maimonides' lifework. It is an invaluable document for explaining the religious considerations that motivated Maimonides to include philosophic themes in his halakhic works.[7]

THE BACKGROUND OF THE ACCUSATION

The *Essay on Resurrection* consists basically of three parts. Maimonides first explains how some readers of his earlier works became confused and began to claim that he denied the resurrection of the dead. Next he defends himself against the accusation of disbelief in this fundamental doctrine of Judaism. Finally, he reinforces the doctrine against doubts that might arise from its relative lack of attestation in the Bible.

Maimonides argues that the source of the public confusion about his belief in resurrection was his decision in earlier writings to explain and restore interest in a doctrine that had been neglected by the community, namely, the immortality of the soul. He regarded the immortality of the soul in the world-to-come as the ultimate reward of a religious life, whereas the community was more interested in the resurrection of the dead to enjoy pleasures in this world before passing to the world-to-come. In order to correct this situation, and to convince his readers that rewards and punishments are not restricted to this world, he had elaborated upon the meaning and importance of immortality, while saying relatively little about the resurrection of the dead. As a result of his emphasis upon immortality, however, people

had begun to question whether he believed in resurrection at all.
Initially, he had chosen to ignore the rumors about his disbelief, but
when noted rabbinic authorities made public accusations against him,
he could no longer remain silent.[8]

While offering this explanation of what had caused their doubts,
Maimonides does not accept it as a justification for their ignoring his
explicit statements about the centrality of the doctrine of resurrection.
In his commentary to the tenth chapter of the talmudic tractate Sanhedrin, he had included resurrection among the thirteen principles of
faith, while in his code of Jewish law, the *Mishneh Torah*, he had
placed those who deny resurrection of the dead in the class of those
who have "no portion in the world-to-come, but are cut off and perish,
and for their great wickedness and sinfulness are condemned for ever
and ever" [*MT Hilkhot Teshuvah* 3:14].

In the light of these unequivocal references to resurrection, Maimonides rebuts those who suspected him of disbelief and attacks them
for their stupidity and distorted attitude toward religion. This group
consists of talmudists who devote themselves to mastering the intricate details of legal argumentation, yet who are ignorant of theology
and philosophy and show no interest in acquiring knowledge of God.
". . . although they consider themselves sages in Israel, [they] are
in fact the most ignorant, and more seriously astray than beasts, their
minds filled with the senseless prattle of old women and noxious
fantasies, like children and women . . . ." (p. 212)

Maimonides reserves his most abusive and derisive language for
those who are ostensibly great scholars and halakhists, but whose
beliefs, e.g., belief in divine corporeality, are tantamount to idolatry.
The urgency of eliminating such false notions of God, and of counter-
acting a halakhic behaviorism that tolerated appalling heresies such
as belief in divine corporeality, was the reason that had led Maimonides to include philosophic-theological sections in his legal writings:

> When I applied myself to this task [i.e., writing a legal compi-
> lation], I realized that it was not correct to strive to explain the
> ramifications of the religious law, and to leave its roots neglected,
> unexplained, and its essentials undiscussed, providing no guid-
> ance. This is especially urgent since I have met some who think
> they are among the sages of Israel—by God, they indeed know
> the way of the Law ever since childhood, and they battle in legal
> discussions—but they are not certain if God is corporeal, with
> eyes, hands, and feet, as the Bible says, or if He has not a body.
> Others, whom I have met in some lands, assert positively that
> He is corporeal, and call anyone who thinks differently a non-
> believer, name him a heretic and Epicurean. (p. 212)

False beliefs concerning God could be even worse than idolatrous forms of worship. While an idolater, though worshiping idols, can yet refer to God in his thoughts, a person with a false conception of God, such as one involving corporeality, cannot truly refer to God at all. Belief in divine corporeality is tantamount to disbelief in the existence of God, because nothing in objective reality corresponds to the content of this belief. In *Hilkhot Teshuvah* Maimonides classifies one who believes in divine corporeality as a *min* (heretic) and in the *Guide* (1:35) as "a hater, an enemy and an adversary of God, much more so than an idolater." The source of this form of idolatry (actually, infidelity) is not the Jewish community's assimilation to the practices of other nations, but rather lies in their ignorance of philosophy and specifically of the logical connection between the unity of God and His incorporeity.

Without offering the detailed and systematic justification of theological beliefs that appears in the *Guide of the Perplexed*, Maimonides presents in a popular and sketchy way philosophical and theological themes in his legal writings. One of the most urgent issues Maimonides faced was that of uprooting anything suggestive of idolatry within the Jewish community. While he could tolerate religious observance that was motivated by self-interest, he was uncompromising in his rejection of belief in divine corporeality and anything that logically implied divine corporeality.[9] Even if the community could not fully grasp the meaning of immaterial existence, or follow rational demonstrations of basic theological truths, he believed that the entire community without exception must be taught to reject false conceptions of God. The community bears witness to the unity of God in its religious utterances and practices even if the truths of divine unity, incorporeity, and the lack of any likeness whatever between God and created things are accepted solely on the basis of the authority of tradition.[10]

Maimonides' overriding concern had been to eliminate the gap between what the philosopher and the community believed with respect to divine unity and incorporeity. The biblical injunction to uproot idolatry was addressed to the community, and thus the community in its entirety was required to bear witness to the reality of God. The philosopher *qua* halakhist must influence the community in order to realize one of the central goals of the Torah: the rejection of idolatry.[11] Maimonides' justification for teaching theoretical truths in his legal writings can be summarized by the rabbinic statement: "Everyone who professes idolatry, disbelieves in the Torah in its entirety; whereas he who disbelieves in idolatry, professes the Torah in its entirety."[12] It was not arid rationalism that had prompted Maimonides to teach philosophy in his legal works, but rather the urgency of uprooting idolatrous beliefs within the halakhic community. A central problem that he, as an observant Jew, could not ignore, was how he could form a community of worship and observance with people who worshiped a nonexistent deity.

A second concern of his, Maimonides writes, had been to make knowledge and love of God the focal point of halakhic practice. He had opposed a type of religious legalism that focused on normative practice to the exclusion of the quest to know God. Halakhic behavior can become a compulsive activity devoid of religious significance when it is severed from the longing to be in the presence of God. Maimonides had therefore included discussions of the principles of faith in his legal works, so that scholars of the law

> . . . will no longer cast the knowledge of God behind their backs, but will exert themselves to the limit of their power to attain what will perfect them and bring them nearer to their Creator, not to what the general public imagines to be perfection. (p. 213)

Preoccupation with the law and its myriad details can become a barrier separating the halakhist from the ultimate purpose of the study and practice of the law: worship of God.

Since in the *Essay on Resurrection* Maimonides makes only brief mention of his earlier discussions on *olam ha-ba* (the world-to-come), it will assist our understanding of the essay to recall them in more detail. His first treatment of resurrection, messianism, and *olam ha-ba* was in his commentary to the tenth chapter of Sanhedrin (usually referred to as *Ḥelek* because of its beginning: "All of Israel have a portion [*ḥelek*] in the world to come"). According to his explanation in *Ḥelek*, eschatological beliefs were the objects of great interest in the community insofar as they involved future material gratification. The doctrine of resurrection inspired heated discussions on how the dead will arise, e.g., whether they will be clothed or not, and messianism became a type of collective fantasy into which people poured their hopes for power, glory, wealth, and all sorts of sensual pleasure.

One result of this obsession with future earthly rewards was that the doctrine of the world-to-come was neglected. This fact provided Maimonides with a justification for emphasizing the importance of *olam ha-ba*. The main purpose, however, of his treatment of this belief was to counteract the community's preoccupation with reward and punishment. He transforms *olam ha-ba* from a typical reward/punishment notion (the threat of being excluded from *olam ha-ba* was considered a severe punishment in the Talmud) into a type of Aristotelian *eudaimonia*, the happiness implicit in having actualized the human potential.[13] For Maimonides, the immortality of the soul is not externally related to human perfection, but is a necessary result of becoming a perfect human being.

> As a decent man, one must cultivate the virtues and avoid the sins. In so doing, he will perfect the specifically human that resides in him and will be genuinely different from the animals. When one becomes fully human, he acquires the nature of the perfect human being; there is no external power to deny his soul eternal life. His soul thus attains the eternal life it has come to know, which is the world-to-come . . .[14]

Aristotle's understanding of the relationship between happiness and the act occasioning happiness throws light on how life in the world-to-come serves as a "reward" for achieving human perfection. When a person maximizes his intellectual powers, acquires the practical and theoretical virtues and directs his thoughts to know God, he necessarily achieves immortality. "There is no external power to deny his soul eternal life" implies that, unlike normal rewards, the "reward" of immortality is not extraneous to the deserving activity in question, but is inherent in the activity itself.

The world-to-come answers to the religious attitude that Maimonides sought to bring about.[15] In general, he distinguishes between two kinds of religious attitude: that based on fear of God (*yirah*) and that based on love of God (*ahavah*).[16] The former attitude is involved whenever an act of worship is motivated by self–interest, such as fear of divine punishment or hope of material rewards in this world. Being motivated by the "reward" of immortality in the world to come, however, presupposes the transformation of a person's motivational framework from one dominated by egocentric interests and desires to one where love of God predominates.

A person's choice to worship God will be based on love, if the anticipated joy of being in God's presence and of reflecting upon His perfection outweighs all other considerations. By making *olam ha-ba* the ultimate goal of Judaism, and emptying it of all human pleasures save the joy of knowledge of God, Maimonides aimed at restoring the quest to know God to the center of halakhic life. Although the language of reward and punishment is still used with regard to *olam ha-ba*, the content of the promised reward is the joy of being in the presence of God. The ultimate reward is that of drawing near to the divine reality.

The connection between the notion of the immortality of the soul and the ideal of the love of God may also be explained in terms of Maimonides' understanding of the nonpersonal nature of the human intellect. Maimonides followed the Aristotelian tradition in regarding matter—thus the body, rather than the soul—as what makes each human being individually different from all others. The human intellect was regarded as universal and thus nonpersonal; it was also the God-like part of man, since the Aristotelian God is a pure intellect without a body.[17] Thus if human perfection consists in realizing the image of God in man, what this implies, in terms of medieval Aristotelianism, is making the nonpersonal the dominant feature of consciousness. For Maimonides, the ultimate realization of love of God consists in knowledge of God in a bodiless state of existence in the world-to-come. Love of God thus involves, in a certain sense, a movement away from individuality. Love of God may be characterized psychologically as a frame of mind where consciousness of one's needs recedes as the reality of God fills one's thoughts. To love God in the manner of the lovesick individual described in *Hilkhot Teshuvah* 10:5 and in the *Guide* 3:51, one must somehow overcome the concerns of individual existence in order to be intellectually absorbed by the perfection of God.

The logic of a religious outlook centering around love of God forced Maimonides to interpret the Torah's frequent references to rewards and punishments to show that the goal of the *mitzvot* (commandments) was to know and love God. The key to his interpretation of biblical rewards and punishments is his characterizing them instrumentally as means which promote or retard fulfillment of the *mitzvot*.

> When we fulfill all the commandments of the Torah, all the good things of this world will come to us. When, however, we transgress the precepts, the evils that are written in the Torah will befall us. But nevertheless, those good things are not the final reward for the fulfilment of the commandments, nor are those evils the last penalty exacted from one who transgresses all the commandments . . . He has further promised us in the Torah, that if we observe its behests joyously and cheerfully, and continually meditate on its wisdom, He will remove from us the obstacles that hinder us in its observance, such as sickness, war, famine and other calamities; and will bestow upon us all the material benefits that will strengthen our ability to fulfill the Law, such as plenty, peace, abundance of silver and gold. Thus we will not be engaged, all our days, in providing for our bodily needs, but will have leisure to study wisdom and fulfill the commandments, and thus attain life in the world-to-come.[18]

For Maimonides, the ultimate justification of biblical rewards and punishments is not the pleasures they provide nor the needs they gratify, but rather their influence upon the community's fulfillment of the Torah. The rewards consist of conditions that enable a person to devote himself to the performance of the *mitzvot* and the acquisition of knowledge of God. The punishments, on the other hand, consist of conditions that impede the realization of these goals.

Maimonides applied this interpretation to all those rewards promised in the Jewish tradition that do not appear to have any connection to love of God. His approach to messianism is a clear case in point.

> . . . when one is troubled here on earth with diseases, war or famine, he does not occupy himself with the acquisition of wisdom or the performance of religious precepts by which life hereafter is gained.
>
> Hence all Israelites, their prophets and sages, longed for the advent of messianic times, that they might have relief from the wicked tyranny that does not permit them properly to occupy themselves with the study of the Torah and the observance of the commandments; that they might have ease, devote themselves to getting wisdom and thus attain to life in the world-to-come.[19]

In *Hilkhot Teshuvah*, Maimonides places his instrumental interpretation of biblical rewards and punishments within the context of his discussion of *olam ha-ba* and of love of God. Maimonides generally discusses the meaning of serving God out of love when he deals with the themes of messianism and *olam ha-ba*. It would hardly make sense to make *olam ha-ba* (as Maimonides understands it) the ultimate goal of Judaism, unless one could show that Judaism revolves around the yearning to serve God out of love. Consequently, he augments his discussion of *olam ha-ba* and love of God with an explanation of how the biblical emphasis upon material rewards and punishments bears upon love and knowledge of God. Similarly in *Ḥelek*, where he explains the notions of messianism and *olam ha-ba*, he also deals with the motivational matrix of religious behavior in order to show that while the rabbinic tradition accepted action motivated by self-interest (*shelo li-shmah*), it regarded such behavior as an initial stage of religious development which ought to be superseded by disinterested performance of the commandments (*li-shmah*).[20]

Although Maimonides' goal was to promote the ideal of love within the community, he used the language of reward and punishment in his description of *olam ha-ba* because this was the motivational framework to which the community was accustomed. In *Ḥelek*, he describes human development in terms of the different rewards that motivate people to act at different stages of their lives. For an adult, power, prestige, wealth, and sensual pleasure are substitutes for the nuts, figs, or bits of sugar that the teacher promises the child to stimulate him to do his lessons. Because Maimonides recognized how difficult it was to transcend action motivated by self-interest, he adopted the language of reward and punishment in the hope that he could use it to foster interest in a joy that, in its deepest sense, expresses love of God.

By stressing the incomparable joy of the immaterial existence of *olam ha-ba*, Maimonides also sought to counteract a prevailing skepticism regarding the reality of incorporeal entities. A number of times throughout the *Essay on Resurrection* he repeats that a major reason why people show little interest in the immortality of the soul, and conceive of God in bodily terms, lies in their inability to conceive of immaterial existence. People reject divine incorporeity and the immateriality of the world-to-come because of this ontological presupposition.

> They [the masses] do not recognize true existence other than in a body. . . . For this reason, most of them believe that God is corporeal, because in their judgment He would not be in existence if He were not. . . . I believe that the angels are not bodies, and that the members of the world-to-come are separated souls, namely, intellects. In my work that I named *Guide of the Perplexed* I have culled proofs of this from the Torah. If one of the simpletons does not care to accept this, and prefers to believe that the angels are bodies and even eat—because the text of the Bible reads *and they ate* [Gen. 18:8]—and that the members of the world-to-come are also bodies, I do not mind. I would this were the extent of the ignorance of any of them. I hope their view of the Creator is free from any acceptance of corporeality. There is no harm in their assuming it for the separated beings. (p. 215)

In saying that he could tolerate the error of conceiving immortality in *olam ha-ba* in material terms, Maimonides in effect admits that he could tolerate nonbelief in *olam ha-ba*. Maimonides believed that the notion of eternal corporeal existence was absurd, since only that which is immaterial could be eternal. Those who believe in *olam ha-ba*, but conceive of it in material terms, in effect believe in that which does not and cannot exist. If, in spite of this, Maimonides claims he could tolerate such a belief, then it is reasonable to conclude that he could also tolerate nonbelief in *olam ha-ba*.

In the light of the foregoing, it would seem clear that *olam ha-ba* was a doctrine whose primary importance for Maimonides was as an instrument to teach divine incorporeity and to shift the focus of worship in the community from *yirah* to *ahavah*. This approach would explain in part why he discusses immortality and *olam ha-ba* in *Sefer ha-Mada* and the *Essay on Resurrection,* but he does not discuss these topics in depth in the *Guide of the Perplexed.* While Maimonides may have taken an agnostic position regarding the permanence of the intellect, as Pines suggests, he certainly believed that the notion of *olam ha-ba* was invaluable as a means to establish belief in divine incorporeity and to instill the ideal of *ahavah* within the community's framework of worship.[21] Consequently, the theses of immortality and *olam ha-ba* play a major role in his legal writings, which are addressed to the community, but are hardly referred to at all in the *Guide of the Perplexed,* which is addressed expressly to philosophically-oriented individuals. When his goal is to influence the community's beliefs, practices, and attitudes, he capitalizes on the authoritative status of the traditional doctrine of *olam ha-ba* and on the widespread interest in rewards and punishments in order to educate the community to accept divine incorporeity and to strive after disinterested love of God. Maimonides does not have to emphasize *olam ha-ba* in the *Guide,* since the intended reader is intellectually prepared to grasp the philosophic underpinnings of both divine incorporeity and love of God.

MAIMONIDES' SELF-DEFENSE

In the second part of the *Essay on Resurrection,* Maimonides defends himself against the charge of disbelief in resurrection by outlining his own justification for regarding resurrection as a fundamental doctrine of Judaism. The justification that he offers betrays an ambivalent attitude toward the importance of resurrection. On the one hand, he equates denial of resurrection with the rejection of such cardinal beliefs as creation, revelation, and prophecy. On the other hand, he does not elaborate upon the specific content or character of resurrection, choosing instead to treat belief in this doctrine as one instance of the general belief in miracles.

The force of Maimonides' argument is not so much *for* belief in resurrection as *against* disbelief in it. He argues that since there are no conclusive reasons for calling this traditional doctrine into question, but at least one reason in its favor, a halakhic Jew ought not to reject resurrection. The argument reveals the conservative attitude of the traditional mind. Rejection of a traditional doctrine requires justification. The onus of proof rests upon those who wish to change what is generally accepted.[22]

The argument may be briefly summarized as follows: Maimonides admits that he regards many biblical statements about resurrection and the messianic era as allegories that are not meant to be taken literally. Nonetheless, given the consensus of belief in resurrection in the community and a biblical text in Daniel in support of this belief, the only conclusive reason for reading the text in Daniel as mere allegory would be if resurrection were logically impossible. Resurrection would be logically impossible if by virtue of its miraculous character it were inconsistent with accepted metaphysical truths. And this would be the case if one believed that every event in our world is the necessary and invariable consequence of earlier events, in which case not only resurrection but belief in all miracles, including belief in revelation and creation, would be untenable. But since, as Maimonides argued in the *Guide*, there are no conclusive rational arguments to decide whether the world was created or has eternally existed, one may accept the traditional doctrine of creation literally. The same goes for the related doctrines of revelation, prophecy, and miracles.[23]

The crucial issue involved in accepting or rejecting the creation of the world is whether God acts at particular moments, i.e., whether there is a principle of divine freedom which permits God to act beyond the constraints of the natural order. If resurrection is rejected because it conflicts with the laws of nature, then, by parity of reason, one ought to reject all miracles including revelation and creation, i.e., all beliefs that presuppose divine freedom and spontaneity. The cost of rejecting resurrection in virtue of its miraculous character is the destruction of the foundation of Judaism as a historical religion.

This argument in defense of resurrection may be characterized as a defense of the Torah. By placing his discussion of resurrection within the broader context of the possibility of miracles as such, he turns the *Essay on Resurrection* into a defense of the principle of divine freedom against the principle of eternal necessity. Belief in resurrection becomes the litmus test of belief in the foundations of Judaism. His argument is thus not so much a defense of resurrection as of the possibility of the election of Israel as a Torah community.

In spite of his powerful defense of resurrection, there are a number of reasons for supposing that Maimonides was actually not greatly interested in the doctrine. To begin with, he discusses only cursorily the content of the belief in resurrection and completely ignores its religious significance.[24] His treatment of the doctrine of resurrection, whether in the *Essay on Resurrection* or in his other works, is exhausted by his including it among the miracles endorsed by the Jewish tradition. By contrast, in those other works he had elaborated on *olam ha-ba* with respect to both its meaning and its religious value. He excuses himself in the essay for this difference of emphasis, claiming that the notion of resurrection requires less explanation than *olam ha-ba* because, in contrast to the latter, 1) its constituent concepts are generally understood and easily grasped and 2) it is justified by authority and not by rational arguments. Notwithstanding this excuse, I believe that Maimonides in fact placed primary emphasis upon the doctrine of *olam ha-ba* because it served as a means of furthering love of God and belief in incorporeal existence. He also devoted considerably more attention to messianism than to resurrection, because of his conviction that without an end to political exploitation and material deprivation, the community as a whole could not be realistically expected to transcend considerations of self-interest and worship God out of love. In contrast to resurrection, messianism and *olam ha-ba* are assimilated into Maimonides' conception of the central goals of Judaism.[25]

As an instance of the general class of miracles in the Jewish tradition, resurrection could be allegorized with no appreciable effect on the character of Judaism. This could hardly be said with regard to such beliefs as creation, revelation, or even messianism. Given Maimonides' socio-political assessment of the requirements of communal life, it is unlikely that he would have thought it possible for any organized society to dispense entirely with reward and punishment or other self-interest directed beliefs. Because the Torah is a system of norms and beliefs meant for a political society, it includes beliefs which promise material benefits for conformity with the commandments.[26]

Offering pragmatic reasons for certain norms or beliefs does not imply their falsity. The question of whether a given belief is required for Judaism to function as a communal normative system should not be confused with the question of whether that belief is true or whether it is a logically necessary presupposition of the system.[27] A strong case can be made to show that Maimonides would have included messianism among such required beliefs of Judaism. Belief in the eventual end to exile and persecution serves to combat despair and hopelessness. Maimonides offers no such rationale for resurrection. He never once explains the social or psychological usefulness of this belief.

The fact that Maimonides dissociated resurrection from immortality and restricted immortality to immaterial and thus bodiless existence further undermines the importance of resurrection. Since resurrection is a temporal event that, except for its own occurrence, involves no change in the natural order (those who are resurrected remain mortal and subject to all the bodily contingencies), it is odd, to say the least, to expect anyone to long for a time when his soul will return to his body after having entered a state of immortal immaterial existence.[28] If one maintains the Aristotelian explanation of human individuality in terms of matter, it is already sufficiently difficult to make sense of the soul's movement between material and immaterial states of existence. It is even more difficult to explain why anyone would want to believe that the soul's separation from matter would be followed by its reunion with matter.

A further consideration is Maimonides' analogy, already quoted, between a king's preference for royalty above the street games of his youth and the superiority of the joy of comprehending God relative to material pleasures. The analogy implies that no one would want bodily pleasures after having entered *olam ha-ba*. "When after death the worthy from among us will reach that exalted stage, he will experience no bodily pleasures, *neither will he have any wish for them . . .*"[29] If *olam ha-ba* is, as Maimonides expressly says, the ultimate goal of Judaism, why should this ultimate goal be followed by a less than ultimate goal?

Maimonides' explanation of why people began to suspect his belief in resurrection thus skirts the entire issue of the pointlessness of maintaining hope for the resurrection of the dead once one accepts his notion of *olam ha-ba*. The justification he offers for the relative lengthiness of his treatment of *olam ha-ba*, i.e., to correct the community's neglect of this doctrine or to expand the scope of rewards and punishments, avoids the basic problem behind the controversy. It was not the physical length of his discussion of *olam ha-ba*, but rather the "logic" of his understanding of immortality and *olam ha-ba* that had led many readers such as the Rabad to wonder whether Maimonides in effect rejected bodily resurrection.[30] If the essence of man is immaterial, if the *tzelem elohim* (image of God) is the intellect, and if the ultimate goal of Judaism is the eternal joy that is only attainable with the separation of the soul from the body after death—then the doctrine of resurrection becomes superfluous and unimportant.

The argument he offers in defense of the doctrine of resurrection is that rejecting this traditional belief can result in the undoing of the entire framework of Judaism, which rests on belief in divine freedom. Although the doctrine of resurrection is not per se an indispensable doctrine without which Judaism would be undermined, it does not follow that the rejection of this belief would have no effect on the community's allegiance to Judaism. Maimonides' refusal to allegorize resurrection may be explained in terms of his appreciation of the dangers involved in introducing change in a traditional society. Allegorizing a doctrine that is widely taken literally may undermine the whole fabric of beliefs of a traditional society. By altering one apparently isolated detail of the tradition, you run the risk of setting into motion a process leading to the disintegration of the entire system.

The upshot of Maimonides' defense of resurrection is a warning against initiating radical changes in beliefs to which a community has become habituated. One must be cautious and conservative when attempting to alter generally accepted beliefs, irrespective of how one evaluates their intrinsic importance. Indeed, Maimonides should have expected the controversial reaction to his writings on messianism and *olam ha-ba*, especially in the light of his commentary on Antigonus of Sokho's statement in Mishnah Avot 1:3: "Be not as servants who serve the master in order to receive a gift, but be as servants who serve the master not in order to receive a gift." While Antigonus intended to teach that one ought to serve God out of love, nonetheless, Maimonides writes, the result was quite different.

> This sage had two disciples, one named Zadok and the other named Boethus. When they heard him deliver this statement they departed from him. The one said to his colleague, "Behold the master expressly stated that man has neither reward nor punishment and there is no expectation at all." [They said this] because they did not understand his intention.[31]

Worship out of love is a dangerous notion if the audience to whom it is addressed is unprepared to receive it. Maimonides stresses repeatedly that, to be effective, change—whether it be in patterns of behavior or of thought—must be gradual. Weaning people away from *yirah* and *she-lo li-shmah* and training them to worship out of love involves a slow and painstaking process.[32] Failure to assess an audience's receptivity to the ideal of love can have disastrous effects. Antigonus' exhortation to worship God out of love rather than in order to receive reward was mistakenly construed as an admission that there were in fact no rewards and punishments.

> But our sages knew how difficult a thing this [love of God] was and that not every one could act up to it. They knew that even the man who reached it would not at once accord with it and think it a true article of faith. For man only does those actions which will either bring him advantage or ward off loss. All other action he holds vain and worthless. Accordingly, how could it be said to one who is learned in the law—"Do these things, but do them not out of fear of God's punishment, nor out of hope for his reward"? This would be exceedingly hard, because it is not every one that comprehends truth, and becomes like Abraham our father. Therefore, in order that the common folk might be established in their convictions, the sages permitted them to perform meritorious actions with the hope of reward, and to avoid the doing of evil out of fear of punishment. They encourage them to these conceptions and their opinions become firmly rooted, until eventually the intelligent among them come to comprehend and know what truth is and what is the most perfect mode of

conduct. It is exactly the way in which we deal with the lad in his studies, as we have explained in our foregoing simile. Antigonus of Sokho was blamed by them for the particular exposition he gave to the multitude and they applied to him the words, "Oh, wise men, be cautious of your words."[33]

Maimonides was fully aware of the reasons why the rabbis reprimanded Antigonus for publicly teaching worship based on love. When the focus of religious discussions is shifted toward the incomparable joy of knowing God and being in His presence, and you totally ignore the gruesome details of the suffering awaiting the wicked or the wondrous pleasures in store for the righteous, i.e., when you turn attention away from the concrete benefits of religious life, you may not only alienate your audience, but also undermine the mainstay of their religious commitment.[34]

Despite his knowledge of Antigonus' mistake of prematurely exposing the ideal of disinterested worship to a spiritually unprepared community, Maimonides, to some extent, repeated that mistake. His guiding passion throughout his writings was to place the ideal of love of God grounded in knowledge at the very center of the halakhic framework of experience. He concluded *Sefer ha-Mada* and the *Mishneh Torah* with the theme of passionate intellectual love of God; he demythologized Judaism's picture of the world and sought to draw his readers' attention to the awe-inspiring wisdom of God within the natural order; he naturalized messianism and made the quest to know God— in *olam ha-ba*—the ultimate goal and purpose of Judaism.

The *Essay on Resurrection*, however, represents a painful reassessment of the wisdom of dealing with the ideal of love of God so explicitly and directly. The community's selective apprehension of his writings and its preoccupation with peripheral matters such as resurrection reminded Maimonides of the gap between what he hoped the community would aspire to and what in fact was the community's understanding of worship of God. In the *Essay on Resurrection* Maimonides gave up hope of inculcating his ideal of love of God into the community. In the entire essay, the themes of love and knowledge of God are notably absent. The notion of *olam ha-ba* is explicated solely in terms of its importance in convincing the community to believe in immaterial existence and to deny divine corporeality. Not a word is mentioned about the connection between *olam ha-ba* and the actualization of the intellect through knowledge.

The reasons Maimonides presents to justify his relative disregard of resurrection in contrast with *olam ha-ba* are basically an apologetic response to the accusation against him. He fails to mention that *olam ha-ba,* unlike resurrection, is systematically connected to the ultimate goals of Judaism: knowledge and love of God. He justifies his naturalized conception of messianism and his allegorization of prophetic texts that suggest radical changes in the natural order by pointing out that there is no binding tradition to the contrary. In *Sefer Shoftim,* by contrast, he had warned people not to devote time and thought to the specific details of when and how the end-of-days promises will materialize and states explicitly that such matters "do not lead to either love or fear of God."[35]

In the *Essay on Resurrection* Maimonides ignores the issue of love of God and the role of knowledge in stimulating a person's quest for God. In contrast to *Ḥelek* and *Sefer ha-Mada,* his treatment of the key eschatological beliefs of Judaism is devoid of any discussion of different levels of worship—e.g., *li-shmah/she-lo li-shmah,* and *ahavah/yirah.* Maimonides' silence suggests that he now took a more sober view of the spiritual capabilities of the community. It would appear that his more modest hope was restricted to eliminating the idolatrous beliefs that had infiltrated the community and gaining a universal consensus of belief in the incorporeity of God.

The first two parts of the essay reflect Maimonides' anger, bitterness, and painful disappointment at a community that forced him to focus on *yirah*-oriented matters such as miracles, reward and punishment, and resurrection, when his overriding religious ideal was love of God. The community seemed to be oblivious to the central guiding ideal of his lifework: to shape a community based on the principles of the rejection of idolatry and the quest to know and love God. Maimonides could have drawn the conclusion that he had failed in his role as religious leader and that it was futile to attempt to narrow the gap between his philosophic-religious orientation and the community's modes of religious life. He could have decided to abandon his deep involvement with the community and to withdraw into the private circle of his religious interests where he could devote undivided attention to love and knowledge of God.

In other words, Maimonides could have decided to abandon the frustrating struggle to "return to the cave" and content himself with furthering his personal quest for love of God. At the end of the *Guide,* he characterizes the highest form of human perfection, which consists of "the conception of intelligibles which teach true opinions concerning the divine things," as that which "gives the individual true perfection, a perfection belonging to him alone."[36] Returning to the community and having to defend your religious integrity do not appear to be conditions that enhance the quest for true human perfection and happiness.

A crucial test of whether the Jewish philosopher returns to the cave or forsakes the community is whether he continues to teach Torah to his community. Maimonides certainly passes this test, as the end of the *Essay on Resurrection* shows. Here he reverts to being the defender of the Torah against the unfounded accusation that the Torah negates the doctrine of resurrection. The shift away from a personal defense to a defense of the Torah is only partially explained by Maimonides' statement:

> After reaching this point in this monograph, which was its objective, and realizing that it is entirely bereft of benefits, because it contains nothing more than repetition of what is written in my commentary to the Mishnah and in my major composition, with some additional explanation for the unintelligent or the skeptic, I think it proper not to deprive it of some new interest. I shall take up two problems relevant to this subject. (p. 225)

If the *Essay on Resurrection* were simply a personal defense of his orthodoxy, Maimonides could have concluded the essay after declaring his belief in the doctrine of resurrection. In the last part of the essay, however, the personal quality of the letter abruptly vanishes and Maimonides assumes the role of a teacher propounding a theory concerning the history of the idea of resurrection. He desists from trying to justify his relatively brief and unimpassioned treatment of resurrection and instead turns to an explanation of the brevity and ambiguity of the Bible's treatment of resurrection. In other words, Maimonides continues to accept the role of spiritual educator of his community.

THE NATURE AND FUNCTION OF MIRACLES

In the last part of his essay, Maimonides turns to the more constructive task of removing two conceivable obstacles to the belief in resurrection: 1) numerous biblical sayings appear to contradict it, despite the statement in Daniel that affirms it, and 2) it is not supported by any statement in the Torah. His answers to these problems require him to say much about the nature of miracles, a category to which resurrection belongs. The *Essay on Resurrection* implies a reassessment by Maimonides of the function of miracles in the religious outlook of the community. In earlier works, he had sought to reduce the scope of miracle, preferring to show that events follow their normal course, whenever this was compatible with the fundamental doctrines of Judaism. But the confusion and misunderstanding caused by his views on *olam ha-ba*, messianism, and resurrection now showed that the notion of miracle was a pivotal religious category within the community. The community's conceptual framework of religious thought and experience revolved, to a great extent, around the notion of miracle.

The predominance of this concept was but one feature of *yirah*-consciousness. This may be characterized as a frame of mind where one's hungers and needs determine the way one relates to the world. *Yirah* in the sense of worship motivated by fear of punishment or expectation of reward is but one instance of a general orientation to life that revolves around the self and its needs. The concept of miracle plays an important role within this framework by channeling interest in God into areas that reveal God's free response to the needs and requests of particular persons. God's miraculous intervention at a particular moment in time serves as a confirmation of God's concern and love for particular persons or groups.

In contrast to the impersonal mode of divine action manifest in nature, the miraculous mode of divine action answers to a person's need for individual divine concern. It gives meaning to the experience of petitional prayer.[37] The language of miracle is a language which involves bodies, i.e., concrete individuals. It is no wonder, therefore, that the doctrine of bodily resurrection aroused such great interest in the community. Resurrection of the body reflects the particularization of the religious outlook, the dominance of the anthropocentric over the theocentric world view.

Maimonides could not ignore the fact that this was the intellectual framework of the community he led and taught.[38] Their thoughts on God focused on rewards and punishments; their view of nature was colored by their overriding interest in miracles; and their hope for messianism, nurtured by their present suffering and deprivation, was for national restoration, power, and material well-being.[39] Maimonides had to come to terms with the limited receptivity of a community unable to go beyond the circle of felt needs and wants. The controversy surrounding his view on resurrection taught him that his effectiveness as a teacher of Torah depended on his working within the conceptual framework of the community. He would have to adapt his mode of teaching to their mode of thought in order not to become embroiled in fruitless controversies. He therefore defended the biblical treatment of resurrection and developed a new theory of how to evaluate God's miraculous acts in history.

The first obstacle, then, to belief in resurrection is that the majority of the biblical texts relevant to this doctrine appear to contradict it. Biblical literature abounds with direct and indirect references to the finality and irreversibility of death. The doctrine of resurrection is even absent from the book of Job, where the central theme is the problem of evil. Indeed, Maimonides knows of only one unequivocal biblical reference to resurrection (Daniel 12).

Maimonides explains the biblical statements that contradict belief in resurrection by pointing out that the majority of biblical texts mirror what ordinarily happens in nature. Ordinary discourse takes the recurrent patterns of nature for granted. This should not be confused with denying the possibility of miracles. These texts merely presuppose that in the vast majority of cases (i.e., *barring* miracles) events conform to the natural order.

Maimonides subtly shows that the concept of miracle presupposes the notion of natural order. Miracles are aberrations from the normal. The predominant feature of the biblical conception of the world is its orderliness and regularity. In order to make sense of the biblical world of experience one must understand the rabbinic notion *olam ke-min-hago noheg* (the world conforms to its usual course).[40]

The other obstacle to belief in resurrection, and one to which Maimonides gives greater attention, is the notable absence of references to resurrection in the Torah. To account for their absence, Maimonides uses the radical theory he had propounded in the *Guide* to explain the reasons behind the commandments. The theory cites specific historical influences upon the content of the revealed Law and is based on Maimonides' general theory of human development. The basic idea of this general psychological theory is that change is a process and not a sudden transition from one state to a completely different one. "For a sudden transition from one opposite to another is impossible. And therefore, man, according to his nature, is not capable of abandoning suddenly all to which he was accustomed."[41]

Although Maimonides claims that such graduated processes of change are not unique to human psychology, but are manifest in many areas studied by natural science (e.g., infant development and physiology), he draws attention to this fact of nature in order to explain how changes in deep-rooted human habits can be achieved. His main thesis is that in order to effect changes in the practices, dispositions, or beliefs of a person or group, one must first compare the existing condition of practice or belief to the desired condition. If the differences require too sudden a change—one to which man "according to his nature" is not capable of adapting—then one must devise a strategy that will graduate the change. If the desired end, the "first intention," is not realizable immediately, then one must compromise in such a way that the practices or ideas one introduces are sufficiently like current practices or ideas to be assimilated by the person(s) in question, yet sufficiently unlike them to set into motion a process leading to their eventual abolition and their replacement by the desired practices or ideas.

The rationale behind such strategies or "ruses" is that since human nature abhors sudden changes, it may be necessary (as in the case of sacrifices) to devise ways of embedding the dynamic for change within frameworks which, on the surface, resemble existing frameworks. Maimonides uses this theory of "ruses" to explain certain narrative and legal sections in the Torah. God's decision to have the people wander and grow hardier in the desert, rather than enter the land of Canaan immediately after leaving Egypt, was based on a "divine ruse" not unlike the "divine ruse" that underlies the inclusion of the sacrificial cult in the Law:

> For just as it is not in the nature of man that, after having been brought up in slavish service occupied with clay, bricks and similar things, he should all of a sudden wash off from his hands the dirt deriving from them and proceed immediately to fight against "the children of Anak," so is it not in his nature that, after having been brought up upon very many modes of worship and of customary practices, which the soul finds so agreeable that they become as it were a primary notion, he should abandon them all of a sudden. And just as the deity used a gracious ruse in causing them to wander perplexedly in the desert until their souls became courageous . . . and until, moreover, people were born who were not accustomed to humiliation and servitude . . . so did this group of laws derive from a divine grace, so that they should be left with the kind of practices to which they were accustomed and so that consequently the belief that constitutes the first intention should be validated in them.[42]

Because the "way of life generally accepted and customary in the whole world and the universal service upon which we were brought up" consisted in animal sacrifices and the burning of incense in temples dedicated to the worship of the stars, God did not abolish these forms of worship in the Torah.

> For one could not then conceive the acceptance of [such a Law], considering the nature of man, which always likes that to which it is accustomed. At that time this would have been similar to the appearance of a prophet in these times, who, calling upon the people to worship God, would say: "God has given you a law forbidding you to pray to Him, to fast, to call upon Him for help in misfortune. Your worship should consist solely in meditation without any works at all."[43]

Rather than proscribe the cultic forms of worship universally practiced at the time, God permitted them to continue, but made Himself—rather than "created or imaginary and unreal things"—the object of worship.

> Through this divine ruse it came about that the memory of idolatry was effaced and that the grandest and true foundation of our belief—namely, the existence and oneness of the deity—was firmly established, while at the same time the souls had no feeling of repugnance and were not repelled because of the abolition of modes of worship to which they were accustomed and other than which no other mode of worship was known at that time.[44]

The centrality of *mitzvah* in Judaism embodies this gradualist approach to behavior modification. According to Maimonides, the commandments mirror the wisdom of God who acts as a patient educator who works within the limitations of given realities.

> God does not change at all the nature of human individuals by means of miracles. . . . It is because of this that there are commandments and prohibitions, rewards and punishments. . . . We do not say this because we believe that the changing of the nature of any human individual is difficult for Him. . . . Rather is it possible and fully within capacity. But according to the foundations of the Law, of the Torah, He has never willed to do it, nor shall He ever will it. For if it were His will that the nature of any human individual should be changed because of what He, may He be exalted, wills from that individual, sending of prophets and all giving of a law would have been useless.[45]

For Maimonides, the meaning of God's giving *mitzvot* implies that God renounces the use of miracles as a way of changing human behavior. Although creation and the unique revelation at Sinai express the miraculous power of God to act at singular moments in history, the content of this revelation points toward God the educator who works within the ordered and limited confines of human behavior. Belief in the possibility of *mitzvah* leads one in the direction of miracles; the understanding and practice of *mitzvah* leads one in the direction of God's wisdom as manifest in the orderly patterns of being.[46] The eternal authority of *mitzvah* in Judaism suggests, for Maimonides, that God affects man in history through the patient process of education rather than through sudden miraculous transformations.

In the *Essay on Resurrection*, Maimonides uses the same historical framework to explain why the Torah fails to mention the promise of resurrection.[47] "Sabean" culture was the dominant culture with which the Torah had to contend. As a result of its widespread influence, people believed in the eternity of the world, in divine corporeality, and in the impossibility of prophecy and miracles.[48] In the light of these beliefs, one of the Torah's primary tasks was to bring about belief in prophecy, revelation, and creation. Consequently, God produced miracles in order to authenticate prophecy and belief in creation. "The genuine miracle," states Maimonides, "is decisive proof of the production of the universe."

Because the concept of miracle was foreign to their conceptual framework, it was necessary to allow the people time to become habituated to the belief in miracles. Until belief in miracles became firmly established in the minds of the community, promises of reward and punishment were restricted to "happenings of this world and the course of nature; this embraces immortality of the soul or its discontinuity." Introducing the doctrine of resurrection was delayed, because it is a miracle in the class of the naturally impossible and therefore might not only have been rejected by the people, but even have destroyed whatever plausibility the notion of miracle had in their minds at that point. Rather than risk undermining the credibility of the Torah and the consequent abandonment of the *mitzvot*, God chose to postpone disclosure of the doctrine of resurrection until the community accepted, beyond any doubt, the authenticity of prophecy, revelation, and miracles.

Maimonides mentions two reasons why resurrection was initially excluded from the rewards and punishments revealed to the community: 1) because it is a blatant miracle and 2) because the benefits it promised lay in the distant future. According to Maimonides, the credibility of the doctrine of reward and punishment was enhanced by the promise of immediate fulfillment. It is clear, therefore, that Maimonides did not consider the doctrine of reward and punishment to be an empirically verified belief. If it were, then the community's belief in reward and punishment could have been verified by observation and would not have been affected at all by Moses' teaching the doctrine of resurrection. The language of reward and punishment is more a language of interpretation and response to reality than a language of description. The plausibility of doctrines such as reward and punishment should not be evaluated in isolation from a person's needs and interests and the other beliefs he holds about the world and about himself. If one presents a person with a doctrine of reward and punishment which also involves belief in resurrection—a belief which that person considers to be absurd—then his belief in the entire system of reward and punishment may be undermined. Moses therefore had to be cautiously selective in revealing doctrinal matters to the community.

Because their commitment to the Torah was tenuous and they were not convinced of the authenticity of revelation and miracles, God had to confine His dogmatic teachings to the people's *yirah* framework of thought. He had to focus on immediate gratification, while allowing nothing (e.g., the doctrine of resurrection) to weaken the effectiveness of a religious system that makes the observance of commandments the necessary and sufficient condition for material prosperity and gratification.

> He knew that when they were informed of the innovation of the return of the dead, they would consider it impossible and would emphatically shun it. They would indulge in sin, since retribution was greatly delayed. For this reason they were warned and threatened with punishment, of which they were quickly persuaded: if you listen, . . . if you do not listen. . . . Their acceptance of that was more immediate and more beneficial. This too is a great benefit as obedience will make their situation in this world prosper and disobedience will hurt it. (p. 230)

The community could learn to accept a doctrine which involved the postponement of gratification only when the belief in miracles and prophetic revelation became deeply entrenched in their minds. According to Maimonides' historical reconstruction, one can gauge progress in biblical history in terms of the growth of belief in the concept of miracle. The process of development begins with total disbelief in creation, revelation, and prophecy and ends with belief in the truly miraculous doctrine of resurrection. In his usual subtle way, Maimonides is possibly arguing for the connection between the community's internalization of the Torah and its ability to live with postponed gratification.

The concluding section of the *Essay on Resurrection* is, on the surface, a striking turnabout in Maimonides' attitude to and mode of dealing with miracles. From a rationalist philosopher with a clear preference for the regularities of the natural order above miracles, he suddenly becomes a classifier of miracles, pointing out criteria for identifying the perfect miracle. Toward the end of the essay, Maimonides surprisingly presents an analysis of the concept of miracle that highlights the miraculous nature of all of Jewish history. This section of the essay constitutes a striking reversal of his declared policy of minimizing the appeal to miracle to clarify Judaism. "It is recognized," writes Maimonides, "that I shun as best I can changes in the physical order." In keeping with this general policy, Maimonides often resorts to allegory in his exegesis of biblical and rabbinic texts.

My endeavor, and that of the select keen-minded people, differs from the quest of the masses. They like nothing better and, in their silliness, enjoy nothing more, than to set the Law and reason at opposite ends, and to move everything far from the explicable. So they claim it to be a miracle, and they shrink from identifying it as a natural incident, whether it is something that happened in the past and is recorded, or something predicted to happen in the future. But I try to reconcile the Law and reason, and wherever possible consider all things as of the natural order. Only when something is explicitly identified as a miracle, and reinterpretation of it cannot be accommodated, only then I feel forced to grant that this is a miracle. (p. 223)

Despite his lifelong struggle to cultivate in his readers a religious appreciation of the wisdom of God revealed in the structure of the natural order, he ends the *Essay on Resurrection* with a brief analysis of the concept of miracles, ostensibly aimed at enabling the community to identify the perfect miracle.

Maimonides begins by dividing the class of miracles into two subclasses. The first subclass involves occurrences that clearly contravene the natural order. Moses' rod turning into a serpent and the splitting of the Red Sea are examples of such "naturally impossible" miracles. One of the distinctive characteristics of such miracles is their short duration. The reason Maimonides offers for their brevity is that otherwise people would begin to doubt whether the events constituting the miracle were genuine occurrences, e.g., whether Moses' rod was really a rod to begin with and not simply a serpent mistakenly identified as a rod.

Contrary to what one might expect from his earlier writings, Maimonides does not use the fact that such miracles are short-lived to reinforce belief in the unchanging order of nature, but rather he uses it to reinforce belief in the genuineness of such miracles.[49] Nature resumes its natural course in order to support belief in miracles.

The second subclass of miracles consists of events that are "in the realm of the naturally possible," but because of specific circumstances are deemed to be miracles. Such occurrences would be regarded as natural were it not for the following conditions: 1) the events occur in fulfillment of a prophetic prediction, 2) the extraordinary character of these particular occurrences relative to others of the same kind (e.g., the plagues of hail and locusts as described in Exodus 9:26 and 10:14, respectively), and 3) the persistence of normally infrequent and highly

improbable conjunctions of occurrences. The causal connection between observance of the commandments and material rewards and
punishments is an example of the latter.[50] Unlike miracles within the
class of the naturally impossible, such miracles presuppose the persistence of the events in question in order to dispel any suspicion that
they occurred by chance.

Although natural regularities appear to be morally indifferent, the
doctrine of rewards and punishments implies that there is a miraculous
connection between a person's moral-religious deserts and what happens to him. In numerous places in his writings, Maimonides offers
naturalistic explanations for rewards and punishments by arguing that
beneficial consequences follow naturally from virtuous behavior and
harmful consequences from sinful behavior.[51] In the *Essay on Resurrection*, however, he characterizes rewards and punishments exclusively as miracles. Also, unlike his treatment of providence in the
Guide,[52] he restricts the miracle of providence to the people of Israel
alone:

> It is written: *They shall serve as signs and proofs against you and
> your offspring for all time* [Deut. 28:46]. This is the basis of the
> rabbinic declaration: "Israel has no star," meaning that their
> success and failure are not the result of natural causes or cus-
> tomary existence, but are linked to their obedience and disobe-
> dience; this is the most convincing sign. I have already stated
> that this applies to the community and to every individual. It is
> clear from that anecdote, which is in harmony with the verse:
> *and your offspring,* and also from the counsel, well known in the
> community: When a person feels that he is being afflicted, let
> him examine his behavior. This same idea is implied in God's
> assertion regarding the singularity of the community: *These the
> Lord your God allotted to the other peoples everywhere under heaven,
> but you the Lord took* [Deut. 4:19–20]. The meaning is that their
> situation does not follow the pattern of the situation of the other
> communities. No, they are singled out by this great miracle:
> success and failure in their activities will always be linked to
> their actions. (pp. 230–231)

The survival of the community of Israel, which depends upon the
observance of the *mitzvot,* is the "continuous miracle" of Jewish history.[53] This interpretation banishes the arbitrary and the accidental
from Jewish religious consciousness. *Teshuvah,* repentance in the sense
of return to God and to the Torah, constitutes one of the ways the
community responds to suffering and misfortune. The doctrine of reward and punishment for the observance of the *mitzvot* enables a person

to interpret his suffering as a message from God calling him to do *teshuvah*.

One of the aims of the halakhic requirement of *teshuvah* is to counteract the belief that suffering is the result of *mikreh*, chance. In the first chapter of *Hilkhot Ta'anit*, in his letter on astrology to the rabbis of Marseilles, and in the section preceding his detailed explanation of the reasons for specific commandments in the *Guide* 3:36, Maimonides discusses the theme of *teshuvah* from the perspective of the Judaic belief in providence. *Teshuvah* as a response to suffering expresses this community's refusal to admit the arbitrary and the accidental into the conceptual network through which it interprets human suffering.[54]

Maimonides' "ruse" in this essay consists in his addressing the suffering community in the language of miracles. Given the community's limitations, his main concern becomes that of fortifying their belief that their suffering and well-being depend upon their observance of the commandments. If they believe this, then they will come to regard their survival as an expression of the greatest of miracles. Rather than seek out the anomalous, the bizarre, and the irrational in order to satisfy their quest for God's loving concern, they can satisfy their religious hunger by focusing on the unique power of the *mitzvot* to guarantee their survival. Israel expresses its unique relationship to God by banishing the morally neutral from its interpretation of events in history. The wondrous power of miracle is revealed within the community's steadfast loyalty to *mitzvot*, irrespective of the events of history.[55] When a community interprets its destiny solely on the basis of its relationship to Torah, then one witnesses the "continuous miracle" of Jewish history.

By redirecting the community's preoccupation with miracles toward the "continuous miracle" underlying their survival, Maimonides shifts the focus away from singular, naturally inexplicable occurrences, neutralizes the potentially disruptive effects of alleged supernatural intrusions into history, and creates an impetus to persevere in loyalty to the Torah.[56] Instead of looking to the splitting of seas, manna from heaven, miraculous plagues, or bizarre promises and actions of charismatic messianic pretenders, the community is educated by Maimonides to perceive the perfect miracle in the connection between their survival as a community and their commitment to the Torah.[57]

EDUCATIONAL APPROACHES OF MAIMONIDES

As one reads the concluding lines of the *Essay on Resurrection*, one senses the complex mixture of emotions that Maimonides feels toward his community. He has no illusions about the people he addresses and

he cannot suppress feelings of anger because of the likelihood that he
will be misunderstood. At the end of the essay, Maimonides shows
that he is fully aware of the vast differences between the intended
readers of the *Guide* and those of the *Essay on Resurrection*, yet he
feels responsible to both groups:

> No intelligent person has the right to blame me for the repetition
> in this essay, the additions to the main idea, or for the extensive
> clarification of what does not really require further light. I wrote
> this tract only for the common people who had begun to doubt
> what I had stated explicitly, and for those who reproached me
> for brevity when I spoke of the Resurrection. Those who are truly
> learned are satisfied with a suggestion; they need neither repe-
> tition nor prolonged exegesis; they need only summary state-
> ments, as I have done with the profound questions in the *Guide*
> and in all my works. I follow the method related by the sages:
> He said to him: Explain it, but he answered: A sage needs no
> explaining. He said: Repeat it, but he answered: A sage requires
> no repetition. From this it becomes clear that discourse with the
> wise stands in need of neither repetition nor elucidation. *Instruct
> a wise man, and he will grow wiser* [Prov. 9:9]. But the common
> people need both, *precept after precept, precept after precept, now
> here, now there* [Isa. 28:13]. The sense of it is that they under-
> stand but little, they comprehend a bit, a little here, a little there.
> But the right thing to do is to address each group according to
> its capacity. (p. 233)

Maimonides draws attention to the difference between this essay
and those other writings in which he felt more confident of his readers'
ability to discern his intended meaning. He concludes the essay with
the painful acknowledgment that, despite his painstaking effort to express himself clearly and precisely, he remains uncertain of whether
he will be understood correctly. Notwithstanding his frank assessment
of the difficulty of teaching the "common folk," he ends by reaffirming
his commitment to "address each group according to its capacity." Just
as the God of revelation as described in the *Guide of the Perplexed*
addresses His "audience" according to its capacity ("The Torah spoke
in the language of human beings"), so too does Maimonides adapt his
teachings to the audiences he addresses. Just as God showed His
patient love for Israel by appreciating their limitations, so too does
Maimonides, the leader of his people, reveal in his *Essay on Resurrection* his struggle to imitate God's patience.[58]

I have tried to show that the *Essay on Resurrection* differs not only
from the *Guide* but, in some important respects, also from his legal

works, the *Commentary to the Mishnah* and the *Mishneh Torah*. I
believe that Maimonides' concluding statement in the *Essay on Resurrection*, which indicates different audiences of his writings, invites the
reader to examine the possible goals he had in mind when he addressed
his different audiences. I shall therefore briefly compare the works
mentioned in order to contrast Maimonides' various approaches as a
religious educator.

In the *Commentary to the Mishnah* and the *Mishneh Torah*— two
major legal works addressed to the community—Maimonides tried *inter
alia* to broaden the religious framework of halakhic experience. As I
showed in my previous book on Maimonides, one of his aims in these
works was to inculcate philosophic-religious sensibilities within the
halakhic community. The *Mishneh Torah* begins with an explication
of the notion of God's necessary existence. In providing the reader of
the *Mishneh Torah* with a minimal philosophic background with which
to understand proofs for the existence of God, Maimonides does not
fear to expose the reader to the Aristotelian thesis of the eternity of
the universe.[59] He does not confine knowledge of God to the study of
the Law, but emphasizes the religious significance of the study of
nature in order to discover the wisdom of God. Comprehension of God's
revelation in nature leads directly to passionate love of God and to
feelings of profound humility, because of His awe-inspiring power and
wisdom. Love and reverential fear of God—the two ultimate goals of
Judaism—may be realized through knowledge of the natural and divine
sciences.

The actualization of the image of God in man, the intellect, is a
crucial condition for realizing the goal of love of God. Maimonides
concludes *Sefer ha-Mada* with this very theme and he concludes the
entire *Mishneh Torah* with the yearning for a historical period that
would be conducive to the unfolding of intellectual love of God described in the second chapter of *Hilkhot Yesodei ha-Torah*. Messianism
serves as the link between the seemingly individualistic ideal of intellectual love of God and the collective framework of Halakhah. Maimonides' explanation of messianism in terms of material conditions
that enable the majority of the community to devote itself to knowledge
and love of God reflects his approach to Judaism as a communal way
of life centering around the quest to know and to love God.

I suggest that for Maimonides, *mitzvah* is a bridging concept that
connects the founding miracle of revelation at Sinai with the ultimate
realization of love of God born of knowledge of God's wisdom as revealed in nature and Torah in the messianic era. The inception of the
Torah is the miracle of revelation and its culmination is the establishment of a society dedicated to the pursuit of knowledge of God whose

wisdom is revealed in the everyday patterns of nature. The purpose of *mitzvah* is to move a person from *yirah* to *ahavah*, from miracle-dependent religiosity to knowledge-oriented passionate love of God.

The *Guide of the Perplexed* points toward a similar religious outlook but, because this work is addressed to individuals and not to the community as a collective unit, messianism is not a crucial theme. The first two chapters of the *Guide* set the tone of a religious journey that is, in certain respects, different from the path charted by the Halakhah.

The *Guide* begins with an analysis of the concept of *tzelem elohim,* the image of God, in terms of the human intellect. While the body is that which explains individuality, the intellect, which is immaterial and nonpersonal, enables a person to share in the divine reality. Prophecy notwithstanding, the intellect provides the primary framework of a person's relationship with God.

In the second chapter of the *Guide,* Maimonides interprets the "fall of man" by distinguishing between two states of man. The original state is determined exclusively by the intellect. In this state, a human being is wholly preoccupied with the true and the false and has no need for a knowledge of moral concepts that are applied in situations involving the problematic influence of the bodily passions. The second state of human existence emerges when the body interferes with the activity of the intellect. Human passions and drives are expressions of the material component of the human being. Self-conscious man, who discovers his "nakedness" in terms of his personal hungers, needs, and pleasures, requires a morality that answers to his personal frame of mind.

The first two chapters of the *Guide* thus indicate the difference between a world view dominated by the non-individualized human essence and the individualized body-oriented framework of morality. The direction man faces is drastically altered when he is compelled to struggle to regain mastery of his body. Revealed morality may be characterized in terms of the individualized framework in which "fallen" man perceives reality.[60] Revelation is thus fundamentally addressed to a community that must struggle to control the inclinations of the body. The individualized "body" morality of revelation requires a metaphysical framework that will make such an individualized relationship between God and man possible. The doctrine of creation serves as the foundation of a religious world view that pictures man as an entity comprised of intellect and body.

Revelation is also conceptually bound up with the notion of miracle. Miracle is perhaps the most vivid example of the particularization of one's relationship with God. Nevertheless, the fact that creation makes miracle possible does not imply that one's view of reality need be dominated by the concept of miracle. Maimonides insists on pointing out that while revelation of Torah presupposes creation, i.e., the rejection of eternity *a parte ante*, it does not imply the rejection of eternity *a parte post*. Revelation is compatible with the belief that, subsequent to the founding miracle of revelation at Sinai, the universe will pursue its natural course to eternity. The compatibility of belief in the Torah and disbelief in an end to history and to the natural order means that one can adopt a largely Aristotelian view of the unchanging order of nature, yet remain within the framework of the Torah.

> I have already made it clear to you that the belief in the production of the world is necessarily the foundation of the entire Law. However, the belief in its passing away after it has come into being and been generated is not, in our opinion, in any respect a foundation of the Law, and none of our beliefs would be hurt through the belief in its permanent duration.[61]

The religious importance of this insight lies in the implied compatibility between Judaism and a philosophic attitude that focuses on the impersonal wisdom of God in nature. The movement from *yirah* to *ahavah* corresponds to the movement from a religious fixation on miracles to a love of God inspired by knowledge of divine actions revealed within the orderly patterns of nature.

According to Maimonides, nature can serve as a model for moral behavior by virtue of the divine attributes of action that are revealed in its workings:

> For instance, one apprehends the kindness of His governance in the production of the embryos of living beings, the bringing of various faculties to existence in them and in those who rear them after birth—faculties that preserve them from destruction and annihilation and protect them against harm and are useful to them in all the doings that are necessary to them. Now actions of this kind proceed from us only after we feel a certain affection and compassion, and this is the meaning of mercy. God, may He be exalted, is said to be merciful, just as it is said, *Like as a father is merciful to his children* [Ps. 103:13], and it says, *And I will pity them, as a man pitieth his own son* [Mal. 3:17]. It is not that He, may He be exalted, is affected and has compassion. But an action similar to that which proceeds from a father in respect to his child and that is attached to compassion, pity and an absolute passion, proceeds from Him, may He be exalted, in reference to His holy ones, not because of a passion or a change.[62]

God's *hesed* (loving-kindness) is manifest in the very existence of the world:

> Now it is known that beneficence includes two notions, one of them consisting in the exercise of beneficence toward one who has no right at all to claim this from you, and the other consisting in the exercise of beneficence toward one who deserves it, but in a greater measure than he deserves it. In most cases the prophetic books use the word *hesed* in the sense of practicing beneficence toward one who has no right at all to claim this from you. Therefore every benefit that comes from Him, may He be exalted, is called *hesed*. Thus it says: *I will make mention of the loving-kindness* [hasdei] *of the Lord* [Ps. 89:3]. Hence this reality as a whole—I mean that He, may He be exalted, has brought it into being—is *hesed*.[63]

The three attributes of *hesed*, *tzedakah* (righteousness), and *mishpat* (judgment) are applicable to God by virtue of existence per se and of the structure of being:

> When refuting the doctrine of divine attributes, we have already explained that every attribute by which God is described in the books of the prophets is an attribute of action. Accordingly He is described as *hasid* [one possessing loving-kindness] because He has brought the all into being; as *saddiq* [righteous] because of His mercy toward the weak—I refer to the governance of the living being by means of its forces; and as *Judge* because of the occurrence in the world of relative good things and of relative great calamities, necessitated by judgment that is consequent upon wisdom. The Torah uses all three terms: *Shall the Judge of all the earth*; Ṣaddiq [*righteous*] *and upright is He*; *And abundant in* hesed [*loving-kindness*].[64]

The *Guide of the Perplexed* begins with an analysis of the concept of *tzelem elohim* in terms of the human intellect. It ends with a description of the philosopher entering the presence of the King, through having ascended the steps leading to the knowledge of God and to his total preoccupation with this knowledge. The actualization of the intellect leads man from a universe in which man is at the center to a universe where all of being is sustained by the quest to know and imitate God.

At the end of the religious journey in the *Guide of the Perplexed*, Maimonides' reader is taught to internalize a morality whose content may be similar to that of the commandments, but whose ground is decidedly different. The morality of the philosopher-lover as described

in the *Guide* 3:54, and of the political statesman as portrayed there
(1:54), is a mode of ethical behavior that seeks to imitate God's action
in nature. Here the framework of moral behavior is not God's revelation
of commandments to a particular people, but rather God's goodness
manifest in the patterns of natural phenomena; this makes a difference
to the manner, if not the content, of moral behavior. The nonpersonal
quality of an ethic of imitation of God in nature is especially evident
with respect to the role of emotions in moral actions. The prophet who
is a political leader imitates God by acting "according to the deserts
of the people who are affected by them [his actions] and not merely
because of his following a passion."[65]
    The morality of imitation of God's actions reflects the actualization
of the nonindividualized *tzelem elohim* in man. At this stage, the framework of a person's religious outlook mirrors the nonpersonal character
of the divine actions he feels drawn to imitate. Miracle, revelation,
reward and punishment—all those beliefs that particularize the religious outlook recede in importance. Such a person feels divine love
in virtue of his very existence as a being endowed with an intellect
capable of transcending the narrow confines of ego-consciousness.
    In transcending his dependence on being emotionally affected (i.e.,
dependence on the body) as a necessary component in his moral behavior, the philosopher-statesman shows that his religious consciousness has been transformed by the love of God that his knowledge
awakened within him. Maimonides knew that such a transformation of
consciousness involved a long and arduous process. The goal of love
and knowledge of God was not only the acquisition of certain metaphysical truths, but also the liberation of one's religious consciousness
from an ego-oriented individualized framework toward self-transcend-
ence.
    Because of the difficulty of realizing this goal, Maimonides often
merely hinted to his readers that this was the ultimate goal of Judaism.
By stressing that Torah does not require an *eschaton* and that the
ultimate goal of Torah—passionate love of God—may be reached without God's miraculous intrusion into the natural order, Maimonides
hoped to make the community more receptive to this ideal.
    Despite the dangers of revealing the ideal of passionate love of God
to people who worship out of *yirah*, and despite the likelihood of being
misunderstood, Maimonides decided to incorporate his views on the
ultimate goals of Judaism within his legal works. He undertook the
task of challenging the community to move toward the ideal of *ahavah*,
even though he believed that without messianic conditions of peace
and prosperity this was unlikely to happen.
    The *Essay on Resurrection* was a consequence of the community's

failure to respond to that challenge. They realized that he had tried to wean them away from miracles; they rejected his attempt at instilling within them an appreciation of the nonmiraculous, impersonal divine actions in nature. They clamored for a religious world view that answered to the suffering condition of man. They focused on Maimonides' problematic treatment of the doctrine of resurrection, for they understood correctly that his philosophy of Judaism undermined the foundations of their *yirah*-based religious world view.

Maimonides was aware of this, I believe, when he wrote his final essay. He was angry at the community and possibly also at himself. He lashes out with anger and sarcasm at those halakhists who are exclusively preoccupied with details of the law and ignore the reality of God. In spite of his painful disappointment, he remains committed to the community and accepts the responsibility of leadership.

The option of withdrawal from the community was not available to Maimonides either from a religious or even from an epistemological perspective. At the end of the *Guide of the Perplexed*, Maimonides indicates that the knowledge comprising ultimate human perfection is practical. As Pines has recently shown, Maimonides believed that

> The only positive knowledge of God of which man is capable is knowledge of the attributes of action and this leads and ought to lead to a sort of political activity which is the highest perfection of man. The practical way of life, the *bios praktikos*, is superior to the theoretical.[66]

Maimonides thus remained within the Platonic cave and continued to try to devise a language the community could understand. His final letter to the community treats of the theme of resurrection and places a great deal of emphasis on the notion of miracle. His classification of miracles implies that the community need not be vulnerable to the dazzling claims of miracle-workers, because the most compelling miracle of their experience is their very survival as a covenantal people. The natural and the accidental are superseded by the continuous miracle of divine providence. Every event of Jewish history mediates God's unique love and concern for the people of Israel. In putting to productive use even the notion of miracle, which his earlier writings had sought to play down, Maimonides demonstrated that his commitment as an educator to his community could survive all setbacks.

CONCLUSION

All of Maimonides' letters share one thing in common: they indicate the loving concern and commitment of a great halakhic leader who struggled to sustain the dignity and the will to persevere of a community that was persistently abused, exploited, and humiliated. When one feels the actual suffering and degradation of the community, as Maimonides does in the *Epistle to Yemen*, then one's notion of love of God includes not only philosophic knowledge of God but also the courageous actions of a community that remains loyal to God and Torah in spite of the tragic circumstances of history. In the *Epistle to Yemen*, in contrast to the *Mishneh Torah* and the *Guide of the Perplexed*, the Song of Songs becomes an allegory of a people silently bearing shame and suffering with dignity.

Maimonides wrote his final essay in order to sustain his community's will to survive by fortifying belief in the miraculous nature of its existence. The *Essay on Resurrection* aims at banishing the accidental and the arbitrary from religious consciousness. Commitment to *mitzvot* makes all of life revelatory; everything that occurs is incorporated into the personalized framework of the Sinai revelation.

Given the world in which Maimonides lived, the goal of love understood by Maimonides must remain an esoteric ideal which one may disclose only to those singular individuals capable of transcending the brutal conditions of Jewish history. The readers of the *Guide of the Perplexed* are taught to strive for love of God in an unredeemed world by responding to the nonpersonal world of divine actions with the religious moral passion of *imitatio dei* found in the tradition; the readers of the *Essay on Resurrection* are shown how to transform the apparent chaos of history into a call for moral renewal. Both sets of readers are taught to live in a world where the miraculous workings of the Lord of history must be rethought if the community is to survive. Both have learned according to their respective frameworks, i.e., *ahavah* and *yirah*, to appropriate the talmudic concept of *olam ke-minhago noheg*, the world conforms to its usual course.[67]

NOTES

All quotations from *Sefer ha-Mada* are from H. Hyamson's translation (Jerusalem: Boys' Town, 1965).

1. See *MT Hilkhot Teshuvah* 10; *Guide* 3:51; Y. Leibowitz, *The Faith of Maimonides* (Hebrew) (Tel Aviv: Ministry of Defense, 1980).

2. See *Eight Chapters* 5; the introduction to the *Mishneh Torah* (where Maimonides explains why he included the laws of circumcision in the "Book of Love," the second book of the *Mishneh Torah*); *MT Hilkhot De'ot* 3:2–3 and *Hilkhot Mezuzah* 6:13. Also D. Hartman, *Maimonides: Torah and Philosophic Quest* (Philadelphia: Jewish Publication Society, 1976), pp. 86–90.

3. *MT Hilkhot Teshuvah* 10:5.

4. Introduction to *Ḥelek*, trans. J. Abelson, in "Maimonides on the Jewish Creed," *Jewish Quarterly Review* 19(1906–07):38. This metaphor may shed light upon how one understands the truth content of different descriptions of God. The relationship between the persuasive significance of religious language and its truth content is a serious question in Maimonidean exegesis; it now seems more complex than as implied in Hartman, *Maimonides*, pp. 76 and 80. See *Guide* 3:28; A. Hyman, "Spinoza's Dogmas of Universal Faith in Light of Their Medieval Jewish Background," in *Biblical and Other Studies*, ed. A. Altmann (Cambridge, Mass.: Harvard University Press, 1963), pp. 183–95.

5. See Plato, *Republic* 514a–521b; Hartman, *Maimonides* p. 246, n. 10, and p. 261, n. 39.

6. See L. Strauss, "The Literary Character of the *Guide for the Perplexed*," in *Persecution and the Art of Writing* (Glencoe, Ill.: The Free Press, 1952), p. 73.

7. See "Philosophy in Maimonides' Legal Works," in Hartman, *Maimonides*, pp. 28–65; I. Twersky, *Introduction to the Code of Maimonides (Mishneh Torah)* (New Haven and London: Yale University Press, 1980), pp. 77–79, 162–164, 215–220, ch. 6.

8. See Maimonides' *Letter to Joseph*, in *Ethical Writings of Maimonides*, ed. R. L. Weiss and C. E. Butterworth (New York: New York University Press, 1975), pp. 115–123; J. L. Teicher, "Maimonides' Letter to Joseph B. Jehudah—A Literary Forgery," *Journal of Jewish Studies* 1 (1948): 35–54. Teicher's suggestion that the letter is incompatible with Maimonides' "humility" is unconvincing. In *Ḥelek* and the *Guide*, Maimonides displays little humility when attacking those talmudists who lack an understanding of philosophy; see *Guide*, introduction and 3:43. Much of Maimonides' writings reflect an intellectual arrogance characteristic of a person who is deeply convinced of the truth of his position.

9. See *Maimonides*, p. 226, n. 92; "The God of Abraham and the God of the Philosophers," in D. Hartman, *Joy and Responsibility* (Jerusalem: Ben Zvi-Posner, 1978), pp. 170–75.

10. See *Guide* 1:33–35; L. Strauss, "How to Begin to Study *The Guide of the Perplexed*," in *The Guide of the Perplexed*, trans. S. Pines (Chicago: Chicago University Press, 1963), pp. xvii–xxiv.

11. Compare Strauss, *Persecution*, pp. 17–21, 32–7.

12. See *Guide* 3:29, *MT Hilkhot Avodah Zarah* 2:4; Sifrei, Deut. *piska* 54, Num. *piska* 111; BT Ḥullin 5a, BT Shevu'ot 29a; also BT Megillah 13a for the application of the term *yehudi* (Jew) to one who repudiates idolatry. For a contemporary understanding of this central principle in Judaism, see Hartman, "Halakhah as a Ground for Creating a Shared Spiritual Language," in *Joy and Responsibility*, pp. 145–50; compare E. E. Urbach, *The Sages: Their Concepts and Beliefs* (Jerusalem: Magnes, 1975), pp. 21–3.

13. See Aristotle, *Nicomachean Ethics* 1177a–1179b; G. E. Lloyd, *Aristotle: The Growth and Structure of his Thought* (Cambridge: Cambridge University Press, 1958), pp. 238–41; S. S. Schwarzschild, "Moral Radicalism and 'Middlingness' in the Ethics of Maimonides," in *Studies in Medieval*

Culture 11 (1978), pp. 65–94. Schwarzschild's serious attempt—in the spirit of Hermann Cohen—to sever any possible connection between Maimonides' concepts of man, *olam ha-ba*, ethics, and Aristotle's positions on these issues is intellectually challenging, but fundamentally mistaken. Schwarzschild's notion of "the ethico-intellectual life in the world to come" (p. 79) is incompatible with Maimonides' understanding of the philosopher's quest for knowledge (*Guide* 3:51). Knowledge of the workings of nature contains moral guidelines, but is not exhausted by the moral (*Guide* 1:54, 3:54). There is also progress in knowledge in Maimonides' conception of negative theology. There is a leading quality to such knowledge. For Maimonides, moreover, love of God is not exhausted by the ethical, although containing it. While there is an element of the ethical universal in Maimonides' thought, it is mistaken to place Maimonides in the Marxian tradition of philosophers who define philosophy as a means to transform the world. See J. Guttman, *Philosophies of Judaism* (New York: Anchor, 1966), pp. 199–200; Maimonides, Introduction to *Commentary to the Mishnah*, trans. J. Kafih (Jerusalem: Mossad Harav Kook, 1963), pp. 22–3.

14. *Ḥelek*, trans. A. J. Wolf, in *A Maimonides Reader*, ed. I. Twersky (New York: Behrman House, 1972), p. 416.

15. See Hartman, *Maimonides*, pp. 76–83.

16. See the discussion of *ahavah* and *yirah* in the discussion of the *Epistle on Martyrdom* in this volume.

17. See Aristotle, *Metaphysics* 1072. Further, Maimonides, *Guide* 1:1, 41, 74; the introduction to the second part, sixteenth premise, 3:22, 27, 51, 54; also MT *Hilkhot Yesodei ha-Torah* 4:8–9; and the vague but suggestive comments on Berakhot 9:7 in his *Commentary to the Mishnah*. Compare H. A. Wolfson, *Crescas' Critique of Aristotle* (Cambridge, Mass.: Harvard University Press, 1929), pp. 108–9, 292–95, 664–68; W. Harvey, *Hasdai Cresca's Critique of the Theory of the Acquired Intellect* (Doctoral Dissertation, Columbia University, 1973), pp. 28–63; Strauss, *Persecution*, p. 76; F. Rahman, *Avicenna's Psychology* (Oxford: Oxford University Press, 1952), pp. 3–19.

18. MT *Hilkhot Teshuvah* 9:2–4.

19. Ibid. 9:7–8.

20. See Sifrei, Deut. *piska* 48; BT Pesaḥim 50b, BT Berakhot 17a, BT Nazir 23b, BT Arakhin 16b, BT Sotah 29b. Notice the different attempts of Tosafot to harmonize the various texts dealing with *li-shmah* and *she-lo li-shmah*, as they shed light on the relationship between action and motive. Tosafot argues that *she-lo li-shmah*, which expresses negative virtues (e.g., studying for the sake of being intellectually aggressive toward others), is not valued by any view in the tradition. For Tosafot, it is important to distinguish between imperfect or mixed motives and clearly negative ones.

Y. Leibowitz seems to be unique in his claim that Maimonides' *taamei ha-mitzvot* (reasons for the commandments) reflect the category of *she-lo li-shmah*. Saying that the *mitzvot* fulfill the purpose of building a moral personality or a just society does not undermine the *li-shmah* quality of religious life, i.e., to serve God out of love and not for the sake of reward. On the contrary, one's love for God is enhanced when one recognizes the wisdom implicit in the commandment. See Leibowitz, *The Faith of Maimonides*; Urbach, *The Sages*, pp. 511–16.

21. See S. Pines, "The Limitations of Human Knowledge According to Al-Farabi, ibn Bajja, and Maimonides," in *Studies in Medieval Jewish History and Literature*, ed. I. Twersky (Cambridge, Mass.: Harvard University Press, 1979), pp. 95–7. Compare Pines' earlier views in "The Philosophic Sources of *The Guide of the Perplexed*," in his translation of the *Guide*, pp. cii–cvii. See A. Altmann, "Ibn Bajja on Man's Ultimate Felicity," in *Studies in Religious Philosophy and Mysticism* (Ithaca, New York: Cornell University Press, 1969), pp. 73–107; "Maimonides' 'four perfections,'" *Israel Oriental Studies* 2 (1972): 22–3. For an informative discussion of the concept of the world-to-come in rabbinic thought, see G. F. Moore, *Judaism*, vol. 2 (Cambridge, Mass.: Harvard University Press, 1954), pp. 279–395.

22. See C. Perelman, "The Justification of Norms," in *Justice, Law, and Argument* (Dordrecht: Reidel, 1980), pp. 107–13; "The Specific Nature of Juridical Proof," in *The Idea of Justice and the Problem of Argument* (New York: Humanities Press, 1963), pp. 98–108.

23. See *Guide* 2:22–25; H. Davidson, "Maimonides' Secret Position on Creation," *Studies in Medieval Jewish History and Literature*, pp. 16–56; A. J. Reines, "Maimonides' Concept of Miracles," *Hebrew Union College Annual* 14 (1975): 243–87. Reines believes that Maimonides accepted the doctrine of creation, but that "his real concept of miracles" as distinct from his apparent or modified view would lead to a totally naturalistic position similar to that of Aristotle. Reines' serious thesis hangs on his claim that Maimonides believed that creation could be rationally demonstrated by prophets whose knowledge is superior to that of philosophers; given Maimonides' rejection of supernaturalistic explanations of prophecy, the prophet's knowledge of creation and miracles is derived naturally. Reines is therefore hard-pressed to explain why Maimonides in *Guide* 2:25 states that relevation at Sinai is impossible within an Aristotelian universe. For Reines, there is no serious difference between the doctrines of creation and eternity as far as the philosophic foundations of Judaism are concerned. One chooses creation for social reasons: "it is on the grounds of its superior social consequences that Maimonides ultimately argues for a theology of creationism" (p. 285).

24. See D. J. Silver, *Maimonidean Criticism and the Maimonidean Controversy 1180–1240* (Leiden: Brill, 1965), ch. 7 and esp. p. 116.

25. The essay in this volume on Maimonides' *Epistle to Yemen* shows that for him messianism is essentially tied to the communal normative structure of Judaism. It is not merely a principle that comforts and offers hope, but a realistic perception of the intrinsic connection between the normative demand of love and the social and material conditions required for its realization in a community. Resurrection, however, is solely a doctrine of reward and punishment. One must strive to work toward the establishment of a messianic society irrespective of how one understands the doctrine of reward and punishment. See Hartman, *Maimonides*, pp. 82–85, 231, n. 43; A. Hyman, "Maimonides' 'Thirteen Principles,' " in *Jewish Medieval and Renaissance*

Studies (Cambridge, Mass.: Harvard University Press, 1967), p. 144. Compare Joseph Albo, *Sefer ha-Ikkarim*, ed. and trans. I. Husik (Philadelphia: Jewish Publication Society, 1946), vol. I, pp. 47, 135–36.

26. See *Guide* 3:29 and compare with Maimonides' description of Abraham in *MT Hilkhot Avodah Zarah* 1. The promising of benefits referred to in the *Guide* is absent in the *Mishneh Torah*, where Abraham's success is characterized solely by his intellectual victory.

27. See Strauss, "How to Begin to Study the Guide," p. xxvi; also Hyman, "Spinoza's Dogmas of Universal Faith," for his discussion of the dialectical rather than sophistic nature of Maimonides' "necessary beliefs."

28. See *The Commentary of R. Hoter Ben Shelomo to the Thirteen Principles of Maimonides*, ed. and trans. D. R. Blumenthal (Leiden: Brill, 1974), pp. 183, 189–90, esp. p. 190, n. 2; Ramban, *The Gate of Reward*, in *Ramban: Writings and Discussions*, vol. II, trans C. B. Chavel (New York: Shilo, 1978), p. 547.

29. Abelson, Introduction to *Helek*, p. 38.

30. See the comments of Rabad to *MT Hilkhot Teshuvah* 8:2. Compare the comments of *Kesef Mishneh* and the startling statement of the Ramban (*The Gate of Reward*, p. 550) regarding the difference between his views and those of Maimonides: "there is no difference between us with the sole exception of a difference in nomenclature." See L. Finkelstein, *Mabo le-Massektot Abot ve-Abot d'Rabbi Nathan* (New York: Jewish Theological Seminary, 1950), pp. xxxiii–xxxvi, 212–33. For the connection with discussions of immortality and resurrection in the Church Fathers, see H. A. Wolfson, *Religious Philosophy* (New York: Atheneum, 1965), pp. 78–83.

31. *The Commentary to Mishnah Aboth*, trans. A. David (New York: Bloch, 1968), 1:3, p. 4.

32. See *MT Hilkhot Teshuvah* 10:5:

> Hence, when instructing the young, women or the illiterate generally, we teach them to serve God out of fear or for the sake of reward, till their knowledge increases and they have attained a large measure of wisdom. Then we reveal to them this mystic truth, little by little, and train them by easy stages till they have grasped and comprehended it, and serve God out of love.

33. Abelson, Introduction to *Helek*, pp. 33–4.

34. See Ramban's vivid and detailed descriptions of the three judgments on Rosh Hashanah, at a person's death, and at the resurrection, as well as those of Gehennah, Gan Eden, etc. Maimonides' brevity and apparent indifference to such themes make even more fascinating the Ramban's claim that the difference between their views is merely verbal.

The following statement from G. Scholem, *Major Trends in Jewish Mysticism* (New York: Schocken, 1941), p. 35, is germane to understanding the differences between the Ramban and Maimonides:

> Mystics and philosophers are, as it were, both aristocrats of thought; yet Kabbalism succeeded in establishing a connection between its own world and certain elemental impulses operative in every human mind. It did not turn its back upon the primitive side of life, that all-important

region where mortals are afraid of life and in fear of death, and derive scant wisdom from rational philosophy. Philosophy ignored these fears, out of whose substance man wove myths, and in turning its back upon the primitive side of man's existence, it paid a high price in losing touch with him altogether.

See also his "Kabbalah and Myth," in *On the Kabbalah and its Symbolism* (New York: Schocken, 1965), pp. 94–100; and Hartman, "Sinai and Messianism: A Halakhic Model for Understanding God's Relationship to History," in *Joy and Responsibility*, pp. 232–58.

35. *MT Hilkhot Melakhim* 12:2.

36. *Guide* 3:54. See Altmann, "Maimonides' 'four perfections' " for the claim that Maimonides "followed the precedent of Ibn Bajja who in his *Tadbir al-mutawahhid* ("The Regimen of the Solitary") advocated the pursuit of the contemplative life as unrelated to the well-being of the body and the moral concerns of the imperfect state" (p. 22). In his introduction to the *Guide*, Pines maintained that Ibn Bajja's position was based upon his belief that "man's supreme goal was union with the Active Intellect, and that this union was not dependent upon living in the ideal philosophic city but could be achieved in solitude" (p. cvii). The difficulty in attributing any such view to Maimonides is the evidence that he was skeptical about the ability of man to acquire metaphysical knowledge. If such knowledge is unattainable, man's ultimate goal can only be the practical and not the theoretical life. At that time, Pines was unwilling to attribute skepticism about metaphysical knowledge to Maimonides: "Yet it seems to me that such agnosticism would stultify all that Maimonides set out to accomplish in the *Guide* and would also be quite irreconcilable with his general views, expressed in quite different contexts, on man's highest destination and man's knowledge" (p. cxi; see also p. cxxi). Strauss took a similar position in *Persecution*, pp. 84–97.

Recently, however, in "The Limitations of Human Knowledge," Pines has resolved his earlier uncertainty and affirmed that Maimonides genuinely believed that there were limitations of the human intellect that prevent the acquisition of metaphysical knowledge.

Both Kant and Maimonides, the first outspokenly and the second partly by implication, have tried to show that because of the limitations of his mind man is incapable of intellecting some of the main objects of the traditional metaphysics. There may be a correlation between this fact and the tendency of both philosophers and also of al-Farabi to accord primacy to the life of action. (p. 100)

See also Pines' introduction to Hartman, *Maimonides*, and pp. 200–206.

37. See Ramban's definition of prayer in terms of crisis situations in the comments on Maimonides' *Sefer ha-Mitzvot*, positive commandment 5; *MT Hilkhot Tefillah* 1:1–3; *Guide* 3:32 on crisis and contemplative prayer; and *Maimonides*, pp. 162–66.

38. The philosophical importance of the *Essay on Resurrection* as a commentary to the *Guide* is obvious in respect of the apparent contradiction in *Guide* 3:54 regarding the relationship between solitude and commitment to the community. Furthermore, the model of imitation of God for the political leader involves not only the attributes of action mentioned at *Guide* 1:54, but

also the statements in the Torah that reveal God as a patient teacher (see *Guide* 3:32).

39. See the beginning of the introduction to *Ḥelek;* also Hartman, *Maimonides,* pp. 68–72.

40. See BT Avodah Zarah 54b; also Hartman, "The God of Abraham and the God of the Philosophers," pp. 181–87. On the paucity of biblical attestation for resurrection, see Y. Kaufmann, *The Religion of Israel,* trans. M. Greenberg (Chicago: University of Chicago Press, 1960), pp. 311–16, 384–85, and E. E. Urbach, "Halakhot yerushah ve-ḥayyei olam," in *Fourth World Congress of Jewish Studies* (Jerusalem: World Union of Jewish Studies, 1967), p. 138.

41. This theory upset many halakhists, because of the obvious dangers involved in offering historical, time-bound reasons to explain the content of revelation. How could Maimonides explain certain commandments, e.g., sacrifices, on the basis of transitory historical conditions, while at the same time including these commandments in a code of law meant to be eternally binding upon the Jewish community? Yet it is this theory of religious history that is used in the *Essay on Resurrection* to reinforce belief in the traditional doctrine of the resurrection of the dead. What a fascinating and ingenious way to teach traditional halakhists not to be frightened by the notion of religious development in history! Maimonides strengthens belief in traditional doctrines by arguing that the generation that witnessed the Sinai revelation did not exemplify the highest level of religious faith. See Hartman, *Maimonides,* pp. 174–86; Strauss, "How to Begin," pp. xxix–xliv.

42. *Guide* 3:32, p. 528.

43. Ibid., p. 526.

44. Ibid., p. 527.

45. Ibid., p. 529.

46. See *Guide* 2:39; 3:25–26, 31, 34, 49; Hartman, *Maimonides,* pp. 166–76.

47. Cf. J. L. Teicher, "Ziyyuf sifruti: maamar tehiyyat ha-metim," *Melilah* 1 (1944): 86–88. My interpretation of the final section of the epistle weakens the philosophical argument given by Teicher to support his claim that the letter on resurrection is a forgery. Teicher emphasizes the difference between the *Guide,* with its doctrine of slow and patient development that in effect neutralizes the need for miracles, and the epistle, which uses the same theory of development to enhance the importance of miracles. But he seems to ignore the educational implication of Maimonides' concept of ruse in the *Guide:* a teacher must always speak in the language of his student. See also Teicher's earlier article, "Maimonides' Letter" (note 8 above), and his "Christian Theology and the Jewish Opposition to Maimonides," *Journal of Theological Studies* 43 (1942): 68–76.

48. See *Guide* 3:29, 41; Pines' introduction to the *Guide,* pp. cxiii–cxxiv; Strauss, "How to Begin," pp. xxi–xxiii. There is a fundamental difference between the effects of the belief in the eternity of the universe on the masses and on the philosopher. See *Guide* 2:15. From the discussion in *Guide* 3:25 one could not infer that Maimonides held that belief in the eternity of the world made one a pagan. The doctrine of *creatio ex nihilo* educates the

community to 1) belief in the existence of God and 2) the elimination of idolatry. See *Guide* 2:31 and compare with 1:71; also compare 2:25 with 2:16, and see 3:37.

49. See *Guide* 2:29; *Eight Chapters*, ch. 8; also Reines, "Maimonides' Concept of Miracles," for his explanation of Maimonides' "temporalization" of miracles. According to Reines, this temporalization points to Maimonides' esoteric doctrine of prophecy as a natural phenomenon—his "real concept of miracles." See pp. 268–69 regarding the relationship between miracles and prophecy.

> A miracle is not created by God's special will, but occurs as an anomaly of nature. The greater the scientific knowledge a person possesses, the greater his ability to predict irregular events of nature and the higher the status of a prophet, the more his scientific knowledge . . . Hence Moses whose scientific knowledge was supreme among prophets and all mankind could predict anomalies as no one else ever could, and consequently, his "miracles" were greater than those of any other prophet.

In contrast to Reines, I maintain that for Maimonides miracles function with respect to prophets as a legal category. The dogma of the eternity of the law establishes Moses as a unique prophet. The unique nature of the knowledge and miracles ascribed to Moses reflects the unique legal status of the Torah.

Furthermore, Maimonides' concern with temporalization in *Guide* 3:29 seeks to convince the reader that structure and order in nature reflect the spirit of Judaism. When Maimonides refers to the rabbinic tradition that places miracles within the six days of creation, he draws the attention of his readers to the "spirit of that passage." In *Guide* 2:29 Maimonides is trying to show that the notion of divine will that makes the "miracle" of creation possible need not exclude a merging of that will in important respects with the notions of permanence, order, and predictability that characterize an Aristotelian description of the universe.

Reines' important and interesting article fails to appreciate the religious and legal dimensions of Maimonides' understanding of creation. As he understands Maimonides, one accepts creation because of the superiority of the prophet's knowledge. But I feel that Pines' understanding of creation and the categories of practical reason ("philosophical theology") mirrors in a deeper way the religious educational impulse that pervades Maimonides' writings. See *Guide* 2:2.

50. See Ramban, *Commentary on the Torah*, Gen. 17:1 and 46:15, Exod. 13:16, Lev. 26:11. It is interesting to compare the Ramban's explanation of the rabbinic statement that "permission is given to the doctor to heal" with Maimonides' explanation in the *Commentary to the Mishnah*, Pesaḥim 4:10. Maimonides categorically rejects any interpretation of one's reliance upon medical science as an indication of one's lack of faith. The natural as an expression of divine will is implicit in Maimonides' attitude to medicine. For Ramban there is no genuine category of the natural.

51. See Maimonides' *Commentary to the Mishnah*, Avot 2:6, Peah 1:1; also Hartman, *Maimonides*, pp. 149–59.

52. *Guide* 3:17. See *MT Hilkhot Issure Biah* 14:3–5, where *olam ha-ba*

is promised only to Israel; and compare with *MT Hilkhot Teshuvah* 3:5 and the end of *MT Hilkhot Shemittah ve-Yovel*.

53. See BT Yoma 69b for the reinterpretation of *norah*, divine awesomeness.

54. See *MT Hilkhot Avel* 13:12 and compare with *Hilkhot Teshuvah* 3:4.

55. See Mekhilta, *Ba-hodesh* 6 on the text "of them who love Me and keep my commandments"; Urbach, *The Sages*, pp. 436–44.

56. See M. Buber, *Moses: The Revelation and the Covenant* (New York: Harper, 1958), for his appropriation of the biblical experience of miracle. In the medieval discussion the problem centered around the logical possibility of miracles, i.e., necessity or freedom with respect to divine action. For Buber the difference between causal and miraculous interpretations of reality is in the eyes of the beholder:

> The concept of miracle which is permissible from the historical approach can be defined at its starting point as an abiding astonishment. The philosophizing and the religious person both wonder at the phenomenon, but the one neutralizes his wonder in ideal knowledge, while the other abides in that wonder; no knowledge, no cognition, can weaken his astonishment. Any causal explanation only deepens the wonder for him . . . Miracle is not something "supernatural" or "superhistorical," but an incident, an event which can be fully included in the objective, scientific nexus of nature and history; the vital meaning of which, however, for the person to whom it occurs, destroys the security of the whole nexus of knowledge for him, and explodes the fixity of the fields of experience named "Nature" and "History." Miracle is simply what happens; in so far as it meets people who are capable of receiving it, or prepared to receive it, as miracle. The extraordinary element favours this coming together, but it is not characteristic of it; the normal and ordinary can also undergo a transfiguration into miracle in the light of the suitable hour. (pp. 75–76)

See E. Fackenheim, *God's Presence in History* (New York: New York University Press, 1970), pp. 8–14; A. J. Heschel, *God in Search of Man* (New York: Farrar, Strauss and Cudahy, 1955), pp. 43–54, 88–101.

57. Maimonides continues a dominant theme in the rabbinic tradition and in Jewish liturgy by making the living Torah the mediating framework that expresses God's love for Israel. See Solomon Schechter, *Aspects of Rabbinic Theology* (New York: Schocken, 1961), pp. 116–126; M. Kadushin, *The Rabbinic Mind* (New York: Bloch, 1972), pp. 194–222; and Hartman, "Soloveitchik's Response to Modernity," in *Joy and Responsibility*, pp. 225–29.

58. See *Sefer ha-Mitzvot*, positive commandment 8; *MT Hilkhot Deot* 1:6 and *Hilkhot Talmud Torah* 1:7; *Guide* 1:54, 3:54; BT Nedarim 37a and commentary of the Rosh. Patience and loving acceptance of human weaknesses are part of God's attributes that a political leader and teacher must emulate.

59. See *MT Hilkhot Yesodei ha-Torah* 1:5; *Guide* 1:71.

60. See Strauss, "How to Begin," pp. xxvi–xxvii; Schwarzschild, "Moral Radicalism and 'Middlingness' in the Ethics of Maimonides." For Schwarzschild the fall of man represents the change from the radical ethics of *imitatio* to

the inferior ethics of the mean. The following statement sheds light on Schwarzschild's concern with distinguishing between Maimonidean ethics of *imitatio* and Aristotelian ethics of the mean:

> Aristotelian ethics of the mean may then be regarded as an adaptation to the world as it is, while Platonic-Maimonidean ethics of *imitatio* are then world-changing, world-reforming. (p. 75)

Schwarzschild's claim that Maimonides makes no reference to the doctrine of the mean in defining the commandment of *imitatio* (p. 68) seems to be untenable in the light of Maimonides' statement in *MT Hilkhot Deot* 1:5. Furthermore, the source of Maimonides' description of *imitatio* is Sifri, *Ekev* 49, which includes graciousness among the divine qualities one must imitate. It is, therefore, mistaken to claim that Maimonides willfully introduced this term to show the "infinite, unattainable, radical character of *imitatio Dei*" (p. 68). While one may question Schwarzschild's understanding of both the Aristotelian "gentlemen's ethos" and Maimonidean radical ethics, his article is nonetheless suggestive and challenges one to rethink the relationship between thought and action in Maimonides' thought.

Since Schwarzschild's argument centers on his claim that knowledge of God is exclusively moral, it is difficult to understand the comments of L. Berman in "Maimonides on the Fall of Man," *AJS Review* 5 (1980): 3, n. 6. Here Berman finds Schwarzschild's analysis "compelling" while stating in the same breath: "I am unable to agree with him that Maimonides posits a sphere of ethical activity which is essentially rational in nature." How can one disagree with Schwarzschild's central claim regarding the rational ground of ethical activity and yet find his article "compelling"?

See W. F. R. Hardie, *Aristotle's Ethical Theory* (Oxford: Oxford University Press), ch. 6, 7; A. MacIntyre, *A Short History of Ethics* (New York: Macmillan, 1966), pp. 57–83.

61. *Guide* 2:27, p. 332; see also 2:29.

62. Ibid. 1:54, p. 125.

63. Ibid. 3:53, p. 631.

64. Ibid., p. 632.

65. Ibid. 1:54, p. 126.

66. "The Limitation of Human Knowledge," p. 100.

67. In the *Mishneh Torah*, Maimonides uses the expression *olam ke-minhago noheg* (the world conforms to its usual course) with regard to messianism in two places: 1) *Hilkhot Teshuvah* 9:2; and 2) *Hilkhot Melakhim* 12:1. The importance of neutralizing the miraculous and the notion of an eschatological rupture in history as fundamental themes in Maimonides' religious teleology has been dealt with in this essay and in the essay on the *Epistle to Yemen* in this volume. Maimonides believes that his use of the concept of *olam keminhago noheg* with regard to messianism was clearly in harmony with the spirit of the rabbinic statement: "The sole difference between the present and the messianic days in delivery from servitude to foreign powers" (BT Sanhedrin 91b).

There are, however, other uses of the concept in the *Mishneh Torah* which are bold and radical and which clearly transmute the spirit and meaning of the talmudic texts in question.

The following text appears in BT Moed Katan 27b:

And furthermore, Rab Judah said, as citing Rab: "Whoever indulges in grief to excess over his dead will weep for another. There was a certain woman that lived in the neighborhood of R. Huna; she had seven sons one of whom died [and] she wept for him rather excessively. R. Huna sent [word] to her: 'Act not thus.' She heeded him not and he sent to her: 'If you heed my word it is well; but if not, are you anxious to make provision for yet another?' He [the next son] died and they all died. In the end he said to her: 'Are you fumbling with provision for yourself?' And she died."

[Our Rabbis taught]: "Weep ye not for the dead, neither bemoan him" [that is], "Weep not for the dead" [that is] in excess, "neither bemoan him"—beyond measure. How is that applied?—Three days for weeping and seven for lamenting and thirty to refrain from cutting the hair and donning pressed clothes; hereafter, the Holy One, blessed be He, says: "Ye are not more compassionate toward him [the departed] than I."

It is obvious from the above text that excessive mourning is treated as a serious sin that warrants divine punishment (the deaths of the woman and of her children). Excessive mourning seems to convey some form of religious heresy that touches upon belief in divine governance of the world.

When the text discusses how the period of mourning should be divided into different levels of intensity, it justifies the graduated lessening of mourning with the ironic theological statement: "Ye are not more compassionate toward him [the departed] than I." Excessive mourning is clearly viewed as a sinful action that is inappropriate for one who believes in divine providence.

Maimonides' treatment of this text in *Hilkhot Avel* 13:11 reveals his philosophic application of the concept *olam ke-minhago noheg* to the experience of tragedy.

One should not indulge in excessive grief over one's dead, for it is said: *Weep ye not for the dead, neither bemoan him* [Jer. 22:10], that is to say, [weep not for him] too much, for that is the way of the world, and he who frets over the way of the world is a fool. What rule should one follow in case of bereavement? [The rule is:] three days for weeping, seven days for lamenting, and thirty days for [abstaining] from cutting the hair and the other four things [forbidden to a mourner].

It is obvious that for Maimonides, excessive mourning is foolish rather than sinful. The reason for such foolishness is that the person in question has not learned to accept the inevitable reality of death. Death is part of *minhago shel olam*. One feels pity for the mourner's foolishness and not moral outrage. Maimonides substitutes *olam ke-minhago noheg* for divine providence. The graduated levels of mourning thus show how Halakhah educates a person to live with the notion of *olam ke-minhago noheg*.

However, when Maimonides relates mourning to the theme of *teshuvah* he subtly makes the mourner conscious of divine providence as it leads a person to moral renewal through the instrument of death.

Whoever does not mourn the dead in the manner enjoined by the Rabbis is cruel. (If one suffers bereavement,) one should be apprehensive, troubled, investigate his conduct, and return in repentance. If one of a company dies, all the members thereof should be troubled. During the first three days the mourner should think of himself as if a sword is resting upon his neck, from the third to the seventh day as if it is lying in the corner, thereafter as if it is moving toward him in the street.

Reflections of this nature will put him on his mettle, he will bestir himself and repent, for it is written: *Thou hast stricken them, but they were not affected* [Jer. 5:3]. He should therefore be wide awake and deeply moved. (*Hilkhot Avel* 13:12)

Twersky (*The Code of Maimonides*) misses completely the implications of the philosophic response to death in the *Mishneh Torah*. Also, his explanation of why the laws of mourning are not treated in the *Guide* is highly implausible.

It is immediately obvious that *Hilkhot Avel* are conspicuous by their omission, and the reason seems equally transparent. In the *Guide* Maimonides sees death as something "which in true reality is salvation from death," for one's intellectual apprehension "becomes stronger at the separation" of the soul from body . . . Clearly there is no room for grief and mourning when death is viewed from such a perspective. (p. 307)

From the philosopher's vantage point, death is not only inevitable but is the "consummation devoutly to be wished" . . . Death is spiritual fulfillment, not physical destruction. It would be difficult to integrate the Laws Concerning Mourning into this Socratic-Platonic perspective concerning the happy liberation of the soul from its bodily incarceration. (p. 438)

Maimonides' description of the joys of *olam ha-ba* in *Ḥelek* and in *Hilkhot Teshuvah* should, if Twersky is correct, also neutralize the importance of the laws of mourning in the *Mishneh Torah*. Also, Maimonides in no way welcomes death in *Guide* 3:51. The context of his treatment of Moses, Aaron, and Miriam is an attempt to offer a new understanding of divine providence and human suffering. Furthermore, the lack of an explicit biblical text dealing with the commandment of mourning may very well explain why Maimonides in the context of the *Guide* does not mention the laws of mourning. Twersky's argument is puzzling given his repeated emphasis upon the unity of the *Guide* and the *Mishneh Torah*. For Maimonides on philosophic training with regard to human tragedy, see *Guide* 3:10, 12, 13. For another instance of Maimonides' substituting *olam ke-minhago noheg* for providence, see BT Sanhedrin 72b, *MT Hilkhot Rotzeah* 1:9, and *Kesef Mishneh*.

In this epistle, Maimonides rejected the possibility that eternal life was possible for human bodily existence. It appears that for Maimonides human death represents the notion of *olam ke-minhago noheg*. Wherever death could be perceived as a miraculous divine intervention Maimonides interprets it in such a way that it becomes the carrier of the principle of ordered regularity in nature. In the *Mishneh Torah*, in contrast to the talmudic context, he guides his reader to accept death as an inseparable part of the human condition. Excessive mourning reflects, in a sense, the yearning for the miraculous, which according to Maimonides was not in harmony with the genuine spirit of Judaism.

Printed in the United States
1326500002B/268-327